ETHAN FROME
AND
SUMMER

SELECTED NEW RIVERSIDE EDITIONS

Series Editor for the American Volumes
Paul Lauter

For a complete listing of our American and British New Riverside
Editions, visit our website at **http://college.hmco.com.**

NEW RIVERSIDE EDITIONS
Series Editor for the American Volumes
Paul Lauter, Trinity College

EDITH WHARTON

Ethan Frome and Summer

Complete Texts with Introduction
Historical Contexts • Critical Essays

Edited by Denise D. Knight
STATE UNIVERSITY OF NEW YORK – CORTLAND

Houghton Mifflin Company
BOSTON • NEW YORK

In memory of Rosie

Publisher: Patricia A. Coryell
Sponsoring Editor: Michael Gillespie
Editorial Associate: Bruce Cantley
Associate Project Editor: Shelley Dickerson
Manufacturing Manager: Florence Cadran
Senior Marketing Manager: Cindy Graff Cohen

Cover image: <To come>

Credits appear on page 324, which is a continuation of the copyright page.

Printed in the U.S.A.

Library of Congress Control Number: 2002114141
ISBN: 0-618-30012-0
1   2   3   4   5   6   7   8   9-QUF-07   06   05   04   03

CONTENTS

ABOUT THIS SERIES
Paul Lauter

The Riverside name dates back well over a century. Readers of this book may have seen — indeed, may own — Riverside Editions of works by the best-known nineteenth-century American writers, such as Emerson, Thoreau, Lowell, Longfellow, and Hawthorne. Houghton Mifflin and its predecessor, Ticknor & Fields, were the primary publishers of the New England authors who constituted much of the undisputed canon of American literature until well into the twentieth century. The Riverside Editions of works by these writers, and of some later writers such as Amy Lowell, became benchmarks for distinguished and useful editions of standard American authors for home, library, and classroom.

In the 1950s and 1960s, the Riverside name was used for another series of texts, primarily for the college classroom, of well-known American and British literary works. These paperback volumes, edited by distinguished critics of that generation, were among the most widely used and appreciated of their day. They provided carefully edited texts in a handsome and readable format, with insightful critical introductions. They were books one kept beyond the exam, the class, or even the college experience.

In the last quarter century, however, ideas about the American literary canon have changed. Many scholars want to see a canon that reflects a broader American heritage, including significant literary works by previously marginalized writers, many of them women or men of color. These changes began to be institutionalized in curricula as well as in textbooks such as *The Heath Anthology of American Literature,* which Houghton Mifflin started publishing in 1998. The older Riverside series, excellent in its day, ran the risk of appearing outdated; the editors were long retired or deceased, and the authors were viewed by some as too exclusive.

Yet the name Riverside and the ideas behind it continued to have appeal. The name stood for distinction and worth in the publication of America's literary heritage. Houghton Mifflin's New Riverside Series, initiated in the year 2000, is designed to uphold the Riverside reputation for excellence while offering a more inclusive range of authors. The Series also provides today's reader with books that contain, in addition to notable literary works, introductions by influential critics, as well as a variety of stimulating materials that bring alive the debates, the conversations, the social and cultural movements within which America's literary classics were formed.

Thus emerged the book you have in hand. Each volume of the New Riverside Editions will contain the basic elements that we think today's readers find interesting and useful: important literary works by significant authors, incisive introductions, and a variety of contextual materials to make the literary text fully engaging. These books will be useful in many kinds of classrooms, but they are also designed to offer the casual reader the enjoyment of a good read in a fresh and accessible format. Among the first group of New Riverside Editions are familiar titles, such as Henry David Thoreau's *Walden* and Mark Twain's *Adventures of Huckleberry Finn.* There are also works in fresh new combinations, such as the collection of early captivity narratives. And there are well-known works in distinctively interesting formats, such as the volume containing Edith Wharton's *The Age of Innocence* and the volume of writings by Stephen Crane. Future books will include classics as well as works drawing renewed attention.

The New Riverside Editions will provide discriminating readers with a wide range of important literary works, contextual materials that vividly illuminate those works, and the best of recent critical commentary and analysis. And because we have not confined our editors to a single monotonous format, we think our readers will find that each volume in this new series has a character appropriate to the literary work it presents.

We expect the New Riverside Editions to bring to the twenty-first century the same literary publishing distinction of its nineteenth- and twentieth-century predecessors.

INTRODUCTION
Denise D. Knight

dith Wharton (1862–1937) is best known for writing works
that explore lives of wealth and privilege among the upper-
class elite. Because she was a member of the old New York social aristocracy, Wharton's social circle included the Astors and Goelets,[1]
and she reaped the benefits of her family's fortune. Her life was marked by
extended European sojourns, elegant dinner parties, exquisite fashions,
and extravagant residences. Not surprisingly, in much of Wharton's fiction,
high society figures prominently. Yet in a bold departure from her more
conventional depictions of pomp and circumstance—and with an un-
canny degree of authenticity—Wharton examined the lives of the rural
poor in two of her most poignant works. As she explained in her autobiography, *A Backward Glance*, "For years I had wanted to draw life as it really
was in the derelict mountain villages of New England [. . .]. In those days,
the snow-bound villages of Western Massachusetts were still grim places,
morally and physically: insanity, incest, and slow mental and moral starvation were hidden away behind the paintless wooden house-fronts of the
long village street, or in the isolated farm-houses on the neighboring hills"
(213–14).[2] Wharton's wish "to draw life as it really was" resulted in *Ethan
Frome* (1911), her most popular novella, and six years later its companion
piece, *Summer* (1917), which Wharton considered one of her best works.

Already an accomplished author by the time *Ethan Frome* was published (*The House of Mirth* appeared in 1905), Wharton claimed in her
memoirs that "It was not until I wrote 'Ethan Frome' that I suddenly felt the

---

[1]The Astors and Goelets were wealthy and prominent members of the New York social circle. The Astors were descended from John Jacob Astor (1763–1848), who made
his fortune in the fur trade and real estate. The Goelets were the second wealthiest
real-estate-owning family in New York; their fortune in the late 1800s was estimated at
over $100 million.

[2]All parenthetical references are to this New Riverside Edition.

artisan's full control of his implements" (213). It was also the work to which she "brought the greatest joy and the fullest ease" (213). Moreover, as Wharton's biographers have argued, the thematic threads of *Ethan Frome* and *Summer* seem to have their origins in Wharton's personal life. Her marriage to Teddy Wharton was devoid of sexual passion, much like the Ethan-Zeena union, and her two-year affair with American journalist Morton Fullerton, which ended the year before *Ethan Frome* was published, was both exhilarating and painful, not unlike Charity's relationship with Lucius Harney in *Summer*.

Autobiographical influences aside, Wharton insisted in *A Backward Glance* that part of the impetus behind writing *Ethan Frome* and *Summer* was her desire to remedy what she believed were "rose-coloured" depictions of New England by her "predecessors, Mary Wilkins [Freeman] and Sarah Orne Jewett" (213). Wishing to infuse into her fiction a degree of realism that she found lacking in Freeman and Jewett, Wharton, a keen observer of human behavior, drew on her ten years in Lenox, Massachusetts, during which she "had come to know well the aspect, dialect, and mental and moral attitude of the hill-people" (215). Wharton began writing *Ethan Frome* as an exercise to perfect her French while she was living in Paris and originally titled the work "*L'Hiver,*" French for "Winter," underscoring its thematic relationship to *Summer*. Like its companion piece, Wharton noted, "'Summer' deals with the same class and type as those portrayed in 'Ethan Frome', and has the same setting [. . .]" (215).

In fact, the novellas share a number of similarities. Both works examine lives marked by isolation, poverty, inarticulateness, and despair, and both feature flawed protagonists who experience the consequences of forbidden passion and the tragedy of thwarted dreams. Each novella explores a triangular relationship (Ethan, Zeena, and Mattie in *Ethan Frome;* Charity, Lawyer Royall, and Harney in *Summer*), and each invokes, to varying degrees, the fictional village of Starkfield, Massachusetts. Moreover, some of the episodes in *Ethan Frome* and *Summer* have their origins in real-life events. The sledding scene in *Ethan Frome* was based on a tragic coasting accident in 1904 that killed one Lenox teenager and seriously injured several others; the death and burial of Charity's mother in *Summer* was taken from the account of a Lenox rector who had been summoned to Bear Mountain — just twelve miles from Wharton's home — to preside over the burial of "a woman of evil reputation" (214). Each novella also hints at incest. Ethan Frome is married to his first cousin, Zeena, although the union seems to be devoid of sexual relations; and in *Summer,* incest is both literal (inbreeding takes place among the Mountain people) and symbolic (Lawyer Royall makes sexual advances toward, and later marries, his daughter figure,

Charity). There are also a number of dichotomies both in and between the two works: summer versus winter; mountain people versus villagers; literacy versus illiteracy; ignorance versus knowledge; dark versus light; illness versus hypochondria; emotional impoverishment versus financial poverty; actual incest versus symbolic incest; and geographic isolation versus emotional isolation, to name a few. Most significantly, however, each novella ends in despair for the protagonists, who are unable to escape their circumstances. Ethan is entrapped for life on the cheerless and dilapidated farm, and Charity is destined to remain in the stifling and dreary North Dormer village that she desperately wanted to flee. Yet, while similarities abound between these two works, each one stands alone as a powerful, and occasionally shocking, dramatization of small-town New England life in the early twentieth century.

———————

Ethan Frome is a chilling tale that takes place in the fictional town of Starkfield, Massachusetts. Set during winter, the novella is narrated by an outsider whose work with an electric-generating station has brought him to Starkfield for several months. His curiosity about the events that left Ethan crippled lead the narrator to reconstruct the tragedy, "bit by bit, from various people" (13). One villager opines that Ethan has "been in Starkfield too many winters" and that "Most of the smart ones get away" (14). For Ethan, however, there is no escape. Forced to abandon his college education to care for his ailing mother, Ethan has few options. He returns to the barren farm and attempts to eke out a living. When his cousin Zeena arrives to help nurse Ethan's dying mother, Ethan is "seized with an unreasoning dread of being left alone on the farm" and, in a moment of weakness, "asked her to stay there with him" (42). Ethan "had often thought since that it would not have happened if his mother had died in spring instead of winter" (42).

Indeed, Wharton invokes winter as the controlling metaphor in *Ethan Frome*; it reinforces the starkness of Ethan's condition, the death of Ethan's dreams, and the lifelessness in his marriage. Significantly, too, the Frome farmhouse has lost its "L"—the section of the structure that is one of "the chief sources of warmth and nourishment" (21). The absence of the "L" becomes emblematic of the lack of both love and life in the Frome household, with the once-vibrant Zeena becoming sickly and querulous. Wharton writes, "Life on an isolated farm was not what she had expected when she married," and "within a year" Zeena is transformed into a whining hypochondriac (42).

It is little wonder, then, when Zeena sends for her vivacious young cousin, Mattie Silver, to help with the household chores, Ethan is immediately captivated. Wharton has created in Mattie—at least initially—the antithesis of Zeena: Mattie is "like the lighting of a fire on a cold hearth" (26). She seems to be everything that Zeena is not. Mattie's "wonder and [Ethan's] laughter ran together like rills in a thaw," and in her presence Ethan feels a "wave of warmth [go] through him" (31, 34). Zeena may be a nagging invalid, but she is no fool, and she possesses an iron will. When she senses Ethan's attraction to Mattie, she contrives to replace her with a "hired girl" who would be stronger than Mattie and "handier" (58, 62). Unskilled and having nowhere to go, Mattie faces a bleak future.

In today's credit-based financial climate, in which consumers use charge cards to buy everything from automobiles to groceries, contemporary readers sometimes puzzle as to why Ethan and Mattie don't simply run off together. Wharton, however, makes it clear that Ethan is shackled by both financial and moral constraints. During the cold, dark, winter night, when he contemplates his future, the reality of Ethan's life becomes clear: "A moment ago he had wondered what he and Mattie were to live on when they reached the West; now he saw that he had not even the money to take her there. [. . .] The inexorable facts closed in on him like prison-warders handcuffing a convict. There was no way out—none. He was a prisoner for life, and now his one ray of light was to be extinguished" (67–8). Ethan briefly contemplates borrowing money from friends to finance his departure, but he cannot bring himself to engage in duplicity: "He was a poor man, the husband of a sickly woman, whom his desertion would leave alone and destitute; and even if he had had the heart to desert her he could have done so only by deceiving two kindly people who had pitied him" (71–72).

It is not only Ethan's moral code and poverty that prevent his escape, however. He is also thwarted by his inability to communicate effectively and by the effects of Zeena's skillful manipulation. There is an enormous disparity between Ethan's private thoughts and his ability to articulate them. Throughout the novella, Wharton alludes to his verbal paralysis: "He vainly struggled for expression" (32); "Again he struggled for the all-expressive word" (33); "Ethan tried to say something befitting the occasion" (40); he was "by nature grave and inarticulate" (41); "He had never learned to say such things" (76). Because Ethan is unable to express himself clearly, he neither can openly declare his love for Mattie, nor can he defend himself against Zeena's verbal attacks. When the two get into a heated exchange over Zeena's decision to banish Mattie from the house, Ethan is "seized with horror of the scene and shame at his own share in it. [. . .] It was the first scene of open anger between the couple in their sad seven years together, and Ethan felt as if he had lost an irretrievable advantage in descending to the level of recrimination" (58–59). Zeena consistently gains the upper hand, leaving Ethan feeling impotent and emasculated: "His wife's retort was like a knife-cut across the sinews and he felt suddenly weak and powerless. [. . .] Now she had mastered him and he abhorred her. [. . .] His manhood was humbled by the part he was compelled to play and by the thought of what Mattie must think of him" (61, 70). The only time that Ethan openly defies Zeena—his insistence on driving Mattie to the train station when Zeena sends her packing—results in a tragic turn of events.

In the novella's most emotionally charged scene, Ethan and Mattie make one last effort at escape through an attempted double suicide, which seals their fate. Zeena recovers her health and becomes caretaker to the paralyzed and droning Mattie; Ethan is forced to bear witness to Mattie's suffering for the remainder of his life. He is condemned to a living hell from which there is no escape.

In contrast to the cold, wintry landscape of *Ethan Frome, Summer,* Wharton's "Hot Ethan," as she characterized the book,[3] is set against the backdrop of a seemingly perfect Berkshire summer. Each day is "a sequence of temperate beauty" (111), but dark themes—incest, prostitution, lust, and betrayal—abound. The novella's first scene introduces Charity Royall, a twenty-one-year-old woman[4] on the threshold of sexual maturity, as she catches sight of Lucius Harney, a handsome young architect from the city who has come to North Dormer to study old houses. Charity is a part-time custodian at the rarely used village library, "for which no new books had been bought for twenty years, and where the old ones mouldered undisturbed on the damp shelves" (92). The description of the library underscores the stagnancy of the town and magnifies Charity's despair. Her hope is "to earn money enough to get away" (102) from North Dormer and from her guardian, Lawyer Royall, who rescued Charity at the age of five from a life of depravity on the Mountain—a remote community of "thieves and outlaws" (118)—and who lives in abject poverty. Throughout *Summer,* the Mountain looms portentously over North Dormer, and Charity knows "it was a bad place, and a shame to have come from [there]" (93). But depravity and shame are not confined to the Mountain.

Wharton creates considerable tension between Charity and Royall from the beginning of the novella. We soon learn why. Wharton alludes to an incident several years earlier, when the widowed Royall had appeared at

---

[3] Wharton, *Letters* 385.
[4] Several critics erroneously state that Mattie is seventeen at the time the novel opens. Lawyer Royall, however, notes that he brought Charity down from the Mountain "sixteen years ago," when she was five (176).

Charity's bedroom door to request sexual favors. Charity, we are told, "was not frightened, she simply felt a deep disgust" and scornfully reminded Royall that "this ain't your wife's room any longer" (101). In recalling the incident, Wharton establishes one of the novella's major themes, what Elizabeth Ammons refers to as "Wharton's bluntest criticism of the patriarchal sexual economy."[5] Indeed, *Summer* effectively underscores the limited options available to women of Charity's class in the early twentieth century. When Royall later proposes marriage, "he seemed like a hideous parody of the fatherly old man [Charity] had always known" (103). She sneeringly rejects his proposal, begins a sexual relationship with Harney, and soon becomes pregnant. After Harney abandons her, Charity impulsively turns to the Mountain to find her biological mother, who had given her up sixteen years earlier. Charity feels "a desperate desire to defend her secret from irreverent eyes, and begin life again among people to whom the harsh code of the village was unknown" (188).

Although Wharton often shows Charity acting on impulse and takes pains to illustrate her intellectual limitations, Charity is not a flat character. The pivotal Fourth of July celebration, for example, symbolically marks the attainment of Charity's short-lived independence and represents the first step in her sexual initiation with Harney. The imagery in the fireworks scene, in which Charity and Harney first share a kiss, is rife with meaning; the language is sexually evocative. Sitting in front of Harney and watching a "dishevelled rocket" (151) exploding in the sky, Charity feels Harney's knees against her bare head. Soon after, "the whole night broke into flower. From every point of the horizon, gold and silver arches sprang up [. . .] sky-orchards broke into blossom, shed their flaming petals and hung their branches with golden fruit; and all the while the air was filled with a soft supernatural hum [. . .]. Charity's heart throbbed with delight. [. . .] and Charity, grasping the hat on her knee, crushed it tight in the effort to restrain her rapture" (151). Though comparatively tame when measured against the erotic lyricism of Wharton's unfinished tale "Beatrice Palmato,"[6] which also deals with sexual initiation, albeit between a father and his daughter, the sensual language in this scene foreshadows Charity's surrender to Harney in the next chapter. It is also noteworthy that Harney's kiss is followed almost immediately by a confrontation with Lawyer Royall, who is accompanied by drunks and streetwalkers. He publicly condemns Charity and calls her a whore. The episode marks a new stage in Charity's quest for independence. She summons the courage to leave the house "of the

[5] Ammons 133.
[6] See pp. 239–241 in this New Riverside Edition.

man who had publicly dishonoured her" (155), vowing to return to the Mountain. Instead, however, she becomes sexually intimate with Lucius Harney (whose name vaguely suggests "horny devil"), and despite the fact that she realizes Harney belongs to a distinctly higher social class into which she will not be admitted, she succumbs to the romantic possibilities of such a union.

Pregnant and abandoned by Harney, who becomes engaged to a young woman of his own social rank, Charity returns to the Mountain to "begin life again among people to whom the harsh code of the village was unknown" (188). In the novella's most intense scene, Charity arrives to find her dead mother, disheveled and bloated, her body lying on a filthy mattress. "There was no sign in it of anything human; she lay there like a dead dog in a ditch" (193). The abandonment by her mother reinforces Charity's obligation to her own unborn child, and although she fears the repercussions of returning to North Dormer, she concludes that "anything, anything was better than to add another life to the nest of misery on the Mountain" (193).

Aside from its thematic emphasis on the politics of gender, one of the strengths of *Summer* is its structure. The novella begins with the promise of freedom, with Charity departing on a warm "June afternoon" (91) from the house of the man she despises; it ends "late [in the] evening, in the cold autumn moonlight" (210) with Charity, pregnant and married to a man she does not love, returning to the home from which she desperately wanted to escape. The juxtaposition of summer and autumn, the shift from departure to arrival, and the movement from freedom to subjugation allow the novella to come full circle. Moreover, Wharton skillfully infuses irony into the text. Charity's response to Royall's sexual overtures early in the work, "I guess you made a mistake [. . .]. This ain't your wife's room any longer" (101), is, at the end of the novella, no longer true. In the domestic climate of the early twentieth century, Lawyer Royall is free to demand, at his pleasure, conjugal relations with his young wife. He does not insist that they consummate their marriage on their wedding night (on the contrary, he sleeps in a chair and leaves her alone in the bed), but it is reasonable to assume that he will expect sexual intimacy. Moreover, Charity's pregnancy compels her dependence on Royall. Like Mattie Silver, Charity is uneducated and unskilled. In addition, given the descriptions of her state of mind in the last two chapters (she is described as "bewildered," "remote," "half-stunned," "frightened," "exhausted," "burdened," "faint," "speechless," "choked," "startled," "shaking," "passive," "confused," "desolate," "dazed," "sick," "disconcerted," "puzzled," and "desperate"), Charity's fate appears to be sealed.

Much of the power of *Summer,* in fact, derives from the subtle ironies that Wharton weaves throughout the text. For example, Charity's first words in the novella, "How I hate everything!" (91), uttered twice, in sequence, reflect her sense of oppression in the small, conservative village of North Dormer. At the end of the novella, her final words, "I guess you're good, too" (210), are in response to her new husband's declaration that she is "a good girl." There is a clear shift from the "hatred" that Charity expressed at the beginning of the novella, to "goodness," yet, at the same time Charity is simply parroting her father/husband's own words. Both linguistically and practically, Royall has appropriated control, and like the "good girl" that Royall has pronounced her to be, the once-rebellious Charity is strikingly deferential. Her sense of confidence has also eroded; the young woman who vociferously declared that she "hated" everything now responds "shyly and quickly," that "I *guess* you're good, too" (210, emphasis added), underscoring her lack of conviction.

Although most of the drama in the novella centers on Charity, Wharton insisted that it was Lawyer Royall who is at the center of *Summer.* To her friend Bernard Berenson she wrote, "I'm so particularly glad you like old man Royall. Of course, *he's* the book!"[7] Wharton, however, leaves many questions about Royall's character unanswered. We don't know, for example, whether his kindness at the end of *Summer* is genuine—a result of the fact that he will no longer be lonely—or whether his actions in "saving" Charity are a calculated maneuver to get her to succumb to his proposal when she is most vulnerable. In his one moment of glory—his speech at the Old Home Week festivities—he seems, in retrospect, to be speaking directly to Charity. Royall remarks that former residents of North Dormer may find themselves in circumstances that bring them "back for good. [...] For *good*" (170, Wharton's emphasis). He continues: "and even if you come back against your will—and thinking it's all a bitter mistake of Fate or Providence—you must try to make the best of it" [...] (170). Royall's emphasis on circumstances that bring people back to North Dormer "for good" is ironically echoed in one of the final scenes when Charity experiences in Royall's presence "a sense of peace and security. She knew that where he was there would be warmth, rest, silence; and for the moment, they were all she wanted" (203). The warmth, peace, and security that Royall apparently offers constitute the "good" to which she returns, pregnant and alone. Still, Wharton emphasizes that Charity is content "for the moment" (203) suggesting that she may very well again fall victim to the despair that enveloped her at the beginning of *Summer.*

---

[7] Wharton. "To Bernard Berenson," 4 Sept. 1917, *Letters* 398.

The fictional landscapes of *Ethan Frome* and *Summer* may be worlds away from the grand foyers and drawing rooms of *The House of Mirth* and *The Age of Innocence* (1920), but the problems that plague Ethan Frome and Charity Royall are no less poignant. The endings of the novellas find both protagonists trapped—victims of circumstances that they cannot escape. In defending herself against a critic who charged that *Ethan Frome* had been "successful" despite the fact that Wharton "knew nothing of New England" (*Backward Glance* 215), Wharton argued that the publication of *Summer* six years later might have confirmed "that I knew something at first hand of the life and the people into whose intimacy I had asked my readers to enter with me on two successive occasions."[8] Indeed, there is little question to modern readers that despite her social advantages and affluence, Wharton understood well the tragic and isolated lives of some of her most memorable characters, as these two masterful novellas attest.

---

[8] Wharton, *Colophon.*

A NOTE ON THE TEXTS
Denise D. Knight

E than Frome first appeared in *Scribner's* from August through October 1911 and was published in book form in October of that year by Charles Scribner's Sons in New York. Six years later, in 1917, D. Appleton and Company published *Summer,* which was originally serialized in *McClure's* magazine. The texts that appear in this volume are taken from first editions so that contemporary readers can experience the works as they originally appeared in book form. I have retained Wharton's spelling, punctuation, ellipses, capitalization, indentations, and italics. My objective has been to preserve, rather than to correct or amend, Wharton's original texts.

Allusions to words, events, people, places, or objects that might be unfamiliar to the contemporary reader, or that might benefit from clarification, are elucidated in footnotes.

Part One

———◆———

ETHAN FROME (1911)

Ethan Frome

Edith Wharton

I had the story, bit by bit, from various people, and, as generally happens in such cases, each time it was a different story.

If you know Starkfield, Massachusetts, you know the post-office. If you know the post-office you must have seen Ethan Frome drive up to it, drop the reins on his hollow-backed bay and drag himself across the brick pavement to the white colonnade; and you must have asked who he was.

It was there that, several years ago, I saw him for the first time; and the sight pulled me up sharp. Even then he was the most striking figure in Starkfield, though he was but the ruin of a man. It was not so much his great height that marked him, for the "natives" were easily singled out by their lank longitude from the stockier foreign breed: it was the careless powerful look he had, in spite of a lameness checking each step like the jerk of a chain. There was something bleak and unapproachable in his face, and he was so stiffened and grizzled that I took him for an old man and was surprised to hear that he was not more than fifty-two. I had this from Harmon Gow, who had driven the stage from Bettsbridge to Starkfield in pre-trolley days and knew the chronicle of all the families on his line.

"He's looked that way ever since he had his smash-up; and that's twenty-four years ago come next February," Harmon threw out between reminiscent pauses.

The "smash-up" it was—I gathered from the same informant—which, besides drawing the red gash across Ethan Frome's forehead, had so shortened and warped his right side that it cost him a visible effort to take the few steps from his buggy to the post-office window. He used to drive in from his farm every day at about noon, and as that was my own hour for fetching my mail I often passed him in the porch or stood beside him while we waited on the motions of the distributing hand behind the grating. I noticed that, though he came so punctually, he seldom received anything but a copy of the *Bettsbridge Eagle,* which he put without a glance into his sagging pocket. At intervals, however, the post-master would hand him an envelope addressed to Mrs. Zenobia—or Mrs. Zeena—Frome, and usually bearing conspicuously in the upper left-hand corner the address of some manufacturer of patent medicine and the name of his specific. These documents my neighbour would also pocket without a glance, as if too much used to them to wonder at their number and variety, and would then turn away with a silent nod to the post-master.

Every one in Starkfield knew him and gave him a greeting tempered to his own grave mien; but his taciturnity was respected and it was only on

---

Starkfield: a fictional town in the Berkshire Mountains of western Massachusetts.
Bettsbridge: a fictional town in the Berkshire Mountains of western Massachusetts.

rare occasions that one of the older men of the place detained him for a word. When this happened he would listen quietly, his blue eyes on the speaker's face, and answer in so low a tone that his words never reached me; then he would climb stiffly into his buggy, gather up the reins in his left hand and drive slowly away in the direction of his farm.

"It was a pretty bad smash-up?" I questioned Harmon, looking after Frome's retreating figure, and thinking how gallantly his lean brown head, with its shock of light hair, must have sat on his strong shoulders before they were bent out of shape.

"Wust kind," my informant assented. "More'n enough to kill most men. But the Fromes are tough. Ethan'll likely touch a hundred."

"Good God!" I exclaimed. At the moment Ethan Frome, after climbing to his seat, had leaned over to assure himself of the security of a wooden box—also with a druggist's label on it—which he had placed in the back of the buggy, and I saw his face as it probably looked when he thought him-self alone. "*That* man touch a hundred? He looks as if he was dead and in hell now!"

Harmon drew a slab of tobacco from his pocket, cut off a wedge and pressed it into the leather pouch of his cheek. "Guess he's been in Starkfield too many winters. Most of the smart ones get away."

"Why didn't *he*?"

"Somebody had to stay and care for the folks. There warn't ever any-body but Ethan. Fust his father—then his mother—then his wife."

"And then the smash-up?"

Harmon chuckled sardonically. "That's so. He *had* to stay then."

"I see. And since then they've had to care for him?"

Harmon thoughtfully passed his tobacco to the other cheek. "Oh, as to that: I guess it's always Ethan done the caring."

Though Harmon Gow developed the tale as far as his mental and moral reach permitted there were perceptible gaps between his facts, and I had the sense that the deeper meaning of the story was in the gaps. But one phrase stuck in my memory and served as the nucleus about which I grouped my subsequent inferences: "Guess he's been in Starkfield too many winters."

Before my own time there was up I had learned to know what that meant. Yet I had come in the degenerate day of trolley, bicycle and rural de-livery, when communication was easy between the scattered mountain vil-lages, and the bigger towns in the valleys, such as Bettsbridge and Shadd's Falls, had libraries, theatres and Y. M. C. A. halls to which the youth of the

---

Shadd's Falls: a fictional town in the Berkshire Mountains of western Massachusetts.

hills could descend for recreation. But when winter shut down on Stark-field, and the village lay under a sheet of snow perpetually renewed from the pale skies, I began to see what life there — or rather its negation — must have been in Ethan Frome's young manhood.

I had been sent up by my employers on a job connected with the big power-house at Corbury Junction, and a long-drawn carpenters' strike had so delayed the work that I found myself anchored at Starkfield — the near-est habitable spot — for the best part of the winter. I chafed at first, and then, under the hypnotising effect of routine, gradually began to find a grim satisfaction in the life. During the early part of my stay I had been struck by the contrast between the vitality of the climate and the deadness of the community. Day by day, after the December snows were over, a blaz-ing blue sky poured down torrents of light and air on the white landscape, which gave them back in an intenser glitter. One would have supposed that such an atmosphere must quicken the emotions as well as the blood; but it seemed to produce no change except that of retarding still more the slug-gish pulse of Starkfield. When I had been there a little longer, and had seen this phase of crystal clearness followed by long stretches of sunless cold; when the storms of February had pitched their white tents about the de-voted village and the wild cavalry of March winds had charged down to their support; I began to understand why Starkfield emerged from its six months' siege like a starved garrison capitulating without quarter. Twenty years earlier the means of resistance must have been far fewer, and the en-emy in command of almost all the lines of access between the beleaguered villages; and, considering these things, I felt the sinister force of Harmon's phrase: "Most of the smart ones get away." But if that were the case, how could any combination of obstacles have hindered the flight of a man like Ethan Frome?

During my stay at Starkfield I lodged with a middle-aged widow collo-quially known as Mrs. Ned Hale. Mrs. Hale's father had been the village lawyer of the previous generation, and "lawyer Varnum's house," where my landlady still lived with her mother, was the most considerable mansion in the village. It stood at one end of the main street, its classic portico and small-paned windows looking down a flagged path between Norway spruces to the slim white steeple of the Congregational church. It was clear that the Varnum fortunes were at the ebb, but the two women did what

---

Corbury Junction: a fictional town in the Berkshire Mountains of western Massa-chusetts.

portico: located at the entrance of a building, a walkway or porch covered by a roof sup-ported by columns.

they could to preserve a decent dignity; and Mrs. Hale, in particular, had a certain wan refinement not out of keeping with her pale old-fashioned house.

In the "best parlour," with its black horse-hair and mahogany weakly illuminated by a gurgling Carcel lamp, I listened every evening to another and more delicately shaded version of the Starkfield chronicle. It was not that Mrs. Ned Hale felt, or affected, any social superiority to the people about her; it was only that the accident of a finer sensibility and a little more education had put just enough distance between herself and her neighbours to enable her to judge them with detachment. She was not unwilling to exercise this faculty, and I had great hopes of getting from her the missing facts of Ethan Frome's story, or rather such a key to his character as should co-ordinate the facts I knew. Her mind was a store-house of innocuous anecdote and any question about her acquaintances brought forth a volume of detail; but on the subject of Ethan Frome I found her unexpectedly reticent. There was no hint of disapproval in her reserve; I merely felt in her an insurmountable reluctance to speak of him or his affairs, a low "Yes, I knew them both . . . it was awful . . ." seeming to be the utmost concession that her distress could make to my curiosity.

So marked was the change in her manner, such depths of sad initiation did it imply, that, with some doubts as to my delicacy, I put the case anew to my village oracle, Harmon Gow; but got for my pains only an uncomprehending grunt.

"Ruth Varnum was always as nervous as a rat; and, come to think of it, she was the first one to see 'em after they was picked up. It happened right below lawyer Varnum's, down at the bend of the Corbury road, just round about the time that Ruth got engaged to Ned Hale. The young folks was all friends, and I guess she just can't bear to talk about it. She's had troubles enough of her own."

All the dwellers in Starkfield, as in more notable communities, had had troubles enough of their own to make them comparatively indifferent to those of their neighbours; and though all conceded that Ethan Frome's had been beyond the common measure, no one gave me an explanation of the look in his face which, as I persisted in thinking, neither poverty nor physical suffering could have put there. Nevertheless, I might have contented myself with the story pieced together from these hints had it not been for

---

best parlour: a room used primarily for conversation or the reception of guests.

Carcel lamp: an oil lamp, named after a French inventor, in which the oil is raised through tubes by clockwork and produces a brilliant light.

the provocation of Mrs. Hale's silence, and—a little later—for the accident of personal contact with the man.

On my arrival at Starkfield, Denis Eady, the rich Irish grocer, who was the proprietor of Starkfield's nearest approach to a livery stable, had entered into an agreement to send me over daily to Corbury Flats, where I had to pick up my train for the Junction. But about the middle of the winter Eady's horses fell ill of a local epidemic. The illness spread to the other Starkfield stables and for a day or two I was put to it to find a means of transport. Then Harmon Gow suggested that Ethan Frome's bay was still on his legs and that his owner might be glad to drive me over.

I stared at the suggestion. "Ethan Frome? But I've never even spoken to him. Why on earth should he put himself out for me?"

Harmon's answer surprised me still more. "I don't know as he would; but I know he wouldn't be sorry to earn a dollar."

I had been told that Frome was poor, and that the saw-mill and the arid acres of his farm yielded scarcely enough to keep his household through the winter; but I had not supposed him to be in such want as Harmon's words implied, and I expressed my wonder.

"Well, matters ain't gone any too well with him," Harmon said. "When a man's been setting round like a hulk for twenty years or more, seeing things that want doing, it eats inter him, and he loses his grit. That Frome farm was always 'bout as bare's a milkpan when the cat's been round; and you know what one of them old water-mills is wuth nowadays. When Ethan could sweat over 'em both from sun-up to dark he kinder choked a living out of 'em; but his folks ate up most everything, even then, and I don't see how he makes out now. Fust his father got a kick, out haying, and went soft in the brain, and gave away money like Bible texts afore he died. Then his mother got queer and dragged along for years as weak as a baby; and his wife Zeena, she's always been the greatest hand at doctoring in the county. Sickness and trouble: that's what Ethan's had his plate full up with, ever since the very first helping."

The next morning, when I looked out, I saw the hollow-backed bay between the Varnum spruces, and Ethan Frome, throwing back his worn bear-skin, made room for me in the sleigh at his side. After that, for a week, he drove me over every morning to Corbury Flats, and on my return in the afternoon met me again and carried me back through the icy night to Starkfield. The distance each way was barely three miles, but the old bay's pace was slow, and even with firm snow under the runners we were nearly

---

Corbury Flats: a fictional town in the Berkshire Mountains of western Massachusetts.

an hour on the way. Ethan Frome drove in silence, the reins loosely held in his left hand, his brown seamed profile, under the helmet-like peak of the cap, relieved against the banks of snow like the bronze image of a hero. He never turned his face to mine, or answered, except in monosyllables, the questions I put, or such slight pleasantries as I ventured. He seemed a part of the mute melancholy landscape, an incarnation of its frozen woe, with all that was warm and sentient in him fast bound below the surface; but there was nothing unfriendly in his silence. I simply felt that he lived in a depth of moral isolation too remote for casual access, and I had the sense that his loneliness was not merely the result of his personal plight, tragic as I guessed that to be, but had in it, as Harmon Gow had hinted, the profound accumulated cold of many Starkfield winters.

Only once or twice was the distance between us bridged for a moment; and the glimpses thus gained confirmed my desire to know more. Once I happened to speak of an engineering job I had been on the previous year in Florida, and of the contrast between the winter landscape about us and that in which I had found myself the year before; and to my surprise Frome said suddenly: "Yes: I was down there once, and for a good while afterward I could call up the sight of it in winter. But now it's all snowed under."

He said no more, and I had to guess the rest from the inflection of his voice and his sharp relapse into silence.

Another day, on getting into my train at the Flats, I missed a volume of popular science—I think it was on some recent discoveries in biochemistry—which I had carried with me to read on the way. I thought no more about it till I got into the sleigh again that evening, and saw the book in Frome's hand.

"I found it after you were gone," he said.

I put the volume into my pocket and we dropped back into our usual silence; but as we began to crawl up the long hill from Corbury Flats to the Starkfield ridge I became aware in the dusk that he had turned his face to mine.

"There are things in that book that I didn't know the first word about," he said.

I wondered less at his words than at the queer note of resentment in his voice. He was evidently surprised and slightly aggrieved at his own ignorance.

"Does that sort of thing interest you?" I asked.

"It used to."

---

popular science: *Popular Science,* a science and technology magazine founded in 1872.

"There are one or two rather new things in the book: there have been some big strides lately in that particular line of research." I waited a moment for an answer that did not come; then I said: "If you'd like to look the book through I'd be glad to leave it with you."

He hesitated, and I had the impression that he felt himself about to yield to a stealing tide of inertia; then, "Thank you—I'll take it," he answered shortly.

I hoped that this incident might set up some more direct communication between us. Frome was so simple and straightforward that I was sure his curiosity about the book was based on a genuine interest in its subject. Such tastes and acquirements in a man of his condition made the contrast more poignant between his outer situation and his inner needs, and I hoped that the chance of giving expression to the latter might at least unseal his lips. But something in his past history, or in his present way of living, had apparently driven him too deeply into himself for any casual impulse to draw him back to his kind. At our next meeting he made no allusion to the book, and our intercourse seemed fated to remain as negative and one-sided as if there had been no break in his reserve.

Frome had been driving me over to the Flats for about a week when one morning I looked out of my window into a thick snow-fall. The height of the white waves massed against the garden-fence and along the wall of the church showed that the storm must have been going on all night, and that the drifts were likely to be heavy in the open. I thought it probable that my train would be delayed; but I had to be at the power-house for an hour or two that afternoon, and I decided, if Frome turned up, to push through to the Flats and wait there till my train came in. I don't know why I put it in the conditional, however, for I never doubted that Frome would appear. He was not the kind of man to be turned from his business by any commotion of the elements; and at the appointed hour his sleigh glided up through the snow like a stage-apparition behind thickening veils of gauze.

I was getting to know him too well to express either wonder or gratitude at his keeping his appointment; but I exclaimed in surprise as I saw him turn his horse in a direction opposite to that of the Corbury road.

"The railroad's blocked by a freight-train that got stuck in a drift below the Flats," he explained, as we jogged off into the stinging whiteness.

"But look here—where are you taking me, then?"

---

power-house: an electric utility generating station.

"Straight to the Junction, by the shortest way," he answered, pointing up School House Hill with his whip.

"To the Junction—in this storm? Why, it's a good ten miles!"

"The bay'll do it if you give him time. You said you had some business there this afternoon. I'll see you get there."

He said it so quietly that I could only answer: "You're doing me the biggest kind of a favour."

"That's all right," he rejoined.

Abreast of the schoolhouse the road forked, and we dipped down a lane to the left, between hemlock boughs bent inward to their trunks by the weight of the snow. I had often walked that way on Sundays, and knew that the solitary roof showing through bare branches near the bottom of the hill was that of Frome's saw-mill. It looked exanimate enough, with its idle wheel looming above the black stream dashed with yellow-white spume, and its cluster of sheds sagging under their white load. Frome did not even turn his head as we drove by, and still in silence we began to mount the next slope. About a mile farther, on a road I had never travelled, we came to an orchard of starved apple-trees writhing over a hillside among outcroppings of slate that nuzzled up through the snow like animals pushing out their noses to breathe. Beyond the orchard lay a field or two, their boundaries lost under drifts; and above the fields, huddled against the white immensities of land and sky, one of those lonely New England farm-houses that make the landscape lonelier.

"That's my place," said Frome, with a sideway jerk of his lame elbow; and in the distress and oppression of the scene I did not know what to answer. The snow had ceased, and a flash of watery sunlight exposed the house on the slope above us in all its plaintive ugliness. The black wraith of a deciduous creeper flapped from the porch, and the thin wooden walls, under their worn coat of paint, seemed to shiver in the wind that had risen with the ceasing of the snow.

"The house was bigger in my father's time: I had to take down the 'L,' a while back," Frome continued, checking with a twitch of the left rein the bay's evident intention of turning in through the broken-down gate.

I saw then that the unusually forlorn and stunted look of the house was partly due to the loss of what is known in New England as the "L": that long

---

exanimate: appearing lifeless

spume: foam.

wraith: ghost.

"L": an addition to a house that gives the whole structure a shape resembling the letter L.

deep-roofed adjunct usually built at right angles to the main house, and connecting it, by way of store-rooms and tool-house, with the wood-shed and cow-barn. Whether because of its symbolic sense, the image it presents of a life linked with the soil, and enclosing in itself the chief sources of warmth and nourishment, or whether merely because of the consolatory thought that it enables the dwellers in that harsh climate to get to their morning's work without facing the weather, it is certain that the "L" rather than the house itself seems to be the centre, the actual hearth-stone, of the New England farm. Perhaps this connection of ideas, which had often occurred to me in my rambles about Starkfield, caused me to hear a wistful note in Frome's words, and to see in the diminished dwelling the image of his own shrunken body.

"We're kinder side-tracked here now," he added, "but there was considerable passing before the railroad was carried through to the Flats." He roused the lagging bay with another twitch; then, as if the mere sight of the house had let me too deeply into his confidence for any farther pretence of reserve, he went on slowly: "I've always set down the worst of mother's trouble to that. When she got the rheumatism so bad she couldn't move around she used to sit up there and watch the road by the hour; and one year, when they was six months mending the Bettsbridge pike after the floods, and Harmon Gow had to bring his stage round this way, she picked up so that she used to get down to the gate most days to see him. But after the trains begun running nobody ever come by here to speak of, and mother never could get it through her head what had happened, and it preyed on her right along till she died."

As we turned into the Corbury road the snow began to fall again, cutting off our last glimpse of the house; and Frome's silence fell with it, letting down between us the old veil of reticence. This time the wind did not cease with the return of the snow. Instead, it sprang up to a gale which now and then, from a tattered sky, flung pale sweeps of sunlight over a landscape chaotically tossed. But the bay was as good as Frome's word, and we pushed on to the Junction through the wild white scene.

In the afternoon the storm held off, and the clearness in the west seemed to my inexperienced eye the pledge of a fair evening. I finished my business as quickly as possible, and we set out for Starkfield with a good chance of getting there for supper. But at sunset the clouds gathered again, bringing an earlier night, and the snow began to fall straight and steadily from a sky without wind, in a soft universal diffusion more confusing than the gusts and eddies of the morning. It seemed to be a part of the thickening darkness, to be the winter night itself descending on us layer by layer.

The small ray of Frome's lantern was soon lost in this smothering medium, in which even his sense of direction, and the bay's homing instinct, finally ceased to serve us. Two or three times some ghostly landmark sprang up to warn us that we were astray, and then was sucked back into the mist; and when we finally regained our road the old horse began to show signs of exhaustion. I felt myself to blame for having accepted Frome's offer, and after a short discussion I persuaded him to let me get out of the sleigh and walk along through the snow at the bay's side. In this way we struggled on for another mile or two, and at last reached a point where Frome, peering into what seemed to me formless night, said: "That's my gate down yonder."

The last stretch had been the hardest part of the way. The bitter cold and the heavy going had nearly knocked the wind out of me, and I could feel the horse's side ticking like a clock under my hand.

"Look here, Frome," I began, "there's no earthly use in your going any farther—" but he interrupted me: "Nor you neither. There's been about enough of this for anybody."

I understood that he was offering me a night's shelter at the farm, and without answering I turned into the gate at his side, and followed him to the barn, where I helped him to unharness and bed down the tired horse. When this was done he unhooked the lantern from the sleigh, stepped out again into the night, and called to me over his shoulder: "This way."

Far off above us a square of light trembled through the screen of snow. Staggering along in Frome's wake I floundered toward it, and in the darkness almost fell into one of the deep drifts against the front of the house. Frome scrambled up the slippery steps of the porch, digging a way through the snow with his heavily booted foot. Then he lifted his lantern, found the latch, and led the way into the house. I went after him into a low unlit passage, at the back of which a ladder-like staircase rose into obscurity. On our right a line of light marked the door of the room which had sent its ray across the night; and behind the door I heard a woman's voice droning querulously.

Frome stamped on the worn oil-cloth to shake the snow from his boots, and set down his lantern on a kitchen chair which was the only piece of furniture in the hall. Then he opened the door.

"Come in," he said; and as he spoke the droning voice grew still. . .

It was that night that I found the clue to Ethan Frome, and began to put together this vision of his story.   .   .   .   .

.   .   .   .

.   .   .   .

I

The village lay under two feet of snow, with drifts at the windy corners. In a sky of iron the points of the Dipper hung like icicles and Orion flashed his cold fires. The moon had set, but the night was so transparent that the white house-fronts between the elms looked gray against the snow, clumps of bushes made black stains on it, and the basement windows of the church sent shafts of yellow light far across the endless undulations.

Young Ethan Frome walked at a quick pace along the deserted street, past the bank and Michael Eady's new brick store and Lawyer Varnum's house with the two black Norway spruces at the gate. Opposite the Varnum gate, where the road fell away toward the Corbury valley, the church reared its slim white steeple and narrow peristyle. As the young man walked toward it the upper windows drew a black arcade along the side wall of the building, but from the lower openings, on the side where the ground sloped steeply down to the Corbury road, the light shot its long bars, illuminating many fresh furrows in the track leading to the basement door, and showing, under an adjoining shed, a line of sleighs with heavily blanketed horses.

The night was perfectly still, and the air so dry and pure that it gave little sensation of cold. The effect produced on Frome was rather of a complete absence of atmosphere, as though nothing less tenuous than ether intervened between the white earth under his feet and the metallic dome overhead. "It's like being in an exhausted receiver," he thought. Four or five years earlier he had taken a year's course at a technological college at Worcester, and dabbled in the laboratory with a friendly professor of physics; and the images supplied by that experience still cropped up, at unexpected moments, through the totally different associations of thought in which he had since been living. His father's death, and the misfortunes following it, had put a premature end to Ethan's studies; but though they had not gone far enough to be of much practical use they had fed his fancy and made him aware of huge cloudy meanings behind the daily face of things.

Orion: a constellation on the equator east of Taurus, represented on charts by the figure of a hunter with a belt and sword.

peristyle: columns surrounding a building or an open space.

receiver: a device for converting signals, such as electromagnetic waves, into audio or visual form.

Worcester: a city in east central Massachusetts.

As he strode along through the snow the sense of such meanings glowed in his brain and mingled with the bodily flush produced by his sharp tramp. At the end of the village he paused before the darkened front of the church. He stood there a moment, breathing quickly, and looking up and down the street, in which not another figure moved. The pitch of the Corbury road, below lawyer Varnum's spruces, was the favourite coasting-ground of Starkfield, and on clear evenings the church corner rang till late with the shouts of the coasters; but to-night not a sled darkened the whiteness of the long declivity. The hush of midnight lay on the village, and all its waking life was gathered behind the church windows, from which strains of dance-music flowed with the broad bands of yellow light.

The young man, skirting the side of the building, went down the slope toward the basement door. To keep out of range of the revealing rays from within he made a circuit through the untrodden snow and gradually approached the farther angle of the basement wall. Thence, still hugging the shadow, he edged his way cautiously forward to the nearest window, holding back his straight spare body and craning his neck till he got a glimpse of the room.

Seen thus, from the pure and frosty darkness in which he stood, it seemed to be seething in a mist of heat. The metal reflectors of the gas-jets sent crude waves of light against the whitewashed walls, and the iron flanks of the stove at the end of the hall looked as though they were heaving with volcanic fires. The floor was thronged with girls and young men. Down the side wall facing the window stood a row of kitchen chairs from which the older women had just risen. By this time the music had stopped, and the musicians—a fiddler, and the young lady who played the harmonium on Sundays—were hastily refreshing themselves at one corner of the supper-table which aligned its devastated pie-dishes and ice-cream saucers on the platform at the end of the hall. The guests were preparing to leave, and the tide had already set toward the passage where coats and wraps were hung, when a young man with a sprightly foot and a shock of black hair shot into the middle of the floor and clapped his hands. The signal took instant effect. The musicians hurried to their instruments, the dancers— some already half-muffled for departure—fell into line down each side of the room, the older spectators slipped back to their chairs, and the lively young man, after diving about here and there in the throng, drew forth a girl who had already wound a cherry-coloured "fascinator" about her

---

harmonium: a small organlike keyboard instrument.
fascinator: a woman's scarf.

head, and, leading her up to the end of the floor, whirled her down its length to the bounding tune of a Virginia reel.

Frome's heart was beating fast. He had been straining for a glimpse of the dark head under the cherry-coloured scarf and it vexed him that another eye should have been quicker than his. The leader of the reel, who looked as if he had Irish blood in his veins, danced well, and his partner caught his fire. As she passed down the line, her light figure swinging from hand to hand in circles of increasing swiftness, the scarf flew off her head and stood out behind her shoulders, and Frome, at each turn, caught sight of her laughing panting lips, the cloud of dark hair about her forehead, and the dark eyes which seemed the only fixed points in a maze of flying lines.

The dancers were going faster and faster, and the musicians, to keep up with them, belaboured their instruments like jockeys lashing their mounts on the home-stretch; yet it seemed to the young man at the window that the reel would never end. Now and then he turned his eyes from the girl's face to that of her partner, which, in the exhilaration of the dance, had taken on a look of almost impudent ownership. Denis Eady was the son of Michael Eady, the ambitious Irish grocer, whose suppleness and effrontery had given Starkfield its first notion of "smart" business methods, and whose new brick store testified to the success of the attempt. His son seemed likely to follow in his steps, and was meanwhile applying the same arts to the conquest of the Starkfield maidenhood. Hitherto Ethan Frome had been content to think him a mean fellow; but now he positively invited a horse-whipping. It was strange that the girl did not seem aware of it: that she could lift her rapt face to her dancer's, and drop her hands into his, without appearing to feel the offence of his look and touch.

Frome was in the habit of walking into Starkfield to fetch home his wife's cousin, Mattie Silver, on the rare evenings when some chance of amusement drew her to the village. It was his wife who had suggested, when the girl came to live with them, that such opportunities should be put in her way. Mattie Silver came from Stamford, and when she entered the Fromes' household to act as her cousin Zeena's aid it was thought best, as she came without pay, not to let her feel too sharp a contrast between the life she had left and the isolation of a Starkfield farm. But for this—as Frome sardonically reflected—it would hardly have occurred to Zeena to take any thought for the girl's amusement.

Virginia reel: an American country dance in which two lines of dancers face each other and each pair in turn performs a series of dance moves.
Stamford: a city in Connecticut.

When his wife first proposed that they should give Mattie an occasional evening out he had inwardly demurred at having to do the extra two miles to the village and back after his hard day on the farm; but not long afterward he had reached the point of wishing that Starkfield might give all its nights to revelry.

Mattie Silver had lived under his roof for a year, and from early morning till they met at supper he had frequent chances of seeing her; but no moments in her company were comparable to those when, her arm in his, and her light step flying to keep time with his long stride, they walked back through the night to the farm. He had taken to the girl from the first day, when he had driven over to the Flats to meet her, and she had smiled and waved to him from the train, crying out "You must be Ethan!" as she jumped down with her bundles, while he reflected, looking over her slight person: "She don't look much on house-work, but she ain't a fretter, anyhow." But it was not only that the coming to his house of a bit of hopeful young life was like the lighting of a fire on a cold hearth. The girl was more than the bright serviceable creature he had thought her. She had an eye to see and an ear to hear: he could show her things and tell her things, and taste the bliss of feeling that all he imparted left long reverberations and echoes he could wake at will.

It was during their night walks back to the farm that he felt most intensely the sweetness of this communion. He had always been more sensitive than the people about him to the appeal of natural beauty. His unfinished studies had given form to this sensibility and even in his unhappiest moments field and sky spoke to him with a deep and powerful persuasion. But hitherto the emotion had remained in him as a silent ache, veiling with sadness the beauty that evoked it. He did not even know whether any one else in the world felt as he did, or whether he was the sole victim of this mournful privilege. Then he learned that one other spirit had trembled with the same touch of wonder: that at his side, living under his roof and eating his bread, was a creature to whom he could say: "That's Orion down yonder; the big fellow to the right is Aldebaran, and the bunch of little ones—like bees swarming—they're the Pleiades . . ." or whom he could hold entranced before a ledge of granite thrusting up through the fern while he unrolled the huge panorama of the ice age, and the long dim stretches of succeeding time. The fact that admiration for his learning

---

Aldebaran: the brightest star of the constellation Taurus.

Pleiades: a conspicuous cluster of stars in the constellation Taurus; it includes six stars in the form of a very small dipper.

mingled with Mattie's wonder at what he taught was not the least part of his pleasure. And there were other sensations, less definable but more exquisite, which drew them together with a shock of silent joy: the cold red of sunset behind winter hills, the flight of cloud-flocks over slopes of golden stubble, or the intensely blue shadows of hemlocks on sunlit snow. When she said to him once: "It looks just as if it was painted!" it seemed to Ethan that the art of definition could go no farther, and that words had at last been found to utter his secret soul. . . .

As he stood in the darkness outside the church these memories came back with the poignancy of vanished things. Watching Mattie whirl down the floor from hand to hand he wondered how he could ever have thought that his dull talk interested her. To him, who was never gay but in her presence, her gaiety seemed plain proof of indifference. The face she lifted to her dancers was the same which, when she saw him, always looked like a window that has caught the sunset. He even noticed two or three gestures which, in his fatuity, he had thought she kept for him: a way of throwing her head back when she was amused, as if to taste her laugh before she let it out, and a trick of sinking her lids slowly when anything charmed or moved her.

The sight made him unhappy, and his unhappiness roused his latent fears. His wife had never shown any jealousy of Mattie, but of late she had grumbled increasingly over the house-work and found oblique ways of attracting attention to the girl's inefficiency. Zeena had always been what Starkfield called "sickly," and Frome had to admit that, if she were as ailing as she believed, she needed the help of a stronger arm than the one which lay so lightly in his during the night walks to the farm. Mattie had no natural turn for house-keeping, and her training had done nothing to remedy the defect. She was quick to learn, but forgetful and dreamy, and not disposed to take the matter seriously. Ethan had an idea that if she were to marry a man she was fond of the dormant instinct would wake, and her pies and biscuits become the pride of the county; but domesticity in the abstract did not interest her. At first she was so awkward that he could not help laughing at her; but she laughed with him and that made them better friends. He did his best to supplement her unskilled efforts, getting up earlier than usual to light the kitchen fire, carrying in the wood overnight, and neglecting the mill for the farm that he might help her about the house during the day. He even crept down on Saturday nights to scrub the kitchen floor after the women had gone to bed; and Zeena, one day, had surprised him at the churn and had turned away silently, with one of her queer looks.

Of late there had been other signs of her disfavour, as intangible but more disquieting. One cold winter morning, as he dressed in the dark, his candle flickering in the draught of the ill-fitting window, he had heard her speak from the bed behind him.

"The doctor don't want I should be left without anybody to do for me," she said in her flat whine.

He had supposed her to be asleep, and the sound of her voice had startled him, though she was given to abrupt explosions of speech after long intervals of secretive silence.

He turned and looked at her where she lay indistinctly outlined under the dark calico quilt, her high-boned face taking a grayish tinge from the whiteness of the pillow.

"Nobody to do for you?" he repeated.

"If you say you can't afford a hired girl when Mattie goes."

Frome turned away again, and taking up his razor stooped to catch the reflection of his stretched cheek in the blotched looking-glass above the wash-stand.

"Why on earth should Mattie go?"

"Well, when she gets married, I mean," his wife's drawl came from behind him.

"Oh, she'd never leave us as long as you needed her," he returned, scraping hard at his chin.

"I wouldn't ever have it said that I stood in the way of a poor girl like Mattie marrying a smart fellow like Denis Eady," Zeena answered in a tone of plaintive self-effacement.

Ethan, glaring at his face in the glass, threw his head back to draw the razor from ear to chin. His hand was steady, but the attitude was an excuse for not making an immediate reply.

"And the doctor don't want I should be left without anybody," Zeena continued. "He wanted I should speak to you about a girl he's heard about, that might come——"

Ethan laid down the razor and straightened himself with a laugh.

"Denis Eady! If that's all I guess there's no such hurry to look round for a girl."

"Well, I'd like to talk to you about it," said Zeena obstinately.

He was getting into his clothes in fumbling haste. "All right. But I haven't got the time now; I'm late as it is," he returned, holding his old silver turnip-watch to the candle.

Zeena, apparently accepting this as final, lay watching him in silence while he pulled his suspenders over his shoulders and jerked his arms into

---

turnip-watch: a large pocket watch.

his coat; but as he went toward the door she said, suddenly and incisively: "I guess you're always late, now you shave every morning."

That thrust had frightened him more than any vague insinuations about Denis Eady. It was a fact that since Mattie Silver's coming he had taken to shaving every day; but his wife always seemed to be asleep when he left her side in the winter darkness, and he had stupidly assumed that she would not notice any change in his appearance. Once or twice in the past he had been faintly disquieted by Zenobia's way of letting things happen without seeming to remark them, and then, weeks afterward, in a casual phrase, revealing that she had all along taken her notes and drawn her inferences. Of late, however, there had been no room in his thoughts for such vague apprehensions. Zeena herself, from an oppressive reality, had faded into an insubstantial shade. All his life was lived in the sight and sound of Mattie Silver, and he could no longer conceive of its being otherwise. But now, as he stood outside the church, and saw Mattie spinning down the floor with Denis Eady, a throng of disregarded hints and menaces wove their cloud about his brain. . .

I I

As the dancers poured out of the hall Frome, drawing back behind the projecting storm-door, watched the segregation of the grotesquely muffled groups, in which a moving lantern ray now and then lit up a face flushed with food and dancing. The villagers, being afoot, were the first to climb the slope to the main street, while the country neighbours packed themselves more slowly into the sleighs under the shed.

"Ain't you riding, Mattie?" a woman's voice called back from the throng about the shed, and Ethan's heart gave a jump. From where he stood he could not see the persons coming out of the hall till they had advanced a few steps beyond the wooden sides of the storm-door; but through its cracks he heard a clear voice answer: "Mercy no! Not on such a night."

She was there, then, close to him, only a thin board between. In another moment she would step forth into the night, and his eyes, accustomed to the obscurity, would discern her as clearly as though she stood in daylight. A wave of shyness pulled him back into the dark angle of the wall, and he stood there in silence instead of making his presence known to her. It had been one of the wonders of their intercourse that from the first, she, the quicker, finer, more expressive, instead of crushing him by the contrast, had given him something of her own ease and freedom; but now he felt as heavy and loutish as in his student days, when he had tried to "jolly" the Worcester girls at a picnic.

He hung back, and she came out alone and paused within a few yards of him. She was almost the last to leave the hall, and she stood looking uncertainly about her as if wondering why he did not show himself. Then a man's figure approached, coming so close to her that under their formless wrappings they seemed merged in one dim outline.

"Gentleman friend gone back on you? Say, Matt, that's tough! No, I wouldn't be mean enough to tell the other girls. I ain't as low-down as that." (How Frome hated his cheap banter!) "But look at here, ain't it lucky I got the old man's cutter down there waiting for us?"

Frome heard the girl's voice, gaily incredulous: "What on earth's your father's cutter doin' down there?"

"Why, waiting for me to take a ride. I got the roan colt too. I kinder knew I'd want to take a ride to-night," Eady, in his triumph, tried to put a sentimental note into his bragging voice.

The girl seemed to waver, and Frome saw her twirl the end of her scarf irresolutely about her fingers. Not for the world would he have made a sign to her, though it seemed to him that his life hung on her next gesture.

"Hold on a minute while I unhitch the colt," Denis called to her, springing toward the shed.

She stood perfectly still, looking after him, in an attitude of tranquil expectancy torturing to the hidden watcher. Frome noticed that she no longer turned her head from side to side, as though peering through the night for another figure. She let Denis Eady lead out the horse, climb into the cutter and fling back the bearskin to make room for her at his side; then, with a swift motion of flight, she turned about and darted up the slope toward the front of the church.

"Good-bye! Hope you'll have a lovely ride!" she called back to him over her shoulder.

Denis laughed, and gave the horse a cut that brought him quickly abreast of her retreating figure.

"Come along! Get in quick! It's as slippery as thunder on this turn," he cried, leaning over to reach out a hand to her.

She laughed back at him: "Good-night! I'm not getting in."

By this time they had passed beyond Frome's earshot and he could only follow the shadowy pantomime of their silhouettes as they continued to

---

jolly: to flatter.
cutter: a light sleigh.

move along the crest of the slope above him. He saw Eady, after a moment, jump from the cutter and go toward the girl with the reins over one arm. The other he tried to slip through hers; but she eluded him nimbly, and Frome's heart, which had swung out over a black void, trembled back to safety. A moment later he heard the jingle of departing sleigh bells and discerned a figure advancing alone toward the empty expanse of snow before the church.

In the black shade of the Varnum spruces he caught up with her and she turned with a quick "Oh!"

"Think I'd forgotten you, Matt?" he asked with sheepish glee.

She answered seriously: "I thought maybe you couldn't come back for me."

"Couldn't? What on earth could stop me?"

"I knew Zeena wasn't feeling any too good to-day."

"Oh, she's in bed long ago." He paused, a question struggling in him. "Then you meant to walk home all alone?"

"Oh, I ain't afraid!" she laughed.

They stood together in the gloom of the spruces, an empty world glimmering about them wide and grey under the stars. He brought his question out.

"If you thought I hadn't come, why didn't you ride back with Denis Eady?"

"Why, where *were* you? How did you know? I never saw you!"

Her wonder and his laughter ran together like spring rills in a thaw. Ethan had the sense of having done something arch and ingenious. To prolong the effect he groped for a dazzling phrase, and brought out, in a growl of rapture: "Come along."

He slipped an arm through hers, as Eady had done, and fancied it was faintly pressed against her side; but neither of them moved. It was so dark under the spruces that he could barely see the shape of her head beside his shoulder. He longed to stoop his cheek and rub it against her scarf. He would have liked to stand there with her all night in the blackness. She moved forward a step or two and then paused again above the dip of the Corbury road. Its icy slope, scored by innumerable runners, looked like a mirror scratched by travellers at an inn.

"There was a whole lot of them coasting before the moon set," she said.

"Would you like to come in and coast with them some night?" he asked.

"Oh, *would* you, Ethan? It would be lovely!"

"We'll come to-morrow if there's a moon."

She lingered, pressing closer to his side. "Ned Hale and Ruth Varnum came just as *near* running into the big elm at the bottom. We were all sure they were killed." Her shiver ran down his arm. "Wouldn't it have been too awful? They're so happy!"

"Oh, Ned ain't much at steering. I guess I can take you down all right!" he said disdainfully.

He was aware that he was "talking big," like Denis Eady; but his reaction of joy had unsteadied him, and the inflection with which she had said of the engaged couple "They're so happy!" made the words sound as if she had been thinking of herself and him.

"The elm *is* dangerous, though. It ought to be cut down," she insisted.

"Would you be afraid of it, with me?"

"I told you I ain't the kind to be afraid," she tossed back, almost indifferently; and suddenly she began to walk on with a rapid step.

These alterations of mood were the despair and joy of Ethan Frome. The motions of her mind were as incalculable as the flit of a bird in the branches. The fact that he had no right to show his feelings, and thus provoke the expression of hers, made him attach a fantastic importance to every change in her look and tone. Now he thought she understood him, and feared; now he was sure she did not, and despaired. To-night the pressure of accumulated misgivings sent the scale drooping toward despair, and her indifference was the more chilling after the flush of joy into which she had plunged him by dismissing Denis Eady. He mounted School House Hill at her side and walked on in silence till they reached the lane leading to the saw-mill; then the need of some definite assurance grew too strong for him.

"You'd have found me right off if you hadn't gone back to have that last reel with Denis," he brought out awkwardly. He could not pronounce the name without a stiffening of the muscles of his throat.

"Why, Ethan, how could I tell you were there?"

"I suppose what folks say is true," he jerked out at her, instead of answering.

She stopped short, and he felt, in the darkness, that her face was lifted quickly to his. "Why, what do folks say?"

"It's natural enough you should be leaving us," he floundered on, following his thought.

"Is that what they say?" she mocked back at him; then, with a sudden drop of her sweet treble: "You mean that Zeena—ain't suited with me any more?" she faltered.

Their arms had slipped apart and they stood motionless, each seeking to distinguish the other's face.

"I know I ain't anything like as smart as I ought to be," she went on, while he vainly struggled for expression. "There's lots of things a hired girl could do that come awkward to me still—and I haven't got much strength in my arms. But if she'd only tell me I'd try. You know she hardly ever says anything, and sometimes I can see she ain't suited, and yet I don't know why." She turned on him with a sudden flash of indignation. "You'd ought to tell me, Ethan Frome—you'd ought to! Unless *you* want me to go too——"

Unless he wanted her to go too! The cry was balm to his raw wound. The iron heavens seemed to melt and rain down sweetness. Again he struggled for the all-expressive word, and again, his arm in hers, found only a deep "Come along."

They walked on in silence through the blackness of the hemlock-shaded lane, where Ethan's saw-mill gloomed through the night, and out again into the comparative clearness of the fields. On the farther side of the hemlock belt the open country rolled away before them grey and lonely under the stars. Sometimes their way led them under the shade of an overhanging bank or through the thin obscurity of a clump of leafless trees. Here and there a farmhouse stood far back among the fields, mute and cold as a grave-stone. The night was so still that they heard the frozen snow crackle under their feet. The crash of a loaded branch falling far off in the woods reverberated like a musket-shot, and once a fox barked, and Mattie shrank closer to Ethan, and quickened her steps.

At length they sighted the group of larches at Ethan's gate, and as they drew near it the sense that the walk was over brought back his words.

"Then you don't want to leave us, Matt?"

He had to stoop his head to catch her stifled whisper: "Where'd I go, if I did?"

The answer sent a pang through him but the tone suffused him with joy. He forgot what else he had meant to say and pressed her against him so closely that he seemed to feel her warmth in his veins.

"You ain't crying are you, Matt?"

"No, of course I'm not," she quavered.

They turned in at the gate and passed under the shaded knoll where, enclosed in a low fence, the Frome grave-stones slanted at crazy angles through the snow. Ethan looked at them curiously. For years that quiet company had mocked his restlessness, his desire for change and freedom. "We never got away—how should you?" seemed to be written on every headstone; and whenever he went in or out of his gate he thought with a shiver: "I shall just go on living here till I join them." But now all desire for change had vanished, and the sight of the little enclosure gave him a warm sense of continuance and stability.

---

larches: any of a genus of cone-bearing trees of the pine family; they are unusual because they are not evergreen—they lose their needle-shaped leaves.

"I guess we'll never let you go, Matt," he whispered, as though even the dead, lovers once, must conspire with him to keep her; and brushing by the graves, he thought: "We'll always go on living here together, and some day she'll lie there beside me."

He let the vision possess him as they climbed the hill to the house. He was never so happy with her as when he abandoned himself to these dreams. Half-way up the slope Mattie stumbled against some unseen ob-struction and clutched his sleeve to steady herself. The wave of warmth that went through him was like the prolongation of his vision. For the first time he stole his arm about her, and she did not resist. They walked on as if they were floating on a summer stream.

Zeena always went to bed as soon as she had had her supper, and the shutterless windows of the house were dark. A dead cucumber-vine dangled from the porch like the crape streamer tied to the door for a death, and the thought flashed through Ethan's brain: "If it was there for Zeena —" Then he had a distinct sight of his wife lying in their bed-room asleep, her mouth slightly open, her false teeth in a tumbler by the bed . . .

They walked around to the back of the house, between the rigid goose-berry bushes. It was Zeena's habit, when they came back late from the vil-lage, to leave the key of the kitchen door under the mat. Ethan stood before the door, his head heavy with dreams, his arm still about Mattie. "Matt —" he began, not knowing what he meant to say.

She slipped out of his hold without speaking, and he stooped down and felt for the key.

"It's not there!" he said, straightening himself with a start.

They strained their eyes at each other through the icy darkness. Such a thing had never happened before.

"Maybe she's forgotten it," Mattie said in a tremulous whisper; but both of them knew that it was not like Zeena to forget.

"It might have fallen off into the snow," Mattie continued, after a pause during which they had stood intently listening.

"It must have been pushed off, then," he rejoined in the same tone. An-other wild thought tore through him. What if tramps had been there — what if . . .

Again he listened, fancying he heard a distant sound in the house; then he felt in his pocket for a match, and kneeling down, passed its light slowly over the rough edges of snow about the doorstep.

He was still kneeling when his eyes, on a level with the lower panel of the door, caught a faint ray beneath it. Who could be stirring in that silent

---

crape streamer: a ribbon of crinkled black fabric tied to a door as a sign of mourning.

house? He heard a step on the stairs, and again for an instant the thought of tramps tore through him. Then the door opened and he saw his wife.

Against the dark background of the kitchen she stood up tall and angular, one hand drawing a quilted counterpane to her flat breast, while the other held a lamp. The light, on a level with her chin, drew out of the darkness her puckered throat and the projecting wrist of the hand that clutched the quilt, and deepened fantastically the hollows and prominences of her high-boned face under its ring of crimping-pins. To Ethan, still in the rosy haze of his hour with Mattie, the sight came with the intense precision of the last dream before waking. He felt as if he had never before known what his wife looked like.

She drew aside without speaking, and Mattie and Ethan passed into the kitchen, which had the deadly chill of a vault after the dry cold of the night.

"Guess you forgot about us, Zeena," Ethan joked, stamping the snow from his boots.

"No. I just felt so mean I couldn't sleep."

Mattie came forward, unwinding her wraps, the colour of cherry scarf in her fresh lips and cheeks. "I'm so sorry, Zeena! Isn't there anything I can do?"

"No; there's nothing." Zeena turned away from her. "You might 'a' shook off that snow outside," she said to her husband.

She walked out of the kitchen ahead of them and pausing in the hall raised the lamp at arm's-length, as if to light them up the stairs.

Ethan paused also, affecting to fumble for the peg on which he hung his coat and cap. The doors of the two bedrooms faced each other across the narrow upper landing, and to-night it was peculiarly repugnant to him that Mattie should see him follow Zeena.

"I guess I won't come up yet awhile," he said, turning as if to go back to the kitchen.

Zeena stopped short and looked at him. "For the land's sake—what you going to do down here?"

"I've got the mill accounts to go over."

She continued to stare at him, the flame of the unshaded lamp bringing out with microscopic cruelty the fretful lines of her face.

"At this time o' night? You'll ketch your death. The fire's out long ago."

Without answering he moved away toward the kitchen. As he did so his glance crossed Mattie's and he fancied that a fugitive warning gleamed

---

counterpane: an embroidered quilt.
mean: ill.

through her lashes. The next moment they sank to her flushed cheeks and she began to mount the stairs ahead of Zeena.

"That's so. It *is* powerful cold down here," Ethan assented; and with lowered head he went up in his wife's wake, and followed her across the threshold of their room.

I I I

There was some hauling to be done at the lower end of the wood-lot, and Ethan was out early the next day.

The winter morning was as clear as crystal. The sunrise burned red in a pure sky, the shadows on the rim of the wood-lot were darkly blue, and beyond the white and scintillating fields patches of far-off forest hung like smoke.

It was in the early morning stillness, when his muscles were swinging to their familiar task and his lungs expanding with long draughts of mountain air, that Ethan did his clearest thinking. He and Zeena had not exchanged a word after the door of their room had closed on them. She had measured out some drops from a medicine-bottle on a chair by the bed and, after swallowing them, and wrapping her head in a piece of yellow flannel, had lain down with her face turned away. Ethan undressed hurriedly and blew out the light so that he should not see her when he took his place at her side. As he lay there he could hear Mattie moving about in her room, and her candle, sending its small ray across the landing, drew a scarcely perceptible line of light under his door. He kept his eyes fixed on the light till it vanished. Then the room grew perfectly black, and not a sound was audible but Zeena's asthmatic breathing. Ethan felt confusedly that there were many things he ought to think about, but through his tingling veins and tired brain only one sensation throbbed: the warmth of Mattie's shoulder against his. Why had he not kissed her when he held her there? A few hours earlier he would not have asked himself the question. Even a few minutes earlier, when they had stood alone outside the house, he would not have dared to think of kissing her. But since he had seen her lips in the lamplight he felt that they were his.

Now, in the bright morning air, her face was still before him. It was part of the sun's red and of the pure glitter on the snow. How the girl had changed since she had come to Starkfield! He remembered what a colourless slip of a thing she had looked the day he had met her at the station. And all the first winter, how she had shivered with cold when the northerly gales shook the thin clapboards and the snow beat like hail against the loose-hung windows!

He had been afraid that she would hate the hard life, the cold and loneliness; but not a sign of discontent escaped her. Zeena took the view that Mattie was bound to make the best of Starkfield since she hadn't any other place to go to; but this did not strike Ethan as conclusive. Zeena, at any rate, did not apply the principle in her own case.

He felt all the more sorry for the girl because misfortune had, in a sense, indentured her to them. Mattie Silver was the daughter of a cousin of Zenobia Frome's, who had inflamed his clan with mingled sentiments of envy and admiration by descending from the hills to Connecticut, where he had married a Stamford girl and succeeded to her father's thriving "drug" business. Unhappily Orin Silver, a man of far-reaching aims, had died too soon to prove that the end justifies the means. His accounts revealed merely what the means had been; and these were such that it was fortunate for his wife and daughter that his books were examined only after his impressive funeral. His wife died of the disclosure, and Mattie, at twenty, was left alone to make her way on the fifty dollars obtained from the sale of her piano. For this purpose her equipment, though varied, was inadequate. She could trim a hat, make molasses candy, recite "Curfew shall not ring to-night," and play "The Lost Chord" and a pot-pourri from "Carmen." When she tried to extend the field of her activities in the direction of stenography and book-keeping her health broke down, and six months on her feet behind the counter of a department store did not tend to restore it. Her nearest relations had been induced to place their savings in her father's hands, and though, after his death, they ungrudgingly acquitted themselves of the Christian duty of returning good for evil by giving his daughter all the advice at their disposal, they could hardly be expected to supplement it by material aid. But when Zenobia's doctor recommended her looking about for some one to help her with the house-work the clan

---

"Curfew shall not ring to-night": a poem published in 1866 by American author Rose Hartwick Thorpe (1850–1939).

"The Lost Chord": a hymn written by London-born poet and philanthropist Adelaide A. Procter (1825–64) and set to music in 1876 by English composer Arthur S. Sullivan (1842–1900), of the famed Gilbert and Sullivan partnership. Though unsuited to congregational singing, the song was tremendously popular around the beginning of the twentieth century.

"Carmen": the 1875 opera by Paris-born composer Georges Bizet (1838–75) tracing the fall of a handsome soldier as he is lured by the fickle Carmen into becoming a convict, a smuggler, and finally a murderer.

instantly saw the chance of exacting a compensation from Mattie. Zenobia, though doubtful of the girl's efficiency, was tempted by the freedom to find fault without much risk of losing her; and so Mattie came to Starkfield.

Zenobia's fault-finding was of the silent kind, but not the less penetrating for that. During the first months Ethan alternately burned with the desire to see Mattie defy her and trembled with fear of the result. Then the situation grew less strained. The pure air, and the long summer hours in the open, gave back life and elasticity to Mattie, and Zeena, with more leisure to devote to her complex ailments, grew less watchful of the girl's omissions; so that Ethan, struggling on under the burden of his barren farm and failing saw-mill, could at least imagine that peace reigned in his house.

There was really, even now, no tangible evidence to the contrary; but since the previous night a vague dread had hung on his sky-line. It was formed of Zeena's obstinate silence, of Mattie's sudden look of warning, of the memory of just such fleeting imperceptible signs as those which told him, on certain stainless mornings, that before night there would be rain.

His dread was so strong that, man-like, he sought to postpone certainty. The hauling was not over till mid-day, and as the lumber was to be delivered to Andrew Hale, the Starkfield builder, it was really easier for Ethan to send Jotham Powell, the hired man, back to the farm on foot, and drive the load down to the village himself. He had scrambled up on the logs, and was sitting astride of them, close over his shaggy grays, when, coming between him and their steaming necks, he had a vision of the warning look that Mattie had given him the night before.

"If there's going to be any trouble I want to be there," was his vague reflection, as he threw to Jotham the unexpected order to unhitch the team and lead them back to the barn.

It was a slow trudge home through the heavy fields, and when the two men entered the kitchen Mattie was lifting the coffee from the stove and Zeena was already at the table. Her husband stopped short at sight of her. Instead of her usual calico wrapper and knitted shawl she wore her best dress of brown merino, and above her thin strands of hair, which still pre-served the tight undulations of the crimping-pins, rose a hard perpendic-ular bonnet, as to which Ethan's clearest notion was that he had to pay five dollars for it at the Bettsbridge Emporium. On the floor beside her stood his old valise and a bandbox wrapped in newspapers.

"Why, where are you going, Zeena?" he exclaimed.

"I've got my shooting pains so bad that I'm going over to Bettsbridge to spend the night with Aunt Martha Pierce and see that new doctor," she an-

---

wrapper: a loose housecoat worn wrapped around the body.

swered in a matter-of-fact tone, as if she had said she was going into the store-room to take a look at the preserves, or up to the attic to go over the blankets.

In spite of her sedentary habits such abrupt decisions were not without precedent in Zeena's history. Twice or thrice before she had suddenly packed Ethan's valise and started off to Bettsbridge, or even Springfield, to seek the advice of some new doctor, and her husband had grown to dread these expeditions because of their cost. Zeena always came back laden with expensive remedies, and her last visit to Springfield had been commemorated by her paying twenty dollars for an electric battery of which she had never been able to learn the use. But for the moment his sense of relief was so great as to preclude all other feelings. He had now no doubt that Zeena had spoken the truth in saying, the night before, that she had sat up because she felt "too mean" to sleep: her abrupt resolve to seek medical advice showed that, as usual, she was wholly absorbed in her health.

As if expecting a protest, she continued plaintively; "If you're too busy with the hauling I presume you can let Jotham Powell drive me over with the sorrel in time to ketch the train at the Flats."

Her husband hardly heard what she was saying. During the winter months there was no stage between Starkfield and Bettsbridge, and the trains which stopped at Corbury Flats were slow and infrequent. A rapid calculation showed Ethan that Zeena could not be back at the farm before the following evening. . . .

"If I'd supposed you'd 'a' made any objection to Jotham Powell's driving me over—" she began again, as though his silence had implied refusal. On the brink of departure she was always seized with a flux of words. "All I know is," she continued, "I can't go on the way I am much longer. The pains are clear away down to my ankles now, or I'd 'a' walked in to Starkfield on my own feet, sooner'n put you out, and asked Michael Eady to let me ride over on his wagon to the Flats, when he sends to meet the train that brings his groceries. I'd 'a' had two hours to wait in the station, but I'd sooner 'a' done it, even with this cold, than to have you say——"

"Of course Jotham'll drive you over," Ethan roused himself to answer. He became suddenly conscious that he was looking at Mattie while Zeena talked to him, and with an effort he turned his eyes to his wife. She sat opposite the window, and the pale light reflected from the banks of snow made her face look more than usually drawn and bloodless, sharpened the three parallel creases between ear and cheek, and drew querulous lines

---

Springfield: a city in south central Massachusetts.
electric battery: a device that delivered electric currents to the body to numb pain.

from her thin nose to the corners of her mouth. Though she was but seven years her husband's senior, and he was only twenty-eight, she was already an old woman.

Ethan tried to say something befitting the occasion, but there was only one thought in his mind: the fact that, for the first time since Mattie had come to live with them, Zeena was to be away for a night. He wondered if the girl were thinking of it too. . . .

He knew that Zeena must be wondering why he did not offer to drive her to the Flats and let Jotham Powell take the lumber to Starkfield, and at first he could not think of a pretext for not doing so; then he said: "I'd take you over myself, only I've got to collect the cash for the lumber."

As soon as the words were spoken he regretted them, not only because they were untrue—there being no prospect of his receiving cash payment from Hale—but also because he knew from experience the imprudence of letting Zeena think he was in funds on the eve of one of her therapeutic excursions. At the moment, however, his one desire was to avoid the long drive with her behind the ancient sorrel who never went out of a walk.

Zeena made no reply: she did not seem to hear what he had said. She had already pushed her plate aside, and was measuring out a draught from a large bottle at her elbow.

"It ain't done me a speck of good, but I guess I might as well use it up," she remarked; adding, as she pushed the empty bottle toward Mattie: "If you can get the taste out it'll do for pickles."

I V

As soon as his wife had driven off Ethan took his coat and cap from the peg. Mattie was washing up the dishes, humming one of the dance tunes of the night before. He said "So long, Matt," and she answered gaily "So long, Ethan"; and that was all.

It was warm and bright in the kitchen. The sun slanted through the south window on the girl's moving figure, on the cat dozing in a chair, and on the geraniums brought in from the door-way, where Ethan had planted them in the summer to "make a garden" for Mattie. He would have liked to linger on, watching her tidy up and then settle down to her sewing; but he wanted still more to get the hauling done and be back at the farm before night.

All the way down to the village he continued to think of his return to Mattie. The kitchen was a poor place, not "spruce" and shining as his mother had kept it in his boyhood; but it was surprising what a homelike look the mere fact of Zeena's absence gave it. And he pictured what it would be like that evening, when he and Mattie were there after supper. For the first time they would be alone together indoors, and they would sit there, one on each side of the stove, like a married couple, he in his stocking feet and smoking his pipe, she laughing and talking in that funny way she had, which was always as new to him as if he had never heard her before.

The sweetness of the picture, and the relief of knowing that his fears of "trouble" with Zeena were unfounded, sent up his spirits with a rush, and he, who was usually so silent, whistled and sang aloud as he drove through the snowy fields. There was in him a slumbering spark of sociability which the long Starkfield winters had not yet extinguished. By nature grave and inarticulate, he admired recklessness and gaiety in others and was warmed to the marrow by friendly human intercourse. At Worcester, though he had the name of keeping to himself and not being much of a hand at a good time, he had secretly gloried in being clapped on the back and hailed as "Old Ethe" or "Old Stiff"; and the cessation of such familiarities had increased the chill of his return to Starkfield.

There the silence had deepened about him year by year. Left alone, after his father's accident, to carry the burden of farm and mill, he had had no time for convivial loiterings in the village; and when his mother fell ill the loneliness of the house grew more oppressive than that of the fields. His mother had been a talker in her day, but after her "trouble" the sound of her voice was seldom heard, though she had not lost the power of speech. Sometimes, in the long winter evenings, when in desperation her son asked her why she didn't "say something," she would lift a finger and answer: "Because I'm listening"; and on stormy nights, when the loud wind was about the house, she would complain, if he spoke to her: "They're talking so out there that I can't hear you."

It was only when she drew toward her last illness, and his cousin Zenobia Pierce came over from the next valley to help him nurse her, that human speech was heard again in the house. After the mortal silence of his long imprisonment Zeena's volubility was music in his ears. He felt that he might have "gone like his mother" if the sound of a new voice had not come to steady him. Zeena seemed to understand his case at a glance. She laughed at him for not knowing the simplest sick-bed duties and told him to "go right along out" and leave her to see to things. The mere fact of obeying her orders, of feeling free to go about his business again and talk with other men, restored his shaken balance and magnified his sense of what he owed her. Her efficiency shamed and dazzled him. She seemed to possess by instinct all the household wisdom that his long apprenticeship had not instilled in him. When the end came it was she who had to tell him to hitch up and go for the undertaker, and she thought it "funny" that he had not settled beforehand who was to have his mother's clothes and the sewing-machine. After the funeral, when he saw her preparing to go away, he was seized with an unreasoning dread of being left alone on the farm; and before he knew what he was doing he had asked her to stay there with him. He had often thought since that it would not have happened if his mother had died in spring instead of winter . . .

When they married it was agreed that, as soon as he could straighten out the difficulties resulting from Mrs. Frome's long illness, they would sell the farm and saw-mill and try their luck in a large town. Ethan's love of nature did not take the form of a taste for agriculture. He had always wanted to be an engineer, and to live in towns, where there were lectures and big libraries and "fellows doing things." A slight engineering job in Florida, put in his way during his period of study at Worcester, increased his faith in his ability as well as his eagerness to see the world; and he felt sure that, with a "smart" wife like Zeena, it would not be long before he had made himself a place in it.

Zeena's native village was slightly larger and nearer to the railway than Starkfield, and she had let her husband see from the first that life on an isolated farm was not what she had expected when she married. But purchasers were slow in coming, and while he waited for them Ethan learned the impossibility of transplanting her. She chose to look down on Starkfield, but she could not have lived in a place which looked down on her. Even Bettsbridge or Shadd's Falls would not have been sufficiently aware of her, and in the greater cities which attracted Ethan she would have suffered a complete loss of identity. And within a year of their marriage she developed the "sickliness" which had since made her notable even in a community rich in pathological instances. When she came to take care of his mother she had seemed to Ethan like the very genius of health, but he soon saw that her skill as a nurse had been acquired by the absorbed observation of her own symptoms.

Then she too fell silent. Perhaps it was the inevitable effect of life on the farm, or perhaps, as she sometimes said, it was because Ethan "never listened." The charge was not wholly unfounded. When she spoke it was only to complain, and to complain of things not in his power to remedy; and to check a tendency to impatient retort he had first formed the habit of not answering her, and finally of thinking of other things while she talked. Of late, however, since he had had reasons for observing her more closely, her silence had begun to trouble him. He recalled his mother's growing taciturnity, and wondered if Zeena were also turning "queer." Women did, he knew. Zeena, who had at her fingers' ends the pathological chart of the whole region, had cited many cases of the kind while she was nursing his mother; and he himself knew of certain lonely farm-houses in the neighbourhood where stricken creatures pined, and of others where sudden tragedy had come of their presence. At times, looking at Zeena's shut face, he felt the chill of such forebodings. At other times her silence seemed deliberately assumed to conceal far-reaching intentions, mysterious conclusions drawn from suspicions and resentments impossible to guess. That supposition was even more disturbing than the other; and it was the one which had come to him the night before, when he had seen her standing in the kitchen door.

Now her departure for Bettsbridge had once more eased his mind, and all his thoughts were on the prospect of his evening with Mattie. Only one thing weighed on him, and that was his having told Zeena that he was to receive cash for the lumber. He foresaw so clearly the consequences of this imprudence that with considerable reluctance he decided to ask Andrew Hale for a small advance on his load.

When Ethan drove into Hale's yard the builder was just getting out of his sleigh.

"Hello, Ethe!" he said. "This comes handy."

Andrew Hale was a ruddy man with a big gray moustache and a stubbly double-chin unconstrained by a collar; but his scrupulously clean shirt was always fastened by a small diamond stud. This display of opulence was misleading, for though he did a fairly good business it was known that his easygoing habits and the demands of his large family frequently kept him what Starkfield called "behind." He was an old friend of Ethan's family, and his house one of the few to which Zeena occasionally went, drawn there by the fact that Mrs. Hale, in her youth, had done more "doctoring" than any other woman in Starkfield, and was still a recognised authority on symptoms and treatment.

Hale went up to the grays and patted their sweating flanks.

"Well, sir," he said, "you keep them two as if they was pets."

Ethan set about unloading the logs and when he had finished his job he pushed open the glazed door of the shed which the builder used as his office. Hale sat with his feet up on the stove, his back propped against a battered desk strewn with papers: the place, like the man, was warm, genial and untidy.

"Sit right down and thaw out," he greeted Ethan.

The latter did not know how to begin, but at length he managed to bring out his request for an advance of fifty dollars. The blood rushed to his thin skin under the sting of Hale's astonishment. It was the builder's custom to pay at the end of three months, and there was no precedent between the two men for a cash settlement.

Ethan felt that if he had pleaded an urgent need Hale might have made shift to pay him; but pride, and an instinctive prudence, kept him from resorting to this argument. After his father's death it had taken time to get his head above water, and he did not want Andrew Hale, or any one else in Starkfield, to think he was going under again. Besides, he hated lying; if he wanted the money he wanted it, and it was nobody's business to ask why. He therefore made his demand with the awkwardness of a proud man who will not admit to himself that he is stooping; and he was not much surprised at Hale's refusal.

The builder refused genially, as he did everything else: he treated the matter as something in the nature of a practical joke, and wanted to know if Ethan meditated buying a grand piano or adding a "cupolo" to his house; offering, in the latter case, to give his services free of cost.

Ethan's arts were soon exhausted, and after an embarrassed pause he wished Hale good day and opened the door of the office. As he passed out the builder suddenly called after him: "See here — you ain't in a tight place, are you?"

"Not a bit," Ethan's pride retorted before his reason had time to intervene.

"Well, that's good! Because I *am*, a shade. Fact is, I was going to ask you to give me a little extra time on that payment. Business is pretty slack, to begin with, and then I'm fixing up a little house for Ned and Ruth when they're married. I'm glad to do it for 'em, but it costs." His look appealed to Ethan for sympathy. "The young people like things nice. You know how it is yourself: it's not so long ago since you fixed up your own place for Zeena."

Ethan left the grays in Hale's stable and went about some other business in the village. As he walked away the builder's last phrase lingered in his ears, and he reflected grimly that his seven years with Zeena seemed to Starkfield "not so long."

The afternoon was drawing to an end, and here and there a lighted pane spangled the cold gray dusk and made the snow look whiter. The bitter weather had driven every one indoors and Ethan had the long rural street to himself. Suddenly he heard the brisk play of sleigh-bells and a cutter passed him, drawn by a free-going horse. Ethan recognised Michael Eady's roan colt, and young Denis Eady, in a handsome new fur cap, leaned forward and waved a greeting. "Hello, Ethe!" he shouted and spun on.

The cutter was going in the direction of the Frome farm, and Ethan's heart contracted as he listened to the dwindling bells. What more likely

---

cupolo: a cupola, a small domelike structure usually mounted on a circular base and placed on top of a roof.

than that Denis Eady had heard of Zeena's departure for Bettsbridge, and was profiting by the opportunity to spend an hour with Mattie? Ethan was ashamed of the storm of jealousy in his breast. It seemed unworthy of the girl that his thoughts of her should be so violent.

He walked on to the church corner and entered the shade of the Varnum spruces, where he had stood with her the night before. As he passed into their gloom he saw an indistinct outline just ahead of him. At his approach it melted for an instant into two separate shapes and then conjoined again, and he heard a kiss, and a half-laughing "Oh!" provoked by the discovery of his presence. Again the outline hastily disunited and the Varnum gate slammed on one half while the other hurried on ahead of him. Ethan smiled at the discomfiture he had caused. What did it matter to Ned Hale and Ruth Varnum if they were caught kissing each other? Everybody in Starkfield knew they were engaged. It pleased Ethan to have surprised a pair of lovers on the spot where he and Mattie had stood with such a thirst for each other in their hearts; but he felt a pang at the thought that these two need not hide their happiness.

He fetched the grays from Hale's stable and started on his long climb back to the farm. The cold was less sharp than earlier in the day and a thick fleecy sky threatened snow for the morrow. Here and there a star pricked through, showing behind it a deep well of blue. In an hour or two the moon would push up over the ridge behind the farm, burn a gold-edged rent in the clouds, and then be swallowed by them. A mournful peace hung on the fields, as though they felt the relaxing grasp of the cold and stretched themselves in their long winter sleep.

Ethan's ears were alert for the jingle of sleigh-bells, but not a sound broke the silence of the lonely road. As he drew near the farm he saw, through the thin screen of larches at the gate, a light twinkling in the house above him. "She's up in her room," he said to himself, "fixing herself up for supper"; and he remembered Zeena's sarcastic stare when Mattie, on the evening of her arrival, had come down to supper with smoothed hair and a ribbon at her neck.

He passed by the graves on the knoll and turned his head to glance at one of the older headstones, which had interested him deeply as a boy because it bore his name.

SACRED TO THE MEMORY OF
ETHAN FROME AND ENDURANCE HIS WIFE,
WHO DWELLED TOGETHER IN PEACE
FOR FIFTY YEARS.

He used to think that fifty years sounded like a long time to live together; but now it seemed to him that they might pass in a flash. Then, with a sudden dart of irony, he wondered if, when their turn came, the same epitaph would be written over him and Zeena.

He opened the barn-door and craned his head into the obscurity, half-fearing to discover Denis Eady's roan colt in the stall beside the sorrel. But the old horse was there alone, mumbling his crib with toothless jaws, and Ethan whistled cheerfully while he bedded down the grays and shook an extra measure of oats into their mangers. His was not a tuneful throat, but harsh melodies burst from it as he locked the barn and sprang up the hill to the house. He reached the kitchen-porch and turned the door-handle; but the door did not yield to his touch.

Startled at finding it locked he rattled the handle violently; then he reflected that Mattie was alone and that it was natural she should barricade herself at nightfall. He stood in the darkness expecting to hear her step. It did not come, and after vainly straining his ears he called out in a voice that shook with joy: "Hello, Matt!"

Silence answered; but in a minute or two he caught a sound on the stairs and saw a line of light about the door-frame, as he had seen it the night before. So strange was the precision with which the incidents of the previous evening were repeating themselves that he half expected, when he heard the key turn, to see his wife before him on the threshold; but the door opened, and Mattie faced him.

She stood just as Zeena had stood, a lifted lamp in her hand, against the black background of the kitchen. She held the light at the same level, and it drew out with the same distinctness her slim young throat and the brown wrist no bigger than a child's. Then, striking upward, it threw a lustrous fleck on her lips, edged her eyes with velvet shade, and laid a milky whiteness above the black curve of her brows.

She wore her usual dress of darkish stuff, and there was no bow at her neck; but through her hair she had run a streak of crimson ribbon. This tribute to the unusual transformed and glorified her. She seemed to Ethan taller, fuller, more womanly in shape and motion. She stood aside, smiling silently, while he entered, and then moved away from him with something soft and flowing in her gait. She set the lamp on the table, and he saw that it was carefully laid for supper, with fresh dough-nuts, stewed blueberries and his favourite pickles in a dish of gay red glass. A bright fire glowed in the stove and the cat lay stretched before it, watching the table with a drowsy eye.

Ethan was suffocated with the sense of well-being. He went out into the passage to hang up his coat and pull off his wet boots. When he came back Mattie had set the teapot on the table and the cat was rubbing itself persuasively against her ankles.

"Why, Puss! I nearly tripped over you," she cried, the laughter sparkling through her lashes.

Again Ethan felt a sudden twinge of jealousy. Could it be his coming that gave her such a kindled face?

"Well, Matt, any visitors?" he threw off, stooping down carelessly to examine the fastening of the stove.

She nodded and laughed "Yes, one," and he felt a blackness settling on his brows.

"Who was that?" he questioned, raising himself up to slant a glance at her beneath his scowl.

Her eyes danced with malice. "Why, Jotham Powell. He came in after he got back, and asked for a drop of coffee before he went down home."

The blackness lifted and light flooded Ethan's brain. "That all? Well, I hope you made out to let him have it." And after a pause he felt it right to add: "I suppose he got Zeena over to the Flats all right?"

"Oh, yes; in plenty of time."

The name threw a chill between them, and they stood a moment looking sideways at each other before Mattie said with a shy laugh: "I guess it's about time for supper."

They drew their seats up to the table, and the cat, unbidden, jumped between them into Zeena's empty chair. "Oh, Puss!" said Mattie, and they laughed again.

Ethan, a moment earlier, had felt himself on the brink of eloquence; but the mention of Zeena had paralysed him. Mattie seemed to feel the contagion of his embarrassment, and sat with downcast lids, sipping her tea, while he feigned an insatiable appetite for dough-nuts and sweet pickles. At last, after casting about for an effective opening, he took a long gulp of tea, cleared his throat, and said: "Looks as if there'd be more snow."

She feigned great interest. "Is that so? Do you suppose it'll interfere with Zeena's getting back?" She flushed red as the question escaped her, and hastily set down the cup she was lifting.

Ethan reached over for another helping of pickles. "You never can tell, this time of year, it drifts so bad on the Flats." The name had benumbed him again, and once more he felt as if Zeena were in the room between them.

"Oh, Puss, you're too greedy!" Mattie cried.

The cat, unnoticed, had crept up on muffled paws from Zeena's seat to the table, and was stealthily elongating its body in the direction of the milk-jug, which stood between Ethan and Mattie. The two leaned forward at the same moment and their hands met on the handle of the jug. Mattie's hand was underneath, and Ethan kept his clasped on it a moment longer than was necessary. The cat, profiting by this unusual demonstration, tried to effect an unnoticed retreat, and in doing so backed into the pickle-dish, which fell to the floor with a crash.

Mattie, in an instant, had sprung from her chair and was down on her knees by the fragments.

"Oh, Ethan, Ethan—it's all to pieces! What will Zeena say?"

But this time his courage was up. "Well, she'll have to say it to the cat, any way!" he rejoined with a laugh, kneeling down at Mattie's side to scrape up the swimming pickles.

She lifted stricken eyes to him. "Yes, but, you see, she never meant it should be used, not even when there was company; and I had to get up on the step-ladder to reach it down from the top shelf of the china-closet, where she keeps it with all her best things, and of course she'll want to know why I did it——"

The case was so serious that it called forth all of Ethan's latent resolution.

"She needn't know anything about it if you keep quiet. I'll get another just like it to-morrow. Where did it come from? I'll go to Shadd's Falls for it if I have to!"

"Oh, you'll never get another even there! It was a wedding present— don't you remember? It came all the way from Philadelphia, from Zeena's aunt that married the minister. That's why she wouldn't ever use it. Oh, Ethan, Ethan, what in the world shall I do?"

She began to cry, and he felt as if every one of her tears were pouring over him like burning lead. "Don't, Matt, don't—oh, *don't!*" he implored her.

She struggled to her feet, and he rose and followed her helplessly while she spread out the pieces of glass on the kitchen dresser. It seemed to him as if the shattered fragments of their evening lay there.

"Here, give them to me," he said in a voice of sudden authority.

She drew aside, instinctively obeying his tone. "Oh, Ethan, what are you going to do?"

Without replying he gathered the pieces of glass into his broad palm and walked out of the kitchen to the passage. There he lit a candle-end, opened the china-closet, and, reaching his long arm up to the highest shelf, laid the pieces together with such accuracy of touch that a close inspection convinced him of the impossibility of detecting from below that the dish was broken. If he glued it together the next morning months might elapse before his wife noticed what had happened, and meanwhile he might after all be able to match the dish at Shadd's Falls or Bettsbridge. Having satisfied himself that there was no risk of immediate discovery he went back to the kitchen with a lighter step, and found Mattie disconsolately removing the last scraps of pickle from the floor.

"It's all right, Matt. Come back and finish supper," he commanded her.

Completely reassured, she shone on him through tear-hung lashes, and his soul swelled with pride as he saw how his tone subdued her. She did not even ask what he had done. Except when he was steering a big log down the mountain to his mill he had never known such a thrilling sense of mastery.

V

They finished supper, and while Mattie cleared the table Ethan went to look at the cows and then took a last turn about the house. The earth lay dark under a muffled sky and the air was so still that now and then he heard a lump of snow come thumping down from a tree far off on the edge of the wood-lot.

When he returned to the kitchen Mattie had pushed up his chair to the stove and seated herself near the lamp with a bit of sewing. The scene was just as he had dreamed of it that morning. He sat down, drew his pipe from his pocket and stretched his feet to the glow. His hard day's work in the keen air made him feel at once lazy and light of mood, and he had a confused sense of being in another world, where all was warmth and harmony and time could bring no change. The only drawback to his complete well-being was the fact that he could not see Mattie from where he sat; but he was too indolent to move and after a moment he said: "Come over here and sit by the stove."

Zeena's empty rocking-chair stood facing him. Mattie rose obediently, and seated herself in it. As her young brown head detached itself against the patch-work cushion that habitually framed his wife's gaunt countenance, Ethan had a momentary shock. It was almost as if the other face, the face of the superseded woman, had obliterated that of the intruder. After a moment Mattie seemed to be affected by the same sense of constraint. She changed her position, leaning forward to bend her head above her work, so that he saw only the foreshortened tip of her nose and the streak of red in her hair; then she slipped to her feet, saying "I can't see to sew," and went back to her chair by the lamp.

Ethan made a pretext of getting up to replenish the stove, and when he returned to his seat he pushed it sideways that he might get a view of her profile and of the lamplight falling on her hands. The cat, who had been a puzzled observer of these unusual movements, jumped up into Zeena's chair, rolled itself into a ball, and lay watching them with narrowed eyes.

Deep quiet sank on the room. The clock ticked above the dresser, a piece of charred wood fell now and then in the stove, and the faint sharp scent of the geraniums mingled with the odour of Ethan's smoke, which began to throw a blue haze about the lamp and to hang its greyish cobwebs in the shadowy corners of the room.

All constraint had vanished between the two, and they began to talk easily and simply. They spoke of every-day things, of the prospect of snow, of the next church sociable, of the loves and quarrels of Starkfield. The commonplace nature of what they said produced in Ethan an illusion of long-established intimacy which no outburst of emotion could have given, and he set his imagination adrift on the fiction that they had always spent their evenings thus and would always go on doing so . . .

"This is the night we were to have gone coasting. Matt," he said at length, with the rich sense, as he spoke, that they could go on any other night they chose, since they had all time before them.

She smiled back at him. "I guess you forgot!"

"No, I didn't forget; but it's as dark as Egypt outdoors. We might go to-morrow if there's a moon."

She laughed with pleasure, her head tilted back, the lamplight sparkling on her lips and teeth. "That would be lovely, Ethan!"

He kept his eyes fixed on her, marvelling at the way her face changed with each turn of their talk, like a wheat-field under a summer breeze. It was intoxicating to find such magic in his clumsy words, and he longed to try new ways of using it.

"Would you be scared to go down the Corbury road with me on a night like this?" he asked.

Her cheeks burned redder. "I ain't any more scared than you are!"

"Well, I'd be scared, then; I wouldn't do it. That's an ugly corner down by the big elm. If a fellow didn't keep his eyes open he'd go plumb into it." He luxuriated in the sense of protection and authority which his words conveyed. To prolong and intensify the feeling he added: "I guess we're well enough here."

She let her lids sink slowly, in the way he loved. "Yes, we're well enough here," she sighed.

Her tone was so sweet that he took the pipe from his mouth and drew his chair up to the table. Leaning forward, he touched the farther end of the strip of brown stuff that she was hemming. "Say, Matt," he began with a smile, "what do you think I saw under the Varnum spruces, coming along home just now? I saw a friend of yours getting kissed."

The words had been on his tongue all the evening, but now that he had spoken them they struck him as inexpressibly vulgar and out of place.

Mattie blushed to the roots of her hair and pulled her needle rapidly twice or thrice through her work, insensibly drawing the end of it away from him. "I suppose it was Ruth and Ned," she said in a low voice, as though he had suddenly touched on something grave.

Ethan had imagined that his allusion might open the way to the accepted pleasantries, and these perhaps in turn to a harmless caress, if only a mere touch on her hand. But now he felt as if her blush had set a flaming guard about her. He supposed it was his natural awkwardness that made him feel so. He knew that most young men made nothing at all of giving a pretty girl a kiss, and he remembered that the night before, when he had put his arm about Mattie, she had not resisted. But that had been out-of-doors, under the open irresponsible night. Now, in the warm lamplit room, with all its ancient implications of conformity and order, she seemed infinitely farther away from him and more unapproachable.

To ease his constraint he said: "I suppose they'll be setting a date before long."

"Yes. I shouldn't wonder if they got married some time along in the summer." She pronounced the word *married* as if her voice caressed it. It seemed a rustling covert leading to enchanted glades. A pang shot through Ethan, and he said, twisting away from her in his chair: "It'll be your turn next, I wouldn't wonder."

She laughed a little uncertainly. "Why do you keep on saying that?"

He echoed her laugh. "I guess I do it to get used to the idea."

He drew up to the table again and she sewed on in silence, with dropped lashes, while he sat in fascinated contemplation of the way in which her hands went up and down above the strip of stuff, just as he had seen a pair of birds make short perpendicular flights over a nest they were building. At length, without turning her head or lifting her lids, she said in a low tone: "It's not because you think Zeena's got anything against me, is it?"

His former dread started up full-armed at the suggestion. "Why, what do you mean?" he stammered.

She raised distressed eyes to his, her work dropping on the table between them. "I don't know. I thought last night she seemed to have."

"I'd like to know what," he growled.

"Nobody can tell with Zeena." It was the first time they had ever spoken so openly of her attitude toward Mattie, and the repetition of the name seemed to carry it to the farther corners of the room and send it back to them in long repercussions of sound. Mattie waited, as if to give the echo time to drop, and then went on: "She hasn't said anything to *you?*"

He shook his head. "No, not a word."

She tossed the hair back from her forehead with a laugh. "I guess I'm just nervous, then. I'm not going to think about it any more."

"Oh, no—don't let's think about it, Matt!"

The sudden heat of his tone made her colour mount again, not with a rush, but gradually, delicately, like the reflection of a thought stealing slowly across her heart. She sat silent, her hands clasped on her work, and it seemed to him that a warm current flowed toward him along the strip of stuff that still lay unrolled between them. Cautiously he slid his hand palm-downward along the table till his finger-tips touched the end of the stuff. A faint vibration of her lashes seemed to show that she was aware of his gesture, and that it had sent a counter-current back to her; and she let her hands lie motionless on the other end of the strip.

As they sat thus he heard a sound behind him and turned his head. The cat had jumped from Zeena's chair to dart at a mouse in the wainscot, and as a result of the sudden movement the empty chair had set up a spectral rocking.

"She'll be rocking in it herself this time to-morrow," Ethan thought. "I've been in a dream, and this is the only evening we'll ever have together." The return to reality was as painful as the return to consciousness after taking an anaesthetic. His body and brain ached with indescribable weariness, and he could think of nothing to say or to do that should arrest the mad flight of the moments.

His alteration of mood seemed to have communicated itself to Mattie. She looked up at him languidly, as though her lids were weighted with sleep and it cost her an effort to raise them. Her glance fell on his hand, which now completely covered the end of her work and grasped it as if it were a part of herself. He saw a scarcely perceptible tremor cross her face, and without knowing what he did he stooped his head and kissed the bit of stuff in his hold. As his lips rested on it he felt it glide slowly from beneath them, and saw that Mattie had risen and was silently rolling up her work. She fastened it with a pin, and then, finding her thimble and scissors, put them with the roll of stuff into the box covered with fancy paper which he had once brought to her from Bettsbridge.

He stood up also, looking vaguely about the room. The clock above the dresser struck eleven.

"Is the fire all right?" she asked in a low voice.

He opened the door of the stove and poked aimlessly at the embers. When he raised himself again he saw that she was dragging toward the stove the old soap-box lined with carpet in which the cat made its bed. Then she recrossed the floor and lifted two of the geranium pots in her arms, moving them away from the cold window. He followed her and brought the other geraniums, the hyacinth bulbs in a cracked custard bowl and the German ivy trained over an old croquet hoop.

When these nightly duties were performed there was nothing left to do but to bring in the tin candle-stick from the passage, light the candle and blow out the lamp. Ethan put the candlestick in Mattie's hand and she went out of the kitchen ahead of him, the light that she carried before her making her dark hair look like a drift of mist on the moon.

"Good night, Matt," he said as she put her foot on the first step of the stairs.

She turned and looked at him a moment. "Good night, Ethan," she answered, and went up.

When the door of her room had closed on her he remembered that he had not even touched her hand.

V I

The next morning at breakfast Jotham Powell was between them, and Ethan tried to hide his joy under an air of exaggerated indifference, lounging back in his chair to throw scraps to the cat, growling at the weather, and not so much as offering to help Mattie when she rose to clear away the dishes.

He did not know why he was so irrationally happy, for nothing was changed in his life or hers. He had not even touched the tip of her fingers or looked her full in the eyes. But their evening together had given him a vision of what life at her side might be, and he was glad now that he had done nothing to trouble the sweetness of the picture. He had a fancy that she knew what had restrained him . . .

There was a last load of lumber to be hauled to the village, and Jotham Powell—who did not work regularly for Ethan in winter—had "come round" to help with the job. But a wet snow, melting to sleet, had fallen in the night and turned the roads to glass. There was more wet in the air and it seemed likely to both men that the weather would "milden" toward afternoon and make the going safer. Ethan therefore proposed to his assistant that they should load the sledge at the wood-lot, as they had done on the previous morning, and put off the "teaming" to Starkfield till later in the day. This plan had the advantage of enabling him to send Jotham to the Flats after dinner to meet Zenobia, while he himself took the lumber down to the village.

He told Jotham to go out and harness up the grays, and for a moment he and Mattie had the kitchen to themselves. She had plunged the breakfast dishes into a tin dish-pan and was bending above it with her slim arms bared to the elbow, the steam from the hot water beading her forehead and

---

milden: to become milder.

tightening her rough hair into little brown rings like the tendrils on the traveller's joy.

Ethan stood looking at her, his heart in his throat. He wanted to say: "We shall never be alone again like this." Instead, he reached down his tobacco-pouch from a shelf of the dresser, put it into his pocket and said: "I guess I can make out to be home for dinner."

She answered "All right, Ethan," and he heard her singing over the dishes as he went.

As soon as the sledge was loaded he meant to send Jotham back to the farm and hurry on foot into the village to buy the glue for the pickle-dish. With ordinary luck he should have had time to carry out this plan; but everything went wrong from the start. On the way over to the wood-lot one of the grays slipped on a glare of ice and cut his knee; and when they got him up again Jotham had to go back to the barn for a strip of rag to bind the cut. Then, when the loading finally began, a sleety rain was coming down once more, and the tree trunks were so slippery that it took twice as long as usual to lift them and get them in place on the sledge. It was what Jotham called a sour morning for work, and the horses, shivering and stamping under their wet blankets, seemed to like it as little as the men. It was long past the dinner-hour when the job was done, and Ethan had to give up going to the village because he wanted to lead the injured horse home and wash the cut himself.

He thought that by starting out again with the lumber as soon as he had finished his dinner he might get back to the farm with the glue before Jotham and the old sorrel had had time to fetch Zenobia from the Flats; but he knew the chance was a slight one. It turned on the state of the roads and on the possible lateness of the Bettsbridge train. He remembered afterward, with a grim flash of self-derision, what importance he had attached to the weighing of these probabilities . . .

As soon as dinner was over he set out again for the wood-lot, not daring to linger till Jotham Powell left. The hired man was still drying his wet feet at the stove, and Ethan could only give Mattie a quick look as he said beneath his breath: "I'll be back early."

He fancied that she nodded her comprehension; and with that scant solace he had to trudge off through the rain.

He had driven his load half-way to the village when Jotham Powell overtook him, urging the reluctant sorrel toward the Flats. "I'll have to hurry up to do it," Ethan mused, as the sleigh dropped down ahead of him over the dip of the school-house hill. He worked like ten at the unloading, and

---

traveller's joy: a climbing plant with white flowers.

when it was over hastened on to Michael Eady's for the glue. Eady and his assistant were both "down street," and young Denis, who seldom deigned to take their place, was lounging by the stove with a knot of the golden youth of Starkfield. They hailed Ethan with ironic compliment and offers of conviviality; but no one knew where to find the glue. Ethan, consumed with the longing for a last moment alone with Mattie, hung about impatiently while Denis made an ineffectual search in the obscurer corners of the store.

"Looks as if we were all sold out. But if you'll wait around till the old man comes along maybe he can put his hand on it."

"I'm obliged to you, but I'll try if I can get it down at Mrs. Homan's," Ethan answered, burning to be gone.

Denis's commercial instinct compelled him to aver on oath that what Eady's store could not produce would never be found at the widow Homan's; but Ethan, heedless of this boast, had already climbed to the sledge and was driving on to the rival establishment. Here, after considerable search, and sympathetic questions as to what he wanted it for, and whether ordinary flour paste wouldn't do as well if she couldn't find it, the widow Homan finally hunted down her solitary bottle of glue to its hiding-place in a medley of cough-lozenges and corset-laces.

"I hope Zeena ain't broken anything she sets store by," she called after him as he turned the grays toward home.

The fitful bursts of sleet had changed into a steady rain and the horses had heavy work even without a load behind them. Once or twice, hearing sleigh-bells, Ethan turned his head, fancying that Zeena and Jotham might overtake him; but the old sorrel was not in sight, and he set his face against the rain and urged on his ponderous pair.

The barn was empty when the horses turned into it and, after giving them the most perfunctory ministrations they had ever received from him, he strode up to the house and pushed open the kitchen door.

Mattie was there alone, as he had pictured her. She was bending over a pan on the stove; but at the sound of his step she turned with a start and sprang to him.

"See, here, Matt, I've got some stuff to mend the dish with! Let me get at it quick," he cried, waving the bottle in one hand while he put her lightly aside; but she did not seem to hear him.

"Oh, Ethan—Zeena's come," she said in a whisper, clutching his sleeve.

They stood and stared at each other, pale as culprits.

"But the sorrel's not in the barn!" Ethan stammered.

"Jotham Powell brought some goods over from the Flats for his wife, and he drove right on home with them," she explained.

He gazed blankly about the kitchen, which looked cold and squalid in the rainy winter twilight.

"How is she?" he asked, dropping his voice to Mattie's whisper.

She looked away from him uncertainly. "I don't know. She went right up to her room."

"She didn't say anything?"

"No."

Ethan let out his doubts in a low whistle and thrust the bottle back into his pocket. "Don't fret; I'll come down and mend it in the night," he said. He pulled on his wet coat again and went back to the barn to feed the grays.

While he was there Jotham Powell drove up with the sleigh, and when the horses had been attended to Ethan said to him: "You might as well come back up for a bite." He was not sorry to assure himself of Jotham's neutralising presence at the supper table, for Zeena was always "nervous" after a journey. But the hired man, though seldom loth to accept a meal not included in his wages, opened his stiff jaws to answer slowly: "I'm obliged to you, but I guess I'll go along back."

Ethan looked at him in surprise. "Better come up and dry off. Looks as if there'd be something hot for supper."

Jotham's facial muscles were unmoved by this appeal and, his vocabulary being limited, he merely repeated: "I guess I'll go along back."

To Ethan there was something vaguely ominous in this stolid rejection of free food and warmth, and he wondered what had happened on the drive to nerve Jotham to such stoicism. Perhaps Zeena had failed to see the new doctor or had not liked his counsels: Ethan knew that in such cases the first person she met was likely to be held responsible for her grievance.

When he re-entered the kitchen the lamp lit up the same scene of shining comfort as on the previous evening. The table had been as carefully laid, a clear fire glowed in the stove, the cat dozed in its warmth, and Mattie came forward carrying a plate of dough-nuts.

She and Ethan looked at each other in silence; then she said, as she had said the night before: "I guess it's about time for supper."

VII

Ethan went out into the passage to hang up his wet garments. He listened for Zeena's step and, not hearing it, called her name up the stairs. She did not answer, and after a moment's hesitation he went up and opened her door. The room was almost dark, but in the obscurity he saw her sitting by the window, bolt upright, and knew by the rigidity of the outline projected against the pane that she had not taken off her travelling dress.

"Well, Zeena," he ventured from the threshold.

She did not move, and he continued: "Supper's about ready. Ain't you coming?"

She replied: "I don't feel as if I could touch a morsel."

It was the consecrated formula, and he expected it to be followed, as usual, by her rising and going down to supper. But she remained seated, and he could think of nothing more felicitous than: "I presume you're tired after the long ride."

Turning her head at this, she answered solemnly: "I'm a great deal sicker than you think."

Her words fell on his ear with a strange shock of wonder. He had often heard her pronounce them before—what if at last they were true?

He advanced a step or two into the dim room. "I hope that's not so, Zeena," he said.

She continued to gaze at him through the twilight with a mien of wan authority, as of one consciously singled out for a great fate. "I've got complications," she said.

Ethan knew the word for one of exceptional import. Almost everybody in the neighbourhood had "troubles," frankly localized and specified; but only the chosen had "complications." To have them was in itself a distinction, though it was also, in most cases, a death-warrant. People struggled on for years with "troubles," but they almost always succumbed to "complications."

Ethan's heart was jerking to and fro between two extremities of feeling, but for the moment compassion prevailed. His wife looked so hard and lonely, sitting there in the darkness with such thoughts.

"Is that what the new doctor told you?" he asked, instinctively lowering his voice.

"Yes. He says any regular doctor would want me to have an operation."

Ethan was aware that, in regard to the important question of surgical intervention, the female opinion of the neighbourhood was divided, some glorying in the prestige conferred by operations while others shunned them as indelicate. Ethan, from motives of economy, had always been glad that Zeena was of the latter faction.

In the agitation caused by the gravity of her announcement he sought a consolatory short cut. "What do you know about this doctor anyway? Nobody ever told you that before."

He saw his blunder before she could take it up: she wanted sympathy, not consolation.

"I didn't need to have anybody tell me I was losing ground every day. Everybody but you could see it. And everybody in Bettsbridge knows about Dr. Buck. He has his office in Worcester, and comes over once a fortnight to Shadd's Falls and Bettsbridge for consultations. Eliza Spears was wasting away with kidney trouble before she went to him, and now she's up and around, and singing in the choir."

"Well, I'm glad of that. You must do just what he tells you," Ethan answered sympathetically.

She was still looking at him. "I mean to," she said. He was struck by a new note in her voice. It was neither whining nor reproachful, but drily resolute.

"What does he want you should do?" he asked, with a mounting vision of fresh expenses.

"He wants I should have a hired girl. He says I oughtn't to have to do a single thing around the house."

"A hired girl?" Ethan stood transfixed.

"Yes. And Aunt Martha found me one right off. Everybody said I was lucky to get a girl to come away out here, and I agreed to give her a dollar extry to make sure. She'll be over to-morrow afternoon."

Wrath and dismay contended in Ethan. He had foreseen an immediate demand for money, but not a permanent drain on his scant resources. He no longer believed what Zeena had told him of the supposed seriousness of her state: he saw in her expedition to Bettsbridge only a plot hatched between herself and her Pierce relations to foist on him the cost of a servant; and for the moment wrath predominated.

"If you meant to engage a girl you ought to have told me before you started," he said.

"How could I tell you before I started? How did I know what Dr. Buck would say?"

"Oh, Dr. Buck—" Ethan's incredulity escaped in a short laugh. "Did Dr. Buck tell you how I was to pay her wages?"

Her voice rose furiously with his. "No, he didn't. For I'd 'a' been ashamed to tell *him* that you grudged me the money to get back my health, when I lost it nursing your own mother!"

"*You* lost your health nursing mother?"

"Yes; and my folks all told me at the time you couldn't do no less than marry me after——"

"Zeena!"

Through the obscurity which hid their faces their thoughts seemed to dart at each other like serpents shooting venom. Ethan was seized with horror of the scene and shame at his own share in it. It was as senseless and savage as a physical fight between two enemies in the darkness.

He turned to the shelf above the chimney, groped for matches and lit the one candle in the room. At first its weak flame made no impression on the shadows; then Zeena's face stood grimly out against the uncurtained pane, which had turned from gray to black.

It was the first scene of open anger between the couple in their sad seven years together, and Ethan felt as if he had lost an irretrievable advantage in descending to the level of recrimination. But the practical problem was there and had to be dealt with.

"You know I haven't got the money to pay for a girl, Zeena. You'll have to send her back: I can't do it."

"The doctor says it'll be my death if I go on slaving the way I've had to. He doesn't understand how I've stood it as long as I have."

"Slaving! —" He checked himself again, "You sha'n't lift a hand, if he says so. I'll do everything round the house myself——"

She broke in: "You're neglecting the farm enough already," and this being true, he found no answer, and left her time to add ironically: "Better send me over to the almshouse and done with it . . . I guess there's been Fromes there afore now."

The taunt burned into him, but he let it pass. "I haven't got the money. That settles it."

There was a moment's pause in the struggle, as though the combatants were testing their weapons. Then Zeena said in a level voice: "I thought you were to get fifty dollars from Andrew Hale for that lumber."

"Andrew Hale never pays under three months." He had hardly spoken when he remembered the excuse he had made for not accompanying his wife to the station the day before; and the blood rose to his frowning brows.

"Why, you told me yesterday you'd fixed it up with him to pay cash down. You said that was why you couldn't drive me over to the Flats."

Ethan had no suppleness in deceiving. He had never before been convicted of a lie, and all the resources of evasion failed him. "I guess that was a misunderstanding," he stammered.

"You ain't got the money?"

"No."

"And you ain't going to get it?"

"No."

"Well, I couldn't know that when I engaged the girl, could I?"

"No." He paused to control his voice. "But you know it now. I'm sorry, but it can't be helped. You're a poor man's wife, Zeena; but I'll do the best I can for you."

---

almshouse: a home for people too poor to support themselves.

For a while she sat motionless, as if reflecting, her arms stretched along the arms of her chair, her eyes fixed on vacancy. "Oh, I guess we'll make out," she said mildly.

The change in her tone reassured him. "Of course we will! There's a whole lot more I can do for you, and Mattie——"

Zeena, while he spoke, seemed to be following out some elaborate mental calculation. She emerged from it to say: "There'll be Mattie's board less, anyhow——"

Ethan, supposing the discussion to be over, had turned to go down to supper. He stopped short, not grasping what he heard. "Mattie's board less—?" he began.

Zeena laughed. It was an odd unfamiliar sound—he did not remember ever having heard her laugh before. "You didn't suppose I was going to keep two girls, did you? No wonder you were scared at the expense!"

He still had but a confused sense of what she was saying. From the beginning of the discussion he had instinctively avoided the mention of Mattie's name, fearing he hardly knew what: criticism, complaints, or vague allusions to the imminent probability of her marrying. But the thought of a definite rupture had never come to him, and even now could not lodge itself in his mind.

"I don't know what you mean," he said. "Mattie Silver's not a hired girl. She's your relation."

"She's a pauper that's hung onto us all after her father'd done his best to ruin us. I've kep' her here a whole year: it's somebody else's turn now."

As the shrill words shot out Ethan heard a tap on the door, which he had drawn shut when he turned back from the threshold.

"Ethan—Zeena!" Mattie's voice sounded gaily from the landing, "do you know what time it is? Supper's been ready half an hour."

Inside the room there was a moment's silence; then Zeena called out from her seat: "I'm not coming down to supper."

"Oh, I'm sorry! Aren't you well? Sha'n't I bring you up a bite of something?"

Ethan roused himself with an effort and opened the door. "Go along down, Matt. Zeena's just a little tired. I'm coming."

He heard her "All right!" and her quick step on the stairs; then he shut the door and turned back into the room. His wife's attitude was unchanged, her face inexorable, and he was seized with the despairing sense of his helplessness.

"You ain't going to do it, Zeena?"

"Do what?" she emitted between flattened lips.

"Send Mattie away—like this?"

"I never bargained to take her for life!"

He continued with rising vehemence: "You can't put her out of the house like a thief—a poor girl without friends or money. She's done her best for you and she's got no place to go to. You may forget she's your kin but everybody else'll remember it. If you do a thing like that what do you suppose folks'll say of you?"

Zeena waited a moment, as if giving him time to feel the full force of the contrast between his own excitement and her composure. Then she replied in the same smooth voice: "I know well enough what they say of my having kep' her here as long as I have."

Ethan's hand dropped from the door-knob, which he had held clenched since he had drawn the door shut on Mattie. His wife's retort was like a knife-cut across the sinews and he felt suddenly weak and powerless. He had meant to humble himself, to argue that Mattie's keep didn't cost much, after all, that he could make out to buy a stove and fix up a place in the attic for the hired girl—but Zeena's words revealed the peril of such pleadings.

"You mean to tell her she's got to go—at once?" he faltered out, in terror of letting his wife complete her sentence.

As if trying to make him see reason she replied impartially; "The girl will be over from Bettsbridge to-morrow, and I presume she's got to have somewheres to sleep."

Ethan looked at her with loathing. She was no longer the listless creature who had lived at his side in a state of sullen self-absorption, but a mysterious alien presence, an evil energy secreted from the long years of silent brooding. It was the sense of his helplessness that sharpened his antipathy. There had never been anything in her that one could appeal to; but as long as he could ignore and command he had remained indifferent. Now she had mastered him and he abhorred her. Mattie was her relation, not his: there were no means by which he could compel her to keep the girl under her roof. All the long misery of his baffled past, of his youth of failure, hardship and vain effort, rose up in his soul in bitterness and seemed to take shape before him in the woman who at every turn had barred his way. She had taken everything else from him; and now she meant to take the one thing that made up for all the others. For a moment such a flame of hate rose in him that it ran down his arm and clenched his fist against her. He took a wild step forward and then stopped.

"You're—you're not coming down?" he said in a bewildered voice.

"No. I guess I'll lay down on the bed a little while," she answered mildly; and he turned and walked out of the room.

In the kitchen Mattie was sitting by the stove, the cat curled up on her knees. She sprang to her feet as Ethan entered and carried the covered dish of meat-pie to the table.

"I hope Zeena isn't sick?" she asked.

"No."

She shone at him across the table. "Well, sit right down then. You must be starving." She uncovered the pie and pushed it over to him. So they were to have one more evening together, her happy eyes seemed to say!

He helped himself mechanically and began to eat; then disgust took him by the throat and he laid down his fork.

Mattie's tender gaze was on him and she marked the gesture.

"Why, Ethan, what's the matter? Don't it taste right?"

"Yes—it's first-rate. Only I—" He pushed his plate away, rose from his chair, and walked around the table to her side. She started up with frightened eyes.

"Ethan, there's something wrong! I *knew* there was!"

She seemed to melt against him in her terror, and he caught her in his arms, held her fast there, felt her lashes beat his cheek like netted butterflies.

"What is it—what is it?" she stammered; but he had found her lips at last and was drinking unconsciousness of everything but the joy they gave him.

She lingered a moment, caught in the same strong current; then she slipped from him and drew back a step or two, pale and troubled. Her look smote him with compunction, and he cried out, as if he saw her drowning in a dream: "You can't go, Matt! I'll never let you!"

"Go—go?" she stammered. "Must I go?"

The words went on sounding between them as though a torch of warning flew from hand to hand through a black landscape.

Ethan was overcome with shame at his lack of self-control in flinging the news at her so brutally. His head reeled and he had to support himself against the table. All the while he felt as if he were still kissing her, and yet dying of thirst for her lips.

"Ethan what has happened? Is Zeena mad with me?"

Her cry steadied him, though it deepened his wrath and pity. "No, no," he assured her, "it's not that. But this new doctor has scared her about herself. You know she believes all they say the first time she sees them. And this one's told her she won't get well unless she lays up and don't do a thing about the house—not for months——"

He paused, his eyes wandering from her miserably. She stood silent a moment, drooping before him like a broken branch. She was so small and weak-looking that it wrung his heart; but suddenly she lifted her head and looked straight at him. "And she wants somebody handier in my place? Is that it?"

"That's what she says to-night."

"If she says it to-night she'll say it to-morrow."

Both bowed to the inexorable truth: they knew that Zeena never changed her mind, and that in her case a resolve once taken was equivalent to an act performed.

There was a long silence between them; then Mattie said in a low voice: "Don't be too sorry, Ethan."

"Oh, God—oh, God," he groaned. The glow of passion he had felt for her had melted to an aching tenderness. He saw her quick lids beating back the tears, and longed to take her in his arms and soothe her.

"You're letting your supper get cold," she admonished him with a pale gleam of gaiety.

"Oh, Matt—Matt—where'll you go to?"

Her lids sank and a tremor crossed her face. He saw that for the first time the thought of the future came to her distinctly. "I might get something to do over at Stamford," she faltered, as if knowing that he knew she had no hope.

He dropped back into his seat and hid his face in his hands. Despair seized him at the thought of her setting out alone to renew the weary quest for work. In the only place where she was known she was surrounded by indifference or animosity; and what chance had she, inexperienced and un-trained, among the million bread-seekers of the cities? There came back to him miserable tales he had heard at Worcester, and the faces of girls whose lives had begun as hopefully as Mattie's. . . . It was not possible to think of such things without a revolt of his whole being. He sprang up suddenly.

"You can't go, Matt! I won't let you! She's always had her way, but I mean to have mine now——"

Mattie lifted her hand with a quick gesture, and he heard his wife's step behind him.

Zeena came into the room with her dragging down-at-the-heel step, and quietly took her accustomed seat between them.

"I felt a little mite better, and Dr. Buck says I ought to eat all I can to keep my stren'th up, even if I ain't got any appetite," she said in her flat whine, reaching across Mattie for the teapot. Her "good" dress had been replaced by the black calico and brown knitted shawl which formed her daily wear, and with them she had put on her usual face and manner. She poured out her tea, added a great deal of milk to it, helped herself largely to pie and pickles, and made the familiar gesture of adjusting her false teeth before she began to eat. The cat rubbed itself ingratiatingly against her, and she said "Good Pussy," stooped to stroke it and gave it a scrap of meat from her plate.

Ethan sat speechless, not pretending to eat, but Mattie nibbled valiantly at her food and asked Zeena one or two questions about her visit to Betts-bridge. Zeena answered in her every-day tone and, warming to the theme, regaled them with several vivid descriptions of intestinal disturbances among her friends and relatives. She looked straight at Mattie as she spoke, a faint smile deepening the vertical lines between her nose and chin.

When supper was over she rose from her seat and pressed her hand to the flat surface over the region of her heart. "That pie of yours always sets a mite heavy, Matt," she said, not ill-naturedly. She seldom abbreviated the girl's name, and when she did so it was always a sign of affability.

"I've a good mind to go and hunt up those stomach powders I got last year over in Springfield," she continued. "I ain't tried them for quite a while, and maybe they'll help the heart-burn."

Mattie lifted her eyes. "Can't I get them for you, Zeena?" she ventured.

"No. They're in a place you don't know about," Zeena answered darkly, with one of her secret looks.

She went out of the kitchen and Mattie, rising, began to clear the dishes from the table. As she passed Ethan's chair their eyes met and clung together desolately. The warm still kitchen looked as peaceful as the night before. The cat had sprung to Zeena's rocking-chair, and the heat of the fire was beginning to draw out the faint sharp scent of the geraniums. Ethan dragged himself wearily to his feet.

"I'll go out and take a look round," he said, going toward the passage to get his lantern.

As he reached the door he met Zeena coming back into the room, her lips twitching with anger, a flush of excitement on her sallow face. The shawl had slipped from her shoulders and was dragging at her down-trodden heels, and in her hands she carried the fragments of the red glass pickle-dish.

"I'd like to know who done this," she said, looking sternly from Ethan to Mattie.

There was no answer, and she continued in a trembling voice: "I went to get those powders I'd put away in father's old spectacle-case, top of the china-closet, where I keep the things I set store by, so's folks sha'n't meddle with them—" Her voice broke, and two small tears hung on her lashless lids and ran slowly down her cheeks. "It takes the step-ladder to get at the top shelf, and I put Aunt Philura Maple's pickle-dish up there o' purpose when we was married, and it's never been down since, 'cept for the spring cleaning, and then I always lifted it with my own hands, so's 't it shouldn't get broke." She laid the fragments reverently on the table. "I want to know who done this," she quavered.

At the challenge Ethan turned back into the room and faced her. "I can tell you, then. The cat done it."

"The *cat?*"

"That's what I said."

She looked at him hard, and then turned her eyes to Mattie, who was carrying the dish-pan to the table.

"I'd like to know how the cat got into my china-closet," she said.

"Chasin' mice, I guess," Ethan rejoined. "There was a mouse round the kitchen all last evening."

Zeena continued to look from one to the other; then she emitted her small strange laugh. "I knew the cat was a smart cat," she said in a high voice, "but I didn't know he was smart enough to pick up the pieces of my pickle-dish and lay 'em edge to edge on the very shelf he knocked 'em off of."

Mattie suddenly drew her arms out of the steaming water. "It wasn't Ethan's fault, Zeena! The cat *did* break the dish; but I got it down from the china-closet, and I'm the one to blame for its getting broken."

Zeena stood beside the ruin of her treasure, stiffening into a stony image of resentment. "*You* got down my pickle-dish—what for?"

A bright flush flew to Mattie's cheeks. "I wanted to make the supper-table pretty," she said.

"You wanted to make the supper-table pretty; and you waited till my back was turned, and took the thing I set most store by of anything I've got, and wouldn't never use it, not even when the minister come to dinner, or Aunt Martha Pierce come over from Bettsbridge—" Zeena paused with a gasp, as if terrified by her own evocation of the sacrilege. "You're a bad girl, Mattie Silver, and I always known it. It's the way your father begun, and I was warned of it when I took you, and I tried to keep my things where you couldn't get at 'em—and now you've took from me the one I cared for most of all—" She broke off in a short spasm of sobs that passed and left her more than ever like a shape of stone.

"If I'd 'a' listened to folks, you'd 'a' gone before now, and this wouldn't 'a' happened," she said; and gathering up the bits of broken glass she went out of the room as if she carried a dead body . . .

VIII

When Ethan was called back to the farm by his father's illness his mother gave him, for his own use, a small room behind the untenanted "best parlour." Here he had nailed up shelves for his books, built himself a box-sofa out of boards and a mattress, laid out his papers on a kitchen-table, hung on the rough plaster wall an engraving of Abraham Lincoln and a calendar with "Thoughts from the Poets," and tried, with these meagre properties to produce some likeness to the study of a "minister" who had been kind to him and lent him books when he was at Worcester. He still took refuge there in summer, but when Mattie came to live at the farm he had had to give her his stove, and consequently the room was uninhabitable for several months of the year.

To this retreat he descended as soon as the house was quiet, and Zeena's steady breathing from the bed had assured him that there was to be no sequel to the scene in the kitchen. After Zeena's departure he and Mattie had stood speechless, neither seeking to approach the other. Then the girl had returned to her task of clearing up the kitchen for the night and he had taken his lantern and gone on his usual round outside the house. The kitchen was empty when he came back to it; but his tobacco-pouch and pipe had been laid on the table, and under them was a scrap of paper torn from the back of a seedsman's catalogue, on which three words were written: "Don't trouble, Ethan."

Going into his cold dark "study" he placed the lantern on the table and, stooping to its light, read the message again and again. It was the first time that Mattie had ever written to him, and the possession of the paper gave him a strange new sense of her nearness; yet it deepened his anguish by reminding him that henceforth they would have no other way of communicating with each other. For the life of her smile, the warmth of her voice, only cold paper and dead words!

Confused motions of rebellion stormed in him. He was too young, too strong, too full of the sap of living, to submit so easily to the destruction of his hopes. Must he wear out all his years at the side of a bitter querulous woman? Other possibilities had been in him, possibilities sacrificed, one by one, to Zeena's narrow-mindedness and ignorance. And what good had come of it? She was a hundred times bitterer and more discontented than when he had married her: the one pleasure left her was to inflict pain on him. All the healthy instincts of self-defence rose up in him against such waste . . .

He bundled himself into his old coon-skin coat and lay down on the box-sofa to think. Under his cheek he felt a hard object with strange protuberances. It was a cushion which Zeena had made for him when they were engaged—the only piece of needlework he had ever seen her do. He flung it across the floor and propped his head against the wall . . .

He knew a case of a man over the mountain—a young fellow of about his own age—who had escaped from just such a life of misery by going West with the girl he cared for. His wife had divorced him, and he had married the girl and prospered. Ethan had seen the couple the summer before at Shadd's Falls, where they had come to visit relatives. They had a little girl with fair curls, who wore a gold locket and was dressed like a princess. The deserted wife had not done badly either. Her husband had given her the farm and she had managed to sell it, and with that and the alimony she had started a lunch-room at Bettsbridge and bloomed into activity and importance. Ethan was fired by the thought. Why should he not leave with Mattie the next day, instead of letting her go alone? He would hide his valise under the seat of the sleigh, and Zeena would suspect nothing till she went upstairs for her afternoon nap and found a letter on the bed . . .

His impulses were still near the surface, and he sprang up, re-lit the lantern, and sat down at the table. He rummaged in the drawer for a sheet of paper, found one, and began to write.

"Zeena, I've done all I could for you, and I don't see as it's been any use. I don't blame you, nor I don't blame myself. Maybe both of us will do better separate. I'm going to try my luck West, and you can sell the farm and mill, and keep the money——"

His pen paused on the word, which brought home to him the relentless conditions of his lot. If he gave the farm and mill to Zeena what would be left him to start his own life with? Once in the West he was sure of picking up work—he would not have feared to try his chance alone. But with Mattie depending on him the case was different. And what of Zeena's fate? Farm and mill were mortgaged to the limit of their value, and even if she found a purchaser—in itself an unlikely chance—it was doubtful if she could clear a thousand dollars on the sale. Meanwhile, how could she keep the farm going? It was only by incessant labour and personal supervision that Ethan drew a meagre living from his land, and his wife, even if she were in better health than she imagined, could never carry such a burden alone.

Well, she could go back to her people, then, and see what they would do for her. It was the fate she was forcing on Mattie—why not let her try it herself? By the time she had discovered his whereabouts, and brought suit for divorce, he would probably—wherever he was—be earning enough to pay her a sufficient alimony. And the alternative was to let Mattie go forth alone, with far less hope of ultimate provision . . .

He had scattered the contents of the table-drawer in his search for a sheet of paper, and as he took up his pen his eye fell on an old copy of the *Bettsbridge Eagle*. The advertising sheet was folded uppermost, and he read the seductive words: "Trips to the West: Reduced Rates."

He drew the lantern nearer and eagerly scanned the fares; then the paper fell from his hand and he pushed aside his unfinished letter. A moment ago he had wondered what he and Mattie were to live on when they reached the West; now he saw that he had not even the money to take her there. Borrowing was out of the question: six months before he had given his only security to raise funds for necessary repairs to the mill, and he knew that without security no one at Starkfield would lend him ten dollars. The inexorable facts closed in on him like prison-warders hand-cuffing a convict. There was no way out—none. He was a prisoner for life, and now his one ray of light was to be extinguished.

He crept back heavily to the sofa, stretching himself out with limbs so leaden that he felt as if they would never move again. Tears rose in his throat and slowly burned their way to his lids.

As he lay there, the window-pane that faced him, growing gradually lighter, inlaid upon the darkness a square of moon-suffused sky. A crooked tree-branch crossed it, a branch of the apple-tree under which, on summer evenings, he had sometimes found Mattie sitting when he came up from the mill. Slowly the rim of the rainy vapours caught fire and burnt away, and a pure moon swung into the blue. Ethan, rising on his elbow, watched the landscape whiten and shape itself under the sculpture of the moon. This was the night on which he was to have taken Mattie coasting, and there hung the lamp to light them! He looked out at the slopes bathed in lustre, the silver-edged darkness of the woods, the spectral purple of the hills against the sky, and it seemed as though all the beauty of the night had been poured out to mock his wretchedness . . .

He fell asleep, and when he woke the chill of the winter dawn was in the room. He felt cold and stiff and hungry, and ashamed of being hungry. He rubbed his eyes and went to the window. A red sun stood over the gray rim of the fields, behind trees that looked black and brittle. He said to himself: "This is Matt's last day," and tried to think what the place would be without her.

As he stood there he heard a step behind him and she entered.

"Oh, Ethan—were you here all night?"

She looked so small and pinched, in her poor dress, with the red scarf wound about her, and the cold light turning her paleness sallow, that Ethan stood before her without speaking.

"You must be frozen," she went on, fixing lustreless eyes on him.

He drew a step nearer. "How did you know I was here?"

"Because I heard you go down stairs again after I went to bed, and I listened all night, and you didn't come up."

All his tenderness rushed to his lips. He looked at her and said: "I'll come right along and make up the kitchen fire."

They went back to the kitchen, and he fetched the coal and kindlings and cleared out the stove for her, while she brought in the milk and the cold remains of the meat-pie. When warmth began to radiate from the stove, and the first ray of sunlight lay on the kitchen floor, Ethan's dark thoughts melted in the mellower air. The sight of Mattie going about her work as he had seen her on so many mornings made it seem impossible that she should ever cease to be a part of the scene. He said to himself that he had doubtless exaggerated the significance of Zeena's threats, and that she too, with the return of daylight, would come to a saner mood.

He went up to Mattie as she bent above the stove, and laid his hand on her arm. "I don't want you should trouble either," he said, looking down into her eyes with a smile.

She flushed up warmly and whispered back: "No, Ethan, I ain't going to trouble."

"I guess things'll straighten out," he added.

There was no answer but a quick throb of her lids, and he went on: "She ain't said anything this morning?"

"No. I haven't seen her yet."

"Don't you take any notice when you do."

With this injunction he left her and went out to the cow-barn. He saw Jotham Powell walking up the hill through the morning mist, and the familiar sight added to his growing conviction of security.

As the two men were clearing out the stalls Jotham rested on his pitchfork to say: "Dan'l Byrne's goin' over to the Flats to-day noon, an' he c'd take Mattie's trunk along, and make it easier ridin' when I take her over in the sleigh."

Ethan looked at him blankly, and he continued: "Mis' Frome said the new girl'd be at the Flats at five, and I was to take Mattie then, so's 't she could ketch the six o'clock train for Stamford."

Ethan felt the blood drumming in his temples. He had to wait a moment before he could find voice to say: "Oh, it ain't so sure about Mattie's going——"

"That so?" said Jotham indifferently; and they went on with their work.

When they returned to the kitchen the two women were already at breakfast. Zeena had an air of unusual alertness and activity. She drank two cups of coffee and fed the cat with the scraps left in the pie-dish; then she rose from her seat and, walking over to the window, snipped two or three yellow leaves from the geraniums. "Aunt Martha's ain't got a faded leaf on 'em; but they pine away when they ain't cared for," she said reflectively. Then she turned to Jotham and asked: "What time'd you say Dan'l Byrne'd be along?"

The hired man threw a hesitating glance at Ethan. "Round about noon," he said.

Zeena turned to Mattie. "That trunk of yours is too heavy for the sleigh, and Dan'l Byrne'll be round to take it over to the Flats," she said.

"I'm much obliged to you, Zeena," said Mattie.

"I'd like to go over things with you first," Zeena continued in an unperturbed voice. "I know there's a huckabuck towel missing; and I can't make out what you done with that match-safe 't used to stand behind the stuffed owl in the parlour."

She went out, followed by Mattie, and when the men were alone Jotham said to his employer: "I guess I better let Dan'l come round, then."

Ethan finished his usual morning tasks about the house and barn; then he said to Jotham: "I'm going down to Starkfield. Tell them not to wait dinner."

The passion of rebellion had broken out in him again. That which had seemed incredible in the sober light of day had really come to pass, and he was to assist as a helpless spectator at Mattie's banishment. His manhood was humbled by the part he was compelled to play and by the thought of what Mattie must think of him. Confused impulses struggled in him as he strode along to the village. He had made up his mind to do something, but he did not know what it would be.

The early mist had vanished and the fields lay like a silver shield under the sun. It was one of the days when the glitter of winter shines through a pale haze of spring. Every yard of the road was alive with Mattie's presence, and there was hardly a branch against the sky or a tangle of brambles on the bank in which some bright shred of memory was not caught. Once, in the stillness, the call of a bird in a mountain ash was so like her laughter that his heart tightened and then grew large; and all these things made him see that something must be done at once.

Suddenly it occurred to him that Andrew Hale, who was a kind-hearted man, might be induced to reconsider his refusal and advance a small sum on the lumber if he were told that Zeena's ill-health made it necessary to hire a servant. Hale, after all, knew enough of Ethan's situation to make it possible for the latter to renew his appeal without too much loss of pride; and, moreover, how much did pride count in the ebullition of passions in his breast?

The more he considered his plan the more hopeful it seemed. If he could get Mrs. Hale's ear he felt certain of success, and with fifty dollars in his pocket nothing could keep him from Mattie . . .

His first object was to reach Starkfield before Hale had started for his work; he knew the carpenter had a job down the Corbury road and was

---

huckabuck: an absorbent durable fabric of cotton, linen, or both.
match-safe: a case, often made of cast iron, for storing and striking matches.
ebullition: a sudden outburst.

likely to leave his house early. Ethan's long strides grew more rapid with the accelerated beat of his thoughts, and as he reached the foot of School House Hill he caught sight of Hale's sleigh in the distance. He hurried forward to meet it, but as it drew nearer he saw that it was driven by the carpenter's youngest boy and that the figure at his side, looking like a large upright cocoon in spectacles, was that of Mrs. Hale. Ethan signed to them to stop, and Mrs. Hale leaned forward, her pink wrinkles twinkling with benevolence.

"Mr. Hale? Why, yes, you'll find him down home now. He ain't going to his work this forenoon. He woke up with a touch o' lumbago, and I just made him put on one of old Dr. Kidder's plasters and set right up into the fire."

Beaming maternally on Ethan, she bent over to add: "I on'y just heard from Mr. Hale 'bout Zeena's going over to Bettsbridge to see that new doctor. I'm real sorry she's feeling so bad again! I hope he thinks he can do something for her? I don't know anybody round here's had more sickness than Zeena. I always tell Mr. Hale I don't know what she'd 'a' done if she hadn't 'a' had you to look after her; and I used to say the same thing 'bout your mother. You've had an awful mean time, Ethan Frome."

She gave him a last nod of sympathy while her son chirped to the horse; and Ethan, as she drove off, stood in the middle of the road and stared after the retreating sleigh.

It was a long time since any one had spoken to him as kindly as Mrs. Hale. Most people were either indifferent to his troubles, or disposed to think it natural that a young fellow of his age should have carried without repining the burden of three crippled lives. But Mrs. Hale had said "You've had an awful mean time, Ethan Frome," and he felt less alone with his misery. If the Hales were sorry for him they would surely respond to his appeal . . .

He started down the road toward their house, but at the end of a few yards he pulled up sharply, the blood in his face. For the first time, in the light of the words he had just heard, he saw what he was about to do. He was planning to take advantage of the Hales' sympathy to obtain money from them on false pretences. That was a plain statement of the cloudy purpose which had driven him in headlong to Starkfield.

With the sudden perception of the point to which his madness had carried him, the madness fell and he saw his life before him as it was. He was a poor man, the husband of a sickly woman, whom his desertion would leave alone and destitute; and even if he had had the heart to desert

---

lumbago: muscle pain in the lower back.
plasters: medicated dressings.

her he could have done so only by deceiving two kindly people who had pitied him.

He turned and walked slowly back to the farm.

IX

At the kitchen door Daniel Byrne sat in his sleigh behind a big-boned gray who pawed the snow and swung his long head restlessly from side to side.

Ethan went into the kitchen and found his wife by the stove. Her head was wrapped in her shawl, and she was reading a book called "Kidney Troubles And Their Cure" on which he had had to pay extra postage only a few days before.

Zeena did not move or look up when he entered, and after a moment he asked: "Where's Mattie?"

Without lifting her eyes from the page she replied: "I presume she's getting down her trunk."

The blood rushed to his face. "Getting down her trunk—alone?"

"Jotham Powell's down in the wood-lot, and Dan'l Byrne says he darsn't leave that horse," she returned.

Her husband, without stopping to hear the end of the phrase, had left the kitchen and sprung up the stairs. The door of Mattie's room was shut, and he wavered a moment on the landing. "Matt," he said in a low voice; but there was no answer, and he put his hand on the door-knob.

He had never been in her room except once, in the early summer, when he had gone there to plaster up a leak in the eaves, but he remembered exactly how everything had looked: the red and white quilt on her narrow bed, the pretty pin-cushion on the chest of drawers, and over it the enlarged photograph of her mother, in an oxydized frame, with a bunch of dyed grasses at the back. Now these and all other tokens of her presence had vanished, and the room looked as bare and comfortless as when Zeena had shown her into it on the day of her arrival. In the middle of the floor stood her trunk, and on the trunk she sat in her Sunday dress, her back turned to the door and her face in her hands. She had not heard Ethan's call because she was sobbing; and she did not hear his step till he stood close behind her and laid his hands on her shoulders.

"Matt—oh, don't—oh, *Matt!*"

She started up, lifting her wet face to his. "Ethan—I thought I wasn't ever going to see you again!"

He took her in his arms, pressing her close, and with a trembling hand smoothed away the hair from her forehead.

"Not see me again? What do you mean?"

She sobbed out: "Jotham said you told him we wasn't to wait dinner for you, and I thought——"

"You thought I meant to cut it?" he finished for her grimly.

She clung to him without answering, and he laid his lips on her hair, which was soft yet springy, like certain mosses on warm slopes, and had the faint woody fragrance of fresh sawdust in the sun.

Through the door they heard Zeena's voice calling out from below: "Dan'l Byrne says you better hurry up if you want him to take that trunk."

They drew apart with stricken faces. Words of resistance rushed to Ethan's lips and died there. Mattie found her handkerchief and dried her eyes; then, bending down, she took hold of a handle of the trunk.

Ethan put her aside. "You let go, Matt," he ordered her.

She answered: "It takes two to coax it round the corner"; and submitting to this argument he grasped the other handle, and together they manoeuvred the heavy trunk out to the landing.

"Now let go," he repeated; then he shouldered the trunk and carried it down the stairs and across the passage to the kitchen. Zeena, who had gone back to her seat by the stove, did not lift her head from her book as he passed. Mattie followed him out of the door and helped him to lift the trunk into the back of the sleigh. When it was in place they stood side by side on the door-step, watching Daniel Byrne plunge off behind his fidgety horse.

It seemed to Ethan that his heart was bound with cords which an unseen hand was tightening with every tick of the clock. Twice he opened his lips to speak to Mattie and found no breath. At length, as she turned to re-enter the house, he laid a detaining hand on her.

"I'm going to drive you over, Matt," he whispered.

She murmured back: "I think Zeena wants I should go with Jotham."

"I'm going to drive you over," he repeated; and she went into the kitchen without answering.

At dinner Ethan could not eat. If he lifted his eyes they rested on Zeena's pinched face, and the corners of her straight lips seemed to quiver away into a smile. She ate well, declaring that the mild weather made her feel better, and pressed a second helping of beans on Jotham Powell, whose wants she generally ignored.

Mattie, when the meal was over, went about her usual task of clearing the table and washing up the dishes. Zeena, after feeding the cat, had returned to her rocking-chair by the stove, and Jotham Powell, who always lingered last, reluctantly pushed back his chair and moved toward the door.

On the threshold he turned back to say to Ethan: "What time'll I come round for Mattie?"

Ethan was standing near the window, mechanically filling his pipe while he watched Mattie move to and fro. He answered: "You needn't come round; I'm going to drive her over myself."

He saw the rise of the colour in Mattie's averted cheek, and the quick lifting of Zeena's head.

"I want you should stay here this afternoon, Ethan," his wife said. "Jotham can drive Mattie over."

Mattie flung an imploring glance at him, but he repeated curtly: "I'm going to drive her over myself."

Zeena continued in the same even tone: "I wanted you should stay and fix up that stove in Mattie's room afore the girl gets here. It ain't been drawing right for nigh on a month now."

Ethan's voice rose indignantly. "If it was good enough for Mattie I guess it's good enough for a hired girl."

"That girl that's coming told me she was used to a house where they had a furnace," Zeena persisted with the same monotonous mildness.

"She'd better ha' stayed there then," he flung back at her; and turning to Mattie he added in a hard voice: "You be ready by three, Matt; I've got business at Corbury."

Jotham Powell had started for the barn, and Ethan strode down after him aflame with anger. The pulses in his temples throbbed and a fog was in his eyes. He went about his task without knowing what force directed him, or whose hands and feet were fulfilling its orders. It was not till he led out the sorrel and backed him between the shafts of the sleigh that he once more became conscious of what he was doing. As he passed the bridle over the horse's head, and wound the traces around the shafts, he remembered the day when he had made the same preparations in order to drive over and meet his wife's cousin at the Flats. It was little more than a year ago, on just such a soft afternoon, with a "feel" of spring in the air. The sorrel, turning the same big ringed eye on him, nuzzled the palm of his hand in the same way; and one by one all the days between rose up and stood before him . . .

He flung the bearskin into the sleigh, climbed to the seat, and drove up to the house. When he entered the kitchen it was empty, but Mattie's bag and shawl lay ready by the door. He went to the foot of the stairs and listened. No sound reached him from above, but presently he thought he heard some one moving about in his deserted study, and pushing open the door he saw Mattie, in her hat and jacket, standing with her back to him near the table.

She started at his approach and turning quickly, said: "Is it time?"

"What are you doing here, Matt?" he asked her.

She looked at him timidly. "I was just taking a look round—that's all," she answered, with a wavering smile.

They went back into the kitchen without speaking, and Ethan picked up her bag and shawl.

"Where's Zeena?" he asked.

"She went upstairs right after dinner. She said she had those shooting pains again, and didn't want to be disturbed."

"Didn't she say good-bye to you?"

"No. That was all she said."

Ethan, looking slowly about the kitchen, said to himself with a shudder that in a few hours he would be returning to it alone. Then the sense of unreality overcame him once more, and he could not bring himself to believe that Mattie stood there for the last time before him.

"Come on," he said almost gaily, opening the door and putting her bag into the sleigh. He sprang to his seat and bent over to tuck the rug about her as she slipped into the place at his side. "Now then, go 'long," he said, with a shake of the reins that sent the sorrel placidly jogging down the hill.

"We got lots of time for a good ride, Matt!" he cried, seeking her hand beneath the fur and pressing it in his. His face tingled and he felt dizzy, as if he had stopped in at the Starkfield saloon on a zero day for a drink.

At the gate, instead of making for Starkfield, he turned the sorrel to the right, up the Bettsbridge road. Mattie sat silent, giving no sign of surprise; but after a moment she said: "Are you going round by Shadow Pond?"

He laughed and answered: "I knew you'd know!"

She drew closer under the bearskin, so that, looking sideways around his coat-sleeve, he could just catch the tip of her nose and a blown brown wave of hair. They drove slowly up the road between fields glistening under the pale sun, and then bent to the right down a lane edged with spruce and larch. Ahead of them, a long way off, a range of hills stained by mottlings of black forest flowed away in round white curves against the sky. The lane passed into a pine-wood with boles reddening in the afternoon sun and delicate blue shadows on the snow. As they entered it the breeze fell and a warm stillness seemed to drop from the branches with the dropping needles. Here the snow was so pure that the tiny tracks of wood-animals had left on it intricate lace-like patterns, and the bluish cones caught in its surface stood out like ornaments of bronze.

Ethan drove on in silence till they reached a part of the wood where the pines were more widely spaced; then he drew up and helped Mattie to get out of the sleigh. They passed between the aromatic trunks, the snow breaking crisply under their feet, till they came to a small sheet of water with steep wooded sides. Across its frozen surface, from the farther bank, a single hill rising against the western sun threw the long conical shadow which gave the lake its name. It was a shy secret spot, full of the same dumb melancholy that Ethan felt in his heart.

He looked up and down the little pebbly beach till his eye lit on a fallen tree-trunk half submerged in snow.

"There's where we sat at the picnic," he reminded her.

The entertainment of which he spoke was one of the few that they had taken part in together: a "church picnic" which, on a long afternoon of the preceding summer, had filled the retired place with merry-making. Mattie had begged him to go with her but he had refused. Then, toward sunset, coming down from the mountain where he had been felling timber, he had been caught by some strayed revellers and drawn into the group by the lake, where Mattie, encircled by facetious youths, and bright as a black-berry under her spreading hat, was brewing coffee over a gipsy fire. He re-membered the shyness he had felt at approaching her in his uncouth clothes, and then the lighting up of her face, and the way she had broken through the group to come to him with a cup in her hand. They had sat for a few minutes on the fallen log by the pond, and she had missed her gold locket, and set the young men searching for it; and it was Ethan who had spied it in the moss . . . That was all; but all their intercourse had been made up of just such inarticulate flashes, when they seemed to come suddenly upon happiness as if they had surprised a butterfly in the winter woods . . .

"It was right there I found your locket," he said, pushing his foot into a dense tuft of blueberry bushes.

"I never saw anybody with such sharp eyes!" she answered.

She sat down on the tree-trunk in the sun and he sat down beside her.

"You were as pretty as a picture in that pink hat," he said.

She laughed with pleasure. "Oh, I guess it was the hat!" she rejoined.

They had never before avowed their inclination so openly, and Ethan, for a moment, had the illusion that he was a free man, wooing the girl he meant to marry. He looked at her hair and longed to touch it again, and to tell her that it smelt of the woods; but he had never learned to say such things.

Suddenly she rose to her feet and said: "We mustn't stay here any longer."

He continued to gaze at her vaguely, only half-roused from his dream. "There's plenty of time," he answered.

They stood looking at each other as if the eyes of each were straining to absorb and hold fast the other's image. There were things he had to say to her before they parted, but he could not say them in that place of summer memories, and he turned and followed her in silence to the sleigh. As they drove away the sun sank behind the hill and the pine-boles turned from red to gray.

By a devious track between the fields they wound back to the Starkfield road. Under the open sky the light was still clear, with a reflection of cold red on the eastern hills. The clumps of trees in the snow seemed to draw together in ruffled lumps, like birds with their heads under their wings; and the sky, as it paled, rose higher, leaving the earth more alone.

As they turned into the Starkfield road Ethan said: "Matt, what do you mean to do?"

She did not answer at once, but at length she said: "I'll try to get a place in a store."

"You know you can't do it. The bad air and the standing all day nearly killed you before."

"I'm a lot stronger than I was before I came to Starkfield."

"And now you're going to throw away all the good it's done you!"

There seemed to be no answer to this, and again they drove on for a while without speaking. With every yard of the way some spot where they had stood, and laughed together or been silent, clutched at Ethan and dragged him back.

"Isn't there any of your father's folks could help you?"

"There isn't any of 'em I'd ask."

He lowered his voice to say: "You know there's nothing I wouldn't do for you if I could."

"I know there isn't."

"But I can't——"

She was silent, but he felt a slight tremor in the shoulder against his.

"Oh, Matt," he broke out, "if I could ha' gone with you now I'd ha' done it——"

She turned to him, pulling a scrap of paper from her breast. "Ethan—I found this," she stammered. Even in the failing light he saw it was the letter to his wife that he had begun the night before and forgotten to destroy. Through his astonishment there ran a fierce thrill of joy. "Matt—" he cried; "if I could ha' done it, would you?"

"Oh, Ethan, Ethan—what's the use?" With a sudden movement she tore the letter in shreds and sent them fluttering off into the snow.

"Tell me, Matt! Tell me!" he adjured her.

She was silent for a moment; then she said, in such a low tone that he had to stoop his head to hear her: "I used to think of it sometimes, summer nights, when the moon was so bright I couldn't sleep."

His heart reeled with the sweetness of it. "As long ago as that?"

She answered, as if the date had long been fixed for her: "The first time was at Shadow Pond."

"Was that why you gave me my coffee before the others?"

"I don't know. Did I? I was dreadfully put out when you wouldn't go to the picnic with me; and then, when I saw you coming down the road, I thought maybe you'd gone home that way o' purpose; and that made me glad."

They were silent again. They had reached the point where the road dipped to the hollow by Ethan's mill and as they descended the darkness descended with them, dropping down like a black veil from the heavy hemlock boughs.

"I'm tied hand and foot, Matt. There isn't a thing I can do," he began again.

"You must write to me sometimes, Ethan."

"Oh, what good'll writing do? I want to put my hand out and touch you. I want to do for you and care for you. I want to be there when you're sick and when you're lonesome."

"You mustn't think but what I'll do all right."

"You won't need me, you mean? I suppose you'll marry!"

"Oh, Ethan!" she cried.

"I don't know how it is you make me feel, Matt. I'd a'most rather have you dead than that!"

"Oh, I wish I was, I wish I was!" she sobbed.

The sound of her weeping shook him out of his dark anger, and he felt ashamed.

"Don't let's talk that way," he whispered.

"Why shouldn't we, when it's true? I've been wishing it every minute of the day."

"Matt! You be quiet! Don't you say it."

"There's never anybody been good to me but you."

"Don't say that either, when I can't lift a hand for you!"

"Yes; but it's true just the same."

They had reached the top of School House Hill and Starkfield lay below them in the twilight. A cutter, mounting the road from the village, passed them by in a joyous flutter of bells, and they straightened themselves and looked ahead with rigid faces. Along the main street lights had begun to shine from the house-fronts and stray figures were turning in here and there at the gates. Ethan, with a touch of his whip, roused the sorrel to a languid trot.

As they drew near the end of the village the cries of children reached them, and they saw a knot of boys, with sleds behind them, scattering across the open space before the church.

"I guess this'll be their last coast for a day or two," Ethan said, looking up at the mild sky.

Mattie was silent, and he added: "We were to have gone down last night."

Still she did not speak and, prompted by an obscure desire to help himself and her through their miserable last hour, he went on discursively: "Ain't it funny we haven't been down together but just that once last winter?"

She answered: "It wasn't often I got down to the village."

"That's so," he said.

They had reached the crest of the Corbury road, and between the indistinct white glimmer of the church and the black curtain of the Varnum spruces the slope stretched away below them without a sled on its length. Some erratic impulse prompted Ethan to say: "How'd you like me to take you down now?"

She forced a laugh. "Why, there isn't time!"

"There's all the time we want. Come along!" His one desire now was to postpone the moment of turning the sorrel toward the Flats.

"But the girl," she faltered. "The girl'll be waiting at the station."

"Well, let her wait. You'd have to if she didn't. Come!"

The note of authority in his voice seemed to subdue her, and when he had jumped from the sleigh he let him help her out, saying only, with a vague feint of reluctance: "But there isn't a sled round any wheres."

"Yes, there is! Right over there under the spruces."

He threw the bearskin over the sorrel, who stood passively by the roadside, hanging a meditative head. Then he caught Mattie's hand and drew her after him toward the sled.

She seated herself obediently and he took his place behind her, so close that her hair brushed his face.

"All right, Matt?" he called out, as if the width of the road had been between them.

She turned her head to say: "It's dreadfully dark. Are you sure you can see?"

He laughed contemptuously: "I could go down this coast with my eyes tied!" and she laughed with him, as if she liked his audacity. Nevertheless he sat still a moment, straining his eyes down the long hill, for it was the most confusing hour of the evening, the hour when the last clearness from the upper sky is merged with the rising night in a blur that disguises landmarks and falsifies distances.

"Now!" he cried.

The sled started with a bound, and they flew on through the dusk, gathering smoothness and speed as they went, with the hollow night opening out below them and the air singing by like an organ. Mattie sat perfectly still, but as they reached the bend at the foot of the hill, where the big elm thrust out a deadly elbow, he fancied that she shrank a little closer.

"Don't be scared, Matt!" he cried exultantly, as they spun safely past it and flew down the second slope; and when they reached the level ground beyond, and the speed of the sled began to slacken, he heard her give a little laugh of glee.

They sprang off and started to walk back up the hill. Ethan dragged the sled with one hand and passed the other through Mattie's arm.

"Were you scared I'd run you into the elm?" he asked with a boyish laugh.

"I told you I was never scared with you," she answered.

The strange exaltation of his mood had brought on one of his rare fits of boastfulness. "It *is* a tricky place, though. The least swerve, and we'd never ha' come up again. But I can measure distances to a hair's-breadth — always could."

She murmured: "I always say you've got the surest eye . . . "

Deep silence had fallen with the starless dusk, and they leaned on each other without speaking; but at every step of their climb Ethan said to himself: "It's the last time we'll ever walk together."

They mounted slowly to the top of the hill. When they were abreast of the church he stooped his head to her to ask: "Are you tired?" and she answered, breathing quickly: "It was splendid!"

With a pressure of his arm he guided her toward the Norway spruces. "I guess this sled must be Ned Hale's. Anyhow I'll leave it where I found it." He drew the sled up to the Varnum gate and rested it against the fence. As he raised himself he suddenly felt Mattie close to him among the shadows.

"Is this where Ned and Ruth kissed each other?" she whispered breathlessly, and flung her arms about him. Her lips, groping for his, swept over his face, and he held her fast in a rapture of surprise.

"Good-bye — good-bye," she stammered, and kissed him again.

"Oh, Matt I can't let you go!" broke from him in the same old cry.

She freed herself from his hold and he heard her sobbing. "Oh, I can't go either!" she wailed.

"Matt! What'll we do? What'll we do?"

They clung to each other's hands like children, and her body shook with desperate sobs.

Through the stillness they heard the church clock striking five.

"Oh, Ethan, it's time!" she cried.

He drew her back to him. "Time for what? You don't suppose I'm going to leave you now?"

"If I missed my train where'd I go?"

"Where are you going if you catch it?"

She stood silent, her hands lying cold and relaxed in his.

"What's the good of either of us going anywheres without the other one now?" he said.

She remained motionless, as if she had not heard him. Then she snatched her hands from his, threw her arms about his neck, and pressed a sudden drenched cheek against his face. "Ethan! Ethan! I want you to take me down again!"

"Down where?"

"The coast. Right off," she panted. "So 't we'll never come up any more."

"Matt! What on earth do you mean?"

She put her lips close against his ear to say: "Right into the big elm. You said you could. So 't we'd never have to leave each other any more."

"Why, what are you talking of? You're crazy!"

"I'm not crazy; but I will be if I leave you."

"Oh, Matt, Matt—" he groaned.

She tightened her fierce hold about his neck. Her face lay close to his face.

"Ethan, where'll I go if I leave you? I don't know how to get along alone. You said so yourself just now. Nobody but you was ever good to me. And there'll be that strange girl in the house . . . and she'll sleep in my bed, where I used to lay nights and listen to hear you come up the stairs. . ."

The words were like fragments torn from his heart. With them came the hated vision of the house he was going back to—of the stairs he would have to go up every night, of the woman who would wait for him there. And the sweetness of Mattie's avowal, the wild wonder of knowing at last that all that had happened to him had happened to her too, made the other vision more abhorrent, the other life more intolerable to return to . . .

Her pleadings still came to him between short sobs, but he no longer heard what she was saying. Her hat had slipped back and he was stroking her hair. He wanted to get the feeling of it into his hand, so that it would sleep there like a seed in winter. Once he found her mouth again, and they seemed to be by the pond together in the burning August sun. But his cheek touched hers, and it was cold and full of weeping, and he saw the road to the Flats under the night and heard the whistle of the train up the line.

The spruces swathed them in blackness and silence. They might have been in their coffins underground. He said to himself; "Perhaps it'll feel like this . . . " and then again: "After this I sha'n't feel anything. . ."

Suddenly he heard the old sorrel whinny across the road, and thought: "He's wondering why he doesn't get his supper. . ."

"Come," Mattie whispered, tugging at his hand.

Her sombre violence constrained him: she seemed the embodied instrument of fate. He pulled the sled out, blinking like a night-bird as he passed from the shade of the spruces into the transparent dusk of the open. The slope below them was deserted. All Starkfield was at supper, and not a figure crossed the open space before the church. The sky, swollen with the clouds that announce a thaw, hung as low as before a summer storm. He strained his eyes through the dimness, and they seemed less keen, less capable than usual.

He took his seat on the sled and Mattie instantly placed herself in front of him. Her hat had fallen into the snow and his lips were in her hair. He stretched out his legs, drove his heels into the road to keep the sled from slipping forward, and bent her head back between his hands. Then suddenly he sprang up again.

"Get up," he ordered her.

It was the tone she always heeded, but she cowered down in her seat, repeating vehemently: "No, no, no!"

"Get up!"

"Why?"

"I want to sit in front."

"No, no! How can you steer in front?"

"I don't have to. We'll follow the track."

They spoke in smothered whispers, as though the night were listening.

"Get up! Get up!" he urged her; but she kept on repeating: "Why do you want to sit in front?"

"Because I—because I want to feel you holding me," he stammered, and dragged her to her feet.

The answer seemed to satisfy her, or else she yielded to the power of his voice. He bent down, feeling in the obscurity for the glassy slide worn by preceding coasters, and placed the runners carefully between its edges. She waited while he seated himself with crossed legs in the front of the sled; then she crouched quickly down at his back and clasped her arms about him. Her breath in his neck set him shuddering again, and he almost sprang from his seat. But in a flash he remembered the alternative. She was right: this was better than parting. He leaned back and drew her mouth to his. . .

Just as they started he heard the sorrel's whinny again, and the familiar wistful call, and all the confused images it brought with it, went with him down the first reach of the road. Half-way down there was a sudden drop, then a rise, and after that another long delirious descent. As they took wing for this it seemed to him that they were flying indeed, flying far up into the cloudy night, with Starkfield immeasurably below them, falling away like a speck in space. . . Then the big elm shot up ahead, lying in wait for them at the bend of the road, and he said between his teeth: "We can fetch it; I know we can fetch it——"

As they flew toward the tree Mattie pressed her arms tighter, and her blood seemed to be in his veins. Once or twice the sled swerved a little under them. He slanted his body to keep it headed for the elm, repeating to himself again and again: "I know we can fetch it"; and little phrases she had spoken ran through his head and danced before him on the air. The big tree loomed bigger and closer, and as they bore down on it he thought: "It's waiting for us: it seems to know." But suddenly his wife's face, with twisted monstrous lineaments, thrust itself between him and his goal, and he made an instinctive movement to brush it aside. The sled swerved in response, but he righted it again, kept it straight, and drove down on the black projecting mass. There was a last instant when the air shot past him like millions of fiery wires; and then the elm . . .

The sky was still thick, but looking straight up he saw a single star and tried vaguely to reckon whether it were Sirius, or — or — The effort tired him too much, and he closed his heavy lids and thought that he would sleep. . . The stillness was so profound that he heard a little animal twittering somewhere near by under the snow. It made a small frightened *cheep* like a field mouse, and he wondered languidly if it were hurt. Then he understood that it must be in pain: pain so excruciating that he seemed, mysteriously, to feel it shooting through his own body. He tried in vain to roll over in the direction of the sound, and stretched his left arm out across the snow. And now it was as though he felt rather than heard the twittering; it seemed to be under his palm, which rested on something soft and springy. The thought of the animal's suffering was intolerable to him and he struggled to raise himself, and could not because a rock, or some huge mass, seemed to be lying on him. But he continued to finger about cautiously with his left hand, thinking he might get hold of the little creature and help it; and all at once he knew that the soft thing he had touched was Mattie's hair and that his hand was on her face.

He dragged himself to his knees, the monstrous load on him moving with him as he moved, and his hand went over and over her face, and he felt that the twittering came from her lips . . .

He got his face down close to hers, with his ear to her mouth, and in the darkness he saw her eyes open and heard her say his name.

"Oh, Matt, I thought we'd fetched it," he moaned; and far off, up the hill, he heard the sorrel whinny, and thought: "I ought to be getting him his feed. . ." .   .   .   .

.   .   .   .

.   .   .   .

Sirius: the brightest star in the night sky, sometimes called the "Dog Star" because it is in the constellation Canis Majoris (Big Dog). Ironically, after the accident, when Ethan looks skyward and wonders whether the star he sees is "Sirius," he unconsciously makes a pun about the seriousness of his own condition.

The querulous drone ceased as I entered Frome's kitchen, and of the two women sitting there I could not tell which had been the speaker.

One of them, on my appearing, raised her tall bony figure from her seat, not as if to welcome me—for she threw me no more than a brief glance of surprise—but simply to set about preparing the meal which Frome's absence had delayed. A slatternly calico wrapper hung from her shoulders and the wisps of her thin gray hair were drawn away from a high forehead and fastened at the back by a broken comb. She had pale opaque eyes which revealed nothing and reflected nothing, and her narrow lips were of the same sallow colour as her face.

The other woman was much smaller and slighter. She sat huddled in an arm-chair near the stove, and when I came in she turned her head quickly toward me, without the least corresponding movement of her body. Her hair was as gray as her companion's, her face as bloodless and shrivelled, but amber-tinted, with swarthy shadows sharpening the nose and hollowing the temples. Under her shapeless dress her body kept its limp immobility, and her dark eyes had the bright witch-like stare that disease of the spine sometimes gives.

Even for that part of the country the kitchen was a poor-looking place. With the exception of the dark-eyed woman's chair, which looked like a soiled relic of luxury bought at a country auction, the furniture was of the roughest kind. Three coarse china plates and a broken-nosed milk-jug had been set on a greasy table scored with knife-cuts, and a couple of straw-bottomed chairs and a kitchen dresser of un-painted pine stood meagrely against the plaster walls.

"My, it's cold here! The fire must be 'most out," Frome said, glancing about him apologetically as he followed me in.

The tall woman, who had moved away from us toward the dresser, took no notice; but the other, from her cushioned niche, answered complainingly, in a high thin voice: "It's on'y just been made up this very minute. Zeena fell asleep and slep' ever so long, and I thought I'd be frozen stiff before I could wake her up and get her to 'tend to it."

I knew then that it was she who had been speaking when we entered.

Her companion, who was just coming back to the table with the remains of a cold mince-pie in a battered pie-dish, set down her unappetising burden without appearing to hear the accusation brought against her.

Frome stood hesitatingly before her as she advanced; then he looked at me and said: "This is my wife, Mis' Frome." After another interval he added, turning toward the figure in the arm-chair: "And this is Miss Mattie Silver. . ."

. . . .

Mrs. Hale, tender soul, had pictured me as lost in the Flats and buried under a snow-drift; and so lively was her satisfaction on seeing me safely restored to her the next morning that I felt my peril had caused me to advance several degrees in her favour.

Great was her amazement, and that of old Mrs. Varnum, on learning that Ethan Frome's old horse had carried me to and from Corbury Junction through the worst blizzard of the winter; greater still their surprise when they heard that his master had taken me in for the night.

Beneath their wondering exclamations I felt a secret curiosity to know what impressions I had received from my night in the Frome household, and divined that the best way of breaking down their reserve was to let them try to penetrate mine. I therefore confined myself to saying, in a matter-of-fact tone, that I had been received with great kindness, and that Frome had made a bed for me in a room on the ground-floor which seemed in happier days to have been fitted up as a kind of writing-room or study.

"Well," Mrs. Hale mused, "in such a storm I suppose he felt he couldn't less than take you in—but I guess it went hard with Ethan. I don't believe but what you're the only stranger has set foot in that house for over twenty years. He's that proud he don't even like his oldest friends to go there; and I don't know as any do, any more, except myself and the doctor. . ."

"You still go there, Mrs. Hale?" I ventured.

"I used to go a good deal after the accident, when I was first married; but after awhile I got to think it made 'em feel worse to see us. And then one thing and another came, and my own troubles . . . But I generally make out to drive over there round about New Year's, and once in the summer. Only I always try to pick a day when Ethan's off somewheres. It's bad enough to see the two women sitting there—but *his* face, when he looks round that bare place, just kills me . . . You see, I can look back and call it up in his mother's day, before their troubles."

Old Mrs. Varnum, by this time, had gone up to bed, and her daughter and I were sitting alone, after supper, in the austere seclusion of the horse-hair parlour. Mrs. Hale glanced at me tentatively, as though trying to see how much footing my conjectures gave her; and I guessed that if she had kept silence till now it was because she had been waiting, through all the years, for some one who should see what she alone had seen.

I waited to let her trust in me gather strength before I said: "Yes, it's pretty bad, seeing all three of them there together."

She drew her mild brows into a frown of pain. "It was just awful from the beginning. I was here in the house when they were carried up—they laid Mattie Silver in the room you're in. She and I were great friends, and she was to have been my brides-maid in the spring . . . When she came to I went up to her and stayed all night. They gave her things to quiet her, and she didn't know much till to'rd morning, and then all of a sudden she woke up just like herself, and looked straight at me out of her big eyes, and said . . . Oh, I don't know why I'm telling you all this," Mrs. Hale broke off, crying.

She took off her spectacles, wiped the moisture from them, and put them on again with an unsteady hand. "It got about the next day," she went on, "that Zeena Frome had sent Mattie off in a hurry because she had a hired girl coming, and the folks here could never rightly tell what she and Ethan were doing that night coasting, when they'd ought to have been on their way to the Flats to ketch the train . . . I never knew myself what Zeena thought—I don't to this day. Nobody knows Zeena's thoughts. Anyhow, when she heard o' the accident she came right in and stayed with Ethan over to the minister's, where they'd carried him. And as soon as the doctors said that Mattie could be moved, Zeena sent for her and took her back to the farm."

"And there she's been ever since?"

Mrs. Hale answered simply: "There was no-where else fo her to go;" and my heart tightened at the thought of the hard compulsions of the poor.

"Yes, there she's been," Mrs. Hale continued, "and Zeena's done for her, and done for Ethan, as good as she could. It was a miracle, considering how sick she was—but she seemed to be raised right up just when the call came to her. Not as she's ever given up doctoring, and she's had sick spells right along; but she's had the strength given her to care for those two for over twenty years, and before the accident came she thought she couldn't even care for herself."

Mrs. Hale paused a moment, and I remained silent, plunged in the vision of what her words evoked. "It's horrible for them all," I murmured.

"Yes: it's pretty bad. And they ain't any of 'em easy people either. Mattie *was,* before the accident; I never knew a sweeter nature. But she's suffered too much—that's what I always say when folks tell me how she's soured. And Zeena, she was always cranky. Not but what she bears with Mattie wonderful—I've seen that myself. But sometimes the two of them get going at each other, and then Ethan's face'd break your heart . . . When I see that, I think it's *him* that suffers most . . . anyhow it ain't Zeena, because she ain't got the time . . . It's a pity, though," Mrs. Hale ended, sighing, "that they're all shut up there'n that one kitchen. In the summertime, on pleasant days, they move Mattie into the parlour, or out in the door-yard, and that makes it easier . . . but winters there's the fires to be thought of; and there ain't a dime to spare up at the Fromes.'"

Mrs. Hale drew a deep breath, as though her memory were eased of its long burden, and she had no more to say; but suddenly an impulse of complete avowal seized her.

She took off her spectacles again, leaned toward me across the bead-work table-cover, and went on with lowered voice: "There was one day, about a week after the accident, when they all thought Mattie couldn't live. Well, I say it's a pity she *did*. I said it right out to our minister once, and he was shocked at me. Only he wasn't with me that morning when she first came to . . . And I say, if she'd ha' died, Ethan might ha' lived; and the way they are now, I don't see's there's much difference between the Fromes up at the farm and the Fromes down in the graveyard; 'cept that down there they're all quiet, and the women have got to hold their tongues."

Part Two

SUMMER (1917)

Summer

Edith Wharton

I

A girl came out of lawyer Royall's house, at the end of the one street of North Dormer, and stood on the doorstep.

It was the beginning of a June afternoon. The springlike transparent sky shed a rain of silver sunshine on the roofs of the village, and on the pastures and larchwoods surrounding it. A little wind moved among the round white clouds on the shoulders of the hills, driving their shadows across the fields and down the grassy road that takes the name of street when it passes through North Dormer. The place lies high and in the open, and lacks the lavish shade of the more protected New England villages. The clump of weeping-willows about the duck pond, and the Norway spruces in front of the Hatchard gate, cast almost the only roadside shadow between lawyer Royall's house and the point where, at the other end of the village, the road rises above the church and skirts the black hemlock wall enclosing the cemetery.

The little June wind, frisking down the street, shook the doleful fringes of the Hatchard spruces, caught the straw hat of a young man just passing under them, and spun it clean across the road into the duck-pond.

As he ran to fish it out the girl on lawyer Royall's doorstep noticed that he was a stranger, that he wore city clothes, and that he was laughing with all his teeth, as the young and careless laugh at such mishaps.

Her heart contracted a little, and the shrinking that sometimes came over her when she saw people with holiday faces made her draw back into the house and pretend to look for the key that she knew she had already put into her pocket. A narrow greenish mirror with a gilt eagle over it hung on the passage wall, and she looked critically at her reflection, wished for the thousandth time that she had blue eyes like Annabel Balch, the girl who sometimes came from Springfield to spend a week with old Miss Hatchard, straightened the sunburnt hat over her small swarthy face, and turned out again into the sunshine.

"How I hate everything!" she murmured.

The young man had passed through the Hatchard gate, and she had the street to herself. North Dormer is at all times an empty place, and at three o'clock on a June afternoon its few able-bodied men are off in the fields or woods, and the women indoors, engaged in languid household drudgery.

North Dormer: a fictional town in the Berkshire Mountains of western Massachusetts.
larchwoods: any of a genus of trees of the pine family with short fascicled deciduous leaves.
Springfield: a city in south central Massachusetts.

The girl walked along, swinging her key on a finger, and looking about her with the heightened attention produced by the presence of a stranger in a familiar place. What, she wondered, did North Dormer look like to people from other parts of the world? She herself had lived there since the age of five, and had long supposed it to be a place of some importance. But about a year before, Mr. Miles, the new Episcopal clergyman at Hepburn, who drove over every other Sunday—when the roads were not ploughed up by hauling—to hold a service in the North Dormer church, had proposed, in a fit of missionary zeal, to take the young people down to Nettleton to hear an illustrated lecture on the Holy Land; and the dozen girls and boys who represented the future of North Dormer had been piled into a farm-waggon, driven over the hills to Hepburn, put into a way-train and carried to Nettleton. In the course of that incredible day Charity Royall had, for the first and only time, experienced railway-travel, looked into shops with plate-glass fronts, tasted cocoanut pie, sat in a theatre, and listened to a gentleman saying unintelligible things before pictures that she would have enjoyed looking at if his explanations had not prevented her from understanding them. This initiation had shown her that North Dormer was a small place, and developed in her a thirst for information that her position as custodian of the village library had previously failed to excite. For a month or two she dipped feverishly and disconnectedly into the dusty volumes of the Hatchard Memorial Library; then the impression of Nettleton began to fade, and she found it easier to take North Dormer as the norm of the universe than to go on reading.

The sight of the stranger once more revived memories of Nettleton, and North Dormer shrank to its real size. As she looked up and down it, from lawyer Royall's faded red house at one end to the white church at the other, she pitilessly took its measure. There it lay, a weather-beaten sunburnt village of the hills, abandoned of men, left apart by railway, trolley, telegraph, and all the forces that link life to life in modern communities. It had no shops, no theatres, no lectures, no "business block"; only a church that was opened every other Sunday if the state of the roads permitted, and a library for which no new books had been bought for twenty years, and where the old ones mouldered undisturbed on the damp shelves. Yet Charity Royall had always been told that she ought to consider it a privilege that her lot had been cast in North Dormer. She knew that, compared to the place she had come from, North Dormer represented all the bless-

---

Hepburn: a fictional town in the Berkshire Mountains of western Massachusetts.
Nettleton: a fictional town in the Berkshire Mountains of western Massachusetts.
way-train: a train that stops at nearly all of the stations on its line.

ings of the most refined civilization. Everyone in the village had told her so ever since she had been brought there as a child. Even old Miss Hatchard had said to her, on a terrible occasion in her life: "My child, you must never cease to remember that it was Mr. Royall who brought you down from the Mountain."

She had been "brought down from the Mountain"; from the scarred cliff that lifted its sullen wall above the lesser slopes of Eagle Range, making a perpetual background of gloom to the lonely valley. The Mountain was a good fifteen miles away, but it rose so abruptly from the lower hills that it seemed almost to cast its shadow over North Dormer. And it was like a great magnet drawing the clouds and scattering them in storm across the valley. If ever, in the purest summer sky, there trailed a thread of vapour over North Dormer, it drifted to the Mountain as a ship drifts to a whirlpool, and was caught among the rocks, torn up and multiplied, to sweep back over the village in rain and darkness.

Charity was not very clear about the Mountain; but she knew it was a bad place, and a shame to have come from, and that, whatever befell her in North Dormer, she ought, as Miss Hatchard had once reminded her, to remember that she had been brought down from there, and hold her tongue and be thankful. She looked up at the Mountain, thinking of these things, and tried as usual to be thankful. But the sight of the young man turning in at Miss Hatchard's gate had brought back the vision of the glittering streets of Nettleton, and she felt ashamed of her old sun-hat, and sick of North Dormer, and jealously aware of Annabel Balch of Springfield, opening her blue eyes somewhere far off on glories greater than the glories of Nettleton.

"How I hate everything!" she said again.

Half way down the street she stopped at a weak-hinged gate. Passing through it, she walked down a brick path to a queer little brick temple with white wooden columns supporting a pediment on which was inscribed in tarnished gold letters: "The Honorius Hatchard Memorial Library, 1832."

Honorius Hatchard had been old Miss Hatchard's great-uncle; though she would undoubtedly have reversed the phrase, and put forward, as her only claim to distinction, the fact that she was his great-niece. For Honorius Hatchard, in the early years of the nineteenth century, had enjoyed a

---

the Mountain: Wharton remarked in *A Backward Glance* that "the lonely peak I have called 'the Mountain' was in reality Bear Mountain, an isolated summit not more than twelve miles from [my] home" in Lenox, Massachusetts. (See p. 214 in this New Riverside Edition).

Eagle Range: a fictional mountain range in western Massachusetts.

modest celebrity. As the marble tablet in the interior of the library informed its infrequent visitors, he had possessed marked literary gifts, written a series of papers called "The Recluse of Eagle Range," enjoyed the acquaintance of Washington Irving and Fitz-Greene Halleck, and been cut off in his flower by a fever contracted in Italy. Such had been the sole link between North Dormer and literature, a link piously commemorated by the erection of the monument where Charity Royall, every Tuesday and Thursday afternoon, sat at her desk under a freckled steel engraving of the deceased author, and wondered if he felt any deader in his grave than she did in his library.

Entering her prison-house with a listless step she took off her hat, hung it on a plaster bust of Minerva, opened the shutters, leaned out to see if there were any eggs in the swallow's nest above one of the windows, and finally, seating herself behind the desk, drew out a roll of cotton lace and a steel crochet hook. She was not an expert workwoman, and it had taken her many weeks to make the half-yard of narrow lace which she kept wound about the buckram back of a disintegrated copy of "The Lamplighter." But there was no other way of getting any lace to trim her summer blouse, and since Ally Hawes, the poorest girl in the village, had shown herself in church with enviable transparencies about the shoulders, Charity's hook had travelled faster. She unrolled the lace, dug the hook into a loop, and bent to the task with furrowed brows.

Suddenly the door opened, and before she had raised her eyes she knew that the young man she had seen going in at the Hatchard gate had entered the library.

Without taking any notice of her he began to move slowly about the long vault-like room, his hands behind his back, his short-sighted eyes peering up and down the rows of rusty bindings. At length he reached the desk and stood before her.

"Have you a card-catalogue?" he asked in a pleasant abrupt voice; and the oddness of the question caused her to drop her work.

Washington Irving: American author (1783–1859) referred to as the "first American man of letters" and is best known for his short stories "The Legend of Sleepy Hollow" and "Rip Van Winkle."

Fitz-Greene Halleck: American poet (1790–1867) and joint author, with Joseph Rodman Drake, of the humorous lampoons "Croaker Papers," most of which were printed in the New York *Evening Post* in 1819.

Minerva: in Roman mythology, the goddess of wisdom, war, and the liberal arts.

buckram: cotton or linen fabric stiffened with sizing and used for bookbinding.

"The Lamplighter": the first novel, published in 1854, by American author Maria S. Cummins (1827–66).

"A *what?*"

"Why, you know——" He broke off, and she became conscious that he was looking at her for the first time, having apparently, on his entrance, included her in his general short-sighted survey as part of the furniture of the library.

The fact that, in discovering her, he lost the thread of his remark, did not escape her attention, and she looked down and smiled. He smiled also.

"No, I don't suppose you *do* know," he corrected himself. "In fact, it would be almost a pity——"

She thought she detected a slight condescension in his tone, and asked sharply: "Why?"

"Because it's so much pleasanter, in a small library like this, to poke about by one's self—with the help of the librarian."

He added the last phrase so respectfully that she was mollified, and rejoined with a sigh: "I'm afraid I can't help you much."

"Why?" he questioned in his turn; and she replied that there weren't many books anyhow, and that she'd hardly read any of them. "The worms are getting at them," she added gloomily.

"Are they? That's a pity, for I see there are some good ones." He seemed to have lost interest in their conversation, and strolled away again, apparently forgetting her. His indifference nettled her, and she picked up her work, resolved not to offer him the least assistance. Apparently he did not need it, for he spent a long time with his back to her, lifting down, one after another, the tall cobwebby volumes from a distant shelf.

"Oh, I say!" he exclaimed; and looking up she saw that he had drawn out his handkerchief and was carefully wiping the edges of the book in his hand. The action struck her as an unwarranted criticism on her care of the books, and she said irritably: "It's not my fault if they're dirty."

He turned around and looked at her with reviving interest. "Ah—then you're not the librarian?"

"Of course I am; but I can't dust all these books. Besides, nobody ever looks at them, now Miss Hatchard's too lame to come round."

"No, I suppose not." He laid down the book he had been wiping, and stood considering her in silence. She wondered if Miss Hatchard had sent him round to pry into the way the library was looked after, and the suspicion increased her resentment. "I saw you going into her house just now, didn't I?" she asked, with the New England avoidance of the proper name. She was determined to find out why he was poking about among her books.

"Miss Hatchard's house? Yes—she's my cousin and I'm staying there," the young man answered; adding, as if to disarm a visible distrust: "My name is Harney—Lucius Harney. She may have spoken of me."

"No, she hasn't," said Charity, wishing she could have said: "Yes, she has."

"Oh, well——" said Miss Hatchard's cousin with a laugh; and after another pause, during which it occurred to Charity that her answer had not been encouraging, he remarked: "You don't seem strong on architecture."

Her bewilderment was complete: the more she wished to appear to understand him the more unintelligible his remarks became. He reminded her of the gentleman who had "explained" the pictures at Nettleton, and the weight of her ignorance settled down on her again like a pall.

"I mean, I can't see that you have any books on the old houses about here. I suppose, for that matter, this part of the country hasn't been much explored. They all go on doing Plymouth and Salem. So stupid. My cousin's house, now, is remarkable. This place must have had a past—it must have been more of a place once." He stopped short, with the blush of a shy man who overhears himself, and fears he has been voluble. "I'm an architect, you see, and I'm hunting up old houses in these parts."

She stared. "Old houses? Everything's old in North Dormer, isn't it? The folks are, anyhow."

He laughed, and wandered away again.

"Haven't you any kind of a history of the place? I think there was one written about 1840: a book or pamphlet about its first settlement," he presently said from the farther end of the room.

She pressed her crochet hook against her lip and pondered. There was such a work, she knew: "North Dormer and the Early Townships of Eagle County." She had a special grudge against it because it was a limp weakly book that was always either falling off the shelf or slipping back and disappearing if one squeezed it in between sustaining volumes. She remembered, the last time she had picked it up, wondering how anyone could have taken the trouble to write a book about North Dormer and its neighbours: Dormer, Hamblin, Creston and Creston River. She knew them all, mere lost clusters of houses in the folds of the desolate ridges: Dormer, where North Dormer went for its apples; Creston River, where there used to be a paper-mill, and its grey walls stood decaying by the stream; and Hamblin, where the first snow always fell. Such were their titles to fame.

She got up and began to move about vaguely before the shelves. But she had no idea where she had last put the book, and something told her that

---

Plymouth and Salem: cities on the Massachusetts coast.

Dormer, Hamblin, Creston and Creston River: fictional towns or places in the Berkshire Mountains of western Massachusetts.

it was going to play her its usual trick and remain invisible. It was not one of her lucky days.

"I guess it's somewhere," she said, to prove her zeal; but she spoke without conviction, and felt that her words conveyed none.

"Oh, well——" he said again. She knew he was going, and wished more than ever to find the book.

"It will be for next time," he added; and picking up the volume he had laid on the desk he handed it to her. "By the way, a little air and sun would do this good; it's rather valuable."

He gave her a nod and smile, and passed out.

I I

The hours of the Hatchard Memorial librarian were from three to five; and Charity Royall's sense of duty usually kept her at her desk until nearly half-past four.

But she had never perceived that any practical advantage thereby accrued either to North Dormer or to herself; and she had no scruple in decreeing, when it suited her, that the library should close an hour earlier. A few minutes after Mr. Harney's departure she formed this decision, put away her lace, fastened the shutters, and turned the key in the door of the temple of knowledge.

The street upon which she emerged was still empty: and after glancing up and down it she began to walk toward her house. But instead of entering she passed on, turned into a field-path and mounted to a pasture on the hillside. She let down the bars of the gate, followed a trail along the crumbling wall of the pasture, and walked on till she reached a knoll where a clump of larches shook out their fresh tassels to the wind. There she lay down on the slope, tossed off her hat and hid her face in the grass.

She was blind and insensible to many things, and dimly knew it; but to all that was light and air, perfume and colour, every drop of blood in her responded. She loved the roughness of the dry mountain grass under her palms, the smell of the thyme into which she crushed her face, the fingering of the wind in her hair and through her cotton blouse, and the creak of the larches as they swayed to it.

She often climbed up the hill and lay there alone for the mere pleasure of feeling the wind and of rubbing her cheeks in the grass. Generally at such times she did not think of anything, but lay immersed in an inarticulate well-being. Today the sense of well-being was intensified by her joy at escaping from the library. She liked well enough to have a friend drop in and talk to her when she was on duty, but she hated to be bothered about books. How could she remember where they were, when they were so seldom asked for? Orma Fry occasionally took out a novel, and her brother Ben was fond of what he called "jography," and of books relating to trade and bookkeeping; but no one else asked for anything except, at intervals, "Uncle Tom's Cabin," or "Opening of a Chestnut Burr," or Longfellow. She had these under her hand, and could have found them in the dark; but unexpected demands came so rarely that they exasperated her like an injustice. . . .

She had liked the young man's looks, and his short-sighted eyes, and his odd way of speaking, that was abrupt yet soft, just as his hands were sunburnt and sinewy, yet with smooth nails like a woman's. His hair was sunburnt-looking too, or rather the colour of bracken after frost; his eyes grey, with the appealing look of the shortsighted, his smile shy yet confident, as if he knew lots of things she had never dreamed of, and yet wouldn't for the world have had her feel his superiority. But she did feel it, and liked the feeling; for it was new to her. Poor and ignorant as she was, and knew herself to be—humblest of the humble even in North Dormer, where to come from the Mountain was the worst disgrace—yet in her narrow world she had always ruled. It was partly, of course, owing to the fact that lawyer Royall was "the biggest man in North Dormer"; so much too big for it, in fact, that outsiders, who didn't know, always wondered how it held him. In spite of everything—and in spite even of Miss Hatchard—lawyer Royall ruled in North Dormer; and Charity ruled in lawyer Royall's house. She had never put it to herself in those terms; but she knew her power, knew what it was made of, and hated it. Confusedly, the young man in the library had made her feel for the first time what might be the sweetness of dependence.

She sat up, brushed the bits of grass from her hair, and looked down on the house where she held sway. It stood just below her, cheerless and untended, its faded red front divided from the road by a "yard" with a path bordered by gooseberry bushes, a stone well overgrown with traveller's joy, and a sickly Crimson Rambler tied to a fan-shaped support, which

---

"Uncle Tom's Cabin": popular antislavery novel, published in 1852, by American author Harriet Beecher Stowe (1811–96).

"Opening of a Chestnut Burr": a novel, published in 1874, by American author Edward Payson Roe (1838–88).

Longfellow: American poet Henry Wadsworth Longfellow (1807–82).

traveller's joy . . . Crimson Rambler: traveller's joy is a climbing plant with white flowers; crimson rambler is a climbing rosebush with small, often double flowers, growing in large clusters.

Mr. Royall had once brought up from Hepburn to please her. Behind the house a bit of uneven ground with clothes-lines strung across it stretched up to a dry wall, and beyond the wall a patch of corn and a few rows of potatoes strayed vaguely into the adjoining wilderness of rock and fern.

Charity could not recall her first sight of the house. She had been told that she was ill of a fever when she was brought down from the Mountain; and she could only remember waking one day in a cot at the foot of Mrs. Royall's bed, and opening her eyes on the cold neatness of the room that was afterward to be hers.

Mrs. Royall died seven or eight years later; and by that time Charity had taken the measure of most things about her. She knew that Mrs. Royall was sad and timid and weak; she knew that lawyer Royall was harsh and violent, and still weaker. She knew that she had been christened Charity (in the white church at the other end of the village) to commemorate Mr. Royall's disinterestedness in "bringing her down," and to keep alive in her a becoming sense of her dependence; she knew that Mr. Royall was her guardian, but that he had not legally adopted her, though everybody spoke of her as Charity Royall; and she knew why he had come back to live at North Dormer, instead of practising at Nettleton, where he had begun his legal career.

After Mrs. Royall's death there was some talk of sending her to a boarding-school. Miss Hatchard suggested it, and had a long conference with Mr. Royall, who, in pursuance of her plan, departed one day for Starkfield to visit the institution she recommended. He came back the next night with a black face; worse, Charity observed, than she had ever seen him; and by that time she had had some experience.

When she asked him how soon she was to start he answered shortly, "You ain't going," and shut himself up in the room he called his office; and the next day the lady who kept the school at Starkfield wrote that "under the circumstances" she was afraid she could not make room just then for another pupil.

Charity was disappointed; but she understood. It wasn't the temptations of Starkfield that had been Mr. Royall's undoing; it was the thought of losing her. He was a dreadfully "lonesome" man; she had made that out because she was so "lonesome" herself. He and she, face to face in that sad house, had sounded the depths of isolation; and though she felt no particular affection for him, and not the slightest gratitude, she pitied him because she was conscious that he was superior to the people about him, and that she was the only being between him and solitude. Therefore, when Miss Hatchard sent for her a day or two later, to talk of a school at Nettleton, and to say that this time a friend of hers would "make the necessary arrangements," Charity cut her short with the announcement that she had decided not to leave North Dormer.

Miss Hatchard reasoned with her kindly, but to no purpose; she simply repeated: "I guess Mr. Royall's too lonesome."

Miss Hatchard blinked perplexedly behind her eye-glasses. Her long frail face was full of puzzled wrinkles, and she leant forward, resting her hands on the arms of her mahogany armchair, with the evident desire to say something that ought to be said.

"The feeling does you credit, my dear."

She looked about the pale walls of her sitting-room, seeking counsel of ancestral daguerreotypes and didactic samplers; but they seemed to make utterance more difficult.

"The fact is, it's not only—not only because of the advantages. There are other reasons. You're too young to understand——"

"Oh, no, I ain't," said Charity harshly; and Miss Hatchard blushed to the roots of her blonde cap. But she must have felt a vague relief at having her explanation cut short, for she concluded, again invoking the daguerreotypes: "Of course I shall always do what I can for you; and in case . . . in case . . . you know you can always come to me. . . ."

Lawyer Royall was waiting for Charity in the porch when she returned from this visit. He had shaved, and brushed his black coat, and looked a magnificent monument of a man; at such moments she really admired him.

"Well," he said, "is it settled?"

"Yes, it's settled. I ain't going."

"Not to the Nettleton school?"

"Not anywhere."

He cleared his throat and asked sternly: "Why?"

"I'd rather not," she said, swinging past him on her way to her room. It was the following week that he brought her up the Crimson Rambler and its fan from Hepburn. He had never given her anything before.

The next outstanding incident of her life had happened two years later, when she was seventeen. Lawyer Royall, who hated to go to Nettleton, had been called there in connection with a case. He still exercised his profession, though litigation languished in North Dormer and its outlying hamlets; and for once he had had an opportunity that he could not afford to refuse. He spent three days in Nettleton, won his case, and came back in high good-humour. It was a rare mood with him, and manifested itself

---

daguerreotypes: early photographs produced on a silver-covered copper plate.

samplers: decorative pieces of needlework on which are embroidered letters of the alphabet or verses as a demonstration of skill.

on this occasion by his talking impressively at the supper-table of the "rousing welcome" his old friends had given him. He wound up confidentially: "I was a damn fool ever to leave Nettleton. It was Mrs. Royall that made me do it."

Charity immediately perceived that something bitter had happened to him, and that he was trying to talk down the recollection. She went up to bed early, leaving him seated in moody thought, his elbows propped on the worn oilcloth of the supper table. On the way up she had extracted from his overcoat pocket the key of the cupboard where the bottle of whiskey was kept.

She was awakened by a rattling at her door and jumped out of bed. She heard Mr. Royall's voice, low and peremptory, and opened the door, fearing an accident. No other thought had occurred to her; but when she saw him in the doorway, a ray from the autumn moon falling on his discomposed face, she understood.

For a moment they looked at each other in silence; then, as he put his foot across the threshold, she stretched out her arm and stopped him.

"You go right back from here," she said, in a shrill voice that startled her; "you ain't going to have that key tonight."

"Charity, let me in. I don't want the key. I'm a lonesome man," he began, in the deep voice that sometimes moved her.

Her heart gave a startled plunge, but she continued to hold him back contemptuously. "Well, I guess you made a mistake, then. This ain't your wife's room any longer."

She was not frightened, she simply felt a deep disgust; and perhaps he divined it or read it in her face, for after staring at her a moment he drew back and turned slowly away from the door. With her ear to her keyhole she heard him feel his way down the dark stairs, and toward the kitchen; and she listened for the crash of the cupboard panel, but instead she heard him, after an interval, unlock the door of the house, and his heavy steps came to her through the silence as he walked down the path. She crept to the window and saw his bent figure striding up the road in the moonlight. Then a belated sense of fear came to her with the consciousness of victory, and she slipped into bed, cold to the bone.

A day or two later poor Eudora Skeff, who for twenty years had been the custodian of the Hatchard library, died suddenly of pneumonia; and the day after the funeral Charity went to see Miss Hatchard, and asked to be appointed librarian. The request seemed to surprise Miss Hatchard: she evidently questioned the new candidate's qualifications.

"Why, I don't know, my dear. Aren't you rather too young?" she hesitated.

"I want to earn some money," Charity merely answered.

"Doesn't Mr. Royall give you all you require? No one is rich in North Dormer."

"I want to earn money enough to get away."

"To get away?" Miss Hatchard's puzzled wrinkles deepened, and there was a distressful pause. "You want to leave Mr. Royall?"

"Yes: or I want another woman in the house with me," said Charity resolutely.

Miss Hatchard clasped her nervous hands about the arms of her chair. Her eyes invoked the faded countenances on the wall, and after a faint cough of indecision she brought out: "The . . . the housework's too hard for you, I suppose?"

Charity's heart grew cold. She understood that Miss Hatchard had no help to give her and that she would have to fight her way out of her difficulty alone. A deeper sense of isolation overcame her; she felt incalculably old. "She's got to be talked to like a baby," she thought, with a feeling of compassion for Miss Hatchard's long immaturity, "Yes, that's it," she said aloud. "The housework's too hard for me: I've been coughing a good deal this fall."

She noted the immediate effect of this suggestion. Miss Hatchard paled at the memory of poor Eudora's taking-off, and promised to do what she could. But of course there were people she must consult: the clergyman, the selectmen of North Dormer, and a distant Hatchard relative at Springfield. "If you'd only gone to school!" she sighed. She followed Charity to the door, and there, in the security of the threshold, said with a glance of evasive appeal: "I know Mr. Royall is . . . trying at times; but his wife bore with him; and you must always remember, Charity, that it was Mr. Royall who brought you down from the Mountain."

Charity went home and opened the door of Mr. Royall's "office." He was sitting there by the stove reading Daniel Webster's speeches. They had met at meals during the five days that had elapsed since he had come to her door, and she had walked at his side at Eudora's funeral; but they had not spoken a word to each other.

He glanced up in surprise as she entered, and she noticed that he was unshaved, and that he looked unusually old; but as she had always thought of him as an old man the change in his appearance did not move her. She told him she had been to see Miss Hatchard, and with what object. She saw that he was astonished; but he made no comment.

---

selectmen: a board of officials elected in New England towns to serve as the chief administrative authority of the town.

Daniel Webster: American statesman, lawyer, and orator, Webster (1782–1852) was his era's foremost advocate of American nationalism.

"I told her the housework was too hard for me, and I wanted to earn the money to pay for a hired girl. But I ain't going to pay for her: you've got to. I want to have some money of my own."

Mr. Royall's bushy black eyebrows were drawn together in a frown, and he sat drumming with inkstained nails on the edge of his desk.

"What do you want to earn money for?" he asked.

"So's to get away when I want to."

"Why do you want to get away?"

Her contempt flashed out. "Do you suppose anybody'd stay at North Dormer if they could help it? You wouldn't, folks say!"

With lowered head he asked: "Where'd you go to?"

"Anywhere where I can earn my living. I'll try here first, and if I can't do it here I'll go somewhere else. I'll go up the Mountain if I have to." She paused on this threat, and saw that it had taken effect. "I want you should get Miss Hatchard and the selectmen to take me at the library: and I want a woman here in the house with me," she repeated.

Mr. Royall had grown exceedingly pale. When she ended he stood up ponderously, leaning against the desk; and for a second or two they looked at each other.

"See here," he said at length as though utterance were difficult, "there's something I've been wanting to say to you; I'd ought to have said it before. I want you to marry me."

The girl still stared at him without moving. "I want you to marry me," he repeated, clearing his throat. "The minister'll be up here next Sunday and we can fix it up then. Or I'll drive you down to Hepburn to the Justice, and get it done there. I'll do whatever you say." His eyes fell under the merciless stare she continued to fix on him, and he shifted his weight uneasily from one foot to the other. As he stood there before her, unwieldy, shabby, disordered, the purple veins distorting the hands he pressed against the desk, and his long orator's jaw trembling with the effort of his avowal, he seemed like a hideous parody of the fatherly old man she had always known.

"Marry you? Me?" she burst out with a scornful laugh. "Was that what you came to ask me the other night? What's come over you, I wonder? How long is it since you've looked at yourself in the glass?" She straightened herself, insolently conscious of her youth and strength. "I suppose you think it would be cheaper to marry me than to keep a hired girl. Everybody knows you're the closest man in Eagle County; but I guess you're not going to get your mending done for you that way twice."

---

closest: stingiest

Mr. Royall did not move while she spoke. His face was ash-coloured and his black eyebrows quivered as though the blaze of her scorn had blinded him. When she ceased he held up his hand.

"That'll do — that'll about do," he said. He turned to the door and took his hat from the hat-peg. On the threshold he paused. "People ain't been fair to me — from the first they ain't been fair to me," he said. Then he went out.

A few days later North Dormer learned with surprise that Charity had been appointed librarian of the Hatchard Memorial at a salary of eight dollars a month, and that old Verena Marsh, from the Creston Almshouse, was coming to live at lawyer Royall's and do the cooking.

III

It was not in the room known at the red house as Mr. Royall's "office" that he received his infrequent clients. Professional dignity and masculine independence made it necessary that he should have a real office, under a different roof; and his standing as the only lawyer of North Dormer required that the roof should be the same as that which sheltered the Town Hall and the post-office.

It was his habit to walk to this office twice a day, morning and afternoon. It was on the ground floor of the building, with a separate entrance, and a weathered name-plate on the door. Before going in he stepped in to the post-office for his mail — usually an empty ceremony — said a word or two to the town-clerk, who sat across the passage in idle state, and then went over to the store on the opposite corner, where Carrick Fry, the storekeeper, always kept a chair for him, and where he was sure to find one or two selectmen leaning on the long counter, in an atmosphere of rope, leather, tar and coffee-beans. Mr. Royall, though monosyllabic at home, was not averse, in certain moods, to imparting his views to his fellow-townsmen; perhaps, also, he was unwilling that his rare clients should surprise him sitting, clerkless and unoccupied, in his dusty office. At any rate, his hours there were not much longer or more regular than Charity's at the library; the rest of the time he spent either at the store or in driving about the country on business connected with the insurance companies that he represented, or in sitting at home reading Bancroft's History of the United States and the speeches of Daniel Webster.

Bancroft's History of the United States: American historian George Bancroft (1800–91) wrote a comprehensive ten-volume study of the United States' origins and development, which earned him the unofficial title "father of American history."

Since the day when Charity had told him that she wished to succeed to Eudora Skeff's post their relations had undefinably but definitely changed. Lawyer Royall had kept his word. He had obtained the place for her at the cost of considerable manoeuvering, as she guessed from the number of rival candidates, and from the acerbity with which two of them, Orma Fry and the eldest Targatt girl, treated her for nearly a year afterward. And he had engaged Verena Marsh to come up from Creston and do the cooking. Verena was a poor old widow, doddering and shiftless: Charity suspected that she came for her keep. Mr. Royall was too close a man to give a dollar a day to a smart girl when he could get a deaf pauper for nothing. But at any rate, Verena was there, in the attic just over Charity, and the fact that she was deaf did not greatly trouble the young girl.

Charity knew that what had happened on that hateful night would not happen again. She understood that, profoundly as she had despised Mr. Royall ever since, he despised himself still more profoundly. If she had asked for a woman in the house it was far less for her own defense than for his humiliation. She needed no one to defend her: his humbled pride was her surest protection. He had never spoken a word of excuse or extenuation; the incident was as if it had never been. Yet its consequences were latent in every word that he and she exchanged, in every glance they instinctively turned from each other. Nothing now would ever shake her rule in the red house.

On the night of her meeting with Miss Hatchard's cousin Charity lay in bed, her bare arms clasped under her rough head, and continued to think of him. She supposed that he meant to spend some time in North Dormer. He had said he was looking up the old houses in the neighbourhood; and though she was not very clear as to his purpose, or as to why anyone should look for old houses, when they lay in wait for one on every roadside, she understood that he needed the help of books, and resolved to hunt up the next day the volume she had failed to find, and any others that seemed related to the subject.

Never had her ignorance of life and literature so weighed on her as in reliving the short scene of her discomfiture. "It's no use trying to be anything in this place," she muttered to her pillow; and she shrivelled at the vision of vague metropolises, shining super-Nettletons, where girls in better clothes than Belle Balch's talked fluently of architecture to young men with hands like Lucius Harney's. Then she remembered his sudden pause when he had come close to the desk and had his first look at her. The sight had made him forget what he was going to say; she recalled the change in his face, and jumping up she ran over the bare boards to her washstand, found the matches, lit a candle, and lifted it to the square of looking-glass on the white-washed wall. Her small face, usually so darkly pale, glowed like a rose in the faint orb of light, and under her rumpled hair her eyes seemed deeper and larger than by day. Perhaps after all it was a mistake to wish they were blue. A clumsy band and button fastened her unbleached night-gown about the throat. She undid it, freed her thin shoulders, and saw herself a bride in low-necked satin, walking down an aisle with Lucius Harney. He would kiss her as they left the church. . . . She put down the candle and covered her face with her hands as if to imprison the kiss. At that moment she heard Mr. Royall's step as he came up the stairs to bed, and a fierce revulsion of feeling swept over her. Until then she had merely despised him; now deep hatred of him filled her heart. He became to her a horrible old man. . . .

The next day, when Mr. Royall came back to dinner, they faced each other in silence as usual. Verena's presence at the table was an excuse for their not talking, though her deafness would have permitted the freest interchange of confidences. But when the meal was over, and Mr. Royall rose from the table, he looked back at Charity, who had stayed to help the old woman clear away the dishes.

"I want to speak to you a minute," he said; and she followed him across the passage, wondering.

He seated himself in his black horse-hair armchair, and she leaned against the window, indifferently. She was impatient to be gone to the library, to hunt for the book on North Dormer.

"See here," he said, "why ain't you at the library the days you're supposed to be there?"

The question, breaking in on her mood of blissful abstraction, deprived her of speech, and she stared at him for a moment without answering.

"Who says I ain't?"

"There's been some complaints made, it appears. Miss Hatchard sent for me this morning——"

Charity's smouldering resentment broke into a blaze. "I know! Orma Fry, and that toad of a Targatt girl—and Ben Fry, like as not. He's going round with her. The low-down sneaks—I always knew they'd try to have me out! As if anybody ever came to the library, anyhow!"

"Somebody did yesterday, and you weren't there."

"Yesterday?" she laughed at her happy recollection. "At what time wasn't I there yesterday, I'd like to know?"

"Round about four o'clock."

Charity was silent. She had been so steeped in the dreamy remembrance of young Harney's visit that she had forgotten having deserted her post as soon as he had left the library.

"Who came at four o'clock?"

"Miss Hatchard did."

"Miss Hatchard? Why, she ain't ever been near the place since she's been lame. She couldn't get up the steps if she tried."

"She can be helped up, I guess. She was yesterday, anyhow, by the young fellow that's staying with her. He found you there, I understand, earlier in the afternoon; and he went back and told Miss Hatchard the books were in bad shape and needed attending to. She got excited, and had herself wheeled straight round; and when she got there the place was locked. So she sent for me, and told me about that, and about the other complaints. She claims you've neglected things, and that she's going to get a trained librarian."

Charity had not moved while he spoke. She stood with her head thrown back against the window-frame, her arms hanging against her sides, and her hands so tightly clenched that she felt, without knowing what hurt her, the sharp edge of her nails against her palms.

Of all Mr. Royall had said she had retained only the phrase: "He told Miss Hatchard the books were in bad shape." What did she care for the other charges against her? Malice or truth, she despised them as she despised her detractors. But that the stranger to whom she had felt herself so mysteriously drawn should have betrayed her! That at the very moment when she had fled up the hillside to think of him more deliciously he should have been hastening home to denounce her shortcomings! She remembered how, in the darkness of her room, she had covered her face to press his imagined kiss closer; and her heart raged against him for the liberty he had not taken.

"Well, I'll go," she said suddenly. "I'll go right off."

"Go where?" She heard the startled note in Mr. Royall's voice.

"Why, out of their old library: straight out, and never set foot in it again. They needn't think I'm going to wait round and let them say they've discharged me!"

"Charity—Charity Royall, you listen——" he began, getting heavily out of his chair; but she waved him aside, and walked out of the room.

Upstairs she took the library key from the place where she always hid it under her pincushion—who said she wasn't careful?—put on her hat, and swept down again and out into the street. If Mr. Royall heard her go he made no motion to detain her: his sudden rages probably made him understand the uselessness of reasoning with hers.

She reached the brick temple, unlocked the door and entered into the glacial twilight. "I'm glad I'll never have to sit in this old vault again when other folks are out in the sun!" she said aloud as the familiar chill took her. She looked with abhorrence at the long dingy rows of books, the sheep-nosed Minerva on her black pedestal, and the mild-faced young man in a high stock whose effigy pined above her desk. She meant to take out of the drawer her roll of lace and the library register, and go straight to Miss Hatchard to announce her resignation. But suddenly a great desolation overcame her, and she sat down and laid her face against the desk. Her heart was ravaged by life's cruelest discovery: the first creature who had come toward her out of the wilderness had brought her anguish instead of joy. She did not cry; tears came hard to her, and the storms of her heart spent themselves inwardly. But as she sat there in her dumb woe she felt her life to be too desolate, too ugly and intolerable.

"What have I ever done to it, that it should hurt me so?" she groaned, and pressed her fists against her lids, which were beginning to swell with weeping.

"I won't—I won't go there looking like a horror!" she muttered, springing up and pushing back her hair as if it stifled her. She opened the drawer, dragged out the register, and turned toward the door. As she did so it opened, and the young man from Miss Hatchard's came in whistling.

IV

He stopped and lifted his hat with a shy smile. "I beg your pardon," he said. "I thought there was no one here."

Charity stood before him, barring his way. "You can't come in. The library ain't open to the public Wednesdays."

"I know it's not; but my cousin gave me her key."

"Miss Hatchard's got no right to give her key to other folks, any more'n I have. I'm the librarian and I know the by-laws. This is my library."

The young man looked profoundly surprised.

"Why, I know it is; I'm so sorry if you mind my coming."

"I suppose you came to see what more you could say to set her against me? But you needn't trouble: it's my library today, but it won't be this time tomorrow. I'm on the way now to take her back the key and the register."

Young Harney's face grew grave, but without betraying the consciousness of guilt she had looked for.

"I don't understand," he said. "There must be some mistake. Why should I say things against you to Miss Hatchard—or to anyone?"

The apparent evasiveness of the reply caused Charity's indignation to overflow. "I don't know why you should. I could understand Orma Fry's doing it, because she's always wanted to get me out of here ever since the first day. I can't see why, when she's got her own home, and her father to work for her; nor Ida Targatt, neither, when she got a legacy from her step-brother on'y last year. But anyway we all live in the same place, and when it's a place like North Dormer it's enough to make people hate each other just to have to walk down the same street every day. But you don't live here, and you don't know anything about any of us, so what did you have to meddle for? Do you suppose the other girls'd have kept the books any better'n I did? Why, Orma Fry don't hardly know a book from a flat-iron! And what if I don't always sit round here doing nothing till it strikes five up at the church? Who cares if the library's open or shut? Do you suppose anybody ever comes here for books? What they'd like to come for is to meet the fellows they're going with—if I'd let 'em. But I wouldn't let Bill Sollas from over the hill hang round here waiting for the youngest Targatt girl, because I know him . . . that's all . . . even if I don't know about books all I ought to. . . ."

She stopped with a choking in her throat. Tremors of rage were running through her, and she steadied herself against the edge of the desk lest he should see her weakness.

What he saw seemed to affect him deeply, for he grew red under his sunburn, and stammered out: "But, Miss Royall, I assure you . . . I assure you . . ."

His distress inflamed her anger, and she regained her voice to fling back: "If I was you I'd have the nerve to stick to what I said!"

The taunt seemed to restore his presence of mind. "I hope I should if I knew; but I don't. Apparently something disagreeable has happened, for which you think I'm to blame. But I don't know what it is, because I've been up on Eagle Ridge ever since the early morning."

"I don't know where you've been this morning, but I know you were here in this library yesterday; and it was you that went home and told your cousin the books were in bad shape, and brought her round to see how I'd neglected them."

Young Harney looked sincerely concerned. "Was that what you were told? I don't wonder you're angry. The books *are* in bad shape, and as some are interesting it's a pity. I told Miss Hatchard they were suffering from dampness and lack of air; and I brought her here to show her how easily the place could be ventilated. I also told her you ought to have some one to help you do the dusting and airing. If you were given a wrong version of what I said I'm sorry; but I'm so fond of old books that I'd rather see them made into a bonfire than left to moulder away like these."

Charity felt her sobs rising and tried to stifle them in words. "I don't care what you say you told her. All I know is she thinks it's all my fault, and I'm going to lose my job, and I wanted it more'n anyone in the village, because I haven't got anybody belonging to me, the way other folks have. All I wanted was to put aside money enough to get away from here sometime.

D'you suppose if it hadn't been for that I'd have kept on sitting day after day in this old vault?"

Of this appeal her hearer took up only the last question. "It *is* an old vault; but need it be? That's the point. And it's my putting the question to my cousin that seems to have been the cause of the trouble." His glance explored the melancholy penumbra of the long narrow room, resting on the blotched walls, the discoloured rows of books, and the stern rosewood desk surmounted by the portrait of the young Honorius. "Of course it's a bad job to do anything with a building jammed against a hill like this ridiculous mausoleum: you couldn't get a good draught through it without blowing a hole in the mountain. But it can be ventilated after a fashion, and the sun can be let in: I'll show you how if you like. . . ." The architect's passion for improvement had already made him lose sight of her grievance, and he lifted his stick instructively toward the cornice. But her silence seemed to tell him that she took no interest in the ventilation of the library, and turning back to her abruptly he held out both hands. "Look here—you don't mean what you said? You don't really think I'd do anything to hurt you?"

A new note in his voice disarmed her: no one had ever spoken to her in that tone.

"Oh, what *did* you do it for then?" she wailed. He had her hands in his, and she was feeling the smooth touch that she had imagined the day before on the hillside.

He pressed her hands lightly and let them go. "Why, to make things pleasanter for you here; and better for the books. I'm sorry if my cousin twisted around what I said. She's excitable, and she lives on trifles: I ought to have remembered that. Don't punish me by letting her think you take her seriously."

It was wonderful to hear him speak of Miss Hatchard as if she were a querulous baby: in spite of his shyness he had the air of power that the experience of cities probably gave. It was the fact of having lived in Nettleton that made lawyer Royall, in spite of his infirmities, the strongest man in North Dormer; and Charity was sure that this young man had lived in bigger places than Nettleton.

She felt that if she kept up her denunciatory tone he would secretly class her with Miss Hatchard; and the thought made her suddenly simple.

"It don't matter to Miss Hatchard how I take her. Mr. Royall says she's going to get a trained librarian; and I'd sooner resign than have the village say she sent me away."

---

penumbra: a shadowy, partially lighted area.

"Naturally you would. But I'm sure she doesn't mean to send you away. At any rate, won't you give me the chance to find out first and let you know? It will be time enough to resign if I'm mistaken."

Her pride flamed into her cheeks at the suggestion of his intervening. "I don't want anybody should coax her to keep me if I don't suit."

He coloured too. "I give you my word I won't do that. Only wait till to-morrow, will you?" He looked straight into her eyes with his shy grey glance. "You can trust me, you know — you really can."

All the old frozen woes seemed to melt in her, and she murmured awkwardly, looking away from him: "Oh, I'll wait."

V

There had never been such a June in Eagle County. Usually it was a month of moods, with abrupt alternations of belated frost and mid-summer heat; this year, day followed day in a sequence of temperate beauty. Every morning a breeze blew steadily from the hills. Toward noon it built up great canopies of white cloud that threw a cool shadow over fields and woods; then before sunset the clouds dissolved again, and the western light rained its unobstructed brightness on the valley.

On such an afternoon Charity Royall lay on a ridge above a sunlit hollow, her face pressed to the earth and the warm currents of the grass running through her. Directly in her line of vision a blackberry branch laid its frail white flowers and blue-green leaves against the sky. Just beyond, a tuft of sweet-fern uncurled between the beaded shoots of the grass, and a small yellow butterfly vibrated over them like a fleck of sunshine. This was all she saw; but she felt, above her and about her, the strong growth of the beeches clothing the ridge, the rounding of pale green cones on countless spruce-branches, the push of myriads of sweet-fern fronds in the cracks of the stony slope below the wood, and the crowding shoots of meadowsweet and yellow flags in the pasture beyond. All this bubbling of sap and slipping of sheaths and bursting of calyxes was carried to her on mingled currents of fragrance. Every leaf and bud and blade seemed to contribute its exhalation to the pervading sweetness in which the pungency of pine-sap prevailed over the spice of thyme and the subtle perfume of fern, and all were merged in a moist earth-smell that was like the breath of some huge sun-warmed animal.

Charity had lain there a long time, passive and sun-warmed as the slope on which she lay, when there came between her eyes and the dancing butterfly the sight of a man's foot in a large worn boot covered with red mud.

"Oh, don't!" she exclaimed, raising herself on her elbow and stretching out a warning hand.

"Don't what?" a hoarse voice asked above her head.

"Don't stamp on those bramble flowers, you dolt!" she retorted, springing to her knees. The foot paused and then descended clumsily on the frail branch, and raising her eyes she saw above her the bewildered face of a slouching man with a thin sunburnt beard, and white arms showing through his ragged shirt.

"Don't you ever *see* anything, Liff Hyatt?" she assailed him, as he stood before her with the look of a man who has stirred up a wasp's nest.

He grinned. "I seen you! That's what I come down for."

"Down from where?" she questioned, stooping to gather up the petals his foot had scattered.

He jerked his thumb toward the heights. "Been cutting down trees for Dan Targatt."

Charity sank back on her heels and looked at him musingly. She was not in the least afraid of poor Liff Hyatt, though he "came from the Mountain," and some of the girls ran when they saw him. Among the more reasonable he passed for a harmless creature, a sort of link between the mountain and civilized folk, who occasionally came down and did a little wood-cutting for a farmer when hands were short. Besides, she knew the Mountain people would never hurt her: Liff himself had told her so once when she was a little girl, and had met him one day at the edge of lawyer Royall's pasture. "They won't any of 'em touch you up there, f'ever you was to come up. . . . But I don't s'pose you will," he had added philosophically, looking at her new shoes, and at the red ribbon that Mrs. Royall had tied in her hair.

Charity had, in truth, never felt any desire to visit her birthplace. She did not care to have it known that she was of the Mountain, and was shy of being seen in talk with Liff Hyatt. But today she was not sorry to have him appear. A great many things had happened to her since the day when young Lucius Harney had entered the doors of the Hatchard Memorial, but none, perhaps, so unforeseen as the fact of her suddenly finding it a convenience to be on good terms with Liff Hyatt. She continued to look up curiously at his freckled weather-beaten face, with feverish hollows below the cheekbones and the pale yellow eyes of a harmless animal. "I wonder if he's related to me?" she thought, with a shiver of disdain.

"Is there any folks living in the brown house by the swamp, up under Porcupine?" she presently asked in an indifferent tone.

Porcupine: a fictional hill in the Berkshire Mountains.

Liff Hyatt, for a while, considered her with surprise; then he scratched his head and shifted his weight from one tattered sole to the other.

"There's always the same folks in the brown house," he said with his vague grin.

"They're from up your way, ain't they?"

"Their name's the same as mine," he rejoined uncertainly.

Charity still held him with resolute eyes. "See here, I want to go there some day and take a gentleman with me that's boarding with us. He's up in these parts drawing pictures."

She did not offer to explain this statement. It was too far beyond Liff Hyatt's limitations for the attempt to be worth making. "He wants to see the brown house, and go all over it," she pursued.

Liff was still running his fingers perplexedly through his shock of straw-colored hair. "Is it a fellow from the city?" he asked.

"Yes. He draws pictures of things. He's down there now drawing the Bonner house." She pointed to a chimney just visible over the dip of the pasture below the wood.

"The Bonner house?" Liff echoed incredulously.

"Yes. You won't understand—and it don't matter. All I say is: he's going to the Hyatts' in a day or two."

Liff looked more and more perplexed. "Bash is ugly sometimes in the afternoons."

"I know. But I guess he won't trouble me." She threw her head back, her eyes full on Hyatt's. "I'm coming too: you tell him."

"They won't none of them trouble you, the Hyatts won't. What d'you want a take a stranger with you, though?"

"I've told you, haven't I? You've got to tell Bash Hyatt."

He looked away at the blue mountains on the horizon; then his gaze dropped to the chimney-top below the pasture.

"He's down there now?"

"Yes."

He shifted his weight again, crossed his arms, and continued to survey the distant landscape. "Well, so long," he said at last, inconclusively; and turning away he shambled up the hillside. From the ledge above her, he paused to call down: "I wouldn't go there a Sunday"; then he clambered on till the trees closed in on him. Presently, from high overhead, Charity heard the ring of his axe.

She lay on the warm ridge, thinking of many things that the woodsman's appearance had stirred up in her. She knew nothing of her early life, and had not felt any curiosity about it: only a sullen reluctance to explore the corner of her memory where certain blurred images lingered. But all that had happened to her within the last few weeks had stirred her to the sleeping depths. She had become absorbingly interesting to herself, and everything that had to do with her past was illuminated by this sudden curiosity.

She hated more than ever the fact of coming from the Mountain; but it was no longer indifferent to her. Everything that in any way affected her was alive and vivid: even the hateful things had grown interesting because they were a part of herself.

"I wonder if Liff Hyatt knows who my mother was?" she mused; and it filled her with a tremor of surprise to think that some woman who was once young and slight, with quick motions of the blood like hers, had carried her in her breast, and watched her sleeping. She had always thought of her mother as so long dead as to be no more than a nameless pinch of earth; but now it occurred to her that the once-young woman might be alive, and wrinkled and elf-locked like the woman she had sometimes seen in the door of the brown house that Lucius Harney wanted to draw.

The thought brought him back to the central point in her mind, and she strayed away from the conjectures roused by Liff Hyatt's presence. Speculations concerning the past could not hold her long when the present was so rich, the future so rosy, and when Lucius Harney, a stone's throw away, was bending over his sketch-book, frowning, calculating, measuring, and then throwing his head back with the sudden smile that had shed its brightness over everything.

She scrambled to her feet, but as she did so she saw him coming up the pasture and dropped down on the grass to wait. When he was drawing and measuring one of "his houses," as she called them, she often strayed away by herself into the woods or up the hillside. It was partly from shyness that she did so: from a sense of inadequacy that came to her most painfully when her companion, absorbed in his job, forgot her ignorance and her inability to follow his least allusion, and plunged into a monologue on art and life. To avoid the awkwardness of listening with a blank face, and also to escape the surprised stare of the inhabitants of the houses before which he would abruptly pull up their horse and open his sketch-book, she slipped away to some spot from which, without being seen, she could watch him at work, or at least look down on the house he was drawing. She had not been displeased, at first, to have it known to North Dormer and the neighborhood that she was driving Miss Hatchard's cousin about the country in the buggy he had hired of lawyer Royall. She had always kept to herself, contemptuously aloof from village love-making, without exactly knowing whether her fierce pride was due to the sense of her tainted origin, or whether she was reserving herself for a more brilliant fate. Sometimes she envied the other girls their sentimental preoccupations, their long hours of inarticulate philandering with one of the few youths who still lingered in the village; but when she pictured herself curling her hair or putting a new ribbon on her hat for Ben Fry or one of the Sollas boys the fever dropped and she relapsed into indifference.

Now she knew the meaning of her disdains and reluctances. She had learned what she was worth when Lucius Harney, looking at her for the first time, had lost the thread of his speech, and leaned reddening on the edge of her desk. But another kind of shyness had been born in her: a terror of exposing to vulgar perils the sacred treasure of her happiness. She was not sorry to have the neighbors suspect her of "going with" a young man from the city; but she did not want it known to all the countryside how many hours of the long June days she spent with him. What she most feared was that the inevitable comments should reach Mr. Royall. Charity was instinctively aware that few things concerning her escaped the eyes of the silent man under whose roof she lived; and in spite of the latitude which North Dormer accorded to courting couples she had always felt that, on the day when she showed too open a preference, Mr. Royall might, as she phrased it, make her "pay for it." How, she did not know; and her fear was the greater because it was undefinable. If she had been accepting the attentions of one of the village youths she would have been less apprehensive: Mr. Royall could not prevent her marrying when she chose to. But everybody knew that "going with a city fellow" was a different and less straightforward affair: almost every village could show a victim of the perilous venture. And her dread of Mr. Royall's intervention gave a sharpened joy to the hours she spent with young Harney, and made her, at the same time, shy of being too generally seen with him.

As he approached she rose to her knees, stretching her arms above her head with the indolent gesture that was her way of expressing a profound well-being.

"I'm going to take you to that house up under Porcupine," she announced.

"What house? Oh, yes; that ramshackle place near the swamp, with the gipsy-looking people hanging about. It's curious that a house with traces of real architecture should have been built in such a place. But the people were a sulky-looking lot—do you suppose they'll let us in?"

"They'll do whatever I tell them," she said with assurance.

He threw himself down beside her. "Will they?" he rejoined with a smile. "Well, I should like to see what's left inside the house. And I should like to have a talk with the people. Who was it who was telling me the other day that they had come down from the Mountain?"

Charity shot a sideward look at him. It was the first time he had spoken of the Mountain except as a feature of the landscape. What else did he know about it, and about her relation to it? Her heart began to beat with the fierce impulse of resistance which she instinctively opposed to every imagined slight.

"The Mountain? I ain't afraid of the Mountain!"

Her tone of defiance seemed to escape him. He lay breast-down on the grass, breaking off sprigs of thyme and pressing them against his lips. Far off, above the folds of the nearer hills, the Mountain thrust itself up menacingly against a yellow sunset.

"I must go up there some day: I want to see it," he continued.

Her heart-beats slackened and she turned again to examine his profile. It was innocent of all unfriendly intention.

"What'd you want to go up the Mountain for?"

"Why, it must be rather a curious place. There's a queer colony up there, you know: sort of outlaws, a little independent kingdom. Of course you've heard them spoken of; but I'm told they have nothing to do with the people in the valleys — rather look down on them, in fact. I suppose they're rough customers; but they must have a good deal of character."

She did not quite know what he meant by having a good deal of character; but his tone was expressive of admiration, and deepened her dawning curiosity. It struck her now as strange that she knew so little about the Mountain. She had never asked, and no one had ever offered to enlighten her. North Dormer took the Mountain for granted, and implied its disparagement by an intonation rather than by explicit criticism.

"It's queer, you know," he continued, "that, just over there, on top of that hill, there should be a handful of people who don't give a damn for anybody."

The words thrilled her. They seemed the clue to her own revolts and defiances, and she longed to have him tell her more.

"I don't know much about them. Have they always been there?"

"Nobody seems to know exactly how long. Down at Creston they told me that the first colonists are supposed to have been men who worked on the railway that was built forty or fifty years ago between Springfield and Nettleton. Some of them took to drink, or got into trouble with the police, and went off — disappeared into the woods. A year or two later there was a report that they were living up on the Mountain. Then I suppose others joined them — and children were born. Now they say there are over a hundred people up there. They seem to be quite outside the jurisdiction of the valleys. No school, no church — and no sheriff ever goes up to see what they're about. But don't people ever talk of them at North Dormer?"

"I don't know. They say they're bad."

He laughed. "Do they? We'll go and see, shall we?"

She flushed at the suggestion, and turned her face to his. "You never heard, I suppose—I come from there. They brought me down when I was little."

"You?" He raised himself on his elbow, looking at her with sudden interest. "You're from the Mountain? How curious! I suppose that's why you're so different...."

Her happy blood bathed her to the forehead. He was praising her—and praising her because she came from the Mountain!

"Am I . . . different?" she triumphed, with affected wonder.

"Oh, awfully!" He picked up her hand and laid a kiss on the sunburnt knuckles.

"Come," he said, "let's be off." He stood up and shook the grass from his loose grey clothes. "What a good day! Where are you going to take me tomorrow?"

V I

That evening after supper Charity sat alone in the kitchen and listened to Mr. Royall and young Harney talking in the porch.

She had remained indoors after the table had been cleared and old Verena had hobbled up to bed. The kitchen window was open, and Charity seated herself near it, her idle hands on her knee. The evening was cool and still. Beyond the black hills an amber west passed into pale green, and then to a deep blue in which a great star hung. The soft hoot of a little owl came through the dusk, and between its calls the men's voices rose and fell.

Mr. Royall's was full of a sonorous satisfaction. It was a long time since he had had anyone of Lucius Harney's quality to talk to: Charity divined that the young man symbolized all his ruined and unforgotten past. When Miss Hatchard had been called to Springfield by the illness of a widowed sister, and young Harney, by that time seriously embarked on his task of drawing and measuring all the old houses between Nettleton and the New Hampshire border, had suggested the possibility of boarding at the red house in his cousin's absence, Charity had trembled lest Mr. Royall should refuse. There had been no question of lodging the young man: there was no room for him. But it appeared that he could still live at Miss Hatchard's if Mr. Royall would let him take his meals at the red house; and after a day's deliberation Mr. Royall consented.

Charity suspected him of being glad of the chance to make a little money. He had the reputation of being an avaricious man; but she was beginning to think he was probably poorer than people knew. His practice had become little more than a vague legend, revived only at lengthening intervals by a summons to Hepburn or Nettleton; and he appeared to depend for his living mainly on the scant produce of his farm, and on the commissions received from the few insurance agencies that he represented in the neighbourhood. At any rate, he had been prompt in accepting Harney's offer to hire the buggy at a dollar and a half a day; and his satisfaction with the bargain had manifested itself, unexpectedly enough, at the end of the first week, by his tossing a ten-dollar bill into Charity's lap as she sat one day retrimming her old hat.

"Here—go get yourself a Sunday bonnet that'll make all the other girls mad," he said, looking at her with a sheepish twinkle in his deep-set eyes; and she immediately guessed that the unwonted present—the only gift of money she had ever received from him—represented Harney's first payment.

But the young man's coming had brought Mr. Royall other than pecuniary benefit. It gave him, for the first time in years, a man's companionship. Charity had only a dim understanding of her guardian's needs; but she knew he felt himself above the people among whom he lived, and she saw that Lucius Harney thought him so. She was surprised to find how well he seemed to talk now that he had a listener who understood him; and she was equally struck by young Harney's friendly deference.

Their conversation was mostly about politics, and beyond her range; but tonight it had a peculiar interest for her, for they had begun to speak of the Mountain. She drew back a little, lest they should see she was in hearing.

"The Mountain? The Mountain?" she heard Mr. Royall say. "Why, the Mountain's a blot—that's what it is, sir, a blot. That scum up there ought to have been run in long ago—and would have, if the people down here hadn't been clean scared of them. The Mountain belongs to this township, and it's North Dormer's fault if there's a gang of thieves and outlaws living over there, in sight of us, defying the laws of their country. Why, there ain't a sheriff or a tax-collector or a coroner'd durst go up there. When they hear of trouble on the Mountain the selectmen look the other way, and pass an appropriation to beautify the town pump. The only man that ever goes up is the minister, and he goes because they send down and get him whenever there's any of them dies. They think a lot of Christian burial on the Mountain—but I never heard of their having the minister up to marry them. And they never trouble the Justice of the Peace either. They just herd together like the heathen."

He went on, explaining in somewhat technical language how the little colony of squatters had contrived to keep the law at bay, and Charity, with burning eagerness, awaited young Harney's comment; but the young man seemed more concerned to hear Mr. Royall's views than to express his own.

"I suppose you've never been up there yourself?" he presently asked.

"Yes, I have," said Mr. Royall with a contemptuous laugh. "The wise-acres down here told me I'd be done for before I got back; but nobody lifted a finger to hurt me. And I'd just had one of their gang sent up for seven years too."

"You went up after that?"

"Yes, sir: right after it. The fellow came down to Nettleton and ran amuck, the way they sometimes do. After they've done a wood-cutting job they come down and blow the money in; and this man ended up with manslaughter. I got him convicted, though they were scared of the Moun-tain even at Nettleton; and then a queer thing happened. The fellow sent for me to go and see him in gaol. I went, and this is what he says: 'The fool that defended me is a chicken-livered son of a —— and all the rest of it,' he says. 'I've got a job to be done for me up on the Mountain, and you're the only man I seen in court that looks as if he'd do it.' He told me he had a child up there—or thought he had—a little girl; and he wanted her brought down and reared like a Christian. I was sorry for the fellow, so I went up and got the child." He paused, and Charity listened with a throbbing heart. "That's the only time I ever went up the Mountain," he concluded.

There was a moment's silence; then Harney spoke. "And the child—had she no mother?"

"Oh, yes: there was a mother. But she was glad enough to have her go. She'd have given her to anybody. They ain't half human up there. I guess the mother's dead by now, with the life she was leading. Anyhow, I've never heard of her from that day to this."

"My God, how ghastly," Harney murmured; and Charity, choking with humiliation, sprang to her feet and ran upstairs. She knew at last: knew that she was the child of a drunken convict and of a mother who wasn't "half human," and was glad to have her go; and she had heard this history of her origin related to the one being in whose eyes she longed to appear superior to the people about her! She had noticed that Mr. Royall had not named her, had even avoided any allusion that might identify her with the child he had brought down from the Mountain; and she knew it was out of regard for her that he had kept silent. But of what use was his discretion, since only that afternoon, misled by Harney's interest in the outlaw colony, she had boasted to him of coming from the Mountain? Now every word that had been spoken showed her how such an origin must widen the distance between them.

During his ten days' sojourn at North Dormer Lucius Harney had not spoken a word of love to her. He had intervened in her behalf with his cousin, and had convinced Miss Hatchard of her merits as a librarian; but that was a simple act of justice, since it was by his own fault that those merits had been questioned. He had asked her to drive him about the country when he hired lawyer Royall's buggy to go on his sketching expeditions; but that too was natural enough, since he was unfamiliar with the region. Lastly, when his cousin was called to Springfield, he had begged Mr. Royall to receive him as a boarder; but where else in North Dormer could he have boarded? Not with Carrick Fry, whose wife was paralysed, and whose large family crowded his table to over-flowing; not with the Targatts, who lived a mile up the road, nor with poor old Mrs. Hawes, who, since her eldest daughter had deserted her, barely had the strength to cook her own meals while Ally picked up her living as a seamstress. Mr. Royall's was the only house where the young man could have been offered a decent hospitality. There had been nothing, therefore, in the outward course of events to raise in Charity's breast the hopes with which it trembled. But beneath the visible incidents resulting from Lucius Harney's arrival there ran an undercurrent as mysterious and potent as the influence that makes the forest break into leaf befor the ice is off the pools.

The business on which Harney had come was authentic; Charity had seen the letter from a New York publisher commissioning him to make a study of the eighteenth century houses in the less familiar districts of New England. But incomprehensible as the whole affair was to her, and hard as she found it to understand why he paused enchanted before certain neglected and paintless houses, while others, refurbished and "improved" by the local builder, did not arrest a glance, she could not but suspect that Eagle County was less rich in architecture than he averred, and that the duration of his stay (which he had fixed at a month) was not unconnected with the look in his eyes when he had first paused before her in the library. Everything that had followed seemed to have grown out of that look: his way of speaking to her, his quickness in catching her meaning, his evident eagerness to prolong their excursions and to seize on every chance of being with her.

The signs of his liking were manifest enough; but it was hard to guess how much they meant, because his manner was so different from anything North Dormer had ever shown her. He was at once simpler and more deferential than any one she had known; and sometimes it was just when he was simplest that she most felt the distance between them. Education and opportunity had divided them by a width that no effort of hers could bridge, and even when his youth and his admiration brought him nearest, some chance word, some unconscious allusion, seemed to thrust her back across the gulf.

Never had it yawned so wide as when she fled up to her room carrying with her the echo of Mr. Royall's tale. Her first confused thought was the prayer that she might never see young Harney again. It was too bitter to picture him as the detached impartial listener to such a story. "I wish he'd go away: I wish he'd go tomorrow, and never come back!" she moaned to her pillow; and far into the night she lay there, in the disordered dress she had forgotten to take off, her whole soul a tossing misery on which her hopes and dreams spun about like drowning straws.

Of all this tumult only a vague heart-soreness was left when she opened her eyes the next morning. Her first thought was of the weather, for Harney had asked her to take him to the brown house under Porcupine, and then around by Hamblin; and as the trip was a long one they were to start at nine. The sun rose without a cloud, and earlier than usual she was in the kitchen, making cheese sandwiches, decanting buttermilk into a bottle, wrapping up slices of apple pie, and accusing Verena of having given away a basket she needed, which had always hung on a hook in the passage. When she came out into the porch, in her pink calico, which had run a little in the washing, but was still bright enough to set off her dark tints, she had such a triumphant sense of being a part of the sunlight and the morning that the last trace of her misery vanished. What did it matter where she came from, or whose child she was, when love was dancing in her veins, and down the road she saw young Harney coming toward her?

Mr. Royall was in the porch too. He had said nothing at breakfast, but when she came out in her pink dress, the basket in her hand, he looked at her with surprise. "Where you going to?" he asked.

"Why—Mr. Harney's starting earlier than usual today," she answered.

"Mr. Harney, Mr. Harney? Ain't Mr. Harney learned how to drive a horse yet?"

She made no answer, and he sat tilted back in his chair, drumming on the rail of the porch. It was the first time he had ever spoken of the young man in that tone, and Charity felt a faint chill of apprehension. After a moment he stood up and walked away toward the bit of ground behind the house, where the hired man was hoeing.

The air was cool and clear, with the autumnal sparkle that a north wind brings to the hills in early summer, and the night had been so still that the dew hung on everything, not as a lingering moisture, but in separate beads that glittered like diamonds on the ferns and grasses. It was a long drive to the foot of Porcupine: first across the valley, with blue hills bounding the open slopes; then down into the beach-woods, following the course of the Creston, a brown brook leaping over velvet ledges; then out again onto the farm-lands about Creston Lake, and gradually up the ridges of the Eagle Range. At last they reached the yoke of the hills, and before them opened another valley, green and wild, and beyond it more blue heights eddying away to the sky like the waves of a receding tide.

Harney tied the horse to a tree-stump, and they unpacked their basket under an aged walnut with a riven trunk out of which bumblebees darted. The sun had grown hot, and behind them was the noonday murmur of the forest. Summer insects danced on the air, and a flock of white butterflies fanned the mobile tips of the crimson fireweed. In the valley below not a house was visible; it seemed as if Charity Royall and young Harney were the only living beings in the great hollow of earth and sky.

Charity's spirits flagged and disquieting thoughts stole back on her. Young Harney had grown silent, and as he lay beside her, his arms under his head, his eyes on the network of leaves above him, she wondered if he were musing on what Mr. Royall had told him, and if it had really debased her in his thoughts. She wished he had not asked her to take him that day to the brown house; she did not want him to see the people she came from while the story of her birth was fresh in his mind. More than once she had been on the point of suggesting that they should follow the ridge and drive straight to Hamblin, where there was a little deserted house he wanted to see; but shyness and pride held her back. "He'd better know what kind of folks I belong to," she said to herself, with a somewhat forced defiance; for in reality it was shame that kept her silent.

Suddenly she lifted her hand and pointed to the sky. "There's a storm coming up."

He followed her glance and smiled. "Is it that scrap of cloud among the pines that frightens you?"

"It's over the Mountain; and a cloud over the Mountain always means trouble."

"Oh, I don't believe half the bad things you all say of the Mountain! But anyhow, we'll get down to the brown house before the rain comes."

He was not far wrong, for only a few isolated drops had fallen when they turned into the road under the shaggy flank of Porcupine, and came upon the brown house. It stood alone beside a swamp bordered with alder thickets and tall bulrushes. Not another dwelling was in sight, and it was hard to

---

alder: toothed-leaved tree or shrub of the birch family.

guess what motive could have actuated the early settler who had made his home in so unfriendly a spot.

Charity had picked up enough of her companion's erudition to understand what had attracted him to the house. She noticed the fan-shaped tracery of the broken light above the door, the flutings of the paintless pilasters at the corners, and the round window set in the gable; and she knew that, for reasons that still escaped her, these were things to be admired and recorded. Still, they had seen other houses far more "typical" (the word was Harney's); and as he threw the reins on the horse's neck he said with a slight shiver of repugnance: "We won't stay long."

Against the restless alders turning their white lining to the storm the house looked singularly desolate. The paint was almost gone from the clapboards, the window-panes were broken and patched with rags, and the garden was a poisonous tangle of nettles, burdocks and tall swamp-weeds over which big blue-bottles hummed.

At the sound of wheels a child with a tow-head and pale eyes like Liff Hyatt's peered over the fence and then slipped away behind an out-house. Harney jumped down and helped Charity out; and as he did so the rain broke on them. It came slant-wise, on a furious gale, laying shrubs and young trees flat, tearing off their leaves like an autumn storm, turning the road into a river, and making hissing pools of every hollow. Thunder rolled incessantly through the roar of the rain, and a strange glitter of light ran along the ground under the increasing blackness.

"Lucky we're here after all," Harney laughed. He fastened the horse under a half-roofless shed, and wrapping Charity in his coat ran with her to the house. The boy had not reappeared, and as there was no response to their knocks Harney turned the door-handle and they went in.

There were three people in the kitchen to which the door admitted them. An old woman with a handkerchief over her head was sitting by the window. She held a sickly-looking kitten on her knees, and whenever it jumped down and tried to limp away she stooped and lifted it back without any change of her aged, unnoticing face. Another woman, the unkempt creature that Charity had once noticed in driving by, stood leaning against the window-frame and stared at them; and near the stove an unshaved man in a tattered shirt sat on a barrel asleep.

The place was bare and miserable and the air heavy with the smell of dirt and stale tobacco. Charity's heart sank. Old derided tales of the Mountain people came back to her, and the woman's stare was so disconcerting, and the face of the sleeping man so sodden and bestial, that her disgust was

---

pilaster: a rectangular column projecting about one-third of their width from a wall.

tinged with a vague dread. She was not afraid for herself; she knew the Hyatts would not be likely to trouble her; but she was not sure how they would treat a "city fellow."

Lucius Harney would certainly have laughed at her fears. He glanced about the room, uttered a general "How are you?" to which no one responded, and then asked the younger woman if they might take shelter till the storm was over.

She turned her eyes away from him and looked at Charity.

"You're the girl from Royall's, ain't you?"

The colour rose in Charity's face. "I'm Charity Royall," she said, as if asserting her right to the name in the very place where it might have been most open to question.

The woman did not seem to notice. "You kin stay," she merely said; then she turned away and stooped over a dish in which she was stirring something.

Harney and Charity sat down on a bench made of a board resting on two starch boxes. They faced a door hanging on a broken hinge, and through the crack they saw the eyes of the tow-headed boy and of a pale little girl with a scar across her cheek. Charity smiled, and signed to the children to come in; but as soon as they saw they were discovered they slipped away on bare feet. It occurred to her that they were afraid of rousing the sleeping man; and probably the woman shared their fear, for she moved about as noiselessly and avoided going near the stove.

The rain continued to beat against the house, and in one or two places it sent a stream through the patched panes and ran into pools on the floor. Every now and then the kitten mewed and struggled down, and the old woman stooped and caught it, holding it tight in her bony hands; and once or twice the man on the barrel half woke, changed his position and dozed again, his head falling forward on his hairy breast. As the minutes passed, and the rain still streamed against the windows, a loathing of the place and the people came over Charity. The sight of the weak-minded old woman, of the cowed children, and the ragged man sleeping off his liquor, made the setting of her own life seem a vision of peace and plenty. She thought of the kitchen at Mr. Royall's, with its scrubbed floor and dresser full of china, and the peculiar smell of yeast and coffee and soft-soap that she had always hated, but that now seemed the very symbol of household order. She saw Mr. Royall's room, with the high-backed horsehair chair, the faded rag carpet, the row of books on a shelf, the engraving of "The Surrender of Burgoyne"

"**Surrender of Burgoyne**": British general John Burgoyne surrendered to American forces in Saratoga Springs, New York, in 1777, during the U.S. War of Independence.

over the stove, and the mat with a brown and white spaniel on a moss-green border. And then her mind travelled to Miss Hatchard's house, where all was freshness, purity and fragrance, and compared to which the red house had always seemed so poor and plain.

"This is where I belong—this is where I belong," she kept repeating to herself; but the words had no meaning for her. Every instinct and habit made her a stranger among these poor swamp-people living like vermin in their lair. With all her soul she wished she had not yielded to Harney's curiosity, and brought him there.

The rain had drenched her, and she began to shiver under the thin folds of her dress. The younger woman must have noticed it, for she went out of the room and came back with a broken tea-cup which she offered to Charity. It was half full of whiskey, and Charity shook her head; but Harney took the cup and put his lips to it. When he had set it down Charity saw him feel in his pocket and draw out a dollar; he hesitated a moment, and then put it back, and she guessed that he did not wish her to see him offering money to people she had spoken of as being her kin.

The sleeping man stirred, lifted his head and opened his eyes. They rested vacantly for a moment on Charity and Harney, and then closed again, and his head drooped; but a look of anxiety came into the woman's face. She glanced out of the window and then came up to Harney. "I guess you better go along now," she said. The young man understood and got to his feet. "Thank you," he said, holding out his hand. She seemed not to notice the gesture, and turned away as they opened the door.

The rain was still coming down, but they hardly noticed it: the pure air was like balm in their faces. The clouds were rising and breaking, and between their edges the light streamed down from remote blue hollows. Harney untied the horse, and they drove off through the diminishing rain, which was already beaded with sunlight.

For a while Charity was silent, and her companion did not speak. She looked timidly at his profile: it was graver than usual, as though he too were oppressed by what they had seen. Then she broke out abruptly: "Those people back there are the kind of folks I come from. They may be my relations, for all I know." She did not want him to think that she regretted having told him her story.

"Poor creatures," he rejoined. "I wonder why they came down to that fever-hole."

She laughed ironically. "To better themselves! It's worse up on the Mountain. Bash Hyatt married the daughter of the farmer that used to own the brown house. That was him by the stove, I suppose."

Harney seemed to find nothing to say and she went on: "I saw you take out a dollar to give to that poor woman. Why did you put it back?"

He reddened, and leaned forward to flick a swamp-fly from the horse's neck. "I wasn't sure——"

"Was it because you knew they were my folks, and thought I'd be ashamed to see you give them money?"

He turned to her with eyes full of reproach. "Oh, Charity——" It was the first time he had ever called her by her name. Her misery welled over.

"I ain't—I ain't ashamed. They're my people, and I ain't ashamed of them," she sobbed.

"My dear . . ." he murmured, putting his arm about her; and she leaned against him and wept out her pain.

It was too late to go around to Hamblin, and all the stars were out in a clear sky when they reached the North Dormer valley and drove up to the red house.

VII

Since her reinstatement in Miss Hatchard's favour Charity had not dared to curtail by a moment her hours of attendance at the library. She even made a point of arriving before the time, and showed a laudable indignation when the youngest Targatt girl, who had been engaged to help in the cleaning and rearranging of the books, came trailing in late and neglected her task to peer through the window at the Sollas boy. Nevertheless, "library days" seemed more than ever irksome to Charity after her vivid hours of liberty; and she would have found it hard to set a good example to her subordinate if Lucius Harney had not been commissioned, before Miss Hatchard's departure, to examine with the local carpenter the best means of ventilating the "Memorial."

He was careful to prosecute this inquiry on the days when the library was open to the public; and Charity was therefore sure of spending part of the afternoon in his company. The Targatt girl's presence, and the risk of being interrupted by some passer-by suddenly smitten with a thirst for letters, restricted their intercourse to the exchange of commonplaces; but there was a fascination to Charity in the contrast between these public civilities and their secret intimacy.

The day after their drive to the brown house was "library day," and she sat at her desk working at the revised catalogue, while the Targatt girl, one eye on the window, chanted out the titles of a pile of books. Charity's thoughts were far away, in the dismal house by the swamp, and under the twilight sky during the long drive home, when Lucius Harney had consoled her with endearing words. That day, for the first time since he had been boarding with them, he had failed to appear as usual at the midday meal. No message had come to explain his absence, and Mr. Royall, who was more than usually taciturn, had betrayed no surprise, and made no comment. In itself this indifference was not particularly significant, for Mr. Royall, in common with most of his fellow-citizens, had a way of accepting events passively, as if he had long since come to the conclusion that no one who lived in North Dormer could hope to modify them. But to Charity, in the reaction from her mood of passionate exaltation, there was something disquieting in his silence. It was almost as if Lucius Harney had never had a part in their lives: Mr. Royall's imperturbable indifference seemed to relegate him to the domain of unreality.

As she sat at work, she tried to shake off her disappointment at Harney's non-appearing. Some trifling incident had probably kept him from joining them at midday; but she was sure he must be eager to see her again, and that he would not want to wait till they met at supper, between Mr. Royall and Verena. She was wondering what his first words would be, and trying to devise a way of getting rid of the Targatt girl before he came, when she heard steps outside, and he walked up the path with Mr. Miles.

The clergyman from Hepburn seldom came to North Dormer except when he drove over to officiate at the old white church which, by an unusual chance, happened to belong to the Episcopal communion. He was a brisk affable man, eager to make the most of the fact that a little nucleus of "church-people" had survived in the sectarian wilderness, and resolved to undermine the influence of the ginger-bread-coloured Baptist chapel at the other end of the village; but he was kept busy by parochial work at Hepburn, where there were paper-mills and saloons, and it was not often that he could spare time for North Dormer.

Charity, who went to the white church (like all the best people in North Dormer), admired Mr. Miles, and had even, during the memorable trip to Nettleton, imagined herself married to a man who had such a straight nose and such a beautiful way of speaking, and who lived in a brown-stone rectory covered with Virginia creeper. It had been a shock to discover that the privilege was already enjoyed by a lady with crimped hair and a large baby; but the arrival of Lucius Harney had long since banished Mr. Miles from Charity's dreams, and as he walked up the path at Harney's side she saw him as he really was: a fat middle-aged man with a baldness showing under his clerical hat, and spectacles on his Grecian nose. She wondered what had called him to North Dormer on a week-day, and felt a little hurt that Harney should have brought him to the library.

It presently appeared that his presence there was due to Miss Hatchard. He had been spending a few days at Springfield, to fill a friend's pulpit, and had been consulted by Miss Hatchard as to young Harney's plan for ventilating the "Memorial." To lay hands on the Hatchard ark was a grave matter, and Miss Hatchard, always full of scruples about her scruples (it was Harney's phrase), wished to have Mr. Miles's opinion before deciding.

"I couldn't," Mr. Miles explained, "quite make out from your cousin what changes you wanted to make, and as the other trustees did not understand either I thought I had better drive over and take a look—though I'm sure," he added, turning his friendly spectacles on the young man, "that no one could be more competent—but of course this spot has its peculiar sanctity!"

"I hope a little fresh air won't desecrate it," Harney laughingly rejoined; and they walked to the other end of the library while he set forth his idea to the Rector.

Mr. Miles had greeted the two girls with his usual friendliness, but Charity saw that he was occupied with other things, and she presently became aware, by the scraps of conversation drifting over to her, that he was still under the charm of his visit to Springfield, which appeared to have been full of agreeable incidents.

"Ah, the Coopersons . . . yes, you know them, of course," she heard. "That's a fine old house! And Ned Cooperson has collected some really remarkable impressionist pictures. . . ." The names he cited were unknown to Charity. "Yes; yes; the Schaefer quartette played at Lyric Hall on Saturday evening; and on Monday I had the privilege of hearing them again at the Towers. Beautifully done . . . Bach and Beethoven . . . a lawn-party first . . . I saw Miss Balch several times, by the way . . . looking extremely handsome. . . ."

Charity dropped her pencil and forgot to listen to the Targatt girl's sing-song. Why had Mr. Miles suddenly brought up Annabel Balch's name?

"Oh, really?" she heard Harney rejoin; and, raising his stick, he pursued: "You see, my plan is to move these shelves away, and open a round window in this wall, on the axis of the one under the pediment."

"I suppose she'll be coming up here later to stay with Miss Hatchard?" Mr. Miles went on, following on his train of thought; then, spinning about and tilting his head back: "Yes, yes, I see—I understand: that will give a draught without materially altering the look of things. I can see no objection."

The discussion went on for some minutes, and gradually the two men moved back toward the desk. Mr. Miles stopped again and looked

---

Schaefer quartette . . . Lyric Hall: a fictional instrumental quartet and music hall.
the Towers: a fictional theater.

thoughtfully at Charity. "Aren't you a little pale, my dear? Not overworking? Mr. Harney tells me you and Mamie are giving the library a thorough overhauling." He was always careful to remember his parishioners' Christian names, and at the right moment he bent his benignant spectacles on the Targatt girl.

Then he turned to Charity. "Don't take things hard, my dear; don't take things hard. Come down and see Mrs. Miles and me some day at Hepburn," he said, pressing her hand and waving a farewell to Mamie Targatt. He went out of the library, and Harney followed him.

Charity thought she detected a look of constraint in Harney's eyes. She fancied he did not want to be alone with her; and with a sudden pang she wondered if he repented the tender things he had said to her the night before. His words had been more fraternal than lover-like; but she had lost their exact sense in the caressing warmth of his voice. He had made her feel that the fact of her being a waif from the Mountain was only another reason for holding her close and soothing her with consolatory murmurs; and when the drive was over, and she got out of the buggy, tired, cold, and aching with emotion, she stepped as if the ground were a sunlit wave and she the spray on its crest.

Why, then, had his manner suddenly changed, and why did he leave the library with Mr. Miles? Her restless imagination fastened on the name of Annabel Balch: from the moment it had been mentioned she fancied that Harney's expression had altered. Annabel Balch at a garden-party at Springfield, looking "extremely handsome" . . . perhaps Mr. Miles had seen her there at the very moment when Charity and Harney were sitting in the Hyatts' hovel, between a drunkard and a half-witted old woman! Charity did not know exactly what a garden-party was, but her glimpse of the flower-edged lawns of Nettleton helped her to visualize the scene, and envious recollections of the "old things" which Miss Balch avowedly "wore out" when she came to North Dormer made it only too easy to picture her in her splendour. Charity understood what associations the name must have called up, and felt the uselessness of struggling against the unseen influences in Harney's life.

When she came down from her room for supper he was not there; and while she waited in the porch she recalled the tone in which Mr. Royall had commented the day before on their early start. Mr. Royall sat at her side, his chair tilted back, his broad black boots with side-elastics resting against the lower bar of the railings. His rumpled grey hair stood up above his forehead like the crest of an angry bird, and the leather-brown of his veined cheeks was blotched with red. Charity knew that those red spots were the signs of a coming explosion.

Suddenly he said: "Where's supper? Has Verena Marsh slipped up again on her soda-biscuits?"

Charity threw a startled glance at him. "I presume she's waiting for Mr. Harney."

"Mr. Harney, is she? She'd better dish up, then. He ain't coming." He stood up, walked to the door, and called out, in the pitch necessary to penetrate the old woman's tympanum: "Get along with the supper, Verena."

Charity was trembling with apprehension. Something had happened—she was sure of it now—and Mr. Royall knew what it was. But not for the world would she have gratified him by showing her anxiety. She took her usual place, and he seated himself opposite, and poured out a strong cup of tea before passing her the tea-pot. Verena brought some scrambled eggs, and he piled his plate with them. "Ain't you going to take any?" he asked. Charity roused herself and began to eat.

The tone with which Mr. Royall had said "He's not coming" seemed to her full of an ominous satisfaction. She saw that he had suddenly begun to hate Lucius Harney, and guessed herself to be the cause of this change of feeling. But she had no means of finding out whether some act of hostility on his part had made the young man stay away, or whether he simply wished to avoid seeing her again after their drive back from the brown house. She ate her supper with a studied show of indifference, but she knew that Mr. Royall was watching her and that her agitation did not escape him.

After supper she went up to her room. She heard Mr. Royall cross the passage, and presently the sounds below her window showed that he had returned to the porch. She seated herself on her bed and began to struggle against the desire to go down and ask him what had happened. "I'd rather die than do it," she muttered to herself. With a word he could have relieved her uncertainty: but never would she gratify him by saying it.

She rose and leaned out of the window. The twilight had deepened into night, and she watched the frail curve of the young moon dropping to the edge of the hills. Through the darkness she saw one or two figures moving down the road; but the evening was too cold for loitering, and presently the strollers disappeared. Lamps were beginning to show here and there in the windows. A bar of light brought out the whiteness of a clump of lilies in the Hawes's yard: and farther down the street Carrick Fry's Rochester lamp cast its bold illumination on the rustic flower-tub in the middle of his grass-plot.

---

tympanum: a membrane covering the middle ear.

Rochester lamp: a decorative oil lamp manufactured by the Rochester Lamp Company of New York.

For a long time she continued to lean in the window. But a fever of unrest consumed her, and finally she went downstairs, took her hat from its hook, and swung out of the house. Mr. Royall sat in the porch, Verena beside him, her old hands crossed on her patched skirt. As Charity went down the steps Mr. Royall called after her: "Where you going?" She could easily have answered: "To Orma's," or "Down to the Targatts'"; and either answer might have been true, for she had no purpose. But she swept on in silence, determined not to recognize his right to question her.

At the gate she paused and looked up and down the road. The darkness drew her, and she thought of climbing the hill and plunging into the depths of the larch-wood above the pasture. Then she glanced irresolutely along the street, and as she did so a gleam appeared through the spruces at Miss Hatchard's gate. Lucius Harney was there, then—he had not gone down to Hepburn with Mr. Miles, as she had at first imagined. But where had he taken his evening meal, and what had caused him to stay away from Mr. Royall's? The light was positive proof of his presence, for Miss Hatchard's servants were away on a holiday, and her farmer's wife came only in the mornings, to make the young man's bed and prepare his coffee. Beside that lamp he was doubtless sitting at this moment. To know the truth Charity had only to walk half the length of the village, and knock at the lighted window. She hesitated a minute or two longer, and then turned toward Miss Hatchard's.

She walked quickly, straining her eyes to detect anyone who might be coming along the street; and before reaching the Frys' she crossed over to avoid the light from their window. Whenever she was unhappy she felt herself at bay against a pitiless world, and a kind of animal secretiveness possessed her. But the street was empty, and she passed unnoticed through the gate and up the path to the house. Its white front glimmered indistinctly through the trees, showing only one oblong of light on the lower floor. She had supposed that the lamp was in Miss Hatchard's sitting-room; but she now saw that it shone through a window at the farther corner of the house. She did not know the room to which this window belonged, and she paused under the trees, checked by a sense of strangeness. Then she moved on, treading softly on the short grass, and keeping so close to the house that whoever was in the room, even if roused by her approach, would not be able to see her.

The window opened on a narrow verandah with a trellised arch. She leaned close to the trellis, and parting the sprays of clematis that covered it looked into a corner of the room. She saw the foot of a mahogany bed, an engraving on the wall, a wash-stand on which a towel had been tossed, and one end of the green-covered table which held the lamp. Half of the lamp-shade projected into her field of vision, and just under it two smooth sunburnt hands, one holding a pencil and the other a ruler, were moving to and fro over a drawing-board.

Her heart jumped and then stood still. He was there, a few feet away; and while her soul was tossing on seas of woe he had been quietly sitting at his drawing-board. The sight of those two hands, moving with their usual skill and precision, woke her out of her dream. Her eyes were opened to the disproportion between what she had felt and the cause of her agitation; and she was turning away from the window when one hand abruptly pushed aside the drawing-board and the other flung down the pencil.

Charity had often noticed Harney's loving care of his drawings, and the neatness and method with which he carried on and concluded each task. The impatient sweeping aside of the drawing-board seemed to reveal a new mood. The gesture suggested sudden discouragement, or distaste for his work and she wondered if he too were agitated by secret perplexities. Her impulse of flight was checked; she stepped up on the verandah and looked into the room.

Harney had put his elbows on the table and was resting his chin on his locked hands. He had taken off his coat and waistcoat, and unbuttoned the low collar of his flannel shirt; she saw the vigorous lines of his young throat, and the root of the muscles where they joined the chest. He sat staring straight ahead of him, a look of weariness and self-disgust on his face: it was almost as if he had been gazing at a distorted reflection of his own features. For a moment Charity looked at him with a kind of terror, as if he had been a stranger under familiar lineaments; then she glanced past him and saw on the floor an open portmanteau half full of clothes. She understood that he was preparing to leave, and that he had probably decided to go without seeing her. She saw that the decision, from whatever cause it was taken, had disturbed him deeply; and she immediately concluded that his change of plan was due to some surreptitious interference of Mr. Royall's. All her old resentments and rebellions flamed up, confusedly mingled with the yearning roused by Harney's nearness. Only a few hours earlier she had felt secure in his comprehending pity; now she was flung back on herself, doubly alone after that moment of communion.

Harney was still unaware of her presence. He sat without moving, moodily staring before him at the same spot in the wall-paper. He had not even had the energy to finish his packing, and his clothes and papers lay on the floor about the portmanteau. Presently he unlocked his clasped hands

---

waistcoat: a vest.

portmanteau: a large suitcase.

and stood up; and Charity, drawing back hastily, sank down on the step of the verandah. The night was so dark that there was not much chance of his seeing her unless he opened the window and before that she would have time to slip away and be lost in the shadow of the trees. He stood for a minute or two looking around the room with the same expression of self-disgust, as if he hated himself and everything about him; then he sat down again at the table, drew a few more strokes, and threw his pencil aside. Finally he walked across the floor, kicking the portmanteau out of his way, and lay down on the bed, folding his arms under his head, and staring up morosely at the ceiling. Just so, Charity had seen him at her side on the grass or the pine-needles, his eyes fixed on the sky, and pleasure flashing over his face like the flickers of sun the branches shed on it. But now the face was so changed that she hardly knew it; and grief at his grief gathered in her throat, rose to her eyes and ran over.

She continued to crouch on the steps, holding her breath and stiffening herself into complete immobility. One motion of her hand, one tap on the pane, and she could picture the sudden change in his face. In every pulse of her rigid body she was aware of the welcome his eyes and lips would give her; but something kept her from moving. It was not the fear of any sanction, human or heavenly; she had never in her life been afraid. It was simply that she had suddenly understood what would happen if she went in. It was the thing that *did* happen between young men and girls, and that North Dormer ignored in public and snickered over on the sly. It was what Miss Hatchard was still ignorant of, but every girl of Charity's class knew about before she left school. It was what had happened to Ally Hawes's sister Julia, and had ended in her going to Nettleton, and in people's never mentioning her name.

It did not, of course, always end so sensationally; nor, perhaps, on the whole, so untragically. Charity had always suspected that the shunned Julia's fate might have its compensations. There were others, worse endings that the village knew of, mean, miserable, unconfessed; other lives that went on drearily, without visible change, in the same cramped setting of hypocrisy. But these were not the reasons that held her back. Since the day before, she had known exactly what she would feel if Harney should take her in his arms: the melting of palm into palm and mouth on mouth, and the long flame burning her from head to foot. But mixed with this feeling was another: the wondering pride in his liking for her, the startled softness that his sympathy had put into her heart. Sometimes, when her youth flushed up in her, she had imagined yielding like other girls to furtive caresses in the twilight; but she could not so cheapen herself to Harney. She did not know why he was going; but since he was going she felt she must do nothing to deface the image of her that he carried away. If he wanted her he must seek her: he must not be surprised into taking her as girls like Julia Hawes were taken. . . .

No sound came from the sleeping village, and in the deep darkness of the garden she heard now and then a secret rustle of branches, as though some night-bird brushed them. Once a footfall passed the gate, and she shrank back into her corner; but the steps died away and left a profounder quiet. Her eyes were still on Harney's tormented face: she felt she could not move till he moved. But she was beginning to grow numb from her constrained position, and at times her thoughts were so indistinct that she seemed to be held there only by a vague weight of weariness.

A long time passed in this strange vigil. Harney still lay on the bed, motionless and with fixed eyes, as though following his vision to its bitter end. At last he stirred and changed his attitude slightly, and Charity's heart began to tremble. But he only flung out his arms and sank back into his former position. With a deep sigh he tossed the hair from his forehead; then his whole body relaxed, his head turned sideways on the pillow, and she saw that he had fallen asleep. The sweet expression came back to his lips, and the haggardness faded from his face, leaving it as fresh as a boy's.

She rose and crept away.

VIII

She had lost the sense of time, and did not know how late it was till she came out into the street and saw that all the windows were dark between Miss Hatchard's and the Royall house.

As she passed from under the black pall of the Norway spruces she fancied she saw two figures in the shade about the duck-pond. She drew back and watched; but nothing moved, and she had stared so long into the lamp-lit room that the darkness confused her, and she thought she must have been mistaken.

She walked on, wondering whether Mr. Royall was still in the porch. In her exalted mood she did not greatly care whether he was waiting for her or not: she seemed to be floating high over life, on a great cloud of misery beneath which everyday realities had dwindled to mere specks in space. But the porch was empty, Mr. Royall's hat hung on its peg in the passage, and the kitchen lamp had been left to light her to bed. She took it and went up.

The morning hours of the next day dragged by without incident. Charity had imagined that, in some way or other, she would learn whether Harney had already left; but Verena's deafness prevented her being a source of news, and no one came to the house who could bring enlightenment.

Mr. Royall went out early, and did not return till Verena had set the table for the midday meal. When he came in he went straight to the kitchen and shouted to the old woman: "Ready for dinner——" then he turned into the dining-room, where Charity was already seated. Harney's plate was in its usual place, but Mr. Royall offered no explanation of his absence, and Charity asked none. The feverish exaltation of the night before had dropped, and she said to herself that he had gone away, indifferently, almost callously, and that now her life would lapse again into the narrow rut out of which he had lifted it. For a moment she was inclined to sneer at herself for not having used the arts that might have kept him.

She sat at table till the meal was over, lest Mr. Royall should remark on her leaving; but when he stood up she rose also, without waiting to help Verena. She had her foot on the stairs when he called to her to come back.

"I've got a headache. I'm going up to lie down."

"I want you should come in here first; I've got something to say to you."

She was sure from his tone that in a moment she would learn what every nerve in her ached to know; but as she turned back she made a last effort of indifference.

Mr. Royall stood in the middle of the office, his thick eyebrows beetling, his lower jaw trembling a little. At first she thought he had been drinking; then she saw that he was sober, but stirred by a deep and stern emotion totally unlike his usual transient angers. And suddenly she understood that, until then, she had never really noticed him or thought about him. Except on the occasion of his one offense he had been to her merely the person who is always there, the unquestioned central fact of life, as inevitable but as uninteresting as North Dormer itself, or any of the other conditions fate had laid on her. Even then she had regarded him only in relation to herself, and had never speculated as to his own feelings, beyond instinctively concluding that he would not trouble her again in the same way. But now she began to wonder what he was really like.

He had grasped the back of his chair with both hands, and stood looking hard at her. At length he said: "Charity, for once let's you and me talk together like friends."

Instantly she felt that something had happened, and that he held her in his hand.

"Where is Mr. Harney? Why hasn't he come back? Have you sent him away?" she broke out, without knowing what she was saying.

The change in Mr. Royall frightened her. All the blood seemed to leave his veins and against his swarthy pallor the deep lines in his face looked black.

"Didn't he have time to answer some of those questions last night? You was with him long enough!" he said.

Charity stood speechless. The taunt was so unrelated to what had been happening in her soul that she hardly understood it. But the instinct of self-defense awoke in her.

"Who says I was with him last night?"

"The whole place is saying it by now."

"Then it was you that put the lie into their mouths. — Oh, how I've always hated you!" she cried.

She had expected a retort in kind, and it startled her to hear her exclamation sounding on through silence.

"Yes, I know," Mr. Royall said slowly. "But that ain't going to help us much now."

"It helps me not to care a straw what lies you tell about me!"

"If they're lies, they're not my lies: my Bible oath on that, Charity. I didn't know where you were: I wasn't out of this house last night."

She made no answer and he went on: "Is it a lie that you were seen coming out of Miss Hatchard's nigh onto midnight?"

She straightened herself with a laugh, all her reckless insolence recovered. "I didn't look to see what time it was."

"You lost girl . . . you . . . you . . . Oh, my God, why did you tell me?" he broke out, dropping into his chair, his head bowed down like an old man's.

Charity's self-possession had returned with the sense of her danger. "Do you suppose I'd take the trouble to lie to *you?* Who are you, anyhow, to ask me where I go to when I go out at night?"

Mr. Royall lifted his head and looked at her. His face had grown quiet and almost gentle, as she remembered seeing it sometimes when she was a little girl, before Mrs. Royall died.

"Don't let's go on like this, Charity. It can't do any good to either of us. You were seen going into that fellow's house . . . you were seen coming out of it. . . . I've watched this thing coming, and I've tried to stop it. As God sees me, I have. . . ."

"Ah, it *was* you, then? I knew it was you that sent him away!"

He looked at her in surprise. "Didn't he tell you so? I thought he understood." He spoke slowly, with difficult pauses, "I didn't name you to him: I'd have cut my hand off sooner. I just told him I couldn't spare the horse any longer; and that the cooking was getting too heavy for Verena. I guess he's the kind that's heard the same thing before. Anyhow, he took it quietly enough. He said his job here was about done, anyhow; and there didn't another word pass between us. . . . If he told you otherwise he told you an untruth."

Charity listened in a cold trance of anger. It was nothing to her what the village said . . . but all this fingering of her dreams!

"I've told you he didn't tell me anything. I didn't speak with him last night."

"You didn't speak with him?"

"No. . . . It's not that I care what any of you say . . . but you may as well know. Things ain't between us the way you think . . . and the other people in this place. He was kind to me; he was my friend; and all of a sudden he stopped coming, and I knew it was you that done it—*you!*" All her unreconciled memory of the past flamed out at him. "So I went there last night to find out what you'd said to him: that's all."

Mr. Royall drew a heavy breath. "But, then—if he wasn't there, what were you doing there all that time?—Charity, for pity's sake, tell me. I've got to know, to stop their talking."

This pathetic abdication of all authority over her did not move her: she could feel only the outrage of his interference.

"Can't you see that I don't care what anybody says? It's true I went there to see him; and he was in his room, and I stood outside for ever so long and watched him; but I dursn't go in for fear he'd think I'd come after him. . . ." She felt her voice breaking, and gathered it up in a last defiance. "As long as I live I'll never forgive you!" she cried.

Mr. Royall made no answer. He sat and pondered with sunken head, his veined hands clasped about the arms of his chair. Age seemed to have come down on him as winter comes on the hills after a storm. At length he looked up.

"Charity, you say you don't care; but you're the proudest girl I know, and the last to want people to talk against you. You know there's always eyes watching you: you're handsomer and smarter than the rest, and that's enough. But till lately you've never given them a chance. Now they've got it, and they're going to use it. I believe what you say, but they won't. . . . It was Mrs. Tom Fry seen you going in . . . and two or three of them watched for you to come out again. . . . You've been with the fellow all day long every day since he come here . . . and I'm a lawyer, and I know how hard slander dies." He paused, but she stood motionless, without giving him any sign of acquiescence or even of attention. "He's a pleasant fellow to talk to—I liked having him here myself. The young men up here ain't had his chances. But there's one thing as old as the hills and as plain as daylight: if he'd wanted you the right way he'd have said so."

Charity did not speak. It seemed to her that nothing could exceed the bitterness of hearing such words from such lips.

Mr. Royall rose from his seat. "See here, Charity Royall: I had a shameful thought once, and you've made me pay for it. Isn't that score pretty near wiped out? . . . There's a streak in me I ain't always master of; but I've always acted straight to you but that once. And you've known I would—you've trusted me. For all your sneers and your mockery you've always known I loved you the way a man loves a decent woman. I'm a good many years older than you, but I'm head and shoulders above this place and everybody in it, and you know that too. I slipped up once, but that's no reason for not starting again. If you'll come with me I'll do it. If you'll marry me we'll leave here and settle in some big town, where there's men, and business, and things doing. It's not too late for me to find an opening. . . . I can see it by the way folks treat me when I go down to Hepburn or Nettleton. . . ."

Charity made no movement. Nothing in his appeal reached her heart, and she thought only of words to wound and wither. But a growing lassitude restrained her. What did anything matter that he was saying? She saw the old life closing in on her, and hardly heeded his fanciful picture of renewal.

"Charity—Charity—say you'll do it," she heard him urge, all his lost years and wasted passion in his voice.

"Oh, what's the use of all this? When I leave here it won't be with you."

She moved toward the door as she spoke, and he stood up and placed himself between her and the threshold. He seemed suddenly tall and strong, as though the extremity of his humiliation had given him new vigour.

"That's all, is it? It's not much." He leaned against the door, so towering and powerful that he seemed to fill the narrow room. "Well, then—look here. . . . You're right: I've no claim on you—why should you look at a broken man like me? You want the other fellow . . . and I don't blame you. You picked out the best when you seen it . . . well, that was always my way." He fixed his stern eyes on her, and she had the sense that the struggle within him was at its highest. "Do you want him to marry you?" he asked.

They stood and looked at each other for a long moment, eye to eye, with the terrible equality of courage that sometimes made her feel as if she had his blood in her veins.

"Do you want him to—say? I'll have him here in an hour if you do. I ain't been in the law thirty years for nothing. He's hired Carrick Fry's team to take him to Hepburn, but he ain't going to start for another hour. And I can put things to him so he won't be long deciding. . . . He's soft: I could see that. I don't say you won't be sorry afterward—but, by God, I'll give you the chance to be, if you say so."

She heard him out in silence, too remote from all he was feeling and saying for any sally of scorn to relieve her. As she listened, there flitted through her mind the vision of Liff Hyatt's muddy boot coming down on the white bramble-flowers. The same thing had happened now; something transient and exquisite had flowered in her, and she had stood by and seen it trampled to earth. While the thought passed through her she was aware of Mr. Royall, still leaning against the door, but crestfallen, diminished, as though her silence were the answer he most dreaded.

"I don't want any chance you can give me: I'm glad he's going away," she said.

He kept his place a moment longer, his hand on the door-knob. "Charity!" he pleaded. She made no answer, and he turned the knob and went out. She heard him fumble with the latch of the front door, and saw him walk down the steps. He passed out of the gate, and his figure, stooping and heavy, receded slowly up the street.

For a while she remained where he had left her. She was still trembling with the humiliation of his last words, which rang so loud in her ears that it seemed as though they must echo through the village, proclaiming her a creature to lend herself to such vile suggestions. Her shame weighed on her like a physical oppression: the roof and walls seemed to be closing in on her, and she was seized by the impulse to get away, under the open sky, where there would be room to breathe. She went to the front door, and as she did so Lucius Harney opened it.

He looked graver and less confident than usual, and for a moment or two neither of them spoke. Then he held out his hand. "Are you going out?" he asked. "May I come in?"

Her heart was beating so violently that she was afraid to speak, and stood looking at him with tear-dilated eyes; then she became aware of what her silence must betray, and said quickly: "Yes: come in."

She led the way into the dining-room, and they sat down on opposite sides of the table, the cruet-stand and japanned bread-basket between them. Harney had laid his straw hat on the table, and as he sat there, in his easy-looking summer clothes, a brown tie knotted under his flannel collar, and his smooth brown hair brushed back from his forehead, she pictured him, as she had seen him the night before, lying on his bed, with the tossed locks falling into his eyes, and his bare throat rising out of his unbuttoned shirt. He had never seemed so remote as at the moment when that vision flashed through her mind.

"I'm so sorry it's good-bye: I suppose you know I'm leaving," he began, abruptly and awkwardly; she guessed that he was wondering how much she knew of his reasons for going.

"I presume you found your work was over quicker than what you expected," she said.

---

japanned: coated with a hard, glossy finish; lacquered.

"Well, yes—that is, no: there are plenty of things I should have liked to do. But my holiday's limited; and now that Mr. Royall needs the horse for himself it's rather difficult to find means of getting about."

"There ain't any too many teams for hire around here," she acquiesced; and there was another silence.

"These days here have been—awfully pleasant: I wanted to thank you for making them so," he continued, his colour rising.

She could not think of any reply, and he went on: "You've been wonderfully kind to me, and I wanted to tell you. . . . I wish I could think of you as happier, less lonely. . . . Things are sure to change for you by and by. . . ."

"Things don't change at North Dormer: people just get used to them."

The answer seemed to break up the order of his pre-arranged consolations, and he sat looking at her uncertainly. Then he said, with his sweet smile: "That's not true of you. It can't be."

The smile was like a knife-thrust through her heart: everything in her began to tremble and break loose. She felt her tears run over, and stood up.

"Well, good-bye," she said.

She was aware of his taking her hand, and of feeling that his touch was lifeless.

"Good-bye." He turned away, and stopped on the threshold. "You'll say good-bye for me to Verena?"

She heard the closing of the outer door and the sound of his quick tread along the path. The latch of the gate clicked after him.

The next morning when she arose in the cold dawn and opened her shutters she saw a freckled boy standing on the other side of the road and looking up at her. He was a boy from a farm three or four miles down the Creston road, and she wondered what he was doing there at that hour, and why he looked so hard at her window. When he saw her he crossed over and leaned against the gate unconcernedly. There was no one stirring in the house, and she threw a shawl over her night-gown and ran down and let herself out. By the time she reached the gate the boy was sauntering down the road, whistling carelessly; but she saw that a letter had been thrust between the slats and the crossbar of the gate. She took it out and hastened back to her room.

The envelope bore her name, and inside was a leaf torn from a pocket-diary.

DEAR CHARITY:

I can't go away like this. I am staying for a few days at Creston River. Will you come down and meet me at Creston pool? I will wait for you till evening.

I X

Charity sat before the mirror trying on a hat which Ally Hawes, with much secrecy, had trimmed for her. It was of white straw, with a drooping brim and cherry-coloured lining that made her face glow like the inside of the shell on the parlour mantelpiece.

She propped the square of looking-glass against Mr. Royall's black leather Bible, steadying it in front with a white stone on which a view of the Brooklyn Bridge was painted; and she sat before her reflection, bending the brim this way and that, while Ally Hawes's pale face looked over her shoulder like the ghost of wasted opportunities.

"I look awful, don't I?" she said at last with a happy sigh.

Ally smiled and took back the hat. "I'll stitch the roses on right here, so's you can put it away at once."

Charity laughed, and ran her fingers through her rough dark hair. She knew that Harney liked to see its reddish edges ruffled about her forehead and breaking into little rings at the nape. She sat down on her bed and watched Ally stoop over the hat with a careful frown.

"Don't you ever feel like going down to Nettleton for a day?" she asked.

Ally shook her head without looking up. "No, I always remember that awful time I went down with Julia—to that doctor's."

"Oh, Ally——"

"I can't help it. The house is on the corner of Wing Street and Lake Avenue. The trolley from the station goes right by it, and the day the minister took us down to see those pictures I recognized it right off, and couldn't seem to see anything else. There's a big black sign with gold letters all across the front—'Private Consultations.' She came as near as anything to dying. . . ."

"Poor Julia!" Charity sighed from the height of her purity and her security. She had a friend whom she trusted and who respected her. She was going with him to spend the next day—the Fourth of July—at Nettleton. Whose business was it but hers, and what was the harm? The pity of it was that girls like Julia did not know how to choose, and to keep bad fellows at a distance. . . . Charity slipped down from the bed, and stretched out her hands.

"Is it sewed? Let me try it on again." She put the hat on, and smiled at her image. The thought of Julia had vanished. . . .

The next morning she was up before dawn, and saw the yellow sunrise broaden behind the hills, and the silvery luster preceding a hot day tremble across the sleeping fields.

Her plans had been made with great care. She had announced that she was going down to the Band of Hope picnic at Hepburn, and as no one else from North Dormer intended to venture so far it was not likely that her absence from the festivity would be reported. Besides, if it were she would not greatly care. She was determined to assert her independence, and if she stooped to fib about the Hepburn picnic it was chiefly from the secretive instinct that made her dread the profanation of her happiness. Whenever she was with Lucius Harney she would have liked some impenetrable mountain mist to hide her.

It was arranged that she should walk to a point of the Creston road where Harney was to pick her up and drive her across the hills to Hepburn in time for the nine-thirty train to Nettleton. Harney at first had been rather lukewarm about the trip. He declared himself ready to take her to Nettleton, but urged her not to go on the Fourth of July, on account of the crowds, the probable lateness of the trains, the difficulty of her getting back before night; but her evident disappointment caused him to give way, and even to affect a faint enthusiasm for the adventure. She understood why he was not more eager: he must have seen sights beside which even a Fourth of July at Nettleton would seem tame. But she had never seen anything; and a great longing possessed her to walk the streets of a big town on a holiday, clinging to his arm and jostled by idle crowds in their best clothes. The only cloud on the prospect was the fact that the shops would be closed; but she hoped he would take her back another day, when they were open.

She started out unnoticed in the early sunlight, slipping through the kitchen while Verena bent above the stove. To avoid attracting notice, she carried her new hat carefully wrapped up, and had thrown a long grey veil of Mrs. Royall's over the new white muslin dress which Ally's clever fingers had made for her. All of the ten dollars Mr. Royall had given her, and a part of her own savings as well, had been spent on renewing her wardrobe; and when Harney jumped out of the buggy to meet her she read her reward in his eyes.

The freckled boy who had brought her the note two weeks earlier was to wait with the buggy at Hepburn till their return. He perched at Charity's feet, his legs dangling between the wheels, and they could not say much because of his presence. But it did not greatly matter, for their past was now rich enough to have given them a private language; and with the long day stretching before them like the blue distance beyond the hills there was a delicate pleasure in postponement.

Band of Hope: a temperance organization for youth, founded in England in 1847.

When Charity, in response to Harney's message, had gone to meet him at the Creston pool her heart had been so full of mortification and anger that his first words might easily have estranged her. But it happened that he had found the right word, which was one of simple friendship. His tone had instantly justified her, and put her guardian in the wrong. He had made no allusion to what had passed between Mr. Royall and himself, but had simply let it appear that he had left because means of conveyance were hard to find at North Dormer, and because Creston River was a more convenient centre. He told her that he had hired by the week the buggy of the freckled boy's father, who served as livery-stable keeper to one or two melancholy summer boarding-houses on Creston Lake, and had discovered, within driving distance, a number of houses worthy of his pencil; and he said that he could not, while he was in the neighbourhood, give up the pleasure of seeing her as often as possible.

When they took leave of each other she promised to continue to be his guide; and during the fortnight which followed they roamed the hills in happy comradeship. In most of the village friendships between youths and maidens lack of conversation was made up for by tentative fondling; but Harney, except when he had tried to comfort her in her trouble on their way back from the Hyatts', had never put his arm about her, or sought to betray her into any sudden caress. It seemed to be enough for him to breathe her nearness like a flower's; and since his pleasure at being with her, and his sense of her youth and her grace, perpetually shone in his eyes and softened the inflection of his voice, his reserve did not suggest coldness, but the deference due to a girl of his own class.

The buggy was drawn by an old trotter who whirled them along so briskly that the pace created a little breeze; but when they reached Hepburn the full heat of the airless morning descended on them. At the railway station the platform was packed with a sweltering throng, and they took refuge in the waiting-room, where there was another throng, already dejected by the heat and the long waiting for retarded trains. Pale mothers were struggling with fretful babies, or trying to keep their older offspring from the fascination of the track; girls and their "fellows" were giggling and shoving, and passing about candy in sticky bags, and older men, collarless and perspiring, were shifting heavy children from one arm to the other, and keeping a haggard eye on the scattered members of their families.

At last the train rumbled in, and engulfed the waiting multitude. Harney swept Charity up on to the first car and they captured a bench for two, and sat in happy isolation while the train swayed and roared along through rich fields and languid tree-clumps. The haze of the morning had become a sort of clear tremor over everything, like the colourless vibration about a flame;

and the opulent landscape seemed to droop under it. But to Charity the heat was a stimulant: it enveloped the whole world in the same glow that burned at her heart. Now and then a lurch of the train flung her against Harney, and through her thin muslin she felt the touch of his sleeve. She steadied herself, their eyes met, and the flaming breath of the day seemed to enclose them.

The train roared into the Nettleton station, the descending mob caught them on its tide, and they were swept out into a vague dusty square thronged with seedy "hacks" and long curtained omnibuses drawn by horses with tasselled fly-nets over their withers, who stood swinging their depressed heads drearily from side to side.

A mob of 'bus and hack drivers were shouting "To the Eagle House," "To the Washington House," "This way to the Lake," "Just starting for Greytop;" and through their yells came the popping of fire-crackers, the explosion of torpedoes, the banging of toy-guns, and the crash of a fire-men's band trying to play the Merry Widow while they were being packed into a waggonette streaming with bunting.

The ramshackle wooden hotels about the square were all hung with flags and paper lanterns, and as Harney and Charity turned into the main street, with its brick and granite business blocks crowding out the old low-storied shops, and its towering poles strung with innumerable wires that seemed to tremble and buzz in the heat, they saw the double line of flags and lanterns tapering away gaily to the park at the other end of the perspective. The noise and colour of this holiday vision seemed to transform Nettleton into a metropolis. Charity could not believe that Springfield or even Boston had anything grander to show, and she wondered if, at this very moment, Annabel Balch, on the arm of as brilliant a young man, were threading her way through scenes as resplendent.

"Where shall we go first?" Harney asked; but as she turned her happy eyes on him he guessed the answer and said: "We'll take a look round, shall we?"

The street swarmed with their fellow-travellers, with other excursionists arriving from other directions, with Nettleton's own population, and with the mill-hands trooping in from the factories on the Creston. The shops were closed, but one would scarcely have noticed it, so numerous were the glass doors swinging open on saloons, on restaurants, on drug-stores gushing from every soda-water tap, on fruit and confectionery shops stacked with strawberry-cake, cocoanut drops, trays of glistening molasses candy,

---

withers: the highest part of a horse's back, located between the shoulder bones.
The Merry Widow: an operetta by Hungarian composer Franz Lehar (1870–1948).

boxes of caramels and chewing-gum, baskets of sodden strawberries, and dangling branches of bananas. Outside of some of the doors were trestles with banked-up oranges and apples, spotted pears and dusty raspberries; and the air reeked with the smell of fruit and stale coffee, beer and sarsa-parilla and fried potatoes.

Even the shops that were closed offered, through wide expanses of plate-glass, hints of hidden riches. In some, waves of silk and ribbon broke over shores of imitation moss from which ravishing hats rose like tropical orchids. In others, the pink throats of gramophones opened their giant convolutions in a soundless chorus; or bicycles shining in neat ranks seemed to await the signal of an invisible starter; or tiers of fancy-goods in leatherette and paste and celluloid dangled their insidious graces; and, in one vast bay that seemed to project them into exciting contact with the public, wax ladies in daring dresses chatted elegantly, or, with gestures in-timate yet blameless, pointed to their pink corsets and transparent hosiery.

Presently Harney found that his watch had stopped, and turned in at a small jeweller's shop which chanced to be still open. While the watch was being examined Charity leaned over the glass counter where, on a back-ground of dark blue velvet, pins, rings and brooches glittered like the moon and stars. She had never seen jewellery so near by, and she longed to lift the glass lid and plunge her hand among the shining treasures. But al-ready Harney's watch was repaired, and he laid his hand on her arm and drew her from her dream.

"Which do you like best?" he asked leaning over the counter at her side.

"I don't know. . . ." She pointed to a gold lily-of-the-valley with white flowers.

"Don't you think the blue pin's better?" he suggested, and immediately she saw that the lily of the valley was mere trumpery compared to the small round stone, blue as a mountain lake, with little sparks of light all round it. She coloured at her want of discrimination.

"It's so lovely I guess I was afraid to look at it," she said.

He laughed, and they went out of the shop; but a few steps away he ex-claimed: "Oh, by Jove, I forgot something," and turned back and left her in the crowd. She stood staring down a row of pink gramophone throats till he rejoined her and slipped his arm through hers.

"You mustn't be afraid of looking at the blue pin any longer, because it belongs to you," he said; and she felt a little box being pressed into her hand. Her heart gave a leap of joy, but it reached her lips only in a shy stam-mer. She remembered other girls whom she had heard planning to extract

---

gramophones: phonographs.

presents from their fellows, and was seized with a sudden dread lest Harney should have imagined that she had leaned over the pretty things in the glass case in the hope of having one given to her. . . .

A little farther down the street they turned in at a glass doorway opening on a shining hall with a mahogany staircase, and brass cages in its corners. "We must have something to eat," Harney said; and the next moment Charity found herself in a dressing-room all looking-glass and lustrous surfaces, where a party of showy-looking girls were dabbing on powder and straightening immense plumed hats. When they had gone she took courage to bathe her hot face in one of the marble basins, and to straighten her own hat-brim, which the parasols of the crowd had indented. The dresses in the shops had so impressed her that she scarcely dared look at her reflection; but when she did so, the glow of her face under her cherry-coloured hat, and the curve of her young shoulders through the transparent muslin, restored her courage; and when she had taken the blue brooch from its box and pinned it on her bosom she walked toward the restaurant with her head high, as if she had always strolled through tessellated halls beside young men in flannels.

Her spirit sank a little at the sight of the slim-waisted waitresses in black, with bewitching mob-caps on their haughty heads, who were moving disdainfully between the tables. "Not f'r another hour," one of them dropped to Harney in passing; and he stood doubtfully glancing about him.

"Oh, well, we can't stay sweltering here," he decided; "let's try somewhere else—" and with a sense of relief Charity followed him from that scene of inhospitable splendour.

That "somewhere else" turned out—after more hot tramping, and several failures—to be, of all things, a little open-air place in a back street that called itself a French restaurant, and consisted in two or three rickety tables under a scarlet-runner, between a patch of zinnias and petunias and a big elm bending over from the next yard. Here they lunched on queerly flavoured things, while Harney, leaning back in a crippled rocking-chair, smoked cigarettes between the courses and poured into Charity's glass a pale yellow wine which he said was the very same one drank in just such jolly places in France.

Charity did not think the wine as good as sarsaparilla, but she sipped a mouthful for the pleasure of doing what he did, and of fancying herself alone with him in foreign countries. The illusion was increased by their being served by a deep-bosomed woman with smooth hair and a pleasant

tessellated halls: halls adorned with mosaic tiles.

laugh, who talked to Harney in unintelligible words, and seemed amazed and overjoyed at his answering her in kind. At the other tables other people sat, mill-hands probably, homely but pleasant looking, who spoke the same shrill jargon, and looked at Harney and Charity with friendly eyes; and between the table-legs a poodle with bald patches and pink eyes nosed about for scraps, and sat up on his hind legs absurdly.

Harney showed no inclination to move, for hot as their corner was, it was at least shaded and quiet; and, from the main thoroughfares came the clanging of trolleys, the incessant popping of torpedoes, the jingle of street-organs, the bawling of megaphone men and the loud murmur of increasing crowds. He leaned back, smoking his cigar, patting the dog, and stirring the coffee that steamed in their chipped cups. "It's the real thing, you know," he explained; and Charity hastily revised her previous conception of the beverage.

They had made no plans for the rest of the day, and when Harney asked her what she wanted to do next she was too bewildered by rich possibilities to find an answer. Finally she confessed that she longed to go to the Lake, where she had not been taken on her former visit, and when he answered, "Oh, there's time for that—it will be pleasanter later," she suggested seeing some pictures like the ones Mr. Miles had taken her to. She thought Harney looked a little disconcerted; but he passed his fine handkerchief over his warm brow, said gaily, "Come along, then," and rose with a last pat for the pink-eyed dog.

Mr. Miles's pictures had been shown in an austere Y.M.C.A. hall, with white walls and an organ; but Harney led Charity to a glittering place—everything she saw seemed to glitter—where they passed, between immense pictures of yellow-haired beauties stabbing villains in evening dress, into a velvet-curtained auditorium packed with spectators to the last limit of compression. After that, for a while, everything was merged in her brain in swimming circles of heat and blinding alternations of light and darkness. All the world has to show seemed to pass before her in a chaos of palms and minarets, charging cavalry regiments, roaring lions, comic policemen and scowling murderers; and the crowd around her, the hundreds of hot sallow candy-munching faces, young, old, middle-aged, but all kindled with the same contagious excitement, became part of the spectacle, and danced on the screen with the rest.

Presently the thought of the cool trolley-run to the Lake grew irresistible, and they struggled out of the theatre. As they stood on the pavement,

---

minarets: tall slender towers attached to a mosque and having one or more balconies.

Harney pale with the heat, and even Charity a little confused by it, a young man drove by in an electric run-about with a calico band bearing the words: "Ten dollars to take you round the Lake." Before Charity knew what was happening, Harney had waved a hand, and they were climbing in. "Say, for twenny-five I'll run you out to see the ball-game and back," the driver proposed with an insinuating grin; but Charity said quickly: "Oh, I'd rather go rowing on the Lake." The street was so thronged that progress was slow; but the glory of sitting in the little carriage while it wriggled its way between laden omnibuses and trolleys made the moments seem too short. "Next turn is Lake Avenue," the young man called out over his shoulder; and as they paused in the wake of a big omnibus groaning with Knights of Pythias in cocked hats and swords, Charity looked up and saw on the corner a brick house with a conspicuous black and gold sign across its front. "Dr. Merkle; Private Consultations at all hours. Lady Attendants," she read; and suddenly she remembered Ally Hawes's words: "The house was at the corner of Wing Street and Lake Avenue . . . there's a big black sign across the front. . . ." Through all the heat and the rapture a shiver of cold ran over her.

X

The Lake at last—a sheet of shining metal brooded over by drooping trees. Charity and Harney had secured a boat and, getting away from the wharves and the refreshment-booths, they drifted idly along, hugging the shadow of the shore. Where the sun struck the water its shafts flamed back blindingly at the heat-veiled sky; and the least shade was black by contrast. The Lake was so smooth that the reflection of the trees on its edge seemed enamelled on a solid surface; but gradually, as the sun declined, the water grew transparent, and Charity, leaning over, plunged her fascinated gaze into depths so clear that she saw the inverted tree-tops interwoven with the green growths of the bottom.

They rounded a point at the farther end of the Lake, and entering an inlet pushed their bow against a protruding tree-trunk. A green veil of willows overhung them. Beyond the trees, wheat-fields sparkled in the sun; and all along the horizon the clear hills throbbed with light. Charity leaned back in the stern, and Harney unshipped the oars and lay in the bottom of the boat without speaking.

---

run-about: a light, horse-drawn open carriage.
Knights of Pythias: an international fraternity founded in Washington, DC, in 1864.

Ever since their meeting at the Creston pool he had been subject to these brooding silences, which were as different as possible from the pauses when they ceased to speak because words were needless. At such times his face wore the expression she had seen on it when she had looked in at him from the darkness and again there came over her a sense of the mysterious distance between them; but usually his fits of abstraction were followed by bursts of gaiety that chased away the shadow before it chilled her.

She was still thinking of the ten dollars he had handed to the driver of the run-about. It had given them twenty minutes of pleasure, and it seemed unimaginable that anyone should be able to buy amusement at that rate. With ten dollars he might have bought her an engagement ring; she knew that Mrs. Tom Fry's, which came from Springfield, and had a diamond in it, had cost only eight seventy-five. But she did not know why the thought had occurred to her. Harney would never buy her an engagement ring: they were friends and comrades, but no more. He had been perfectly fair to her: he had never said a word to mislead her. She wondered what the girl was like whose hand was waiting for his ring. . . .

Boats were beginning to thicken on the Lake and the clang of incessantly arriving trolleys announced the return of the crowds from the ball-field. The shadows lengthened across the pearl-grey water and two white clouds near the sun were turning golden. On the opposite shore men were hammering hastily at a wooden scaffolding in a field. Charity asked what it was for.

"Why, the fireworks. I suppose there'll be a big show." Harney looked at her and a smile crept into his moody eyes. "Have you never seen any good fireworks?"

"Miss Hatchard always sends up lovely rockets on the Fourth," she answered doubtfully.

"Oh——" his contempt was unbounded. "I mean a big performance like this, illuminated boats, and all the rest."

She flushed at the picture. "Do they send them up from the Lake, too?"

"Rather. Didn't you notice that big raft we passed? It's wonderful to see the rockets completing their orbits down under one's feet." She said nothing, and he put the oars into the rowlocks. "If we stay we'd better go and pick up something to eat."

"But how can we get back afterwards?" she ventured, feeling it would break her heart if she missed it.

He consulted a time-table, found a ten o'clock train and reassured her. "The moon rises so late that it will be dark by eight, and we'll have over an hour of it."

Twilight fell, and lights began to show along the shore. The trolleys roaring out from Nettleton became great luminous serpents coiling in and out among the trees. The wooden eating-houses at the Lake's edge danced with lanterns, and the dusk echoed with laughter and shouts and the clumsy splashing of oars.

Harney and Charity had found a table in the corner of a balcony built over the Lake, and were patiently awaiting an unattainable chowder. Close under them the water lapped the piles, agitated by the evolutions of a little white steamboat trellised with coloured globes which was to run passengers up and down the Lake. It was already black with them as it sheered off on its first trip.

Suddenly Charity heard a woman's laugh behind her. The sound was familiar, and she turned to look. A band of showily dressed girls and dapper young men wearing badges of secret societies, with new straw hats tilted far back on their square-clipped hair, had invaded the balcony and were loudly clamouring for a table. The girl in the lead was the one who had laughed. She wore a large hat with a long white feather, and from under its brim her painted eyes looked at Charity with amused recognition.

"Say! if this ain't like Old Home Week," she remarked to the girl at her elbow; and giggles and glances passed between them. Charity knew at once that the girl with the white feather was Julia Hawes. She had lost her freshness, and the paint under her eyes made her face seem thinner; but her lips had the same lovely curve, and the same cold mocking smile, as if there were some secret absurdity in the person she was looking at, and she had instantly detected it.

Charity flushed to the forehead and looked away. She felt herself humiliated by Julia's sneer, and vexed that the mockery of such a creature should affect her. She trembled lest Harney should notice that the noisy troop had recognized her; but they found no table free, and passed on tumultuously.

Presently there was a soft rush through the air and a shower of silver fell from the blue evening sky. In another direction, pale Roman candles shot up singly through the trees, and a fire-haired rocket swept the horizon like a portent. Between these intermittent flashes the velvet curtains of the darkness were descending, and in the intervals of eclipse the voices of the crowds seemed to sink to smothered murmurs.

Charity and Harney, dispossessed by newcomers, were at length obliged to give up their table and struggle through the throng about the boat-landings. For a while there seemed no escape from the tide of late arrivals; but finally Harney secured the last two places on the stand from which the more privileged were to see the fireworks. The seats were at the end of a

---

Old Home Week: a celebration where former residents, old friends, neighbors, and family members gather to commemorate their town and its history.

row, one above the other. Charity had taken off her hat to have an unin-terrupted view; and whenever she leaned back to follow the curve of some dishevelled rocket she could feel Harney's knees against her head.

After a while the scattered fireworks ceased. A longer interval of dark-ness followed, and then the whole night broke into flower. From every point of the horizon, gold and silver arches sprang up and crossed each other, sky-orchards broke into blossom, shed their flaming petals and hung their branches with golden fruit; and all the while the air was filled with a soft supernatural hum, as though great birds were building their nests in those invisible tree-tops.

Now and then there came a lull, and a wave of moonlight swept the Lake. In a flash it revealed hundreds of boats, steel-dark against lustrous ripples; then it withdrew as if with a furling of vast translucent wings. Charity's heart throbbed with delight. It was as if all the latent beauty of things had been unveiled to her. She could not imagine that the world held anything more wonderful; but near her she heard someone say, "You wait till you see the set piece," and instantly her hopes took a fresh flight. At last, just as it was beginning to seem as though the whole arch of the sky were one great lid pressed against her dazzled eyeballs, and striking out of them continuous jets of jewelled light, the velvet darkness settled down again, and a murmur of expectation ran through the crowd.

"Now—now!" the same voice said excitedly; and Charity, grasping the hat on her knee, crushed it tight in the effort to restrain her rapture.

For a moment the night seemed to grow more impenetrably black; then a great picture stood out against it like a constellation. It was surmounted by a golden scroll bearing the inscription, "Washington crossing the Dela-ware," and across a flood of motionless golden ripples the National Hero passed, erect, solemn and gigantic, standing with folded arms in the stern of a slowly moving golden boat.

A long "Oh-h-h" burst from the spectators: the stand creaked and shook with their blissful trepidations. "Oh-h-h," Charity gasped: she had forgotten where she was, had at last forgotten even Harney's nearness. She seemed to have been caught up into the stars. . . .

The picture vanished and darkness came down. In the obscurity she felt her head clasped by two hands: her face was drawn backward, and Harney's lips were pressed on hers. With sudden vehemence he wound his arms

---

"Washington crossing the Delaware": a famous painting completed in 1851 by artist Emanuel Leutze depicting the historic moment when General George Washington led American revolutionary troops across the Delaware River in order to surprise the En-glish and Hessian troops in the Battle of Trenton the day after Christmas in 1776.

about her, holding her head against his breast while she gave him back his kisses. An unknown Harney had revealed himself, a Harney who dominated her and yet over whom she felt herself possessed of a new mysterious power.

But the crowd was beginning to move, and he had to release her. "Come," he said in a confused voice. He scrambled over the side of the stand, and holding up his arm caught her as she sprang to the ground. He passed his arm about her waist, steadying her against the descending rush of people; and she clung to him, speechless, exultant, as if all the crowding and confusion about them were a mere vain stirring of the air.

"Come," he repeated, "we must try to make the trolley." He drew her along, and she followed, still in her dream. They walked as if they were one, so isolated in ecstasy that the people jostling them on every side seemed impalpable. But when they reached the terminus the illuminated trolley was already clanging on its way, its platforms black with passengers. The cars waiting behind it were as thickly packed; and the throng about the terminus was so dense that it seemed hopeless to struggle for a place.

"Last trip up the Lake," a megaphone bellowed from the wharf; and the lights of the little steam-boat came dancing out of the darkness.

"No use waiting here; shall we run up the Lake?" Harney suggested.

They pushed their way back to the edge of the water just as the gang-plank lowered from the white side of the boat. The electric light at the end of the wharf flashed full on the descending passengers, and among them Charity caught sight of Julia Hawes, her white feather askew, and the face under it flushed with coarse laughter. As she stepped from the gang-plank she stopped short, her dark-ringed eyes darting malice.

"Hullo, Charity Royall!" she called out; and then, looking back over her shoulder: "Didn't I tell you it was a family party? Here's grandpa's little daughter come to take him home!"

A snigger ran through the group; and then, towering above them, and steadying himself by the hand-rail in a desperate effort at erectness, Mr. Royall stepped stiffly ashore. Like the young men of the party, he wore a secret society emblem in the buttonhole of his black frock-coat. His head was covered by a new Panama hat, and his narrow black tie, half undone, dangled down on his rumpled shirt-front. His face, a livid brown, with red blotches of anger and lips sunken in like an old man's, was a lamentable ruin in the searching glare.

He was just behind Julia Hawes, and had one hand on her arm; but as he left the gang-plank he freed himself, and moved a step or two away from his companions. He had seen Charity at once, and his glance passed slowly from her to Harney, whose arm was still about her. He stood staring at them, and trying to master the senile quiver of his lips; then he drew himself up with the tremulous majesty of drunkenness, and stretched out his arm.

"You whore—you damn—bare-headed whore, you!" he enunciated slowly.

There was a scream of tipsy laughter from the party, and Charity involuntarily put her hands to her head. She remembered that her hat had fallen from her lap when she jumped up to leave the stand; and suddenly she had a vision of herself, hatless, dishevelled, with a man's arm about her, confronting that drunken crew, headed by her guardian's pitiable figure. The picture filled her with shame. She had known since childhood about Mr. Royall's "habits": had seen him, as she went up to bed, sitting morosely in his office, a bottle at his elbow; or coming home, heavy and quarrelsome, from his business expeditions to Hepburn or Springfield; but the idea of his associating himself publicly with a band of disreputable girls and barroom loafers was new and dreadful to her.

"Oh——" she said in a gasp of misery; and releasing herself from Harney's arm she went straight up to Mr. Royall.

"You come home with me—you come right home with me," she said in a low stern voice, as if she had not heard his apostrophe; and one of the girls called out: "Say, how many fellers does she want?"

There was another laugh, followed by a pause of curiosity, during which Mr. Royall continued to glare at Charity. At length his twitching lips parted. "I said, 'You—damn—whore!'" he repeated with precision, steadying himself on Julia's shoulder.

Laughs and jeers were beginning to spring up from the circle of people beyond their group; and a voice called out from the gangway: "Now, then, step lively there—all *aboard!*" The pressure of approaching and departing passengers forced the actors in the rapid scene apart, and pushed them back into the throng. Charity found herself clinging to Harney's arm and sobbing desperately. Mr. Royall had disappeared, and in the distance she heard the receding sound of Julia's laugh.

The boat, laden to the taffrail, was puffing away on her last trip.

X I

At two o'clock in the morning the freckled boy from Creston stopped his sleepy horse at the door of the red house, and Charity got out. Harney had taken leave of her at Creston River, charging the boy to drive her home.

---

taffrail: the rail around the stern of a boat.

Her mind was still in a fog of misery, and she did not remember very clearly what had happened, or what they said to each other, during the interminable interval since their departure from Nettleton; but the secretive instinct of the animal in pain was so strong in her that she had a sense of relief when Harney got out and she drove on alone.

The full moon hung over North Dormer, whitening the mist that filled the hollows between the hills and floated transparently above the fields. Charity stood a moment at the gate, looking out into the waning night. She watched the boy drive off, his horse's head wagging heavily to and fro; then she went around to the kitchen door and felt under the mat for the key. She found it, unlocked the door and went in. The kitchen was dark, but she discovered a box of matches, lit a candle and went upstairs. Mr. Royall's door, opposite hers, stood open on his unlit room; evidently he had not come back. She went into her room, bolted her door and began slowly to untie the ribbon about her waist, and to take off her dress. Under the bed she saw the paper bag in which she had hidden her new hat from inquisitive eyes. . . .

She lay for a long time sleepless on her bed, staring up at the moonlight on the low ceiling; dawn was in the sky when she fell asleep, and when she woke the sun was on her face.

She dressed and went down to the kitchen. Verena was there alone: she glanced at Charity tranquilly, with her old deaf-looking eyes. There was no sign of Mr. Royall about the house and the hours passed without his reappearing. Charity had gone up to her room, and sat there listlessly, her hands on her lap. Puffs of sultry air fanned her dimity window curtains and flies buzzed stiflingly against the bluish panes.

At one o'clock Verena hobbled up to see if she were not coming down to dinner; but she shook her head, and the old woman went away, saying: "I'll cover up, then."

The sun turned and left her room, and Charity seated herself in the window, gazing down the village street through the half-opened shutters. Not a thought was in her mind; it was just a dark whirlpool of crowding images; and she watched the people passing along the street, Dan Targatt's team hauling a load of pine-trunks down to Hepburn, the sexton's old white horse grazing on the bank across the way, as if she looked at these familiar sights from the other side of the grave.

She was roused from her apathy by seeing Ally Hawes come out of the Frys' gate and walk slowly toward the red house with her uneven limping

---

dimity: a sheer, cotton fabric, in which checks or stripes are woven in heavier thread.

step. At the sight Charity recovered her severed contact with reality. She divined that Ally was coming to hear about her day: no one else was in the secret of the trip to Nettleton, and it had flattered Ally profoundly to be allowed to know of it.

At the thought of having to see her, of having to meet her eyes and answer or evade her questions, the whole horror of the previous night's adventure rushed back upon Charity. What had been a feverish nightmare became a cold and unescapable fact. Poor Ally, at that moment, represented North Dormer, with all its mean curiosities, its furtive malice, its sham unconsciousness of evil. Charity knew that, although all relations with Julia were supposed to be severed, the tender-hearted Ally still secretly communicated with her; and no doubt Julia would exult in the chance of retailing the scandal of the wharf. The story, exaggerated and distorted, was probably already on its way to North Dormer.

Ally's dragging pace had not carried her far from the Frys' gate when she was stopped by old Mrs. Sollas, who was a great talker, and spoke very slowly because she had never been able to get used to her new teeth from Hepburn. Still, even this respite would not last long; in another ten minutes Ally would be at the door, and Charity would hear her greeting Verena in the kitchen, and then calling up from the foot of the stairs.

Suddenly it became clear that flight, and instant flight, was the only thing conceivable. The longing to escape, to get away from familiar faces, from places where she was known, had always been strong in her in moments of distress. She had a childish belief in the miraculous power of strange scenes and new faces to transform her life and wipe out bitter memories. But such impulses were mere fleeting whims compared to the cold resolve which now possessed her. She felt she could not remain an hour longer under the roof of the man who had publicly dishonoured her, and face to face with the people who would presently be gloating over all the details of her humiliation.

Her passing pity for Mr. Royall had been swallowed up in loathing: everything in her recoiled from the disgraceful spectacle of the drunken old man apostrophizing her in the presence of a band of loafers and street-walkers. Suddenly, vividly, she relived again the horrible moment when he had tried to force himself into her room, and what she had before supposed to be a mad aberration now appeared to her as a vulgar incident in a debauched and degraded life.

While these thoughts were hurrying through her she had dragged out her old canvas school-bag, and was thrusting into it a few articles of clothing and the little packet of letters she had received from Harney. From under her pincushion she took the library key, and laid it in full view; then she felt at the back of a drawer for the blue brooch that Harney had given her. She would not have dared to wear it openly at North Dormer, but now she fastened it on her bosom as if it were a talisman to protect her in her flight. These preparations had taken but a few minutes, and when they were finished Ally Hawes was still at the Frys' corner talking to old Mrs. Sollas. . . .

She had said to herself, as she always said in moments of revolt: "I'll go to the Mountain—I'll go back to my own folks." She had never really meant it before; but now, as she considered her case, no other course seemed open. She had never learned any trade that would have given her independence in a strange place, and she knew no one in the big towns of the valley, where she might have hoped to find employment. Miss Hatchard was still away; but even had she been at North Dormer she was the last person to whom Charity would have turned, since one of the motives urging her to flight was the wish not to see Lucius Harney. Travelling back from Nettleton, in the crowded brightly-lit train, all exchange of confidence between them had been impossible; but during their drive from Hepburn to Creston River she had gathered from Harney's snatches of consolatory talk—again hampered by the freckled boy's presence—that he intended to see her the next day. At the moment she had found a vague comfort in the assurance; but in the desolate lucidity of the hours that followed she had come to see the impossibility of meeting him again. Her dream of comradeship was over; and the scene on the wharf—vile and disgraceful as it had been—had after all shed the light of truth on her minute of madness. It was as if her guardian's words had stripped her bare in the face of the grinning crowd and proclaimed to the world the secret admonitions of her conscience.

She did not think these things out clearly; she simply followed the blind propulsion of her wretchedness. She did not want, ever again, to see anyone she had known; above all, she did not want to see Harney. . . .

She climbed the hill-path behind the house and struck through the woods by a short-cut leading to the Creston road. A lead-coloured sky hung heavily over the fields, and in the forest the motionless air was stifling; but she pushed on, impatient to reach the road which was the shortest way to the Mountain.

To do so, she had to follow the Creston road for a mile or two, and go within half a mile of the village; and she walked quickly, fearing to meet Harney. But there was no sign of him, and she had almost reached the branch road when she saw the flanks of a large white tent projecting through the trees by the roadside. She supposed that it sheltered a travelling circus which had come there for the Fourth; but as she drew nearer she saw, over the folded-back flap, a large sign bearing the inscription, "Gospel Tent." The interior seemed to be empty; but a young man in a black alpaca coat, his lank hair parted over a round white face, stepped from under the flap and advanced toward her with a smile.

"Sister, your Saviour knows everything. Won't you come in and lay your guilt before Him?" he asked insinuatingly, putting his hand on her arm.

Charity started back and flushed. For a moment she thought the evangelist must have heard a report of the scene at Nettleton; then she saw the absurdity of the supposition.

"I on'y wish't I had any to lay!" she retorted, with one of her fierce flashes of self-derision; and the young man murmured, aghast: "Oh, Sister, don't speak blasphemy. . . ."

But she had jerked her arm out of his hold, and was running up the branch road, trembling with the fear of meeting a familiar face. Presently she was out of sight of the village, and climbing into the heart of the forest. She could not hope to do the fifteen miles to the Mountain that afternoon; but she knew of a place half-way to Hamblin where she could sleep, and where no one would think of looking for her. It was a little deserted house on a slope in one of the lonely rifts of the hills. She had seen it once, years before, when she had gone on a nutting expedition to the grove of walnuts below it. The party had taken refuge in the house from a sudden mountain storm, and she remembered that Ben Sollas, who liked frightening girls, had told them that it was said to be haunted.

She was growing faint and tired, for she had eaten nothing since morning, and was not used to walking so far. Her head felt light and she sat down for a moment by the roadside. As she sat there she heard the click of a bicycle-bell, and started up to plunge back into the forest; but before she could move the bicycle had swept around the curve of the road, and Harney, jumping off, was approaching her with outstretched arms.

"Charity! What on earth are you doing here?"

She stared as if he were a vision, so startled by the unexpectedness of his being there that no words came to her.

"Where were you going? Had you forgotten that I was coming?" he continued, trying to draw her to him; but she shrank from his embrace.

"I was going away—I don't want to see you—I want you should leave me alone," she broke out wildly.

He looked at her and his face grew grave, as though the shadow of a premonition brushed it.

"Going away—from me, Charity?"

"From everybody. I want you should leave me."

He stood glancing doubtfully up and down the lonely forest road that stretched away into sunflecked distances.

"Where were you going?"

"Home."

"Home—this way?"

She threw her head back defiantly. "To my home—up yonder: to the Mountain."

As she spoke she became aware of a change in his face. He was no longer listening to her, he was only looking at her, with the passionate absorbed expression she had seen in his eyes after they had kissed on the stand at Nettleton. He was the new Harney again, the Harney abruptly revealed in that embrace, who seemed so penetrated with the joy of her presence that he was utterly careless of what she was thinking or feeling.

He caught her hands with a laugh. "How do you suppose I found you?" he said gaily. He drew out the little packet of his letters and flourished them before her bewildered eyes.

"You dropped them, you imprudent young person—dropped them in the middle of the road, not far from here; and the young man who is running the Gospel tent picked them up just as I was riding by." He drew back, holding her at arm's length, and scrutinizing her troubled face with the minute searching gaze of his short-sighted eyes.

"Did you really think you could run away from me? You see you weren't meant to," he said; and before she could answer he had kissed her again, not vehemently, but tenderly, almost fraternally, as if he had guessed her confused pain, and wanted her to know he understood it. He wound his fingers through hers.

"Come—let's walk a little. I want to talk to you. There's so much to say."

He spoke with a boy's gaiety, carelessly and confidently, as if nothing had happened that could shame or embarrass them; and for a moment, in the sudden relief of her release from lonely pain, she felt herself yielding to his mood. But he had turned, and was drawing her back along the road by which she had come. She stiffened herself and stopped short.

"I won't go back," she said.

They looked at each other a moment in silence; then he answered gently: "Very well: let's go the other way, then."

She remained motionless, gazing silently at the ground, and he went on: "Isn't there a house up here somewhere—a little abandoned house—you meant to show me some day?" Still she made no answer, and he continued, in the same tone of tender reassurance: "Let us go there now and sit down and talk quietly." He took one of the hands that hung by her side and pressed his lips to the palm. "Do you suppose I'm going to let you send me away? Do you suppose I don't understand?"

The little old house — its wooden walls sun-bleached to a ghostly gray — stood in an orchard above the road. The garden palings had fallen, but the broken gate dangled between its posts, and the path to the house was marked by rose-bushes run wild and hanging their small pale blossoms above the crowding grasses. Slender pilasters and an intricate fan-light framed the opening where the door had hung; and the door itself lay rotting in the grass, with an old apple-tree fallen across it.

Inside, also, wind and weather had blanched everything to the same wan silvery tint; the house was as dry and pure as the interior of a long-empty shell. But it must have been exceptionally well built, for the little rooms had kept something of their human aspect: the wooden mantels with their neat classic ornaments were in place, and the corners of one ceiling retained a light film of plaster tracery.

Harney had found an old bench at the back door and dragged it into the house. Charity sat on it, leaning her head against the wall in a state of drowsy lassitude. He had guessed that she was hungry and thirsty, and had brought her some tablets of chocolate from his bicycle-bag, and filled his drinking-cup from a spring in the orchard; and now he sat at her feet, smoking a cigarette, and looking up at her without speaking. Outside, the afternoon shadows were lengthening across the grass, and through the empty window-frame that faced her she saw the Mountain thrusting its dark mass against a sultry sunset. It was time to go.

She stood up, and he sprang to his feet also, and passed his arm through hers with an air of authority. "Now, Charity, you're coming back with me."

She looked at him and shook her head. "I ain't ever going back. You don't know."

"What don't I know?" She was silent, and he continued: "What happened on the wharf was horrible — it's natural you should feel as you do. But it doesn't make any real difference: you can't be hurt by such things. You must try to forget. And you must try to understand that men . . . men sometimes . . ."

"I know about men. That's why."

He coloured a little at the retort, as though it had touched him in a way she did not suspect.

"Well, then . . . you must know one has to make allowances. . . . He'd been drinking. . . ."

"I know all that, too. I've seen him so before. But he wouldn't have dared speak to me that way if he hadn't . . ."

"Hadn't what? What do you mean?"

---

palings: fences.

"Hadn't wanted me to be like those other girls. . . ." She lowered her voice and looked away from him. "So's 't he wouldn't have to go out. . . ."

Harney stared at her. For a moment he did not seem to seize her meaning; then his face grew dark. "The damned hound! The villainous low hound!" His wrath blazed up, crimsoning him to the temples. "I never dreamed—good God, it's too vile," he broke off, as if his thoughts recoiled from the discovery.

"I won't never go back there," she repeated doggedly.

"No——" he assented.

There was a long interval of silence, during which she imagined that he was searching her face for more light on what she had revealed to him; and a flush of shame swept over her.

"I know the way you must feel about me," she broke out, " . . . telling you such things. . . ."

But once more, as she spoke, she became aware that he was no longer listening. He came close and caught her to him as if he were snatching her from some imminent peril: his impetuous eyes were in hers, and she could feel the hard beat of his heart as he held her against it.

"Kiss me again—like last night," he said, pushing her hair back as if to draw her whole face up into his kiss.

XII

One afternoon toward the end of August a group of girls sat in a room at Miss Hatchard's in a gay confusion of flags, turkey-red, blue and white paper muslin, harvest sheaves and illuminated scrolls.

North Dormer was preparing for its Old Home Week. That form of sentimental decentralization was still in its early stages, and, precedents being few, and the desire to set an example contagious, the matter had become a subject of prolonged and passionate discussion under Miss Hatchard's roof. The incentive to the celebration had come rather from those who had left North Dormer than from those who had been obliged to stay there, and there was some difficulty in rousing the village to the proper state of enthusiasm. But Miss Hatchard's pale prim drawing-room was the centre of constant comings and goings from Hepburn, Nettleton, Springfield and even more distant cities; and whenever a visitor arrived he was led across the hall, and treated to a glimpse of the group of girls deep in their pretty preparations.

"All the old names . . . all the old names. . . ." Miss Hatchard would be heard, tapping across the hall on her crutches. "Targatt . . . Sollas . . . Fry:

this is Miss Orma Fry sewing the stars on the drapery for the organ-loft. Don't move, girls . . . and this is Miss Ally Hawes, our cleverest needle-woman . . . and Miss Charity Royall making our garlands of evergreen. . . . I like the idea of its all being home-made, don't you? We haven't had to call in any foreign talent: my young cousin Lucius Harney, the architect—you know he's up here preparing a book on Colonial houses—he's taken the whole thing in hand so cleverly; but you must come and see his sketch for the stage we're going to put up in the Town Hall."

One of the first results of the Old Home Week agitation had, in fact, been the reappearance of Lucius Harney in the village street. He had been vaguely spoken of as being not far off, but for some weeks past no one had seen him at North Dormer, and there was a recent report of his having left Creston River, where he was said to have been staying, and gone away from the neighbourhood for good. Soon after Miss Hatchard's return, however, he came back to his old quarters in her house, and began to take a leading part in the planning of the festivities. He threw himself into the idea with extraordinary good-humour, and was so prodigal of sketches, and so inex-haustible in devices, that he gave an immediate impetus to the rather lan-guid movement, and infected the whole village with his enthusiasm.

"Lucius has such a feeling for the past that he has roused us all to a sense of our privileges," Miss Hatchard would say, lingering on the last word, which was a favourite one. And before leading her visitor back to the drawing-room she would repeat, for the hundredth time, that she sup-posed he thought it very bold of little North Dormer to start up and have a Home Week of its own, when so many bigger places hadn't thought of it yet; but that, after all, Associations counted more than the size of the pop-ulation, didn't they? And of course North Dormer was so full of Associa-tions . . . historic, literary (here a filial sigh for Honorius) and ecclesiastical . . . he knew about the old pewter communion service imported from En-gland in 1769, she supposed? And it was so important, in a wealthy materi-alistic age, to set the example of reverting to the old ideals, the family and the homestead, and so on. This peroration usually carried her half-way back across the hall, leaving the girls to return to their interrupted activities.

The day on which Charity Royall was weaving hemlock garlands for the procession was the last before the celebration. When Miss Hatchard called upon the North Dormer maidenhood to collaborate in the festal preparations Charity had at first held aloof; but it had been made clear to her that her non-appearance might excite conjecture, and, reluctantly, she

---

old pewter communion service: typically a pewter flagon, pewter chalices, and a pewter communion plate used in church for the sacrament of communion.

had joined the other workers. The girls, at first shy and embarrassed, and puzzled as to the exact nature of the projected commemoration, had soon become interested in the amusing details of their task, and excited by the notice they received. They would not for the world have missed their afternoons at Miss Hatchard's, and, while they cut out and sewed and draped and pasted, their tongues kept up such an accompaniment to the sewing-machine that Charity's silence sheltered itself unperceived under their chatter.

In spirit she was still almost unconscious of the pleasant stir about her. Since her return to the red house, on the evening of the day when Harney had overtaken her on her way to the Mountain, she had lived at North Dormer as if she were suspended in the void. She had come back there because Harney, after appearing to agree to the impossibility of her doing so, had ended by persuading her that any other course would be madness. She had nothing further to fear from Mr. Royall. Of this she had declared herself sure, though she had failed to add, in his exoneration, that he had twice offered to make her his wife. Her hatred of him made it impossible, at the moment, for her to say anything that might partly excuse him in Harney's eyes.

Harney, however, once satisfied of her security, had found plenty of reasons for urging her to return. The first, and the most unanswerable, was that she had nowhere else to go. But the one on which he laid the greatest stress was that flight would be equivalent to avowal. If—as was almost inevitable—rumours of the scandalous scene at Nettleton should reach North Dormer, how else would her disappearance be interpreted? Her guardian had publicly taken away her character, and she immediately vanished from his house. Seekers after motives could hardly fail to draw an unkind conclusion. But if she came back at once, and was seen leading her usual life, the incident was reduced to its true proportions, as the outbreak of a drunken old man furious at being surprised in disreputable company. People would say that Mr. Royall had insulted his ward to justify himself, and the sordid tale would fall into its place in the chronicle of his obscure debaucheries.

Charity saw the force of the argument; but if she acquiesced it was not so much because of that as because it was Harney's wish. Since that evening in the deserted house she could imagine no reason for doing or not doing anything except the fact that Harney wished or did not wish it. All her tossing contradictory impulses were merged in a fatalistic acceptance of his will. It was not that she felt in him any ascendency of character—there were moments already when she knew she was the stronger—but that all the rest of life had become a mere cloudy rim about the central glory of their passion. Whenever she stopped thinking about that for a moment she felt as she sometimes did after lying on the grass and staring up too long at the sky; her eyes were so full of light that everything about her was a blur.

Each time that Miss Hatchard, in the course of her periodical incursions into the work-room, dropped an allusion to her young cousin, the architect, the effect was the same on Charity. The hemlock garland she was wearing fell to her knees and she sat in a kind of trance. It was so manifestly absurd that Miss Hatchard should talk of Harney in that familiar possessive way, as if she had any claim on him, or knew anything about him. She, Charity Royall, was the only being on earth who really knew him, knew him from the soles of his feet to the rumpled crest of his hair, knew the shifting lights in his eyes, and the inflexions of his voice, and the things he liked and disliked, and everything there was to know about him, as minutely and yet unconsciously as a child knows the walls of the room it wakes up in every morning. It was this fact, which nobody about her guessed, or would have understood, that made her life something apart and inviolable, as if nothing had any power to hurt or disturb her as long as her secret was safe.

The room in which the girls sat was the one which had been Harney's bedroom. He had been sent upstairs, to make room for the Home Week workers; but the furniture had not been moved, and as Charity sat there she had perpetually before her the vision she had looked in on from the midnight garden. The table at which Harney had sat was the one about which the girls were gathered; and her own seat was near the bed on which she had seen him lying. Sometimes, when the others were not looking, she bent over as if to pick up something, and laid her cheek for a moment against the pillow.

Toward sunset the girls disbanded. Their work was done, and the next morning at daylight the draperies and garlands were to be nailed up, and the illuminated scrolls put in place in the Town Hall. The first guests were to drive over from Hepburn in time for the midday banquet under a tent in Miss Hatchard's field; and after that the ceremonies were to begin. Miss Hatchard, pale with fatigue and excitement, thanked her young assistants, and stood in the porch, leaning on her crutches and waving a farewell as she watched them troop away down the street.

Charity had slipped off among the first; but at the gate she heard Ally Hawes calling after her, and reluctantly turned.

"Will you come over now and try on your dress?" Ally asked, looking at her with wistful admiration. "I want to be sure the sleeves don't ruck up the same as they did yesterday."

Charity gazed at her with dazzled eyes. "Oh, it's lovely," she said, and hastened away without listening to Ally's protest. She wanted her dress to be as pretty as the other girls' — wanted it, in fact, to outshine the rest, since she was to take part in the "exercises"—but she had no time just then to fix her mind on such matters. . . .

She sped up the street to the library, of which she had the key about her neck. From the passage at the back she dragged forth a bicycle, and guided it to the edge of the street. She looked about to see if any of the girls were approaching; but they had drifted away together toward the Town Hall, and she sprang into the saddle and turned toward the Creston road. There was an almost continual descent to Creston, and with her feet against the pedals she floated through the still evening air like one of the hawks she had often watched slanting downward on motionless wings. Twenty minutes from the time when she had left Miss Hatchard's door she was turning up the wood-road on which Harney had overtaken her on the day of her flight; and a few minutes afterward she had jumped from her bicycle at the gate of the deserted house.

In the gold-powdered sunset it looked more than ever like some frail shell dried and washed by many seasons; but at the back, whither Charity advanced, drawing her bicycle after her, there were signs of recent habitation. A rough door made of boards hung in the kitchen doorway, and pushing it open she entered a room furnished in primitive camping fashion. In the window was a table, also made of boards, with an earthenware jar holding a big bunch of wild asters, two canvas chairs stood near by, and in one corner was a mattress with a Mexican blanket over it.

The room was empty, and leaning her bicycle against the house Charity clambered up the slope and sat down on a rock under an old apple-tree. The air was perfectly still, and from where she sat she would be able to hear the tinkle of a bicycle-bell a long way down the road. . . .

She was always glad when she got to the little house before Harney. She liked to have time to take in every detail of its secret sweetness—the shadows of the apple-trees swaying on the grass, the old walnuts rounding their domes below the road, the meadows sloping westward in the afternoon light—before his first kiss blotted it all out. Everything unrelated to the hours spent in that tranquil place was as faint as the remembrance of a dream. The only reality was the wondrous unfolding of her new self, the reaching out to the light of all her contracted tendrils. She had lived all her life among people whose sensibilities seemed to have withered for lack of use; and more wonderful, at first, than Harney's endearments were the words that were a part of them. She had always thought of love as something confused and furtive, and he made it as bright and open as the summer air.

On the morrow of the day when she had shown him the way to the deserted house he had packed up and left Creston River for Boston; but at the first station he had jumped off the train with a hand-bag and scrambled up into the hills. For two golden rainless August weeks he had camped in the house, getting eggs and milk from the solitary farm in the valley, where no one knew him, and doing his cooking over a spirit-lamp. He got up every day with the sun, took a plunge in a brown pool he knew of, and spent long hours lying in the scented hemlock-woods above the house, or wandering along the yoke of the Eagle Ridge, far above the misty blue valleys that swept away east and west between the endless hills. And in the afternoon Charity came to him.

With part of what was left of her savings she had hired a bicycle for a month, and every day after dinner, as soon as her guardian started to his office, she hurried to the library, got out her bicycle, and flew down the Creston road. She knew that Mr. Royall, like everyone else in North Dormer, was perfectly aware of her acquisition: possibly he, as well as the rest of the village, knew what use she made of it. She did not care: she felt him to be so powerless that if he had questioned her she would probably have told him the truth. But they had never spoken to each other since the night on the wharf at Nettleton. He had returned to North Dormer only on the third day after that encounter, arriving just as Charity and Verena were sitting down to supper. He had drawn up his chair, taken his napkin from the sideboard drawer, pulled it out of its ring, and seated himself as unconcernedly as if he had come in from his usual afternoon session at Carrick Fry's; and the long habit of the household made it seem almost natural that Charity should not so much as raise her eyes when he entered. She had simply let him understand that her silence was not accidental by leaving the table while he was still eating, and going up without a word to shut herself into her room. After that he formed the habit of talking loudly and genially to Verena whenever Charity was in the room; but otherwise there was no apparent change in their relations.

She did not think connectedly of these things while she sat waiting for Harney, but they remained in her mind as a sullen background against which her short hours with him flamed out like forest fires. Nothing else mattered, neither the good nor the bad, or what might have seemed so before she knew him. He had caught her up and carried her away into a new world, from which, at stated hours, the ghost of her came back to perform certain customary acts, but all so thinly and insubstantially that she sometimes wondered that the people she went about among could see her. . . .

Behind the swarthy Mountain the sun had gone down in waveless gold. From a pasture up the slope a tinkle of cow-bells sounded; a puff of smoke hung over the farm in the valley, trailed on the pure air and was gone. For

---

spirit lamp: a lamp in which alcohol or methylated spirit is burned.

a few minutes, in the clear light that is all shadow, fields and woods were outlined with an unreal precision; then the twilight blotted them out, and the little house turned gray and spectral under its wizened apple-branches.

Charity's heart contracted. The first fall of night after a day of radiance often gave her a sense of hidden menace: it was like looking out over the world as it would be when love had gone from it. She wondered if some day she would sit in that same place and watch in vain for her lover. . . .

His bicycle-bell sounded down the lane, and in a minute she was at the gate and his eyes were laughing in hers. They walked back through the long grass, and pushed open the door behind the house. The room at first seemed quite dark and they had to grope their way in hand in hand. Through the window-frame the sky looked light by contrast, and above the black mass of asters in the earthern jar one white star glimmered like a moth.

"There was such a lot to do at the last minute," Harney was explaining, "and I had to drive down to Creston to meet someone who has come to stay with my cousin for the show."

He had his arms about her, and his kisses were in her hair and on her lips. Under his touch things deep down in her struggled to the light and sprang up like flowers in sunshine. She twisted her fingers into his, and they sat down side by side on the improvised couch. She hardly heard his excuses for being late: in his absence a thousand doubts tormented her, but as soon as he appeared she ceased to wonder where he had come from, what had delayed him, who had kept him from her. It seemed as if the places he had been in, and the people he had been with, must cease to exist when he left them, just as her own life was suspended in his absence.

He continued, now, to talk to her volubly and gaily, deploring his lateness, grumbling at the demands on his time, and good-humouredly mimicking Miss Hatchard's benevolent agitation. "She hurried off Miles to ask Mr. Royall to speak at the Town Hall tomorrow: I didn't know till it was done." Charity was silent, and he added: "After all, perhaps it's just as well. No one else could have done it."

Charity made no answer: She did not care what part her guardian played in the morrow's ceremonies. Like all the other figures peopling her meagre world he had grown non-existent to her. She had even put off hating him.

"Tomorrow I shall only see you from far off," Harney continued. "But in the evening there'll be the dance in the Town Hall. Do you want me to promise not to dance with any other girl?"

Any other girl? Were there any others? She had forgotten even that peril, so enclosed did he and she seem in their secret world. Her heart gave a frightened jerk.

"Yes, promise."

He laughed and took her in his arms. "You goose—not even if they're hideous?"

He pushed the hair from her forehead, bending her face back, as his way was, and leaning over so that his head loomed black between her eyes and the paleness of the sky, in which the white star floated . . .

Side by side they sped back along the dark wood-road to the village. A late moon was rising, full orbed and fiery, turning the mountain ranges from fluid gray to a massive blackness, and making the upper sky so light that the stars looked as faint as their own reflections in water. At the edge of the wood, half a mile from North Dormer, Harney jumped from his bicycle, took Charity in his arms for a last kiss, and then waited while she went on alone.

They were later than usual, and instead of taking the bicycle to the library she propped it against the back of the wood-shed and entered the kitchen of the red house. Verena sat there alone; when Charity came in she looked at her with mild impenetrable eyes and then took a plate and a glass of milk from the shelf and set them silently on the table. Charity nodded her thanks, and sitting down, fell hungrily upon her piece of pie and emptied the glass. Her face burned with her quick flight through the night, and her eyes were dazzled by the twinkle of the kitchen lamp. She felt like a night-bird suddenly caught and caged.

"He ain't come back since supper," Verena said. "He's down to the Hall."

Charity took no notice. Her soul was still winging through the forest. She washed her plate and tumbler, and then felt her way up the dark stairs. When she opened her door a wonder arrested her. Before going out she had closed her shutters against the afternoon heat, but they had swung partly open, and a bar of moonlight, crossing the room, rested on her bed and showed a dress of China silk laid out on it in virgin whiteness. Charity had spent more than she could afford on the dress, which was to surpass those of all the other girls; she had wanted to let North Dormer see that she was worthy of Harney's admiration. Above the dress, folded on the pillow, was the white veil which the young women who took part in the exercises were to wear under a wreath of asters; and beside the veil a pair of slim white satin shoes that Ally had produced from an old trunk in which she stored mysterious treasures.

Charity stood gazing at all the outspread whiteness. It recalled a vision that had come to her in the night after her first meeting with Harney. She no longer had such visions . . . warmer splendours had displaced them . . . but it was stupid of Ally to have paraded all those white things on her bed, exactly as Hattie Targatt's wedding dress from Springfield had been spread out for the neighbours to see when she married Tom Fry. . . .

Charity took up the satin shoes and looked at them curiously. By day, no doubt, they would appear a little worn, but in the moonlight they seemed carved of ivory. She sat down on the floor to try them on and they fitted her perfectly, though when she stood up she lurched a little on the high heels. She looked down at her feet, which the graceful mould of the slippers had marvellously arched and narrowed. She had never seen such shoes before, even in the shop-windows at Nettleton . . . never, except . . . yes, once, she had noticed a pair of the same shape on Annabel Balch.

A blush of mortification swept over her. Ally sometimes sewed for Miss Balch when that brilliant being descended on North Dormer, and no doubt she picked up presents of cast-off clothing: the treasures in the mysterious trunk all came from the people she worked for; there could be no doubt that the white slippers were Annabel Balch's. . . .

As she stood there, staring down moodily at her feet, she heard the triple click-click-click of a bicycle-bell under her window. It was Harney's secret signal as he passed on his way home. She stumbled to the window on her high heels, flung open the shutters and leaned out. He waved to her and sped by, his black shadow dancing merrily ahead of him down the empty moonlit road; and she leaned there watching him till he vanished under the Hatchard spruces.

XIII

The Town Hall was crowded and exceedingly hot. As Charity marched into it third in the white muslin file headed by Orma Fry, she was conscious mainly of the brilliant effect of the wreathed columns framing the green-carpeted stage toward which she was moving; and of the unfamiliar faces turning from the front rows to watch the advance of the procession.

But it was all a bewildering blur of eyes and colours till she found herself standing at the back of the stage, her great bunch of asters and golden-rod held well in front of her, and answering the nervous glance of Lambert Sollas, the organist from Mr. Miles's church, who had come up from Nettleton to play the harmonium and sat behind it, his conductor's eye running over the fluttered girls.

A moment later Mr. Miles, pink and twinkling, emerged from the background, as if buoyed up on his broad white gown, and briskly dominated the bowed heads in the front rows. He prayed energetically and briefly and then retired, and a fierce nod from Lambert Sollas warned the girls that they were to follow at once with "Home, Sweet Home." It was a joy to Charity to sing: it seemed as though, for the first time, her secret rapture might burst from her and flash its defiance at the world. All the glow in her blood, the breath of the summer earth, the rustle of the forest, the fresh call of birds at sunrise, and the brooding midday languors, seemed to pass into her untrained voice, lifted and led by the sustaining chorus.

And then suddenly the song was over, and after an uncertain pause, during which Miss Hatchard's pearl-grey gloves started a furtive signalling down the hall, Mr. Royall, emerging in turn, ascended the steps of the stage and appeared behind the flower-wreathed desk. He passed close to Charity, and she noticed that his gravely set face wore the look of majesty that used to awe and fascinate her childhood. His frock-coat had been carefully brushed and ironed, and the ends of his narrow black tie were so nearly even that the tying must have cost him a protracted struggle. His appearance struck her all the more because it was the first time she had looked him full in the face since the night at Nettleton, and nothing in his grave and impressive demeanour revealed a trace of the lamentable figure on the wharf.

He stood a moment behind the desk, resting his finger-tips against it, and bending slightly toward his audience; then he straightened himself and began.

At first she paid no heed to what he was saying: only fragments of sentences, sonorous quotations, allusions to illustrious men, including the obligatory tribute to Honorius Hatchard, drifted past her inattentive ears. She was trying to discover Harney among the notable people in the front row; but he was nowhere near Miss Hatchard, who, crowned by a pearl-grey hat that matched her gloves, sat just below the desk, supported by Mrs. Miles and an important-looking unknown lady. Charity was near one end of the stage, and from where she sat the other end of the first row of seats was cut off by the screen of foliage masking the harmonium. The effort to see Harney around the corner of the screen, or through its interstices, made her unconscious of everything else; but the effort was unsuccessful, and gradually she found her attention arrested by her guardian's discourse.

She had never heard him speak in public before, but she was familiar with the rolling music of his voice when he read aloud, or held forth to the selectmen about the stove at Carrick Fry's. Today his inflections were richer and graver than she had ever known them: he spoke slowly, with pauses that seemed to invite his hearers to silent participation in his thought; and Charity perceived a light of response in their faces.

He was nearing the end of his address . . . "Most of you," he said, "most of you who have returned here today, to take contact with this little place for a brief hour, have come only on a pious pilgrimage, and will go back presently to busy cities and lives full of larger duties. But that is not the only way of coming back to North Dormer. Some of us, who went out from here in our youth . . . went out, like you, to busy cities and larger duties . . . have come back in another way—come back for good. I am one of those, as many of you know. . . ." He paused, and there was a sense of suspense in the listening hall. "My history is without interest, but it has its lesson: not so much for those of you who have already made your lives in other places, as for the young men who are perhaps planning even now to leave these quiet hills and go down into the struggle. Things they cannot foresee may send some of those young men back some day to the little township and the old homestead: they may come back for good. . . ." He looked about him, and repeated gravely: "For *good*. There's the point I want to make . . . North Dormer is a poor little place, almost lost in a mighty landscape: perhaps, by this time, it might have been a bigger place, and more in scale with the landscape, if those who had to come back had come with that feeling in their minds—that they wanted to come back for *good* . . . and not for bad . . . or just for indifference. . . .

"Gentlemen, let us look at things as they are. Some of us have come back to our native town because we'd failed to get on elsewhere. One way or other, things had gone wrong with us . . . what we'd dreamed of hadn't come true. But the fact that we had failed elsewhere is no reason why we should fail here. Our very experiments in larger places, even if they were unsuccessful, ought to have helped us to make North Dormer a larger place . . . and you young men who are preparing even now to follow the call of ambition, and turn your back on the old homes—well, let me say this to you, that if ever you do come back to them it's worth while to come back to them for their good. . . . And to do that, you must keep on loving them while you're away from them; and even if you come back against your will—and thinking it's all a bitter mistake of Fate or Providence—you must try to make the best of it, and to make the best of your old town; and after a while—well, ladies and gentlemen, I give you my recipe for what it's worth; after a while, I believe you'll be able to say, as I can say today: 'I'm glad I'm here.' Believe me, all of you, the best way to help the places we live in is to be glad we live there."

He stopped, and a murmur of emotion and surprise ran through the audience. It was not in the least what they had expected, but it moved them more than what they had expected would have moved them. "Hear, hear!" a voice cried out in the middle of the hall. An outburst of cheers caught up the cry, and as they subsided Charity heard Mr. Miles saying to someone near him: "That was a *man* talking——" He wiped his spectacles.

Mr. Royall had stepped back from the desk, and taken his seat in the row of chairs in front of the harmonium. A dapper white-haired gentleman—

a distant Hatchard—succeeded him behind the golden-rod, and began to say beautiful things about the old oaken bucket, patient white-haired mothers, and where the boys used to go nutting . . . and Charity began again to search for Harney. . . .

Suddenly Mr. Royall pushed back his seat, and one of the maple branches in front of the harmonium collapsed with a crash. It uncovered the end of the first row and in one of the seats Charity saw Harney, and in the next a lady whose face was turned toward him, and almost hidden by the brim of her drooping hat. Charity did not need to see the face. She knew at a glance the slim figure, the fair hair heaped up under the hat-brim, the long pale wrinkled gloves with bracelets slipping over them. At the fall of the branch Miss Balch turned her head toward the stage, and in her pretty thin-lipped smile there lingered the reflection of something her neighbour had been whispering to her. . . .

Someone came forward to replace the fallen branch, and Miss Balch and Harney were once more hidden. But to Charity the vision of their two faces had blotted out everything. In a flash they had shown her the bare reality of her situation. Behind the frail screen of her lover's caresses was the whole inscrutable mystery of his life: his relations with other people—with other women—his opinions, his prejudices, his principles, the net of influences and interests and ambitions in which every man's life is entangled. Of all these she knew nothing, except what he had told her of his architectural aspirations. She had always dimly guessed him to be in touch with important people, involved in complicated relations—but she felt it all to be so far beyond her understanding that the whole subject hung like a luminous mist on the farthest verge of her thoughts. In the foreground, hiding all else, there was the glow of his presence, the light and shadow of his face, the way his short-sighted eyes, at her approach, widened and deepened as if to draw her down into them; and, above all, the flush of youth and tenderness in which his words enclosed her.

Now she saw him detached from her, drawn back into the unknown, and whispering to another girl things that provoked the same smile of mischievous complicity he had so often called to her own lips. The feeling possessing her was not one of jealousy: she was too sure of his love. It was rather a terror of the unknown, of all the mysterious attractions that must even now be dragging him away from her, and of her own powerlessness to contend with them.

She had given him all she had—but what was it compared to the other gifts life held for him? She understood now the case of girls like herself to whom this kind of thing happened. They gave all they had, but their all was not enough: it could not buy more than a few moments. . . .

The heat had grown suffocating—she felt it descend on her in smothering waves, and the faces in the crowded hall began to dance like the pictures
flashed on the screen at Nettleton. For an instant Mr. Royall's countenance
detached itself from the general blur. He had resumed his place in front of
the harmonium, and sat close to her, his eyes on her face; and his look
seemed to pierce to the very centre of her confused sensations. . . . A feeling of physical sickness rushed over her—and then deadly apprehension.
The light of the fiery hours in the little house swept back on her in a glare
of fear. . . .

She forced herself to look away from her guardian, and became aware
that the oratory of the Hatchard cousin had ceased, and that Mr. Miles was
again flapping his wings. Fragments of his peroration floated through her
bewildered brain. . . . "A rich harvest of hallowed memories. . . . A
sanctified hour to which, in moments of trial, your thoughts will prayer-
fully return. . . . And now, O Lord, let us humbly and fervently give thanks
for this blessed day of reunion, here in the old home to which we have
come back from so far. Preserve it to us, O Lord, in times to come, in all its
homely sweetness—in the kindliness and wisdom of its old people, in the
courage and industry of its young men, in the piety and purity of this group
of innocent girls——" He flapped a white wing in their direction, and at the
same moment Lambert Sollas, with his fierce nod, struck the opening bars
of "Auld Lang Syne." . . . Charity stared straight ahead of her and then,
dropping her flowers, fell face downward at Mr. Royall's feet.

XIV

North Dormer's celebration naturally included the villages attached to its
township, and the festivities were to radiate over the whole group, from
Dormer and the two Crestons to Hamblin, the lonely hamlet on the north
slope of the Mountain where the first snow always fell. On the third day
there were speeches and ceremonies at Creston and Creston River; on
the fourth the principal performers were to be driven in buck-boards to
Dormer and Hamblin.

It was on the fourth day that Charity returned for the first time to the
little house. She had not seen Harney alone since they had parted at the
wood's edge the night before the celebrations began. In the interval she

---

buck-boards: four-wheeled horse-drawn vehicles with floors made of long springy
boards.

had passed through many moods, but for the moment the terror which had seized her in the Town Hall had faded to the edge of consciousness. She had fainted because the hall was stiflingly hot, and because the speakers had gone on and on. . . . Several other people had been affected by the heat, and had had to leave before the exercises were over. There had been thunder in the air all the afternoon, and everyone said afterward that something ought to have been done to ventilate the hall. . . .

At the dance that evening—where she had gone reluctantly, and only because she feared to stay away, she had sprung back into instant reassurance. As soon as she entered she had seen Harney waiting for her, and he had come up with kind gay eyes, and swept her off in a waltz. Her feet were full of music, and though her only training had been with the village youths she had no difficulty in tuning her steps to his. As they circled about the floor all her vain fears dropped from her, and she even forgot that she was probably dancing in Annabel Balch's slippers.

When the waltz was over Harney, with a last hand-clasp, left her to meet Miss Hatchard and Miss Balch, who were just entering. Charity had a moment of anguish as Miss Balch appeared; but it did not last. The triumphant fact of her own greater beauty, and of Harney's sense of it, swept her apprehensions aside. Miss Balch, in an unbecoming dress, looked sallow and pinched, and Charity fancied there was a worried expression in her pale-lashed eyes. She took a seat near Miss Hatchard and it was presently apparent that she did not mean to dance. Charity did not dance often either. Harney explained to her that Miss Hatchard had begged him to give each of the other girls a turn; but he went through the form of asking Charity's permission each time he led one out, and that gave her a sense of secret triumph even completer than when she was whirling about the room with him. . . .

She was thinking of all this as she waited for him in the deserted house. The late afternoon was sultry, and she had tossed aside her hat and stretched herself at full length on the Mexican blanket because it was cooler indoors than under the trees. She lay with her arms folded beneath her head, gazing out at the shaggy shoulder of the Mountain. The sky behind it was full of the splintered glories of the descending sun, and before long she expected to hear Harney's bicycle-bell in the lane. He had bicycled to Hamblin, instead of driving there with his cousin and her friends, so that he might be able to make his escape earlier and stop on the way back at the deserted house, which was on the road to Hamblin. They had smiled together at the joke of hearing the crowded buck-boards roll by on the return, while they lay close in their hiding above the road. Such childish triumphs still gave her a sense of reckless security.

Nevertheless she had not wholly forgotten the vision of fear that had opened before her in the Town Hall. The sense of lastingness was gone from her and every moment with Harney would now be ringed with doubt.

The Mountain was turning purple against a fiery sunset from which it seemed to be divided by a knife-edge of quivering light; and above this wall of flame the whole sky was a pure pale green, like some cold mountain lake in shadow. Charity lay gazing up at it, and watching for the first white star. . . .

Her eyes were still fixed on the upper reaches of the sky when she became aware that a shadow had flitted across the glory-flooded room: it must have been Harney passing the window against the sunset. . . . She half raised herself, and then dropped back on her folded arms. The combs had slipped from her hair, and it trailed in a rough dark rope across her breast. She lay quite still, a sleepy smile on her lips, her indolent lids half shut. There was a fumbling at the padlock and she called out: "Have you slipped the chain?" The door opened, and Mr. Royall walked into the room.

She started up, sitting back against the cushions, and they looked at each other without speaking. Then Mr. Royall closed the door-latch and advanced a few steps.

Charity jumped to her feet. "What have you come for?" she stammered.

The last glare of the sunset was on her guardian's face, which looked ash-coloured in the yellow radiance.

"Because I knew you were here," he answered simply.

She had become conscious of the hair hanging loose across her breast, and it seemed as though she could not speak to him till she had set herself in order. She groped for her comb, and tried to fasten up the coil. Mr. Royall silently watched her.

"Charity," he said, "he'll be here in a minute. Let me talk to you first."

"You've got no right to talk to me. I can do what I please."

"Yes. What is it you mean to do?"

"I needn't answer that, or anything else."

He had glanced away, and stood looking curiously about the illuminated room. Purple asters and red-maple-leaves filled the jar on the table; on a shelf against the wall stood a lamp, the kettle, a little pile of cups and saucers. The canvas chairs were grouped about the table.

"So this is where you meet," he said.

His tone was quiet and controlled, and the fact disconcerted her. She had been ready to give him violence for violence, but this calm acceptance of things as they were left her without a weapon.

"See here, Charity—you're always telling me I've got no rights over you. There might be two ways of looking at that—but I ain't going to argue it.

All I know is I raised you as good as I could, and meant fairly by you always—except once, for a bad half-hour. There's no justice in weighing that half-hour against the rest, and you know it. If you hadn't, you wouldn't have gone on living under my roof. Seems to me the fact of your doing that gives me some sort of a right; the right to try and keep you out of trouble. I'm not asking you to consider any other."

She listened in silence, and then gave a slight laugh. "Better wait till I'm in trouble," she said.

He paused a moment, as if weighing her words. "Is that all your answer?"

"Yes, that's all."

"Well—I'll wait."

He turned away slowly, but as he did so the thing she had been waiting for happened; the door opened again and Harney entered.

He stopped short with a face of astonishment, and then, quickly controlling himself, went up to Mr. Royall with a frank look.

"Have you come to see me, sir?" he said coolly, throwing his cap on the table with an air of proprietorship.

Mr. Royall again looked slowly about the room; then his eyes turned to the young man.

"Is this your house?" he inquired.

Harney laughed: "Well—as much as it's anybody's. I come here to sketch occasionally."

"And to receive Miss Royall's visits?"

"When she does me the honour——"

"Is this the home you propose to bring her to when you get married?"

There was an immense and oppressive silence. Charity, quivering with anger, started forward, and then stood silent, too humbled for speech. Harney's eyes had dropped under the old man's gaze; but he raised them presently, and looking steadily at Mr. Royall, said: "Miss Royall is not a child. Isn't it rather absurd to talk of her as if she were? I believe she considers herself free to come and go as she pleases, without any questions from anyone." He paused and added: "I'm ready to answer any she wishes to ask me."

Mr. Royall turned to her. "Ask him when he's going to marry you, then——" There was another silence, and he laughed in his turn—a broken laugh, with a scraping sound in it. "You darsn't!" he shouted out with sudden passion. He went close up to Charity, his right arm lifted, not in menace but in tragic exhortation.

"You darsn't, and you know it—and you know why!" He swung back again upon the young man. "And you know why you ain't asked her to marry you, and why you don't mean to. It's because you hadn't need to; nor any other man either. I'm the only one that was fool enough not to know that; and I guess nobody'll repeat my mistake—not in Eagle County, anyhow. They all know what she is, and what she came from. They all know her mother was a woman of the town from Nettleton, that followed one of those Mountain fellows up to his place and lived there with him like a heathen. I saw her there sixteen years ago, when I went to bring this child down. I went to save her from the kind of life her mother was leading— but I'd better have left her in the kennel she came from. . . ." He paused and stared darkly at the two young people, and out beyond them, at the menacing Mountain with its rim of fire; then he sat down beside the table on which they had so often spread their rustic supper, and covered his face with his hands. Harney leaned in the window, a frown on his face: he was twirling between his fingers a small package that dangled from a loop of string. . . . Charity heard Mr. Royall draw a hard breath or two, and his shoulders shook a little. Presently he stood up and walked across the room. He did not look again at the young people: they saw him feel his way to the door and fumble for the latch; and then he went out into the darkness.

After he had gone there was a long silence. Charity waited for Harney to speak; but he seemed at first not to find anything to say. At length he broke out irrelevantly: "I wonder how he found out?"

She made no answer and he tossed down the package he had been holding, and went up to her.

"I'm so sorry, dear . . . that this should have happened. . . ."

She threw her head back proudly. "I ain't ever been sorry—not a minute!"

"No."

She waited to be caught into his arms, but he turned away from her irresolutely. The last glow was gone from behind the Mountain. Everything in the room had turned grey and indistinct, and an autumnal dampness crept up from the hollow below the orchard, laying its cold touch on their flushed faces. Harney walked the length of the room, and then turned back and sat down at the table.

"Come," he said imperiously.

She sat down beside him, and he untied the string about the package and spread out a pile of sandwiches.

"I stole them from the love-feast at Hamblin," he said with a laugh, pushing them over to her. She laughed too, and took one, and began to eat.

"Didn't you make the tea?"

"No," she said. "I forgot——"

Eagle County: the fictional county in which North Dormer and other small towns in the novel are set.

"Oh, well—it's too late to boil the water now." He said nothing more, and sitting opposite to each other they went on silently eating the sandwiches. Darkness had descended in the little room, and Harney's face was a dim blur to Charity. Suddenly he leaned across the table and laid his hand on hers.

"I shall have to go off for a while—a month or two, perhaps—to arrange some things; and then I'll come back . . . and we'll get married."

His voice seemed like a stranger's: nothing was left in it of the vibrations she knew. Her hand lay inertly under his, and she left it there, and raised her head, trying to answer him. But the words died in her throat. They sat motionless, in their attitude of confident endearment, as if some strange death had surprised them. At length Harney sprang to his feet with a slight shiver. "God! it's damp—we couldn't have come here much longer." He went to the shelf, took down a tin candle-stick and lit the candle; then he propped an unhinged shutter against the empty window-frame and put the candle on the table. It threw up a queer shadow on his frowning forehead, and made the smile on his lips a grimace.

"But it's been good, though, hasn't it, Charity? . . . What's the matter—why do you stand there staring at me? Haven't the days here been good?" He went up to her and caught her to his breast. "And there'll be others—lots of others . . . jollier . . . even jollier . . . won't there, darling?"

He turned her head back, feeling for the curve of her throat below the ear, and kissing here there, and on the hair and eyes and lips. She clung to him desperately, and as he drew her to his knees on the couch she felt as if they were being sucked down together into some bottomless abyss.

XV

That night, as usual, they said good-bye at the wood's edge.

Harney was to leave the next morning early. He asked Charity to say nothing of their plans till his return, and, strangely even to herself, she was glad of the postponement. A leaden weight of shame hung on her, benumbing every other sensation, and she bade him good-bye with hardly a sign of emotion. His reiterated promises to return seemed almost wounding. She had no doubt that he intended to come back; her doubts were far deeper and less definable.

Since the fanciful vision of the future that had flitted through her imagination at their first meeting she had hardly ever thought of his marrying her. She had not had to put the thought from her mind; it had not been there. If ever she looked ahead she felt instinctively that the gulf between them was too deep, and that the bridge their passion had flung across it was as insubstantial as a rainbow. But she seldom looked ahead; each day was so rich that it absorbed her. . . . Now her first feeling was that everything would be different, and that she herself would be a different being to Harney. Instead of remaining separate and absolute, she would be compared with other people, and unknown things would be expected of her. She was too proud to be afraid, but the freedom of her spirit drooped. . . .

Harney had not fixed any date for his return; he had said he would have to look about first, and settle things. He had promised to write as soon as there was anything definite to say, and had left her his address, and asked her to write also. But the address frightened her. It was in New York, at a club with a long name in Fifth Avenue: it seemed to raise an insurmountable barrier between them. Once or twice, in the first days, she got out a sheet of paper, and sat looking at it, and trying to think what to say; but she had the feeling that her letter would never reach its destination. She had never written to anyone farther away than Hepburn.

Harney's first letter came after he had been gone about ten days. It was tender but grave, and bore no resemblance to the gay little notes he had sent her by the freckled boy from Creston River. He spoke positively of his intention of coming back, but named no date, and reminded Charity of their agreement that their plans should not be divulged till he had had time to "settle things." When that would be he could not yet foresee; but she could count on his returning as soon as the way was clear.

She read the letter with a strange sense of its coming from immeasurable distances and having lost most of its meaning on the way; and in reply she sent him a coloured post-card of Creston Falls, on which she wrote: "With love from Charity." She felt the pitiful inadequacy of this, and understood, with a sense of despair, that in her inability to express herself she must give him an impression of coldness and reluctance; but she could not help it. She could not forget that he had never spoken to her of marriage till Mr. Royall had forced the word from his lips; though she had not had the strength to shake off the spell that bound her to him she had lost all spontaneity of feeling, and seemed to herself to be passively awaiting a fate she could not avert.

She had not seen Mr. Royall on her return to the red house. The morning after her parting from Harney, when she came down from her room, Verena told her that her guardian had gone off to Worcester and Portland. It was the time of year when he usually reported to the insurance agencies

---

Worcester . . . Portland: Worcester is a city in east central Massachusetts; Portland is a coastal city in southern Maine.

he represented, and there was nothing unusual in his departure except its suddenness. She thought little about him, except to be glad he was not there. . . .

She kept to herself for the first days, while North Dormer was recovering from its brief plunge into publicity, and the subsiding agitation left her unnoticed. But the faithful Ally could not be long avoided. For the first few days after the close of the Old Home Week festivities Charity escaped her by roaming the hills all day when she was not at her post in the library; but after that a period of rain set in, and one pouring afternoon, Ally, sure that she would find her friend indoors, came around to the red house with her sewing.

The two girls sat upstairs in Charity's room. Charity, her idle hands in her lap, was sunk in a kind of leaden dream, through which she was only half-conscious of Ally, who sat opposite her in a low rush-bottomed chair, her work pinned to her knee, and her thin lips pursed up as she bent above it.

"It was my idea running a ribbon through the gauging," she said proudly, drawing back to contemplate the blouse she was trimming. "It's for Miss Balch: she was awfully pleased." She paused and then added, with a queer tremor in her piping voice: "I darsn't have told her I got the idea from one I saw on Julia."

Charity raised her eyes listlessly. "Do you still see Julia sometimes?"

Ally reddened, as if the allusion had escaped her unintentionally. "Oh, it was a long time ago I seen her with those gaugings. . . ."

Silence fell again, and Ally presently continued: "Miss Balch left me a whole lot of things to do over this time."

"Why—has she gone?" Charity inquired with an inner start of apprehension.

"Didn't you know? She went off the morning after they had the celebration at Hamblin. I seen her drive by early with Mr. Harney."

There was another silence, measured by the steady tick of the rain against the window, and, at intervals, by the snipping sound of Ally's scissors.

Ally gave a meditative laugh. "Do you know what she told me before she went away? She told me she was going to send for me to come over to Springfield and make some things for her wedding."

Charity again lifted her heavy lids and stared at Ally's pale pointed face, which moved to and fro above her moving fingers.

"Is she going to get married?"

Ally let the blouse sink to her knee, and sat gazing at it. Her lips seemed suddenly dry, and she moistened them a little with her tongue.

"Why, I presume so . . . from what she said. . . . Didn't you know?"

"Why should I know?"

Ally did not answer. She bent above the blouse, and began picking out a basting thread with the point of the scissors.

"Why should I know?" Charity repeated harshly.

"I didn't know but what . . . folks here say she's engaged to Mr. Harney."

Charity stood up with a laugh, and stretched her arms lazily above her head.

"If all the people got married that folks say are going to you'd have your time full making wedding-dresses," she said ironically.

"Why—don't you believe it?" Ally ventured.

"It would not make it true if I did—nor prevent it if I didn't."

"That's so. . . . I only know I seen her crying the night of the party because her dress didn't set right. That was why she wouldn't dance any. . . ."

Charity stood absently gazing down at the lacy garment on Ally's knee. Abruptly she stooped and snatched it up.

"Well, I guess she won't dance in this either," she said with sudden violence; and grasping the blouse in her strong young hands she tore it in two and flung the tattered bits to the floor.

"Oh, Charity——" Ally cried, springing up. For a long interval the two girls faced each other across the ruined garment. Ally burst into tears.

"Oh, what'll I say to her? What'll I do? It was real lace!" she wailed between her piping sobs.

Charity glared at her unrelentingly. "You'd oughtn't to have brought it here," she said, breathing quickly. "I hate other people's clothes—it's just as if they was there themselves." The two stared at each other again over this avowal, till Charity brought out, in a gasp of anguish: "Oh, go—go—go—or I'll hate you too. . . ."

When Ally left her, she fell sobbing across her bed.

The long storm was followed by a north-west gale, and when it was over, the hills took on their first umber tints, the sky grew more densely blue, and the big white clouds lay against the hills like snow-banks. The first crisp maple-leaves began to spin across Miss Hatchard's lawn, and the Virginia creeper on the Memorial splashed the white porch with scarlet. It was a golden triumphant September. Day by day the flame of the Virginia creeper spread to the hillsides in wider waves of carmine and crimson, the larches glowed like the thin yellow halo about a fire, the maples blazed and smouldered, and the black hemlocks turned to indigo against the incandescence of the forest.

The nights were cold, with a dry glitter of stars so high up that they seemed smaller and more vivid. Sometimes, as Charity lay sleepless on her bed through the long hours, she felt as though she were bound to those wheeling fires and swinging with them around the great black vault. At night she planned many things . . . it was then she wrote to Harney. But the letters were never put on paper, for she did not know how to express what she wanted to tell him. So she waited. Since her talk with Ally she had felt sure that Harney was engaged to Annabel Balch, and that the process of "settling things" would involve the breaking of this tie. Her first rage of jealousy over, she felt no fear on this score. She was still sure that Harney would come back, and she was equally sure that, for the moment at least, it was she whom he loved and not Miss Balch. Yet the girl, no less, remained a rival, since she represented all the things that Charity felt herself most incapable of understanding or achieving. Annabel Balch was, if not the girl Harney ought to marry, at least the kind of girl it would be natural for him to marry. Charity had never been able to picture herself as his wife; had never been able to arrest the vision and follow it out in its daily consequences; but she could perfectly imagine Annabel Balch in that relation to him.

The more she thought of these things the more the sense of fatality weighed on her: she felt the uselessness of struggling against the circumstances. She had never known how to adapt herself; she could only break and tear and destroy. The scene with Ally had left her stricken with shame at her own childish savagery. What would Harney have thought if he had witnessed it? But when she turned the incident over in her puzzled mind she could not imagine what a civilized person would have done in her place. She felt herself too unequally pitted against unknown forces. . . .

At length this feeling moved her to sudden action. She took a sheet of letter paper from Mr. Royall's office, and sitting by the kitchen lamp, one night after Verena had gone to bed, began her first letter to Harney. It was very short:

I want you should marry Annabel Balch if you promised to. I think maybe you were afraid I'd feel too bad about it. I feel I'd rather you acted right.

Your loving

CHARITY.

She posted the letter early the next morning, and for a few days her heart felt strangely light. Then she began to wonder why she received no answer.

One day as she sat alone in the library pondering these things the walls of books began to spin around her, and the rosewood desk to rock under her elbows. The dizziness was followed by a wave of nausea like that she had felt on the day of the exercises in the Town Hall. But the Town Hall had been crowded and stiflingly hot, and the library was empty, and so chilly that she had kept on her jacket. Five minutes before she had felt perfectly well; and now it seemed as if she were going to die. The bit of lace at which she still languidly worked dropped from her fingers, and the steel crochet hook clattered to the floor. She pressed her temples hard between her damp hands, steadying herself against the desk while the wave of sickness swept over her. Little by little it subsided, and after a few minutes she stood up, shaken and terrified, groped for her hat, and stumbled out into the air. But the whole sunlit autumn whirled, reeled and roared around her as she dragged herself along the interminable length of the road home.

As she approached the red house she saw a buggy standing at the door, and her heart gave a leap. But it was only Mr. Royall who got out, his travelling-bag in hand. He saw her coming, and waited in the porch. She was conscious that he was looking at her intently, as if there was something strange in her appearance, and she threw back her head with a desperate effort at ease. Their eyes met, and she said: "You back?" as if nothing had happened, and he answered: "Yes, I'm back," and walked in ahead of her, pushing open the door of his office. She climbed to her room, every step of the stairs holding her fast as if her feet were lined with glue.

Two days later, she descended from the train at Nettleton, and walked out of the station into the dusty square. The brief interval of cold weather was over, and the day was as soft, and almost as hot, as when she and Harney had emerged on the same scene on the Fourth of July. In the square the same broken-down hacks and carry-alls stood drawn up in a despondent line, and the lank horses with fly-nets over their withers swayed their heads drearily to and fro. She recognized the staring signs over the eating-houses and billiard saloons, and the long lines of wires on lofty poles tapering down the main street to the park at its other end. Taking the way the wires pointed, she went on hastily, with bent head, till she reached a wide transverse street with a brick building at the corner. She crossed this street and glanced furtively up at the front of the brick building; then she returned, and entered a door opening on a flight of steep brass-rimmed stairs. On the second landing she rang a bell, and a mulatto girl with a bushy head and a frilled apron let her into a hall where a stuffed fox on his hind legs proffered a brass card-tray to visitors. At the back of the hall was a glazed door marked: "Office." After waiting a few minutes in a handsomely furnished room, with plush sofas surmounted by large gold-framed photographs of showy young women, Charity was shown into the office. . . .

When she came out of the glazed door Dr. Merkle followed, and led her into another room, smaller, and still more crowded with plush and gold frames. Dr. Merkle was a plump woman with small bright eyes, an im-

---

carry-alls: light, covered, horse-drawn carriages for four or more persons.

mense mass of black hair coming down low on her forehead, and unnaturally white and even teeth. She wore a rich black dress, with gold chains and charms hanging from her bosom. Her hands were large and smooth, and quick in all their movements; and she smelt of musk and carbolic acid

She smiled on Charity with all her faultless teeth. "Sit down, my dear. Wouldn't you like a little drop of something to pick you up? . . . No. . . . Well, just lay back a minute then. . . . There's nothing to be done just yet; but in about a month, if you'll step round again . . . I could take you right into my own house for two or three days, and there wouldn't be a mite of trouble. Mercy me! The next time you'll know better'n to fret like this. . . ."

Charity gazed at her with widening eyes. This woman with the false hair, the false teeth, the false murderous smile—what was she offering her but immunity from some unthinkable crime? Charity, till then, had been conscious only of a vague self-disgust and a frightening physical distress; now, of a sudden, there came to her the grave surprise of motherhood. She had come to this dreadful place because she knew of no other way of making sure that she was not mistaken about her state; and the woman had taken her for a miserable creature like Julia. . . . The thought was so horrible that she sprang up, white and shaking, one of her great rushes of anger sweeping over her.

Dr. Merkle, still smiling, also rose. "Why do you run off in such a hurry? You can stretch out right here on my sofa. . . ." She paused, and her smile grew more motherly. "Afterwards—if there's been any talk at home, and you want to get away for a while. . . I have a lady friend in Boston who's looking for a companion . . . you're the very one to suit her, my dear. . . ."

Charity had reached the door. "I don't want to stay. I don't want to come back here," she stammered, her hand on the knob; but with a swift movement, Dr. Merkle edged her from the threshold.

"Oh, very well. Five dollars, please."

Charity looked helplessly at the doctor's tight lips and rigid face. Her last savings had gone in repaying Ally for the cost of Miss Balch's ruined blouse, and she had had to borrow four dollars from her friend to pay for her railway ticket and cover the doctor's fee. It had never occurred to her that medical advice could cost more than two dollars.

"I didn't know . . . I haven't got that much . . ." she faltered, bursting into tears.

Dr. Merkle gave a short laugh which did not show her teeth, and inquired with concision if Charity supposed she ran the establishment for her own

---

carbolic acid: a disinfectant and antiseptic.

amusement? She leaned her firm shoulders against the door as she spoke, like a grim gaoler making terms with her captive.

"You say you'll come round and settle later? I've heard that pretty often too. Give me your address, and if you can't pay me I'll send the bill to your folks. . . . What? I can't understand what you say. . . . That don't suit you either? My, you're pretty particular for a girl that ain't got enough to settle her own bills. . . ." She paused, and fixed her eyes on the brooch with a blue stone that Charity had pinned to her blouse.

"Ain't you ashamed to talk that way to a lady that's got to earn her living, when you go about with jewellery like that on you? . . . It ain't in my line, and I do it only as a favour . . . but if you're a mind to leave that brooch as a pledge, I don't say no. . . . Yes, of course, you can get it back when you bring me my money. . . ."

On the way home, she felt an immense and unexpected quietude. It had been horrible to have to leave Harney's gift in the woman's hands, but even at that price the news she brought away had not been too dearly bought. She sat with half-closed eyes as the train rushed through the familiar landscape; and now the memories of her former journey, instead of flying before her like dead leaves, seemed to be ripening in her blood like sleeping grain. She would never again know what it was to feel herself alone. Everything seemed to have grown suddenly clear and simple. She no longer had any difficulty in picturing herself as Harney's wife now that she was the mother of his child; and compared to her sovereign right Annabel Balch's claim seemed no more than a girl's sentimental fancy.

That evening, at the gate of the red house, she found Ally waiting in the dusk. "I was down at the post-office just as they were closing up, and Will Targatt said there was a letter for you, so I brought it."

Ally held out the letter, looking at Charity with piercing sympathy. Since the scene of the torn blouse there had been a new and fearful admiration in the eyes she bent on her friend.

Charity snatched the letter with a laugh. "Oh, thank you—good-night," she called out over her shoulder as she ran up the path. If she had lingered a moment she knew she would have had Ally at her heels.

She hurried upstairs and felt her way into her dark room. Her hands trembled as she groped for the matches and lit her candle, and the flap of the envelope was so closely stuck that she had to find her scissors and slit it open. At length she read:

---

gaoler: jailer.

Dear Charity:

I have your letter, and it touches me more than I can say. Won't you trust me, in return, to do my best? There are things it is hard to explain, much less to justify; but your generosity makes everything easier. All I can do now is to thank you from my soul for understanding. Your telling me that you wanted me to do right has helped me beyond expression. If ever there is a hope of realizing what we dreamed of you will see me back on the instant; and I haven't yet lost that hope.

She read the letter with a rush; then she went over and over it, each time more slowly and painstakingly. It was so beautifully expressed that she found it almost as difficult to understand as the gentleman's explanation of the Bible pictures at Nettleton; but gradually she became aware that the gist of its meaning lay in the last few words. "If ever there is a hope of realizing what we dreamed of . . ."

But then he wasn't even sure of that? She understood now that every word and every reticence was an avowal of Annabel Balch's prior claim. It was true that he was engaged to her, and that he had not yet found a way of breaking his engagement.

As she read the letter over Charity understood what it must have cost him to write it. He was not trying to evade an importunate claim; he was honestly and contritely struggling between opposing duties. She did not even reproach him in her thoughts for having concealed from her that he was not free: she could not see anything more reprehensible in his conduct than in her own. From the first she had needed him more than he had wanted her, and the power that had swept them together had been as far beyond resistance as a great gale loosening the leaves of the forest. . . . Only, there stood between them, fixed and upright in the general upheaval, the indestructible figure of Annabel Balch. . . .

Face to face with his admission of the fact, she sat staring at the letter. A cold tremor ran over her, and the hard sobs struggled up into her throat and shook her from head to foot. For a while she was caught and tossed on great waves of anguish that left her hardly conscious of anything but the blind struggle against their assaults. Then, little by little, she began to re-live, with a dreadful poignancy, each separate stage of her poor romance. Foolish things she had said came back to her, gay answers Harney had made, his first kiss in the darkness between the fireworks, their choosing the blue brooch together, the way he had teased her about the letters she had dropped in her flight from the evangelist. All these memories, and a thousand others, hummed through her brain till his nearness grew so vivid that she felt his fingers in her hair, and his warm breath on her cheek as he bent her head back like a flower. These things were hers; they had passed into her blood, and become a part of her, they were building the child in her womb; it was impossible to tear asunder strands of life so interwoven.

The conviction gradually strengthened her, and she began to form in her mind the first words of the letter she meant to write to Harney. She wanted to write it at once, and with feverish hands she began to rummage in her drawer for a sheet of letter paper. But there was none left; she must go downstairs to get it. She had a superstitious feeling that the letter must be written on the instant, that setting down her secret in words would bring her reassurance and safety; and taking up her candle she went down to Mr. Royall's office.

At that hour she was not likely to find him there: he had probably had his supper and walked over to Carrick Fry's. She pushed open the door of the unlit room, and the light of her lifted candle fell on his figure, seated in the darkness in his high-backed chair. His arms lay along the arms of the chair, and his head was bent a little; but he lifted it quickly as Charity entered. She started back as their eyes met, remembering that her own were red with weeping, and that her face was livid with the fatigue and emotion of her journey. But it was too late to escape, and she stood and looked at him in silence.

He had risen from his chair, and came toward her with outstretched hands. The gesture was so unexpected that she let him take her hands in his and they stood thus, without speaking, till Mr. Royall said gravely: "Charity—was you looking for me?"

She freed herself abruptly and fell back. "Me? No——" She set down the candle on his desk. "I wanted some letter-paper, that's all."

His face contracted, and the bushy brows jutted forward over his eyes. Without answering he opened the drawer of the desk, took out a sheet of paper and an envelope, and pushed them toward her. "Do you want a stamp too?" he asked.

She nodded, and he gave her the stamp. As he did so she felt that he was looking at her intently, and she knew that the candle light flickering up on her white face must be distorting her swollen features and exaggerating the dark rings about her eyes. She snatched up the paper, her reassurance dissolving under his pitiless gaze, in which she seemed to read the grim perception of her state, and the ironic recollection of the day when, in that very room, he had offered to compel Harney to marry her. His look seemed to say that he knew she had taken the paper to write to her lover, who had left her as he had warned her she would be left. She remembered the scorn with which she had turned from him that day, and knew, if he guessed the truth, what a list of old scores it must settle. She turned and fled upstairs; but when she got back to her room all the words that had been waiting had vanished. . . .

If she could have gone to Harney it would have been different; she would only have had to show herself to let his memories speak for her. But she had no money left, and there was no one from whom she could have borrowed enough for such a journey. There was nothing to do but to write, and await his reply. For a long time she sat bent above the blank page; but she found nothing to say that really expressed what she was feeling. . . .

Harney had written that she had made it easier for him, and she was glad it was so; she did not want to make things hard. She knew she had it in her power to do that; she held his fate in her hands. All she had to do was to tell him the truth; but that was the very fact that held her back. . . . Her five minutes face to face with Mr. Royall had stripped her of her last illusion, and brought her back to North Dormer's point of view. Distinctly and pitilessly there rose before her the fate of the girl who was married "to make things right." She had seen too many village love-stories end in that way. Poor Rose Coles's miserable marriage was of the number; and what good had come of it for her or for Halston Skeff? They had hated each other from the day the minister married them; and whenever old Mrs. Skeff had a fancy to humiliate her daughter-in-law she had only to say: "Who'd ever think the baby's only two? And for a seven months' child—ain't it a wonder what a size he is?" North Dormer had treasures of indulgence for brands in the burning, but only derision for those who succeeded in getting snatched from it; and Charity had always understood Julia Hawes's refusal to be snatched. . . .

Only—was there no alternative but Julia's? Her soul recoiled from the vision of the white-faced woman among the plush sofas and gilt frames. In the established order of things as she knew them she saw no place for her individual adventure. . . .

She sat in her chair without undressing till faint grey streaks began to divide the black slats of the shutters. Then she stood up and pushed them open, letting in the light. The coming of a new day brought a sharper consciousness of ineluctable reality, and with it a sense of the need of action. She looked at herself in the glass, and saw her face, white in the autumn dawn, with pinched cheeks and dark-ringed eyes, and all the marks of her state that she herself would never have noticed, but that Dr. Merkle's diagnosis had made plain to her. She could not hope that those signs would escape the watchful village; even before her figure lost its shape she knew her face would betray her.

Leaning from her window she looked out on the dark and empty scene; the ashen houses with shuttered windows, the grey road climbing the slope to the hemlock belt above the cemetery, and the heavy mass of the Mountain black against a rainy sky. To the east a space of light was broadening above the forest; but over that also the clouds hung. Slowly her gaze travelled across the fields to the rugged curve of the hills. She had looked out so often on that lifeless circle, and wondered if anything could ever happen to anyone who was enclosed in it. . . .

Almost without conscious thought her decision had been reached; as her eyes had followed the circle of the hills her mind had also travelled the old round. She supposed it was something in her blood that made the Mountain the only answer to her questioning, the inevitable escape from all that hemmed her in and beset her. At any rate it began to loom against the rainy dawn; and the longer she looked at it the more clearly she understood that now at last she was really going there.

XVI

The rain held off, and an hour later, when she started, wild gleams of sunlight were blowing across the fields.

After Harney's departure she had returned her bicycle to its owner at Creston, and she was not sure of being able to walk all the way to the Mountain. The deserted house was on the road; but the idea of spending the night there was unendurable, and she meant to try to push on to Hamblin, where she could sleep under a wood-shed if her strength should fail her. Her preparations had been made with quiet forethought. Before starting she had forced herself to swallow a glass of milk and eat a piece of bread; and she had put in her canvas satchel a little packet of the chocolate that Harney always carried in his bicycle bag. She wanted above all to keep up her strength, and reach her destination without attracting notice. . . .

Mile by mile she retraced the road over which she had so often flown to her lover. When she reached the turn where the wood-road branched off from the Creston highway she remembered the Gospel tent — long since folded up and transplanted — and her start of involuntary terror when the fat evangelist had said: "Your Saviour knows everything. Come and confess your guilt." There was no sense of guilt in her now, but only a desperate desire to defend her secret from irreverent eyes, and begin life again among people to whom the harsh code of the village was unknown. The impulse did not shape itself in thought: she only knew she must save her baby, and hide herself with it somewhere where no one would ever come to trouble them.

She walked on and on, growing more heavy-footed as the day advanced. It seemed a cruel chance that compelled her to retrace every step of the way to the deserted house; and when she came in sight of the orchard, and the silver-gray roof slanting crookedly through the laden branches, her strength failed her and she sat down by the road-side. She sat there a long time, trying to gather the courage to start again, and walk past the broken gate and the untrimmed rose-bushes strung with scarlet hips. A few drops of rain were falling, and she thought of the warm evenings when she and Harney had sat embraced in the shadowy room, and the noise of summer showers on the roof had rustled through their kisses. At length she understood that if she stayed any longer the rain might compel her to take shelter in the house overnight, and she got up and walked on, averting her eyes as she came abreast of the white gate and the tangled garden.

The hours wore on, and she walked more and more slowly, pausing now and then to rest, and to eat a little bread and an apple picked up from the roadside. Her body seemed to grow heavier with every yard of the way, and she wondered how she would be able to carry her child later, if already he laid such a burden on her. . . . A fresh wind had sprung up, scattering the rain and blowing down keenly from the mountain. Presently the clouds lowered again, and a few white darts struck her in the face: it was the first snow falling over Hamblin. The roofs of the lonely village were only half a mile ahead, and she was resolved to push beyond it, and try to reach the Mountain that night. She had no clear plan of action, except that, once in the settlement, she meant to look for Liff Hyatt, and get him to take her to her mother. She herself had been born as her own baby was going to be born; and whatever her mother's subsequent life had been, she could hardly help remembering the past, and receiving a daughter who was facing the trouble she had known.

Suddenly the deadly faintness came over her once more and she sat down on the bank and leaned her head against a tree-trunk. The long road and the cloudy landscape vanished from her eyes, and for a time she seemed to be circling about in some terrible wheeling darkness. Then that too faded.

She opened her eyes, and saw a buggy drawn up beside her, and a man who had jumped down from it and was gazing at her with a puzzled face. Slowly consciousness came back, and she saw that the man was Liff Hyatt.

She was dimly aware that he was asking her something, and she looked at him in silence, trying to find strength to speak. At length her voice stirred in her throat, and she said in a whisper: "I'm going up the Mountain."

"Up the Mountain?" he repeated, drawing aside a little; and as he moved she saw behind him, in the buggy, a heavily coated figure with a familiar pink face and gold spectacles on the bridge of a Grecian nose.

"Charity! What on earth are you doing here?" Mr. Miles exclaimed, throwing the reins on the horse's back and scrambling down from the buggy.

She lifted her heavy eyes to his. "I'm going to see my mother."

The two men glanced at each other, and for a moment neither of them spoke.

Then Mr. Miles said: "You look ill, my dear, and it's a long way. Do you think it's wise?"

Charity stood up. "I've got to go to her."

A vague mirthless grin contracted Liff Hyatt's face, and Mr. Miles again spoke uncertainly. "You know, then—you'd been told?"

She stared at him. "I don't know what you mean. I want to go to her."

Mr. Miles was examining her thoughtfully. She fancied she saw a change in his expression, and the blood rushed to her forehead. "I just want to go to her," she repeated.

He laid his hand on her arm. "My child, your mother is dying. Liff Hyatt came down to fetch me. . . . Get in and come with us."

He helped her up to the seat at his side, Liff Hyatt clambered in at the back, and they drove off toward Hamblin. At first Charity had hardly grasped what Mr. Miles was saying; the physical relief of finding herself seated in the buggy, and securely on her road to the Mountain, effaced the impression of his words. But as her head cleared she began to understand. She knew the Mountain had but the most infrequent intercourse with the valleys; she had often enough heard it said that no one ever went up there except the minister, when someone was dying. And now it was her mother who was dying . . . and she would find herself as much alone on the Mountain as anywhere else in the world. The sense of unescapable isolation was all she could feel for the moment; then she began to wonder at the strangeness of its being Mr. Miles who had undertaken to perform this grim errand. He did not seem in the least like the kind of man who would care to go up the Mountain. But here he was at her side, guiding the horse with a firm hand, and bending on her the kindly gleam of his spectacles, as if there were nothing unusual in their being together in such circumstances.

For a while she found it impossible to speak, and he seemed to understand this, and made no attempt to question her. But presently she felt her tears rise and flow down over her drawn cheeks; and he must have seen them too, for he laid his hand on hers, and said in a low voice: "Won't you tell me what is troubling you?"

She shook her head, and he did not insist: but after a while he said, in the same low tone, so that they should not be overheard: "Charity, what do you know of your childhood, before you came down to North Dormer?"

She controlled herself, and answered: "Nothing only what I heard Mr. Royall say one day. He said he brought me down because my father went to prison."

"And you've never been up there since?"

"Never."

Mr. Miles was silent again, then he said: "I'm glad you're coming with me now. Perhaps we may find your mother alive, and she may know that you have come."

They had reached Hamblin, where the snow-flurry had left white patches in the rough grass on the roadside, and in the angles of the roofs facing north. It was a poor bleak village under the granite flank of the Mountain, and as soon as they left it they began to climb. The road was steep and full of ruts, and the horse settled down to a walk while they mounted and mounted, the world dropping away below them in great mottled stretches of forest and field, and stormy dark blue distances.

Charity had often had visions of this ascent of the Mountain but she had not known it would reveal so wide a country, and the sight of those strange lands reaching away on every side gave her a new sense of Harney's remoteness. She knew he must be miles and miles beyond the last range of hills that seemed to be the outmost verge of things, and she wondered how she had ever dreamed of going to New York to find him. . . .

As the road mounted the country grew bleaker, and they drove across fields of faded mountain grass bleached by long months beneath the snow. In the hollows a few white birches trembled, or a mountain ash lit its scarlet clusters; but only a scant growth of pines darkened the granite ledges. The wind was blowing fiercely across the open slopes; the horse faced it with bent head and straining flanks, and now and then the buggy swayed so that Charity had to clutch its side.

Mr. Miles had not spoken again; he seemed to understand that she wanted to be left alone. After a while the track they were following forked, and he pulled up the horse, as if uncertain of the way. Liff Hyatt craned his head around from the back, and shouted against the wind: "Left——" and they turned into a stunted pine-wood and began to drive down the other side of the Mountain.

A mile or two farther on they came out on a clearing where two or three low houses lay in stony fields, crouching among the rocks as if to brace themselves against the wind. They were hardly more than sheds, built of logs and rough boards, with tin stove-pipes sticking out of their roofs. The sun was setting, and dusk had already fallen on the lower world, but a yellow glare still lay on the lonely hillside and the crouching houses. The next moment it faded and left the landscape in dark autumn twilight.

"Over there," Liff called out, stretching his long arm over Mr. Miles's shoulder. The clergyman turned to the left, across a bit of bare ground over grown with docks and nettles, and stopped before the most ruinous of the sheds. A stove-pipe reached its crooked arm out of one window, and the broken panes of the other were stuffed with rags and paper. In contrast to such a dwelling the brown house in the swamp might have stood for the home of plenty.

As the buggy drew up two or three mongrel dogs jumped out of the twilight with a great barking, and a young man slouched to the door and stood there staring. In the twilight Charity saw that his face had the same sodden look as Bash Hyatt's, the day she had seen him sleeping by the stove. He made no effort to silence the dogs, but leaned in the door, as if roused from a drunken lethargy, while Mr. Miles got out of the buggy.

"Is it here?" the clergyman asked Liff in a low voice; and Liff nodded.

Mr. Miles turned to Charity. "Just hold the horse a minute, my dear: I'll go in first," he said, putting the reins in her hands. She took them passively, and sat staring straight ahead of her at the darkening scene while Mr. Miles and Liff Hyatt went up to the house. They stood a few minutes talking with the man in the door, and then Mr. Miles came back. As he came close, Charity saw that his smooth pink face wore a frightened solemn look.

"Your mother is dead, Charity; you'd better come with me," he said.

She got down and followed him while Liff led the horse away. As she approached the door she said to herself: "This is where I was born . . . this is where I belong. . . ." She had said it to herself often enough as she looked across the sunlit valleys at the Mountain; but it had meant nothing then, and now it had become a reality. Mr. Miles took her gently by the arm, and they entered what appeared to be the only room in the house. It was so dark that she could just discern a group of a dozen people sitting or sprawling about a table made of boards laid across two barrels. They looked up listlessly as Mr. Miles and Charity came in, and a woman's thick voice said: "Here's the preacher." But no one moved.

Mr. Miles paused and looked about him; then he turned to the young man who had met them at the door.

"Is the body here?" he asked.

The young man, instead of answering, turned his head toward the group. "Where's the candle? I tole yer to bring a candle," he said with sudden harshness to a girl who was lolling against the table. She did not answer, but another man got up and took from some corner a candle stuck into a bottle.

"How'll I light it? The stove's out," the girl grumbled.

Mr. Miles fumbled under his heavy wrappings and drew out a matchbox. He held a match to the candle, and in a moment or two a faint circle of light fell on the pale aguish heads that started out of the shadow like the heads of nocturnal animals.

"Mary's over there," someone said; and Mr. Miles, taking the bottle in his hand, passed behind the table. Charity followed him, and they stood before a mattress on the floor in a corner of the room. A woman lay on it, but she did not look like a dead woman; she seemed to have fallen across her squalid bed in a drunken sleep, and to have been left lying where she fell, in her ragged disordered clothes. One arm was flung above her head, one leg drawn up under a torn skirt that left the other bare to the knee: a swollen glistening leg with a ragged stocking rolled down about the ankle. The woman lay on her back, her eyes staring up unblinkingly at the candle that trembled in Mr. Miles's hand.

"She jus' dropped off," a woman said, over the shoulder of the others; and the young man added "I jus' come in and found her."

An elderly man with lank hair and a feeble grin pushed between them. "It was like this: I says to her on'y the night before: if you don't take and quit, I says to her . . ."

Someone pulled him back and sent him reeling against a bench along the wall, where he dropped down muttering his unheeded narrative.

There was a silence; then the young woman who had been lolling against the table suddenly parted the group, and stood in front of Charity. She was healthier and robuster looking than the others, and her weather-beaten face had a certain sullen beauty.

"Who's the girl? Who brought her here?" she said, fixing her eyes mistrustfully on the young man who had rebuked her for not having a candle ready.

Mr. Miles spoke. "I brought her; she is Mary Hyatt's daughter."

"What? Her too?" the girl sneered; and the young man turned on her with an oath. "Shut your mouth, damn you, or get out of here," he said; then he relapsed into his former apathy, and dropped down on the bench, leaning his head against the wall.

Mr. Miles had set the candle on the floor and taken off his heavy coat. He turned to Charity. "Come and help me," he said.

He knelt down by the mattress, and pressed the lids over the dead woman's eyes. Charity, trembling and sick, knelt beside him, and tried to compose her mother's body. She drew the stocking over the dreadful glistening leg, and pulled the skirt down to the battered upturned boots. As she did so, she looked at her mother's face, thin yet swollen, with lips parted in a frozen gasp above the broken teeth. There was no sign in it of anything human: she lay there like a dead dog in a ditch. Charity's hands grew cold as they touched her.

Mr. Miles drew the woman's arms across her breast and laid his coat over her. Then he covered her face with his handkerchief, and placed the bottle with the candle in it at her head. Having done this he stood up.

"Is there no coffin?" he asked, turning to the group behind him.

There was a moment of bewildered silence; then the fierce girl spoke up. "You'd oughter brought it with you. Where'd we get one here, I'd like ter know?"

Mr. Miles, looking at the others, repeated: "Is it possible you have no coffin ready?"

"That's what I say: them that has it sleeps better," an old woman murmured. "But then she never had no bed. . . ."

"And the stove warn't hers," said the lank-haired man, on the defensive.

Mr. Miles turned away from them and moved a few steps apart. He had drawn a book from his pocket, and after a pause he opened it and began to read, holding the book at arm's length and low down, so that the pages caught the feeble light. Charity had remained on her knees by the mattress: now that her mother's face was covered it was easier to stay near her, and avoid the sight of the living faces which too horribly showed by what stages hers had lapsed into death.

"I am the Resurrection and the Life," Mr. Miles began; "he that believeth in me, though he were dead, yet shall he live. . . . Though after my skin worms destroy my body, yet in my flesh shall I see God. . . ."

In my flesh shall I see God! Charity thought of the gaping mouth and stony eyes under the handkerchief, and of the glistening leg over which she had drawn the stocking. . . .

"We brought nothing into this world and we shall take nothing out of it——"

There was a sudden muttering and a scuffle at the back of the group. "I brought the stove," said the elderly man with lank hair, pushing his way between the others. "I wen' down to Creston'n bought it . . . n' I got a right to take it outer here . . . n' I'll lick any feller says I ain't. . . ."

"Sit down, damn you!" shouted the tall youth who had been drowsing on the bench against the wall.

"For man walketh in a vain shadow, and disquieteth himself in vain; he heapeth up riches and cannot tell who shall gather them . . ."

"Well, it *are* his," a woman in the background interjected in a frightened whine.

The tall youth staggered to his feet. "If you don't hold your mouths I'll turn you all out o' here, the whole lot of you," he cried with many oaths. "G'wan, minister . . . don't let 'em faze you. . . ."

"Now is Christ risen from the dead and become the first-fruits of them that slept. . . . Behold, I show you a mystery. We shall not all sleep, but we shall all be changed, in a moment, in the twinkling of an eye, at the last trump. . . . For this corruptible must put on incorruption and this mortal must put on immortality. So when this corruption shall have put on incorruption, and when this mortal shall have put on immortality, then shall be brought to pass the saying that is written, Death is swallowed up in Victory. . . ."

One by one the mighty words fell on Charity's bowed head, soothing the horror, subduing the tumult, mastering her as they mastered the drink-dazed creatures at her back. Mr. Miles read to the last word, and then closed the book.

"Is the grave ready?" he asked.

Liff Hyatt, who had come in while he was reading, nodded a "Yes," and pushed forward to the side of the mattress. The young man on the bench who seemed to assert some sort of right of kinship with the dead woman, got to his feet again, and the proprietor of the stove joined him. Between them they raised up the mattress; but their movements were unsteady, and the coat slipped to the floor, revealing the poor body in its helpless misery. Charity, picking up the coat, covered her mother once more. Liff had brought a lantern, and the old woman who had already spoken took it up, and opened the door to let the little procession pass out. The wind had dropped, and the night was very dark and bitterly cold. The old woman walked ahead, the lantern shaking in her hand and spreading out before her a pale patch of dead grass and coarse-leaved weeds enclosed in an immensity of blackness.

Mr. Miles took Charity by the arm, and side by side they walked behind the mattress. At length the old woman with the lantern stopped, and Charity saw the light fall on the stooping shoulders of the bearers and on a ridge of upheaved earth over which they were bending. Mr. Miles released her arm and approached the hollow on the other side of the ridge; and while the men stooped down, lowering the mattress into the grave, he began to speak again.

"Man that is born of woman hath but a short time to live and is full of misery. . . . He cometh up and is cut down . . . he fleeth as it were a shadow. . . . Yet, O Lord God most holy, O Lord most mighty, O holy and merciful Saviour, deliver us not into the bitter pains of eternal death . . ."

"Easy there . . . is she down?" piped the claimant to the stove; and the young man called over his shoulder: "Lift the light there, can't you?"

There was a pause, during which the light floated uncertainly over the open grave. Someone bent over and pulled out Mr. Miles's coat — ("No, no — leave the handkerchief," he interposed) — and then Liff Hyatt, coming forward with a spade, began to shovel in the earth.

"Forasmuch as it hath pleased Almighty God of His great mercy to take unto Himself the soul of our dear sister here departed, we therefore commit her body to the ground; earth to earth, ashes to ashes, dust to dust . . ." Liff's gaunt shoulders rose and bent in the lantern light as he dashed the clods of earth into the grave. "God — it's froze a'ready," he muttered, spitting into his palm and passing his ragged shirt-sleeve across his perspiring face.

"Through our Lord Jesus Christ, who shall change our vile body that it may be like unto His glorious body, according to the mighty working, whereby He is able to subdue all things unto Himself . . ." The last spade-ful of earth fell on the vile body of Mary Hyatt, and Liff rested on his spade, his shoulder blades still heaving with the effort.

"Lord, have mercy upon us, Christ have mercy upon us, Lord have mercy upon us. . . ."

Mr. Miles took the lantern from the old woman's hand and swept its light across the circle of bleared faces. "Now kneel down, all of you," he commanded, in a voice of authority that Charity had never heard. She knelt down at the edge of the grave, and the others, stiffly and hesitatingly, got to their knees beside her. Mr. Miles knelt, too. "And now pray with me — you know this prayer," he said, and he began: "Our Father which art in Heaven . . ." One or two of the women falteringly took the words up, and when he ended, the lank-haired man flung himself on the neck of the tall youth. "It was this way," he said. "I tole her the night before, I says to her . . ." The reminiscence ended in a sob.

Mr. Miles had been getting into his coat again. He came up to Charity, who had remained passively kneeling by the rough mound of earth.

"My child, you must come. It's very late."

She lifted her eyes to his face: he seemed to speak out of another world.

"I ain't coming: I'm going to stay here."

"Here? Where? What do you mean?"

"These are my folks. I'm going to stay with them."

Mr. Miles lowered his voice. "But it's not possible — you don't know what you are doing. You can't stay among these people: you must come with me."

She shook her head and rose from her knees. The group about the grave had scattered in the darkness, but the old woman with the lantern stood waiting. Her mournful withered face was not unkind, and Charity went up to her.

"Have you got a place where I can lie down for the night?" she asked. Liff came up, leading the buggy out of the night. He looked from one to the other with his feeble smile. "She's my mother. She'll take you home," he said; and he added, raising his voice to speak to the old woman: "It's the girl from lawyer Royall's — Mary's girl . . . you remember. . . ."

The woman nodded and raised her sad old eyes to Charity's. When Mr. Miles and Liff clambered into the buggy she went ahead with the lantern to show them the track they were to follow; then she turned back, and in silence she and Charity walked away together through the night.

XVII

Charity lay on the floor on a mattress, as her dead mother's body had lain. The room in which she lay was cold and dark and low-ceilinged, and even poorer and barer than the scene of Mary Hyatt's earthly pilgrimage. On the other side of the fireless stove Liff Hyatt's mother slept on a blanket, with two children—her grandchildren, she said—rolled up against her like sleeping puppies. They had their thin clothes spread over them, having given the only other blanket to their guest.

Through the small square of glass in the opposite wall Charity saw a deep funnel of sky, so black, so remote, so palpitating with frosty stars that her very soul seemed to be sucked into it. Up there somewhere, she supposed, the God whom Mr. Miles had invoked was waiting for Mary Hyatt to appear. What a long flight it was! And what would she have to say when she reached Him?

Charity's bewildered brain laboured with the attempt to picture her mother's past, and to relate it in any way to the designs of a just but merciful God; but it was impossible to imagine any link between them. She herself felt as remote from the poor creature she had seen lowered into her hastily dug grave as if the height of the heavens divided them. She had seen poverty and misfortune in her life; but in a community where poor thrifty Mrs. Hawes and the industrious Ally represented the nearest approach to destitution there was nothing to suggest the savage misery of the Mountain farmers.

As she lay there, half-stunned by her tragic initiation, Charity vainly tried to think herself into the life about her. But she could not even make out what relationship these people bore to each other, or to her dead mother; they seemed to be herded together in a sort of passive promiscuity in which their common misery was the strongest link. She tried to picture to herself what her life would have been if she had grown up on the Mountain, running wild in rags, sleeping on the floor curled up against her mother, like the pale-faced children huddled against old Mrs. Hyatt, and turning into a fierce bewildered creature like the girl who had apostrophized her in such strange words. She was frightened by the secret affinity she had felt with this girl, and by the light it threw on her own beginnings. Then she remembered what Mr. Royall had said in telling her story to Lucius Harney: "Yes, there was a mother; but she was glad to have the child go. She'd have given her to anybody. . . ."

Well! after all, was her mother so much to blame? Charity, since that day, had always thought of her as destitute of all human feeling; now she seemed merely pitiful. What mother would not want to save her child from such a life? Charity thought of the future of her own child, and tears welled into her aching eyes, and ran down over her face. If she had been less exhausted, less burdened with his weight, she would have sprung up then and there and fled away. . . .

The grim hours of the night dragged themselves slowly by, and at last the sky paled and dawn threw a cold blue beam into the room. She lay in her corner staring at the dirty floor, the clothes-line hung with decaying rags, the old woman huddled against the cold stove, and the light gradually spreading across the wintry world, and bringing with it a new day in which she would have to live, to choose, to act, to make herself a place among these people — or to go back to the life she had left. A mortal lassitude weighed on her. There were moments when she felt that all she asked was to go on lying there unnoticed; then her mind revolted at the thought of becoming one of the miserable herd from which she sprang, and it seemed as though, to save her child from such a fate, she would find strength to travel any distance, and bear any burden life might put on her.

Vague thoughts of Nettleton flitted through her mind. She said to herself that she would find some quiet place where she could bear her child, and give it to decent people to keep; and then she would go out like Julia Hawes and earn its living and hers. She knew that girls of that kind sometimes made enough to have their children nicely cared for; and every other consideration disappeared in the vision of her baby, cleaned and combed and rosy, and hidden away somewhere where she could run in and kiss it, and bring it pretty things to wear. Anything, anything was better than to add another life to the nest of misery on the Mountain. . . .

The old woman and the children were still sleeping when Charity rose from her mattress. Her body was stiff with cold and fatigue, and she moved slowly lest her heavy steps should rouse them. She was faint with hunger, and had nothing left in her satchel; but on the table she saw the half of a stale loaf. No doubt it was to serve as the breakfast of old Mrs. Hyatt and the children; but Charity did not care; she had her own baby to think of. She broke off a piece of the bread and ate it greedily; then her glance fell on the thin faces of the sleeping children, and filled with compunction she rummaged in her satchel for something with which to pay for what she had taken. She found one of the pretty chemises that Ally had made for her, with a blue ribbon run through its edging. It was one of the dainty things on which she had squandered her savings, and as she looked at it the blood rushed to her forehead. She laid the chemise on the table, and stealing across the floor lifted the latch and went out. . . .

The morning was icy cold and a pale sun was just rising above the eastern shoulder of the Mountain. The houses scattered on the hillside lay cold and smokeless under the sun-flecked clouds, and not a human being was in sight. Charity paused on the threshold and tried to discover the road by which she had come the night before. Across the field surrounding Mrs. Hyatt's shanty she saw the tumble-down house in which she supposed the funeral service had taken place. The trail ran across the ground between the two houses and disappeared in the pine-wood on the flank of the Mountain; and a little way to the right, under a wind-beaten thorn, a mound of fresh earth made a dark spot on the fawn-coloured stubble. Charity walked across the field to the ground. As she approached it she heard a bird's note in the still air, and looking up she saw a brown song-sparrow perched in an upper branch of the thorn above the grave. She stood a minute listening to his small solitary song; then she rejoined the trail and began to mount the hill to the pine-wood.

Thus far she had been impelled by the blind instinct of flight; but each step seemed to bring her nearer to the realities of which her feverish vigil had given only a shadowy image. Now that she walked again in a daylight world, on the way back to familiar things, her imagination moved more soberly. On one point she was still decided: she could not remain at North Dormer, and the sooner she got away from it the better. But everything beyond was darkness.

As she continued to climb the air grew keener, and when she passed from the shelter of the pines to the open grassy roof of the Mountain the cold wind of the night before sprang out on her. She bent her shoulders and struggled on against it for a while; but presently her breath failed, and she sat down under a ledge of rock overhung by shivering birches. From where she sat she saw the trail wandering across the bleached grass in the direction of Hamblin, and the granite wall of the Mountain falling away to infinite distances. On that side of the ridge the valleys still lay in wintry shadow; but in the plain beyond the sun was touching village roofs and steeples, and gilding the haze of smoke over far-off invisible towns.

Charity felt herself a mere speck in the lonely circle of the sky. The events of the last two days seemed to have divided her forever from her short dream of bliss. Even Harney's image had been blurred by that crushing experience: she thought of him as so remote from her that he seemed hardly more than a memory. In her fagged and floating mind only one sensation had the weight of reality; it was the bodily burden of her child. But for it she would have felt as rootless as the whiffs of thistledown the wind blew past her. Her child was like a load that held her down, and yet like a hand that pulled her to her feet. She said to herself that she must get up and struggle on. . . .

Her eyes turned back to the trail across the top of the Mountain, and in the distance she saw a buggy against the sky. She knew its antique outline, and the gaunt build of the old horse pressing forward with lowered head;

and after a moment she recognized the heavy bulk of the man who held the reins. The buggy was following the trail and making straight for the pine-wood through which she had climbed; and she knew at once that the driver was in search of her. Her first impulse was to crouch down under the ledge till he had passed; but the instinct of concealment was overruled by the relief of feeling that someone was near her in the awful emptiness. She stood up and walked toward the buggy.

Mr. Royall saw her, and touched the horse with the whip. A minute or two later he was abreast of Charity; their eyes met, and without speaking he leaned over and helped her up into the buggy. She tried to speak, to stammer out some explanation, but no words came to her; and as he drew the cover over her knees he simply said: "The minister told me he'd left you up here, so I come up for you."

He turned the horse's head, and they began to jog back toward Hamblin. Charity sat speechless, staring straight ahead of her, and Mr. Royall occasionally uttered a word of encouragement to the horse: "Get along there, Dan. . . . I gave him a rest at Hamblin; but I brought him along pretty quick, and it's a stiff pull up here against the wind."

As he spoke it occurred to her for the first time that to reach the top of the Mountain so early he must have left North Dormer at the coldest hour of the night, and have travelled steadily but for the halt at Hamblin; and she felt a softness at her heart which no act of his had ever produced since he had brought her the Crimson Rambler because she had given up boarding-school to stay with him.

After an interval he began again: "It was a day just like this, only spitting snow, when I come up here for you the first time." Then, as if fearing that she might take his remark as a reminder of past benefits, he added quickly: "I dunno's you think it was such a good job, either."

"Yes, I do," she murmured, looking straight ahead of her.

"Well," he said, "I tried——"

He did not finish the sentence, and she could think of nothing more to say.

"Ho, there, Dan, step out," he muttered, jerking the bridle. "We ain't home yet.—You cold?" he asked abruptly.

She shook her head, but he drew the cover higher up, and stooped to tuck it in about the ankles. She continued to look straight ahead. Tears of weariness and weakness were dimming her eyes and beginning to run over, but she dared not wipe them away lest he should observe the gesture.

They drove in silence, following the long loops of the descent upon Hamblin, and Mr. Royall did not speak again till they reached the outskirts of the village. Then he let the reins droop on the dash-board and drew out his watch.

"Charity," he said, "you look fair done up, and North Dormer's a good-ish way off. I've figured out that we'd do better to stop here long enough for you to get a mouthful of breakfast and then drive down to Creston and take the train."

She roused herself from her apathetic musing. "The train—what train?"

Mr. Royall, without answering, let the horse jog on till they reached the door of the first house in the village. "This is old Mrs. Hobart's place," he said. "She'll give us something hot to drink."

Charity, half unconsciously, found herself getting out of the buggy and following him in at the open door. They entered a decent kitchen with a fire crackling in the stove. An old woman with a kindly face was setting out cups and saucers on the table. She looked up and nodded as they came in, and Mr. Royall advanced to the stove, clapping his numb hands together.

"Well, Mrs. Hobart, you got any breakfast for this young lady? You can see she's cold and hungry."

Mrs. Hobart smiled on Charity and took a tin coffee-pot from the fire. "My, you do look pretty mean," she said compassionately.

Charity reddened, and sat down at the table. A feeling of complete passiveness had once more come over her, and she was conscious only of the pleasant animal sensations of warmth and rest.

Mrs. Hobart put bread and milk on the table, and then went out of the house: Charity saw her leading the horse away to the barn across the yard. She did not come back, and Mr. Royall and Charity sat alone at the table with the smoking coffee between them. He poured out a cup for her, and put a piece of bread in the saucer, and she began to eat.

As the warmth of the coffee flowed through her veins her thoughts cleared and she began to feel like a living being again; but the return to life was so painful that the food choked in her throat and she sat staring down at the table in silent anguish.

After a while Mr. Royall pushed back his chair. "Now, then," he said, "if you're a mind to go along——" She did not move, and he continued: "We can pick up the noon train for Nettleton if you say so."

The words sent the blood rushing to her face, and she raised her startled eyes to his. He was standing on the other side of the table looking at her kindly and gravely; and suddenly she understood what he was going to say. She continued to sit motionless, a leaden weight upon her lips.

"You and me have spoke some hard things to each other in our time, Charity; and there's no good that I can see in any more talking now. But I'll never feel any way but one about you; and if you say so we'll drive down in time to catch that train, and go straight to the minister's house; and when you come back home you'll come as Mrs. Royall."

His voice had the grave persuasive accent that had moved his hearers at the Home Week festival; she had a sense of depths of mournful tolerance under that easy tone. Her whole body began to tremble with the dread of her own weakness.

"Oh, I can't——" she burst out desperately.

"Can't what?"

She herself did not know: she was not sure if she was rejecting what he offered, or already struggling against the temptation of taking what she no longer had a right to. She stood up, shaking and bewildered, and began to speak:

"I know I ain't been fair to you always; but I want to be now. . . . I want you to know . . . I want . . ." Her voice failed her and she stopped.

Mr. Royall leaned against the wall. He was paler than usual, but his face was composed and kindly and her agitation did not appear to perturb him.

"What's all this about wanting?" he said as she paused. "Do you know what you really want? I'll tell you. You want to be took home and took care of. And I guess that's all there is to say."

"No . . . it's not all. . . ."

"Ain't it?" He looked at his watch. "Well, I'll tell you another thing. All *I* want is to know if you'll marry me. If there was anything else, I'd tell you so; but there ain't. Come to my age, a man knows the things that matter and the things that don't; that's about the only good turn life does us."

His tone was so strong and resolute that it was like a supporting arm about her. She felt her resistance melting, her strength slipping away from her as he spoke.

"Don't cry, Charity," he exclaimed in a shaken voice. She looked up, startled at his emotion, and their eyes met.

"See here," he said gently, "old Dan's come a long distance, and we've got to let him take it easy the rest of the way. . . ."

He picked up the cloak that had slipped to her chair and laid it about her shoulders. She followed him out of the house, and then walked across the yard to the shed, where the horse was tied. Mr. Royall unblanketed him and led him out into the road. Charity got into the buggy and he drew the cover about her and shook out the reins with a cluck. When they reached the end of the village he turned the horse's head toward Creston.

XVIII

They began to jog down the winding road to the valley at old Dan's languid pace. Charity felt herself sinking into deeper depths of weariness, and as they descended through the bare woods there were moments when she lost the exact sense of things, and seemed to be sitting beside her lover with the leafy arch of summer bending over them. But this illusion was faint and transitory. For the most part she had only a confused sensation of slipping down a smooth irresistible current; and she abandoned herself to the feeling as a refuge from the torment of thought.

Mr. Royall seldom spoke, but his silent presence gave her, for the first time, a sense of peace and security. She knew that where he was there would be warmth, rest, silence; and for the moment they were all she wanted. She shut her eyes, and even these things grew dim to her. . . .

In the train, during the short run from Creston to Nettleton, the warmth aroused her, and the consciousness of being under strange eyes gave her a momentary energy. She sat upright, facing Mr. Royall, and stared out of the window at the denuded country. Forty-eight hours earlier, when she had last traversed it, many of the trees still held their leaves; but the high wind of the last two nights had stripped them, and the lines of the landscape were as finely pencilled as in December. A few days of autumn cold had wiped out all trace of the rich fields and languid groves through which she had passed on the Fourth of July; and with the fading of the landscape those fervid hours had faded, too. She could no longer believe that she was the being who had lived them; she was someone to whom something irreparable and overwhelming had happened, but the traces of the steps leading up to it had almost vanished.

When the train reached Nettleton and she walked out into the square at Mr. Royall's side the sense of unreality grew more overpowering. The physical strain of the night and day had left no room in her mind for new sensations and she followed Mr. Royall as passively as a tired child. As in a confused dream she presently found herself sitting with him in a pleasant room, at a table with a red and white table-cloth on which hot food and tea were placed. He filled her cup and plate and whenever she lifted her eyes from them she found his resting on her with the same steady tranquil gaze that had reassured and strengthened her when they had faced each other in old Mrs. Hobart's kitchen. As everything else in her consciousness grew more and more confused and immaterial, became more and more like the universal shimmer that dissolves the world to failing eyes, Mr. Royall's presence began to detach itself with rocky firmness from this elusive background. She had always thought of him — when she thought of him at all — as of someone hateful and obstructive, but whom she could outwit and dominate when she chose to make the effort. Only once, on the day of the Old Home Week celebration, while the stray fragments of his address drifted across her troubled mind, had she caught a glimpse of another being, a being so different from the dull-witted enemy with whom she had supposed herself to be living that even through the burning mist of her own dreams he had stood out with startling distinctness. For a moment, then, what he said—and something in his way of saying it—had made her see why he had always struck her as such a lonely man. But the mist of her dreams had hidden him again, and she had forgotten that fugitive impression.

It came back to her now, as they sat at the table, and gave her, through her own immeasurable desolation, a sudden sense of their nearness to each other. But all these feelings were only brief streaks of light in the grey blur of her physical weakness. Through it she was aware that Mr. Royall presently left her sitting by the table in the warm room, and came back after an interval with a carriage from the station—a closed "hack" with sunburnt blue silk blinds—in which they drove together to a house covered with creepers and standing next to a church with a carpet of turf before it. They got out at this house, and the carriage waited while they walked up the path and entered a wain-scoted hall and then a room full of books. In this room a clergyman whom Charity had never seen received them pleasantly, and asked them to be seated for a few minutes while witnesses were being summoned.

Charity sat down obediently, and Mr. Royall, his hands behind his back, paced slowly up and down the room. As he turned and faced Charity, she noticed that his lips were twitching a little; but the look in his eyes was grave and calm. Once he paused before her and said timidly: "Your hair's got kinder loose with the wind," and she lifted her hands and tried to smooth back the locks that had escaped from her braid. There was a looking-glass in a carved frame on the wall, but she was ashamed to look at herself in it, and she sat with her hands folded on her knee till the clergyman returned. Then they went out again, along a sort of arcaded passage, and into a low vaulted room with a cross on an altar, and rows of benches. The clergyman, who had left them at the door, presently reappeared before the altar in a surplice, and a lady who was probably his wife, and a man in a blue shirt who had been raking dead leaves on the lawn, came in and sat on one of the benches.

The clergyman opened a book and signed to Charity and Mr. Royall to approach. Mr. Royall advanced a few steps, and Charity followed him as she had followed him to the buggy when they went out of Mrs. Hobart's kitchen; she had the feeling that if she ceased to keep close to him, and do what he told her to do, the world would slip away from beneath her feet.

The clergyman began to read, and on her dazed mind there rose the memory of Mr. Miles, standing the night before in the desolate house of the Mountain, and reading out of the same book words that had the same dread sound of finality:

"I require and charge you both, as ye will answer at the dreadful day of judgment when the secrets of all hearts shall be disclosed, that if either of you know any impediment whereby ye may not be lawfully joined together . . ."

Charity raised her eyes and met Mr. Royall's. They were still looking at her kindly and steadily. "I will!" she heard him say a moment later, after another interval of words that she had failed to catch. She was so busy trying to understand the gestures that the clergyman was signalling to her to make that she no longer heard what was being said. After another interval the lady on the bench stood up, and taking her hand put it in Mr. Royall's. It lay enclosed in his strong palm and she felt a ring that was too big for her being slipped on her thin finger. She understood then that she was married. . . .

Late that afternoon Charity sat alone in a bedroom of the fashionable hotel where she and Harney had vainly sought a table on the Fourth of July. She had never before been in so handsomely furnished a room. The mirror above the dressing-table reflected the high head-board and fluted pillow-slips of the double bed, and a bedspread so spotlessly white that she had hesitated to lay her hat and jacket on it. The humming radiator diffused an atmosphere of drowsy warmth, and through a half-open door she saw the glitter of the nickel taps above twin marble basins.

For a while the long turmoil of the night and day had slipped away from her and she sat with closed eyes, surrendering herself to the spell of warmth and silence. But presently this merciful apathy was succeeded by the sudden acuteness of vision with which sick people sometimes wake out of a heavy sleep. As she opened her eyes they rested on the picture that hung above the bed. It was a large engraving with a dazzling white margin enclosed in a wide frame of bird's-eye maple with an inner scroll of gold. The engraving represented a young man in a boat on a lake overhung with trees. He was leaning over to gather water-lilies for the girl in a light dress who lay among the cushions in the stern. The scene was full of a drowsy midsummer radiance, and Charity averted her eyes from it and, rising from her chair, began to wander restlessly about the room.

It was on the fifth floor, and its broad window of plate glass looked over the roofs of the town. Beyond them stretched a wooded landscape in which the last fires of sunset were picking out a steely gleam. Charity gazed at the gleam with startled eyes. Even through the gathering twilight she recognized the contour of the soft hills encircling it, and the way the meadows sloped to its edge. It was Nettleton Lake that she was looking at.

She stood a long time in the window staring out at the fading water. The sight of it had roused her for the first time to a realization of what she had done. Even the feeling of the ring on her hand had not brought her this sharp sense of the irretrievable. For an instant the old impulse of flight swept through her; but it was only the lift of a broken wing. She heard the door open behind her, and Mr. Royall came in.

He had gone to the barber's to be shaved, and his shaggy grey hair had been trimmed and smoothed. He moved strongly and quickly, squaring his shoulders and carrying his head high, as if he did not want to pass unnoticed.

"What are you doing in the dark?" he called out in a cheerful voice. Charity made no answer. He went up to the window to draw the blind, and putting his finger on the wall flooded the room with a blaze of light from the central chandelier. In this unfamiliar illumination husband and wife faced each other awkwardly for a moment; then Mr. Royall said: "We'll step down and have some supper, if you say so."

The thought of food filled her with repugnance; but not daring to confess it she smoothed her hair and followed him to the lift.

An hour later, coming out of the glare of the dining-room, she waited in the marble-panelled hall while Mr. Royall, before the brass lattice of one of the corner counters, selected a cigar and bought an evening paper. Men were lounging in rocking chairs under the blazing chandeliers, travellers coming and going, bells ringing, porters shuffling by with luggage. Over Mr. Royall's shoulder, as he leaned against the counter, a girl with her hair puffed high smirked and nodded at a dapper drummer who was getting his key at the desk across the hall.

Charity stood among these cross-currents of life as motionless and inert as if she had been one of the tables screwed to the marble floor. All her soul was gathered up into one sick sense of coming doom, and she watched Mr. Royall in fascinated terror while he pinched the cigars in successive boxes and unfolded his evening paper with a steady hand.

Presently he turned and joined her. "You go right along up to bed—I'm going to sit down here and have my smoke," he said. He spoke as easily and naturally as if they had been an old couple, long used to each other's ways, and her contracted heart gave a flutter of relief. She followed him to the lift, and he put her in and enjoined the buttoned and braided boy to show her to her room.

She groped her way in through the darkness, forgetting where the electric button was, and not knowing how to manipulate it. But a white autumn moon had risen, and the illuminated sky put a pale light in the room. By it she undressed, and after folding up the ruffled pillow-slips crept timidly under the spotless counterpane. She had never felt such smooth

---

drummer: traveling salesman.

sheets or such light warm blankets; but the softness of the bed did not soothe her. She lay there trembling with a fear that ran through her veins like ice. "What have I done? Oh, what have I done?" she whispered, shuddering to her pillow; and pressing her face against it to shut out the pale landscape beyond the window she lay in the darkness straining her ears, and shaking at every footstep that approached. . . .

Suddenly she sat up and pressed her hands against her frightened heart. A faint sound had told her that someone was in the room; but she must have slept in the interval, for she had heard no one enter. The moon was setting beyond the opposite roofs, and in the darkness outlined against the grey square of the window, she saw a figure seated in the rocking-chair. The figure did not move: it was sunk deep in the chair, with bowed head and folded arms, and she saw that it was Mr. Royall who sat there. He had not undressed, but had taken the blanket from the foot of the bed and laid it across his knees. Trembling and holding her breath she watched him, fearing that he had been roused by her movement; but he did not stir, and she concluded that he wished her to think he was asleep.

As she continued to watch him ineffable relief stole slowly over her, relaxing her strained nerves and exhausted body. He knew, then . . . he knew . . . it was because he knew that he had married her, and that he sat there in the darkness to show her she was safe with him. A stir of something deeper than she had ever felt in thinking of him flitted through her tired brain, and cautiously, noiselessly, she let her head sink on the pillow. . . .

When she woke the room was full of morning light, and her first glance showed her that she was alone in it. She got up and dressed, and as she was fastening her dress the door opened, and Mr. Royall came in. He looked old and tired in the bright daylight, but his face wore the same expression of grave friendliness that had reassured her on the Mountain. It was as if all the dark spirits had gone out of him.

They went downstairs to the dining-room for breakfast, and after breakfast he told her he had some insurance business to attend to. "I guess while I'm doing it you'd better step out and buy yourself whatever you need." He smiled, and added with an embarrassed laugh: "You know I always wanted you to beat all the other girls." He drew something from his pocket, and pushed it across the table to her; and she saw that he had given her two twenty-dollar bills. "If it ain't enough there's more where that come from—I want you to beat 'em all hollow," he repeated.

She flushed and tried to stammer out her thanks, but he had pushed back his chair and was leading the way out of the dining-room. In the hall he paused a minute to say that if it suited her they would take the three o'clock train back to North Dormer; then he took his hat and coat from the rack and went out.

A few minutes later Charity went out, too. She had watched to see in what direction he was going, and she took the opposite way and walked quickly down the main street to the brick building on the corner of Lake Avenue. There she paused to look cautiously up and down the thoroughfare, and then climbed the brass-bound stairs to Dr. Merkle's door. The same bushy-headed mulatto girl admitted her, and after the same interval of waiting in the red plush parlor she was once more summoned to Dr. Merkle's office. The doctor received her without surprise, and led her into the inner plush sanctuary.

"I thought you'd be back, but you've come a mite too soon: I told you to be patient and not fret," she observed, after a pause of penetrating scrutiny.

Charity drew the money from her breast. "I've come to get my blue brooch," she said, flushing.

"Your brooch?" Dr. Merkle appeared not to remember. "My, yes—I get so many things of that kind. Well, my dear, you'll have to wait while I get it out of the safe. I don't leave valuables like that laying round like the noospaper."

She disappeared for a moment, and returned with a bit of twisted-up tissue paper from which she unwrapped the brooch.

Charity, as she looked at it, felt a stir of warmth at her heart. She held out an eager hand.

"Have you got the change?" she asked a little breathlessly, laying one of the twenty-dollar bills on the table.

"Change? What'd I want to have change for? I only see two twenties there," Dr. Merkle answered brightly.

Charity paused, disconcerted. "I thought . . . you said it was five dollars a visit. . . ."

"For *you,* as a favour—I did. But how about the responsibility and the insurance? I don't s'pose you ever thought of that? This pin's worth a hundred dollars easy. If it had got lost or stole, where'd I been when you come to claim it?"

Charity remained silent, puzzled and half-convinced by the argument, and Dr. Merkle promptly followed up her advantage. "I didn't ask you for your brooch, my dear. I'd a good deal ruther folks paid me my regular charge than have 'em put me to all this trouble."

She paused, and Charity, seized with a desperate longing to escape, rose to her feet and held out one of the bills.

"Will you take that?" she asked.

"No, I won't take that, my dear; but I'll take it with its mate, and hand you over a signed receipt if you don't trust me."

"Oh, but I can't—it's all I've got," Charity exclaimed.

Dr. Merkle looked up at her pleasantly from the plush sofa. "It seems you got married yesterday, up to the 'Piscopal church; I heard all about the wedding from the minister's chore-man. It would be a pity, wouldn't it, to let Mr. Royall know you had an account running here? I just put it to you as your own mother might."

Anger flamed up in Charity, and for an instant she thought of abandoning the brooch and letting Dr. Merkle do her worst. But how could she leave her only treasure with that evil woman? She wanted it for her baby: she meant it, in some mysterious way, to be a link between Harney's child and its unknown father. Trembling and hating herself while she did it, she laid Mr. Royall's money on the table, and catching up the brooch fled out of the room and the house. . . .

In the street she stood still, dazed by this last adventure. But the brooch lay in her bosom like a talisman, and she felt a secret lightness of heart. It gave her strength, after a moment, to walk on slowly in the direction of the post office, and go in through the swinging doors. At one of the windows she bought a sheet of letter-paper, an envelope and a stamp; then she sat down at a table and dipped the rusty post office pen in ink. She had come there possessed with a fear which had haunted her ever since she had felt Mr. Royall's ring on her finger: the fear that Harney might, after all, free himself and come back to her. It was a possibility which had never occurred to her during the dreadful hours after she had received his letter; only when the decisive step she had taken made longing turn to apprehension did such a contingency seem conceivable. She addressed the envelope, and on the sheet of paper she wrote:

I'm married to Mr. Royall. I'll always remember you.

CHARITY.

The last words were not in the least what she had meant to write; they had flowed from her pen irresistibly. She had not had the strength to complete her sacrifice; but, after all, what did it matter? Now that there was no chance of ever seeing Harney again, why should she not tell him the truth?

When she had put the letter in the box she went out into the busy sunlit street and began to walk to the hotel. Behind the plate-glass windows of the department stores she noticed the tempting display of dresses and dress-materials that had fired her imagination on the day when she and Harney had looked in at them together. They reminded her of Mr. Royall's injunction to go out and buy all she needed. She looked down at her shabby dress, and wondered what she should say when he saw her coming back empty-handed. As she drew near the hotel she saw him waiting on the doorstep, and her heart began to beat with apprehension.

He nodded and waved his hand at her approach, and they walked through the hall and went upstairs to collect their possessions, so that Mr. Royall might give up the key of the room when they went down again for their midday dinner. In the bedroom, while she was thrusting back into the satchel the few things she had brought away with her, she suddenly felt that his eyes were on her and that he was going to speak. She stood still, her half-folded night-gown in her hand, while the blood rushed up to her drawn cheeks.

"Well, did you rig yourself out handsomely? I haven't seen any bundles round," he said jocosely.

"Oh, I'd rather let Ally Hawes make the few things I want," she answered.

"That so?" He looked at her thoughtfully for a moment and his eye-brows projected in a scowl. Then his face grew friendly again. "Well, I wanted you to go back looking stylisher than any of them; but I guess you're right. You're a good girl, Charity."

Their eyes met, and something rose in his that she had never seen there: a look that made her feel ashamed and yet secure.

"I guess you're good, too," she said, shyly and quickly. He smiled without answering, and they went out of the room together and dropped down to the hall in the glittering lift.

Late that evening, in the cold autumn moonlight, they drove up to the door of the red house.

Part Three

CONTEXTS

From *A Backward Glance*

Edith Wharton

Wharton published her memoirs, *A Backward Glance,* in 1934, three
years before her death. In the following excerpts, she discusses *Ethan
Frome* and *Summer*. [Ed.]

My two New England tales, "Ethan Frome" and "Summer", were the result
of explorations among villages bedrowsed in a decaying rural existence,
and sad slow-speaking people living in conditions hardly changed since
their forbears held those villages against the Indians. [153–54]

It was not until I wrote "Ethan Frome" that I suddenly felt the artisan's full
control of his implements. When "Ethan Frome" first appeared I was severely criticized by the reviewers for what was considered the clumsy structure of the tale. I had pondered long on this structure, had felt its peculiar
difficulties, and possible awkwardness, but could think of no alternative
which would serve as well in the given case; and though I am far from
thinking "Ethan Frome" my best novel, and am bored and even exasperated when I am told that it is, I am still sure that its structure is not its weak
point. [209]

The book to the making of which I brought the greatest joy and the fullest
ease was "Ethan Frome". For years I had wanted to draw life as it really was
in the derelict mountain villages of New England, a life even in my time,
and a thousandfold more a generation earlier, utterly unlike that seen
through the rose-coloured spectacles of my predecessors, Mary Wilkins
[Freeman] and Sarah Orne Jewett.[1] In those days, the snow-bound villages
of Western Massachusetts were still grim places, morally and physically: in-

---

New York: D. Appleton-Century, 1934.

[1] American authors Mary E. Wilkins Freeman (1852–1930) and Sarah Orne Jewett (1849–
1909) were New England regionalists. [ED.]

sanity, incest, and slow mental and moral starvation were hidden away behind the paintless wooden house-fronts of the long village street, or in the
isolated farm-houses on the neighbouring hills. [. . .] In this connection, I
may mention that every detail about the colony of drunken mountain outlaws described in 'Summer' was given to me by the rector of the church at
Lenox (near which we lived), and that the lonely peak I have called "the
Mountain" was in reality Bear Mountain, an isolated summit not more
than twelve miles from our own home. The rector had been fetched there
by one of the mountain outlaws to read the Burial Service over a woman of
evil reputation; and when he arrived every one in the house of mourning
was drunk, and the service performed as I have related it. The rector's predecessor in the fashionable parish of Lenox had, I believe, once been called
for on a similar errand, but had prudently refused to go; my friend, however, thought it his duty to do so, and drove off alone with the outlaw —
coming back with his eyes full of horror and his heart of anguish and pity.
Needless to say, when "Summer" appeared, this chapter was received with
indignant denial by many reviewers and readers; and not the least vocifer-
ous were the New Englanders who had for years sought the reflection of local life in the rose-and-lavender pages of their favourite authoresses — and
had forgotten to look into Hawthorne's.

   "Ethan Frome" shocked my readers less than "Summer"; but it was frequently criticised as "painful", and at first had much less success than my
previous books. I have a clearer recollection of its beginnings than of those
of my other tales, through the singular accident that its first pages were
written — in French! I had determined, when we came to live in Paris, to
polish and enlarge my French vocabulary; for though I had spoken the language since the age of four I had never had much occasion to talk it, for any
length of time, with cultivated people, having usually, since my marriage,
wandered through France as a tourist. The result was that I had kept up the
language chiefly through reading, and [. . .] to bring my idioms up to date
I asked Charles Du Bos[2] to find, among his friends, a young professor who
would come and talk with me two or three times a week. An amiable young
man was found; but, being too amiable ever to correct my spoken mistakes, he finally hit on the expedient of asking me to prepare an "exercise"
before each visit. The easiest thing for me was to write a story; and thus the
French version of "Ethan Frome" was begun, and carried on for a few
weeks. Then the lessons were given up, and the copy-book containing my
"exercise" vanished forever. But a few years later, during one of our sum-

---

[2] French writer Charles du Bos (1882–1939) was a friend of Wharton and translator of the
French edition of *The House of Mirth*. [Ed.]

mer sojourns at the Mount, a distant glimpse of Bear Mountain brought Ethan back to my memory, and the following winter in Paris I wrote the tale as it now stands, reading my morning's work aloud each evening to Walter Berry,[3] who was as familiar as I was with the lives led in those half-deserted villages before the coming of motor and telephone. We talked the tale over page by page, so that its accuracy of "atmosphere" is doubly assured—and I mention this because not long since, in an article by an American literary critic, I saw "Ethan Frome" cited as an interesting example of a successful New England story written by some one who knew nothing of New England! "Ethan Frome" was written after I had spent ten years in the hill-region where the scene is laid, during which years I had come to know well the aspect, dialect, and mental and moral attitude of the hill-people. The fact that "Summer" deals with the same class and type as those portrayed in "Ethan Frome", and has the same setting, might have sufficed to disprove the legend—but once such a legend is started it echoes on as long as its subject survives. [293–96]

Gradually my intellectual unrest sobered down into activity. I began to write a short novel, "Summer", as remote as possible in setting and subject from the scenes about me; and the work made my other tasks seem lighter. The tale was written at a high pitch of creative joy, but amid a thousand interruptions, and while the rest of my being was steeped in the tragic realities of the war; yet I do not remember ever visualizing with more intensity the inner scene, or the creatures peopling it. [356]

From *The Berkshires: The Purple Hills*

Roderick Peattie et al.

The Berkshire Mountains of western Massachusetts form the backdrop for both *Ethan Frome* and *Summer*. Wharton was a resident of Lenox, Massachusetts, located in the heart of the Berkshires, for ten years in the early part of the twentieth century. [Ed.]

———

What are the Berkshire Hills? Probably many in the outside world think of them chiefly as the hills which ring Stockbridge and Lenox—an idea not

———

New York: Vanguard P, 1948.

[3] American Walter Berry (1859–1927) was a close personal friend of Wharton. [Ed.]

infrequently entertained by the inhabitants of those distinguished villages. Actually they are much more extensive, filling the whole of western Massachusetts from just west of the Connecticut River to the New York State line. The Berkshires are a southern extension of the Green Mountains and the Taconic Range of Vermont, but, unlike the Green Mountains, they have no central spine of pronounced peaks. They form a high, rolling plateau some twenty air-line miles wide, extending from the Vermont boundary into Connecticut, where they change character and become the Litchfield Hills. This plateau, in earlier days rightly called the Berkshire Barrier, rises abruptly from the Connecticut River Valley and drops down abruptly again to the valleys of the Hoosic River north of Pittsfield and the Housatonic River south. Across this depression is the narrow ridge of the Taconics, its western walls dropping into New York, marked by the only truly mountainous peaks in the region. The highest is Greylock at the north (3,491 feet). Mount Everett, or, popularly, the Dome, in the southwest corner of the state, reaches an elevation of only 2,624 feet but by its contours and abrupt leap from the Sheffield plain achieves the beauty and distinction of a true mountain.

The valley between the two ranges, drained northward by the Hoosic and southward by the Housatonic, is the Berkshire region of industry and fashion, of summer music and drama, of schools and colleges. The high plateau of the Barrier is the region of almost forgotten villages, of abandoned farms, of second-growth forest repossessing land once cleared by the pioneers, of ancient roads now choked and often impassable, and of wide prospects from the hills over an undulating sea of treetops.

It was this region I first knew in 1899, before I had ever seen Stockbridge. The season was September, and I decided on a walking trip before going back to college. I took the Fitchburg train out of Boston on a hot, sticky day, and presently we were lurching up the gorge of the Deerfield River. I alighted at a station called Zoar, a few miles short of the tunnel, and drew a deep breath of fresh air. The stage driver was expecting me. His "stage" was a battered carry-all, and after a laconic greeting we began climbing the road northward beside the noisy waters of Pelham Brook.

"How far is it to Rowe?" I asked.

"Ten miles up, two miles down," said he—which added to the right figure.

Up and up we plodded. The air grew cooler and cooler. I could smell the sweet water of the brook, or fancied I could. Finally we leveled off on the village street, where there were a sawmill, a few houses, a little stone church, and a general store. Thence the road ran uphill again to the old center, where I could glimpse the spire of the ancient church, now abandoned. [. . .]

It is difficult to capture a poetic mood from the wheel of a car. Pull up at this abandoned house and barn on the shoulder of a hill and step out. The farm fields have not yet surrendered to the advancing woods, and you can look off a long way. Bryant,[1] looking back down the hill to his native village, saw far more cleared land than you see now, and in spring he would have seen, as he has recorded, acres of pink apple orchards. But he, too, would have looked, as you will, into the gorge cut by the river and walled by forested hills and, far off beyond their green ramparts, at the misty blue waves of the distant Berkshires. Imagine a young man setting off to make his living in the world and looking wistfully back at the embosomed village he calls home, while westward a cold sunset silhouettes a lone bird flying. Then it is not difficult to recapture his inspiration. [. . .]

WINTER

So winter has come to the purple hills. No one knows just when the first sleet will sift through the forest branches and fall rattling through the frozen leaves. Perhaps the snow won't come that way at all. It may appear like a ghost in the silent night and shroud the fields and hills in a soft white blanket. As we step into the fresh clear air, and feel it penetrate deep into our lungs, we accept another season. Snow shoveling, skiing, and skating, and perhaps a long all-day hike with snowshoes when the snow is soft and the air zero crisp. We are startled at the loud reports from frozen hardwood trees but glide silently beneath the towering pines and hemlocks, save for the occasional snap of a lower limb that could not stand our passing pressure.

The contrasting clear white of a large clump of white birches against the evergreen background of hemlocks wins our attention, and we wonder why this combination stands out more now than in summer. Deer tracks, scattered and undecided, tell us of the reluctance of the deer to leave the heavy winter shelter provided by the thick laurel and scattered evergreen trees beneath the mountain ledge. The familiar hopping tracks of the rabbit, the marks of the leaping gray squirrel, and the scuffled snow where a partridge came down to feed from its pine roost, belie the thought that all is dormant.

At first, before the snow is deep, we are reminded of the summer flowers by the persistence of the stiff seed pods. Those of the wild carrots look like giant snowflakes when covered with freshly adhering snow. The milkweed pods rattle and stiffly resist the strong winds, and the cattails stand at

---

[1] William Cullen Bryant (1794–1878) was a Massachusetts-born American poet and editor. Among his best-known works are "Thanatopsis," "To a Waterfowl," and "Autumn Woods." [Ed.]

the edge of the marsh, bordered by lesser sedges, their brown tops conspicuous against the whitened ground. The drooping clusters of the high-bush cranberry fruits must indeed be sour to have survived the sweeping autumn visitations from flocks of robins and a host of other feathered friends. Early in the winter, the beautiful bright red fruit of the black alder, Ilex verticillata, our deciduous holly, stands out on the edge of the swamp.

By February, the woodland snows have piled high, perhaps completely covering the woodsman's four-foot pile of cordwood at the edge of the wind-swept field. But life goes on in a way; the nuthatches and chickadees seem busier than ever, and somewhere up on the side of the mountain a downy woodpecker whales away at something hard. Between storms, the woodland's snow-covered floor becomes soiled with bits of bark and twigs. A flash of red is all we see of a fox whose sense of smell has been sharpened by hunger and the fresh winds of winter.

Late in the season and during early spring, our hills become a richer purple. Is it our imagination, or can it be true that the millions of buds stirred by the first pressure of sap have given the distant hill a richer hue? The blood-red branches of the red osier along the winding meadow brook attract our attention now as the color is heightened. The bluebird has announced spring, but now we have further proof that it is near, for there at the edge of the sugar bush are the farmer and his dog. The farmer has a bitstock in hand, ready to test the first maple for rising sap. As he hangs the pail beneath the spout and turns to sniff the veering south wind, the barking cow dog skids to an abrupt stop in the wet snow, and a red squirrel scampers to safety in the first crotch of the maple tree to be tapped next as sugaring starts. Back in our study, we turn the calendar and make ready for new entries to supplement our still very incomplete notes on Berkshire flora.

"Fatal Coasting Accident"

Berkshire Evening Eagle

Wharton based the sledding scene in *Ethan Frome* on an actual 1904 accident in Lenox, Massachusetts, which took the life of one high school student and seriously injured several others. [Ed.]

———

12 Mar. 1904.

Lenox High School Girl Dashed to Her Death

———

Four Companions Seriously Injured

———

Miss Hazel Crosby, Who Was Steering, Lost Control of "Double Ripper" — Fatal Coasting Accident in Resort Town

———

Miss Hazel Crosby, a junior in the Lenox high school, was fatally and several companions seriously injured in a coasting accident in Lenox yesterday afternoon soon after 4 o'clock.

The young people were on a "double ripper" coasting sled, sweeping down a very steep hill at a tremendous rate of speed, when the fatality occurred. At the foot of the hill the sled veered and crashed into a lamp-post, fatally injuring Miss Crosby and fracturing the limbs of three others.

THE DEAD.

Miss Hazel Crosby, right leg fractured in three places, left leg in one place, lower jaw broken, internal injuries.

THE INJURED.

Miss Crissey Henry, serious concussion of the brain, bad injury to side of face, injured internally.

Miss Lucy Brown, thigh fractured between knee and hip, cut on face under chin, cut in back of head.

Miss Kate Spencer, dislocation of right hip joint.

Mansuit Schmitt, contusions of head and body.

Miss Crosby was taken to the House of Mercy in this city last evening where she died at 11:30 o'clock. The fractures were reduced and everything possible was done for her, but the efforts of the skilled surgeons and doctors were without avail.

Miss Henry was taken to her home, and her condition was such that for a time her recovery was despaired of. Of those who survived the accident, she is the most seriously injured, but will recover.

SCENE OF ACCIDENT.

The scene of the accident is out a short distance from Curtis hotel, in the center of Lenox. The hill leads from Egglestone monument through Stockbridge street in the direction of Stockbridge. The houses of Charles Lanier and W. D. Sloane are on this street.

Court House hill as it is called is exceedingly steep and for some time has been covered with sheet ice. It is in general use for coasting purposes and every afternoon sees a number of parties enjoying the sport at that point. It is the favorite coasting place for all the guests who go to the Curtis hotel for recreation and out of door sport in the wintertime, as, owing to the ice, it is but little used by teams at this season of the year. The smooth condition of the road, with but little snow upon it, affords superior advantages for the sport.

HIGH SPEED ATTAINED.

The road, from the coasters' viewpoint, was never in finer condition than it was yesterday. A speed almost unequaled in all the long history of coasting in Lenox was obtained, and the sport had been indulged in at intervals almost all day. It came to a close by the grim happenings that brought such disaster and sorrow to many homes and shrouded Lenox in gloom. On account of the peculiar circumstances attending the affair and the youth of the victims the accident was especially sad and distressing.

The five injured were but a part of the party who went from the high school building for coasting. They used a large sled, heavily built. Mansuit Schmitt, the only young man in the party, had been steering the sled on its course until the accident. Miss Crosby expressed a desire to guide the sled on one trip, and the permission was reluctantly granted. She took her position in front of the party of coasters.

A young sister of Schmitt was in the party just before the fatal slide was begun. She was invited to participate in the slide, but refused, stating that she was going on an errand and could not delay. As she bade them goodbye the five young people boarded the double-ripper, and started on the coast, which resulted in the death of one and injury of the other members of the party.

Despite the fact that this hill is one of the most popular coasting places in the town it is also very dangerous and numerous narrow escapes from accidents have been reported as taking place there. Just at the foot of the hill Hawthorne street branches off to the southwest. There are two entrances from Hawthorne street to Stockbridge street and the center of these entrances form a triangle. In this triangle is located the lamppost with which the double-ripper collided.

SAW THE PARTY.

So far as can be learned, John Parsons is the only one who saw the accident. Soon after they passed him he heard a shout, presumably uttered by Miss Crosby who had lost control of the sled. It is just possible that one of the runners came in contact with a rut in the road causing the sled to sheer off, but there can be little certainty upon this point. Mr. Parsons turned just in time to witness the collision.

THE START.

The start was made at the brow of the hill, near the Egglestone monument where Schmitt pushed off, and in an instant the sled gained great momentum and fairly vanished from the view of the onlookers at the starting point. Shortly afterward, a crash and shout were heard, and the spectators and residents living along the street hurried to the bend in the road.

There, at the foot of the hill were all five members of the party unconscious. The sled had crashed into a lamp-post at the junction of Hawthorne and Stockbridge streets. Neither the post nor the sled were wrecked. Miss Crosby received the full force of the collision and it is a wonder that she was not instantly killed. Miss Crosby and Miss Spencer were lying close together when found and some distance beyond were the others in a human pile.

INJURED CARED FOR.

Miss Crosby and Miss Henry were carried into the residence of Edward Witherspoon at the Parsons place, and others were taken to the residence of John T. Parsons. Surgeons were telephoned for in all directions. From Lee, Dr. Hassett responded, and Drs. Charles H. Richardson, Henry Colt, and L. C. Swift went from Pittsfield.

The interval between the accident and the arrival of the surgeons was one of high nerve tension in Lenox. Nearly every one in the town hurried to the scene of the accident, and business in the little town was almost suspended. Rumors that at least two were killed were soon afloat, and added to the excitement.

From present indications, the accident was caused by Miss Crosby losing control of the sled at the bottom of the hill, where there is a sharp depression to the right in the road, and causing the sled to leave the track in the road and follow the sheet of ice which stood in the center of a triangle formed by Hawthorne street branch where it joins Stockbridge road.

The "double-ripper" was owned by Herbert Spencer, a brother of one of the girls injured. Twice the four girls had coasted down the hill when young Schmitt put in an appearance. The boy then guided the bobs down the hill. While walking to the top of the hill the Crosby girl requested that she be permitted to steer on the next slide. This request was granted.

WHO VICTIMS ARE.

Miss Crosby was 18 years of age and was the daughter of Mr. and Mrs. Louis Crosby, and, as already stated, a junior in the school. She was a very bright pupil and a general favorite with everybody. She is survived, besides her parents, by four sisters, Lewellyn, Edna, Patience and Constant and by six brothers, Wyland, Harold, Earl, Howard, Sprague and Allida. Three of the brothers are members of the boys' choir of the Episcopal church to which society their parents belong. Hazel was the eldest daughter. The family reside on Stockbridge street. Patience and Constant Crosby are twins. Mr. Crosby was formerly in the meat business but now conducts a gardening business.

Miss Henry was attended by Dr. Hassett. She regained consciousness today, but her condition is still quite serious. She bled quite freely from the eyes and nose today. It is impossible to determine at this time whether her skull is fractured. The family reside on West street. The father is caretaker at the Winthrop, formerly the Robeson place. Miss Henry is a sister of W. G. Henry, who is one of the permanent men at the central fire station in this city. Miss Henry is in her junior year at the high school.

Miss Spencer is a daughter of Mr. and Mrs. Ellery Spencer and the family lives on Fairview avenue. Miss Spencer was the only high school senior in the party, the others being members of the junior class. Her condition today was as comfortable as could be expected and her complete recovery is only a question of time.

The condition of Miss Lucy Brown today is very encouraging. She is a daughter of Mr. and Mrs. Harry A. Brown of Cliffwood street.

Young Schmitt was delirious much of the time today. Although apparently not seriously injured about the body, his head appears to give him some trouble. His condition is rather pitiable from the fact that since the accident he has continually raved about it, giving vent to the feeling that he was entirely responsible for the accident. The boy was a member of the junior class at the high school and is very popular among his schoolmates. In addition to his school duties he acts as Lenox correspondent for the Evening Journal.

HIGH SCHOOL PUPILS MEET.

A meeting of the Lenox high school pupils was held this afternoon to take action anent the accident. It is planned to send a floral tribute to the funeral of Miss Crosby.

Mr. Crosby and Mrs. Arrowsmith, wife of Rev. Harold Arrowsmith, came to Pittsfield this morning and made arrangements for the removal of Miss Crosby's body to Lenox.

FUNERAL MONDAY.

The funeral is to be held Monday afternoon at 2:30 o'clock at the house and at 3 o'clock from the church. Rev. Mr. Arrowsmith is to conduct the services.

From *Essays on Hypochondriacal and Other Nervous Affections*

John Reid, M.D.

Dr. John Reid, a specialist in nervous disorders, including hypochondria, treated hundreds of patients in the late nineteenth and early twentieth century. His observations on hypochrondria offer insights into the complexities of Zeena's medical condition in *Ethan Frome*. [Ed.]

<hr />

Hypochondria

An [*sic*] hypochondriac should be a hermit in abstinence, but not in solitude. [...] The society, in the centre of which a person is placed, may be regarded as the atmosphere of his mind: and to one whose understanding has

---

Philadelphia: M. Carey & Son, 1817.

anent: in regard to.

been improved to any considerable degree of refinement or extent, this mental atmosphere is of more importance to the vigour and proper condition, even of his body, than almost any variety in the modification or proportion of those material ingredients with which his lungs are supplied by the external air. A residence even in a great and polluted city, which affords objects of interest, and motives to exertion, ought to be recommended more especially to an [sic] hypochondriacal or nervous patient, in preference to the most highly oxygenated situation in the country, where there is not enough to rouse the sluggishness, or to fill the vacuity, of the mind.

Hypochondriasis is far from being a metropolitan disease. The multiplicity of external objects, which, in a great capital, are continually giving a new direction to the current of thought, is of course unfavourable to the uniformity and self-absorption of melancholy. There are, in such a situation, so many rival candidates for our attention, as to preclude the exclusive dominion of any single idea. Although a man be not concerned as an actor in the gay or the more serious tumults of the world, he may find, as a simple spectator, sufficient engagement to prevent the dejection of mind which is apt to arise from its being unemployed. [. . .]

A rage for rural charms is at the present day a matter more perhaps of fashion than of feeling. A pretended relish for the beauties of the country is found to be by no means incompatible with a real attachment to vices which are considered as appropriate to the town; although in fact the most degrading kinds of vice are at least as prevalent at a distance from, as in the centre of, the capital. Intemperance, both in eating and drinking, is especially predominant in remote towns and provinces where the inhabitants often devote a large portion of the day to the pleasures of the table, from having no other resource for the disposal of their time. [. . .]

To one who has principally resided in the middle of a great city, an entire and permanent removal from it is a doubtful and somewhat dangerous experiment. The shades of solitude, it is to be feared, may prove too dark for him who has been long used to the sunshine of society. [. . .]

A diseased fancy will not unfrequently produce nearly all the symptoms, or at least all the sensations of bodily disease. But any very serious malady of the latter kind is calculated, on the other hand, to dissipate the clouds which hover over the imagination. Hypochondriasis may often thank calamity for its cure. [. . .]

In the crucible of serious sorrow, the affections are, in general, purified and refined. But trials of a lighter sort have often an undesirable rather than a happy influence upon the character. A high degree of heat *melts,* a lower merely soils and tarnishes the metal which is exposed to its influence. Truly tragical misfortune begets a kind of heroic composure. Distress, when it is profound, becomes the parent of equanimity. It renders our feelings proof against the petty hostilities of fortune. What were before cares, are, under such circumstances, often converted into comforts. [. . .] Adversity, when it assumes its more awful form, lifts us above the level of the earth, so that we are no longer incommoded by the roughness or inequalities of its surface. From this state of elevated sorrow, a man looks down upon the common-place troubles of life with the same sort of contempt or indifference as upon the toys and trifles of his childhood. The mind itself is enlarged by the magnitude of its misery. [. . .]

The advantage of indispensable occupation, is never more unequivocally evinced than in cases of heavy calamity. The apparent aggravation of an evil, will not unfrequently be found to constitute, in fact, the source of its most effectual relief. [. . .] Salutary as occupation in general is, it is far from being so when it consists almost exclusively in an attention to a man's self, and more particularly to his corporeal sensations and infirmities. The hypochondriac often destroys his health, by taking too much care of it. The maker of a watch will tell you, that there is no way more certain of injuring it, than the constantly meddling with its machinery. In like manner, it is impossible to be perpetually tampering with the constitution, without either disordering its movements or impairing the elasticity of its spring. [. . .]

The constitutional or inveterate hypochondriac is apt to view every thing only in the relation which it may bear to his malady. [. . .] He is almost daily employed either in the search after, or in the trial of, remedies for a disease which is often to be cured only by striving to forget it. [. . .]

From *Wharton's New England*

Barbara A. White

Although many of her most famous works take place in urban centers, Wharton set several of her short stories, as well as *Ethan Frome* and *Summer,* in New England. In this excerpt, critic Barbara A. White offers both a historical and a literary context for the New England settings. [Ed.]

———————

Wharton used the western Massachusetts setting not only for *Ethan Frome* and *Summer* but also for a novel, *The Fruit of the Tree* (1907), and

---

Hanover: UP of New England, 1995.

in numerous short stories throughout her career. Long after the Mount was sold, the Whartons divorced, and Edith living out her life in Paris, Starkfield would appear in "Bewitched" (1925). The last story Wharton sent to her publishers before her death was "All Souls'" (1937), another New England witch tale, and she left a number of unpublished fragments with New England settings. A full quarter of Wharton's eighty-five published short stories are set in New England. Of these, three stories, "The Angel at the Grave" (1901), "Xingu" (1911), and "All Souls'" (1937), [. . .], are rated among her very best.

That Wharton felt considerably attached to her New England body of work is shown by the fierceness with which she defended it from attack. Although most reviewers praised her treatment of New England, some thought her settings too bleak — as in *Ethan Frome* and the short story "The Pretext" (1908); others found mistakes, as in her depiction of factories in *The Fruit of the Tree*.[1] Wharton seldom responded to negative reviews, but she was stung by criticisms that she was an outsider who knew nothing of New England. While she quietly corrected the errors, she loudly attributed reviewers' complaints to their desire to avoid dark truths and approach New England as "seen through the rose-colored spectacles of my predecessors, Mary Wilkins [Freeman] and Sarah Orne Jewett."[2] In three articles and her autobiography, Wharton insisted on her firsthand knowledge of the region and the "accuracy of 'atmosphere'" in her works (*BG*, 296).

Wharton was certainly correct about her familiarity with New England. She had summered in the region since childhood in her parents' Newport, Rhode Island, mansion, and as an adolescent she made visits to Bar Harbor, Maine, where she met her lifelong friend Walter Berry. The man she chose to marry was a Bostonian and Harvard graduate; in fact, all the men closest to her — her husband Teddy, Berry, her lover Morton Fullerton, and her art critic friend Bernard Berenson — were Harvard grads, however cosmopolitan and European-oriented they seemed. After her marriage Wharton bought and refurbished a house in Newport, which she named Land's End as it looked out to sea. She became acquainted with Boston through visits to her in-laws, and Teddy's mother also had a summer house in Lenox, Massachusetts. It was thus that Edith found a way to escape the humid climate and (in her view) anti-intellectualism of Newport.

In the eyes of some, Lenox was simply Newport in the mountains. It had become a fashionable resort for the nouveau riche, who lived in million

---

[1]The setting of "The Pretext" is discussed in an anonymous review, "Short Stories by Mrs. Wharton," *New York Times Saturday Review*, Oct. 3, 1908, 541.

[2]Edith Wharton, *A Backward Glance* (New York: D. Appleton-Century, 1934) 293; hereafter cited in the text as *BG*.

dollar "cottages" and built castles with a hundred rooms. With some of these socialites Wharton would not be very popular. Her friend D. B. Updike, founder of the Merrymount Press in Boston, recalled that her neighbors "were sometimes made uncomfortable by the suspicion—by no means unfounded—that Mrs. Wharton was ironically amusing at their expense. I remember one evening in particular when she returned from a dinner remarking, 'The XYZ's have decided, they tell me, to have books in the library.'" [3] Once when a dowager was showing off her house and gushed, "I call this my Louis Quinze room," Wharton reportedly replied, "*Why, my dear?*" [4]

But in spite of the XYZ types, Wharton found fewer of Newport's social "inanities," as she put it, in Lenox (Lewis, 123), and she was intrigued by its literary past. Both Hawthorne and Melville had tramped through the Berkshires and described the area in their works, and one of America's pioneer novelists, Catharine Maria Sedgwick (1789–1867), hailed from nearby Stockbridge. Although Wharton tended to distance herself from her female forerunners, as shown in her remarks on Jewett and Wilkins Freeman, she used Sedgwick's life as a source for an unfinished novel, "The Keys of Heaven," which was set in a town called "Slowbridge."

Wharton spent every summer from 1899 through 1908 in Lenox; in her words, "There for over ten years I lived and gardened and wrote contentedly" (*BG*, 125). The Mount, the home she designed and built to her specifications, was completed in 1902. Although not as costly and ostentatious as the neighboring abodes, it still dwarfed Henry James's description— "a delicate French chateau mirrored in a Massachusetts pond." [5] The Mount, which still stands today and can be visited, is an imposing four-story white stucco building with enough space to house a dozen servants. From the living and dining rooms of the ground floor, French doors lead to a terrace that once overlooked Wharton's profuse flower gardens. To many visitors the gardens were more impressive than the house. Wharton regularly won prizes for her flowers and once confided, "I'm a better landscape gardener than novelist, and this place, every line of which is my own work, far surpasses the House of Mirth." [6]

---

[3] Percy Lubbock, *Portrait of Edith Wharton* (New York: D. Appleton-Century, 1947), 17; subsequent references are noted in the text.

[4] R. W. B. Lewis, *Edith Wharton: A Biography* (New York: Harper, 1975) 148; hereafter cited in the text as Lewis.

[5] *The Letters of Henry James*, ed. Leon Edel (Cambridge: Belknap Press, 1984), 4:325.

[6] *The Letters of Edith Wharton*, ed. R. W. B. Lewis and Nancy Lewis (New York: Scribner's, 1988) 242; hereafter cited in the text as *Letters*.

Wharton was not exactly a "summer visitor" and the Mount a summer home, for she usually spent half the year in Lenox, from June to December (and the other half in New York and Europe). She also participated in village activities, such as rearranging the Lenox Library and serving on the Village Improvement and the Flower Show committees. In ten years she spent a good deal of time in the area, and it was not her choice to leave it. But the Mount became a casualty of the Whartons' marital difficulties: Teddy refused to help manage the estate unless Edith retained him as her trustee; this she declined to do because he had embezzled some of her money to set up a mistress. Thus in 1911 the property was sold, and Edith removed permanently to Europe. Although she felt a "great ache" for the Mount, she was not to see Lenox again except as she re-created it in her fiction (*Letters*, 277).

While living at the Mount, Wharton's pattern was to write in the mornings and spend the afternoons gardening, walking, doing village committee work, or hosting an endless stream of visitors. Most important for her writing was her habit of entertaining visitors with rides through the Berkshires, in the early years by horseback or carriage and later, when the Whartons had acquired an American car, by automobile. Henry James spoke fondly of these auto rides, and Wharton's biographer notes that "as they drove slowly through the little New England villages, Edith regaled the fascinated James with reports that had reached her about the dark unsuspected life — the sexual violence, even the incest — that went on behind the bleak walls of the farmhouses" (Lewis, 140). James was not the only friend with whom Wharton shared her interest in her less wealthy, year-round neighbors. D. B. Updike recalled one windy afternoon when they drove past "a battered two-story house, unpainted, with a neglected dooryard tenanted by hens and chickens, and a few bedraggled children sitting on the stone steps. 'It is about a place like that,' said Mrs. Wharton, 'that I mean to write a story. Only last week I went to the village meeting-house in Lenox and sat there for an hour alone, trying to think what such lives would be, and some day I shall write a story about it'" (Lubbock, 23).

Eventually she would write more than one story. These leisurely rides through the New England countryside (the speed limit was twenty miles per hour and the car often broke down) seem to have deeply inspired Wharton. While her fiction based in Newport tends to be brittle social comedy, and except for the description of Newport in *The Age of Innocence* inferior to her other work, her Lenox observations stimulated her imagination and remained vivid in her mind. Wharton toured with Updike in 1905, but she composed *Ethan Frome* with "the greatest joy and the fullest ease" in 1911 and as late as 1916 wrote *Summer* "at a high pitch of creative joy, but amid a thousand interruptions, and while the rest of my being was steeped in the tragic realities of the war; yet I do not remember ever visualizing with more intensity the inner scene, or the creatures peopling it" (*BG*, 293, 356).

From Wharton's perspective, her auto trips through the Berkshires, and even as far away as Boston, New Hampshire, and Maine, only proved her knowledge of New England. One could, however, take another view of Edith Wharton and guest being chauffeured through the countryside in her luxurious car while they peered at the rustics, trying to envision the inside of a dilapidated farmhouse. This is the pose of the outsider. It could easily be argued that even if Wharton resided in New England, her class status kept her from truly knowing it [. . .]. Wharton was bound to make mistakes, however much she researched local customs and events, and recent critics have found an increasing number of "errors" in Wharton's work. It has been said of *Ethan Frome*, for instance, that Ethan should deliver boards instead of logs, shouldn't shave before he milks the cows, wouldn't waste time coasting downhill, and would never have allowed Mattie to attend a church dance, if there had been such things.

Of course, for every critic who complains that Wharton was an Episcopalian and failed to understand rural Christianity, there are several for whom the dance at the church glows in the imagination. It is important to ask whether Wharton had the desire or intent to portray New England in the thorough, balanced manner of the so-called "local colorist." Rather, she seems to have used New England settings for her own more Hawthornean purposes, as symbolic means of exploring favorite subjects, such as the absence of high culture in modern life, the permeation of the present by the past, and the claustrophobia of female experience. Wharton's New England fiction is most easily characterized by what it is *not* about, not like *The House of Mirth* and *The Age of Innocence* primarily about marriage and divorce, the dishonesty of the socioeconomic system, the power of society to mold individual lives, the turning of women into beautiful objects. With the exception of some Newport stories, it is less socially dense than her other work, more inclined to the probing of psyches than the dissection of manners.

Wharton's New England fiction has a wide range, however, running the gamut from light comedy to horror. One tale [. . .] is a witty satire that makes fun of cultural pretensions ("Xingu"). Others treat the New England past and Puritan legacy in critical but complex ways ("The Lamp of Psyche," "The Angel at the Grave," and "The Pretext"). Finally, in the chilling *Ethan Frome* and her New England ghost stories ("The Triumph of Night," "Bewitched," and "All Souls'"), Wharton undertakes to scare us;

she uses barren settings and cold and snow imagery to create haunting tales shadowed by isolation, crime, and incest. What holds this wide-ranging body of work together are the themes that Wharton sometimes wrote about in her other work but associated most strongly with New England: poverty and decay, moral intolerance ("witch-burning"), cultural emptiness, and oppression by the past.

Poverty and decay are the hallmarks of Wharton's New England. She was clearly less interested in the mansions of her peers than the unpainted farmhouses with bedraggled children on the steps. In her early work the poverty often seems exaggerated, as in "Friends" (1900), one of her first stories set in New England. The heroine's friend lives in a shabby hovel in coastal Sailport while she struggles to support a "crippled" brother and "slatternly" sister.[7] The town is described as a sort of wasteland—the streets are full of dust and garbage, and even "the patches of ground between the houses are not gardens, but waste spaces strewn with nameless refuse" (1:197). Wharton's emphatic opening line, "Sailport is an ugly town" (1:197), recalls her comment that she sought to avoid the rose-colored glasses of her forerunners. One can detect a strong anxiety of influence at work, as Wharton was clearly influenced by Sarah Orne Jewett and Mary Wilkins Freeman, even if she can only acknowledge them in a backhanded way. At the beginning of her career Wharton feared being pigeonholed as a "woman writer" or "local colorist," and along with such male authors as Theodore Dreiser and Stephen Crane, she wanted to announce her departure from the genteel, or rose-colored, tradition in American letters. Thus the exaggerated grimness of Sailport. An early version of the story was in fact rejected for being too negative, and Wharton had to promise her publisher to tone down "the *squalid* part" (*Letters*, 32).

Wharton's portrayal of a decaying New England was realistic to some extent, however. The region's population was shifting westward and into large cities, leaving behind empty farms; the once great sea-faring centers, such as Portsmouth, New Hampshire, lost their power and riches. At the time Wharton began to publish, Boston had already been supplanted by New York as the literary center of the country. Young people made their way in the world by moving out of New England. Thus Wharton could accurately have an old-timer say of Ethan Frome: "Guess he's been in Starkfield too many winters. Most of the smart ones get away." Only Frome's obligation to care for his invalid parents, and later his wife, keeps him from abandoning his "stark field" for greener pastures. [. . .]

---

[7] "Friends," in *The Collected Short Stories of Edith Wharton,* ed. R. W. B. Lewis (New York: Charles Scribner's Sons, 1968), 1:200. This collection is hereafter cited in the text by the volume and page number only.

[. . .] In *Ethan Frome* the protagonist is overcome by the same dark features Wharton attributes to New England in her earlier short stories: grinding poverty, cultural emptiness, and the oppression of a Puritan past. Ethan Frome's poverty, in the form of his "barren farm and failing sawmill," keeps him from realizing his dream of leaving Starkfield for a larger place. Even before he falls in love with Mattie Silver and yearns for the money to take her away, "he had always wanted to be an engineer, and to live in towns, where there were lectures and big libraries." [. . .] Ethan's situation, Wharton indicates, is made particularly painful by the denial of his intellectual aspirations. Before his father's death he had studied engineering at a college in Worcester. Now he expresses "resentment" at his ignorance of scientific advances. Ethan has a great sensitivity to the quiet and beauty of his environment, but like Wharton herself he cannot tolerate the "mental starvation." As much as she loved the Mount, we recall, she could not stay there all year. "I am wretched at being in town," she would tell [her close friend] Sally Norton. "Oh, to live in the country all the year round" (Lewis, 161). But then she would have missed the "mental refreshment" she found in New York and Europe (*Letters*, 104).

Of course it is not only Ethan's poverty that traps him in Starkfield but also his moral scruples. He left college to care for his invalid mother and missed selling the farm and moving to a larger town because of Zeena's illness early in their marriage. As he contemplates going West with Mattie, he recalls that "he was a poor man, the husband of a sickly woman, whom his desertion would leave alone and destitute; and even if he had had the heart to desert her he could have done so only by deceiving two kindly people who had pitied him." The latter are Mr. and Mrs. Hale, from whom Ethan considers borrowing money but rejects the idea because he would be taking advantage of their sympathy in order "to obtain money from them on false pretenses." Here Ethan seems to be making it a moral issue whether the mutton should be roasted or boiled. Although Wharton clearly wants us to admire Ethan's basic honesty and sense of responsibility for others (his positive New England traits), his refusal to budge an inch in relation to the Hales makes him a "prisoner for life."

In Ethan's family graveyard stands a memorial to his ancestors, "ETHAN FROME AND ENDURANCE HIS WIFE, WHO DWELLED TOGETHER IN PEACE FOR FIFTY YEARS." The living Ethan wonders, in a bit of foreshadowing, whether the same epitaph will be written over him and Zeena. Everything repeats itself. It is no accident that Zeena originally came to the Fromes, as Ethan's cousin, to nurse his mother; then Mattie, Zeena's cousin, came to nurse Zeena. Several times the women seem to Ethan to eerily change places, as when Mattie replaces Zeena on the threshold, repeating the previous evening, and Zeena's face "supersedes" Mattie's in the rocking chair.

If the Starkfield women are interchangeable, we are prepared for the ghastly tableau at the end where the fresh and childlike Mattie has turned into Zeena. Mattie is now "witch-like," and critic Elizabeth Ammons has effectively interpreted *Ethan Frome* as a fairy tale in which poverty and isolation turn women into witches (and the men who stay, she might have added, into silent martyrs).[8] The past bears down on the present and links Endurance Frome, with her Puritan name, to Ethan's mother, to Zeena, to Mattie. What seems so grim is not Ethan's or any one character's individual tragedy but the unbroken chain of want and despair.

Fittingly, *Ethan Frome* takes place in winter (in its French version it was known as *L'hiver*). The ubiquitous snow makes the New England farmhouses even more isolated, and the chain of despair seems frozen into place. Wharton, who ranks with the greatest writers in her creation of setting and atmosphere, uses snow and cold to brilliant effect in creating a frightening, voidlike atmosphere. The narrator and Ethan are caught in one storm, for instance, in which the snow falls "straight and steadily from a sky without wind, in a soft universal diffusion. . . . It seemed to be a part of the thickening darkness, to be the winter night itself descending on us layer by layer." The colors of *Ethan Frome* are black and white, with the blank scary white of Herman Melville's *Moby Dick* and only a touch of color provided by Mattie's cheeks and the red pickle dish.

Wharton's snowy settings are organic and not just decorative. The snow becomes an agent in Ethan's unfolding story: it delays him in getting the glue for the broken pickle dish and leads inexorably to the sledding accident. Just as Ethan's maimed body is paralleled in his house, his emotions are mirrored in the frozen landscape. As the narrator describes him, "He seemed a part of the mute melancholy landscape, an incarnation of its frozen woe, with all that was warm and sentient in him fast bound below the surface." The snow is such a "smothering medium" that Ethan has buried his feelings, memories, and perhaps his will. He used to be able to remember his trip to Florida and in winter call up the sight of the sunlit landscape, "but now it's all snowed under." Ethan, "by nature grave and inarticulate," as Wharton tended to see New Englanders, finally lapses into silence in the same way that his mother stopped talking in her last years and Zeena eventually "fell silent." The silence seems to be that of the grave. No wonder Ethan "looks as if he was dead." The novella ends with Mrs. Hale's statement, "I don't see's there's much difference between the Fromes up at the farm and the Fromes down in the graveyard."

[8] Elizabeth Ammons, *Edith Wharton's Argument with America* (Athens: University of Georgia Press, 1980), 59–77.

From "Glimpses of New England Farm Life"

Rowland Evans Robinson

In this excerpt from his 1878 essay, Robinson describes the realities of life on a New England farm, including the grueling labor and difficult winters that farmers face. His descriptions underscore the realism in *Ethan Frome*. [Ed.]

Poets have sung the delights of the farmer's life in strains so enchanting that one might wonder why all the world has not forsaken every other pursuit and betaken itself to the tilling of the soil. But the farmer himself, in the un-shaded hay-field, or plodding in the clayey furrow at the tail of his plow, with a free-holder's right sticking to each boot, or bending, with aching back, between the corn-rows, or breasting the winter storms in the performance of imperative duties, looks at his life from a different point of view. To him this life appears as full of toil and care and evil chances as that of any other toiler. And true it is, the life of an ordinary farmer is hard, with too little to soften it—too much of work, too little of play. But as true is what the poet sang so long ago: "Thrice happy are the husband-men if they could but see their blessings;" for they have independence, more than any others who by the sweat of the brow earn their bread, and the pure air of heaven to breathe, and the blessed privilege of daily communion with nature. [. . .]

Winter is fairly upon us at last, though by such gradual approaches has it come, that we are hardly aware of its presence, for its white seal is not yet set upon the earth. [. . .]

But now comes an afternoon with a breathless chill in it,—"a hard, dull bitterness of cold;" when the gray sky settles down upon the earth, covering, first, the blue, far-away mountains with a gray pall, then the nearer somber hills with a veil through which their rough outlines show but dimly, and are quite hidden when the coming snow-fall makes phantoms of the sturdy trees in the woods hard by. Then roofs and roads and fence-tops and grassless ground begin slowly to whiten, and boughs and twigs are traced with a faint white outline against a gray background, and the dull yellow of the fields grows paler under the falling snow, and a flock of snow-birds drifts across the fading landscape, like larger snow-flakes. The night-fall comes early, and going out on the back stoop, you find yourself on a little

Scribner's Monthly 16 (Aug. 1878).

island in a great sea of misty whiteness, out of which looms dimly the dusky barn, with its freight of live stock, grain and hay, the only ship within hail.

Aroused next morning by the stamping feet of the first risers, who have gone forth to explore, we find that a new world seems to have drifted to us, while we were lying fast anchored to the old chimney. Roofs are heaped and fences coped and trees are whiter than in May with bloom, with the universal snow. The great farm-wagon, standing half-hub deep in it, looks as out of place as if at sea. The dazed fowls peer wonderingly from the poultry-house, or, adventuring short trips therefrom, stop bewildered mid-way in their journey. Presently the gray objects, rising out of the strange white expanse, take on more familiar shapes, and we recognize the barn, the orchard (though it has an unsubstantial look, as if the first wind might blow it away, or an hour's warm sunshine melt it), the well-known trees, the neighbors' houses, the faint lines of the fences tracing the boundaries of fields and farms, the woods, and beyond them, the unchanged outlines of wooded hills and the far-away mountains, but with a new ruggedness in their sides and with new clearings, till now unknown, showing forth in white patches on their slopes. We may take our time, for we shall have long months in which to get acquainted with this changed world. [. . .]

Loads of logs are drawn to the saw-mill, a quaint old structure, whose mossy beams have spanned its swift race-way for half a century or more. The green ooze of the leaky flume turns the icicles to spikes of emerald, and the caves beneath the log dam have crystal portals of fantastic shapes. Heaps of logs and piles of boards and slabs environ it on the landward side, and a pleasant odor of freshly cut pine pervades the neighborhood. Its in-terior is as comfortless in winter as a hill-top, "Cold as a saw-mill" being a New England proverb; and it is often said of one who leaves outer doors open in cold weather, "Guess he was brought up in a saw-mill, where there wa'n't no doors." It is a poor lounging place now for our farmer [. . .].

Though every farm-house now has its sitting-room and parlor, and most a dining-room, the kitchen continues to be a favorite with farming folk, — a liking probably inherited from our grandfathers. In many of their houses this was the only large room, in which the family lived, and where all meals were taken, guests entertained, and merry-makings held. At one end was the great fire-place wherein back-log and fore-stick burned, sending forth warmth and light, intense and bright over the broad hearth, but growing feebler toward the dim corners where Jack Frost lurked and grotesque shadows leaped and danced on the wall. On the crane, sus-pended by hook or trammel, hung the big samp-kettle, bubbling and seething. The open dresser shone with polished pewter mug and trencher. Old-fashioned, splint-bottomed chairs, rude but comfortable, sent their long shadows across the floor. [. . .]

One night in the week, it may be, the young folks all pack off in the big sleigh to the singing-school in the town-house, where they and some scores of others combine to murder psalmody and break the heart of their instructor.

At these gatherings are flirtations and heart-burnings as well as at the "donation parties," which occur once or twice in the winter, when with kindly meant unkindness the poor minister's house is taken possession of by old and young, whose gifts too often but poorly compensate for the up-turning and confusion they have made with their romping games.

So winter drags its hoary length through dreary months, with silent snow-fall, fierce storm and dazzling sunshine. Mows dwindle and stacks disappear, leaving only the empty pens to mark their place, and cisterns fail, making the hauling of snow for melting an added task to the boys' duties. Buck-saw and ax are each day making shorter the long pile of cord-wood and greater the pile of stove-wood.

From "Incest and Resistance: Patterns of Father-Daughter Incest, 1880–1930"

Linda Gordon

Gordon traces actual incidents of father-daughter incest in the time period during which *Summer* is set. Her observations about the psychological impact on the victim help to illuminate the conflicts that Charity Royall undergoes at the end of the novella. Although the "incest" in *Summer* is more symbolic than actual (Royall is not Charity's biological father), there are, nevertheless, similarities in the experiences. [Ed.]

Incest as a form of family violence appeared in 10 percent of case records of Boston child-protection agencies between 1880 and 1930. These were overwhelmingly (98 percent) cases of father-daughter incest, and they shared a common pattern: the family relations made the girl victims into second wives, taking over many of the roles and functions of mothers, including housework, child care, and sexual relations with their father.

Social Problems 33.4 (Apr. 1986).

Despite their apparent obedience and acquiescence in their incestuous families, many of these girls actively sought escape from the family, loitering on the streets where a powerful neighborhood peer culture and their low self-esteem made them easily exploitable. This sex-delinquent behavior was a form of resistance to, even rebellion against, the canons of feminine acquiescence and domesticity which had allowed them to be victimized in the first place.

[. . .] In an uncontrolled qualitative analysis of the incest cases, benefiting also from comparison to nonsexual child abuse cases, it became apparent that one pattern dominated the cases in between 1880 and 1930. In this period, the incestuous relationships grew out of and appeared to participants as part of an overall family pattern of turning girls into second wives. The girls not only became sexual partners to the male heads of household, but also virtual housewives, taking over housework, child care and general family maintenance as well as sexual obligations. I call this pattern "domestic incest."

This historical finding fits with most feminist work on incest, which has emphasized girls' helplessness before fathers who have the combined power of men, parents, and adults. [. . .] Many incest victims do not, perhaps cannot, complain about, let alone prevent, their victimization; and even more difficult, they may enjoy and benefit in some measure from these relationships even as they are also humiliated and terrified. However, I also found a second pattern in the incest case of this period: along with submissive domesticity, these girl victims also displayed energetic resistance and escape tactics which do not match the model of unmitigated victimization. Their resistance often transformed itself, or was transformed by the constriction of their environment, into further victimization. For example, in many cases the girls' attempt to escape from their fathers' homes led them to sexual "delinquency." Nevertheless, the spirit of resistance — as opposed to the resignation and even the deformed gratitude described in many clinical reports — is significant, as I will argue below.

Finding these two patterns, often both in the lives of the same girl at different times, illuminated a contradiction in the dominant standard for daughterly virtue. In the modern version of the sexual double standard, a good girl has been above all sexually pure: a virgin until marriage, innocent of sexual thoughts and experience before that. But she has also been expected to be obedient to and under the protection of her parents. Father-daughter incest creates extreme confusion and double-binds for girls precisely because of their attempts to meet both these criteria of virtue. [. . .] [T]he difficulties of these incest victims are reminders of a daily female uneasiness about virtue, about achieving a feminine balance between modesty and aggression, chastity and vulgarity. On the other hand, in viewing girls' delinquency as a form of escape from victimization by fathers, we see evidence of the girls' willingness to challenge the categories which confined them so tightly in this period. This seems to me cause for optimism, because so much of the damage of sexual abuse for girls is in their blaming themselves.

The common features of the "classic" domestic incest case were an absent or in some way weakened mother; an older daughter who has become the mother and who feels great responsibility towards her whole family, particularly siblings, and is unusually disciplined and self-controlled; and a father committed to and even dependent upon his family yet rigid in his refusal to do the work of family maintenance and in his expectation of being served. [. . .]

The parents in incest families often held strongly conservative views about male supremacy and gender roles in domestic life. Incestuous fathers often voiced moralistic attacks on loose sexual morals in the community. These fathers were unusually tyrannical; the mothers, when present, self-effacing. It followed, in this family logic, that when mothers could not function, daughters took over their work. Often the mother had helped train and orient the daughter towards becoming, to an unusual degree, the substitute housekeeper/mother/wife. Often there were many younger children who depended on the older sister for care, although aspects of the domestic incest pattern remained when there was only one child, a daughter, whose obligations were exclusively towards her father. But in all cases the victim, or at least the first victim, was the eldest daughter. [. . .]

Contemporary clinical studies of father-daughter incest have reported that daughters are often treated well by their fathers, even rewarded with affection and gifts. This "kind" treatment existed in some of our cases [. . .], but in many other cases girls were beaten as well as sexually abused. The fathers were intensely concerned to keep their daughters from telling, and used both rewards and threats to prevent this. In some cases the physical abuse escalated as the sexual abuse stopped, either because the family had discovered it or the girl had become more firm in her refusal [. . .].

However, the power of fathers in the family cannot be measured by or equated with physical violence. Indeed, violence at times indicated the presence of a challenge to the father's power, and the most authoritarian fathers may have been able to impose their wills *without* force. There is a circularity in attempting to measure the father's power, because one index of that power is the result he was able to achieve. The incest itself, which we are trying to explain, is also evidence for the existence of an extremely male-dominant family power structure, which is being considered as a cause. This circularity is, however, part of reality, not a flaw in deductive logic. The victim and other knowing family members colluded in viewing the father as irresistibly powerful in order to rationalize their acquiescence and preserve their self-respect.

The most long-lasting domestic incest cases were characterized by the creation of an alternate psychosocial order within the family. This order, imposed by the father, could be relatively stable despite its contradictory relationship to larger community patterns. Indeed, perhaps the most extraordinary and frightening characteristic of domestic incest is that it could take on the appearance of the ordinary, and could be experienced within the family as normal. This is not to say that victims or other family members believed these incestuous relations to be legitimate. The necessity for secrecy would be enough to make that unlikely, as would the response of any outsiders who sensed the existence of the family secret. However, the assimilation of the sexual relationship with other aspects of the family dynamics and division of labor created an alternative normality, logic, and order. Here it bears repeating that most incestuous relations continued for years. This deviant but quotidian order within the family was more stable when family members were relatively secluded, geographically and/or socially. Isolated, sometimes hardly ever allowed out of the house, the daughters had no access to outside help nor even to outside verification of the possibility of escape. The importance of seclusion is underscored by the prominence of semi-rural cases of domestic incest, even within the highly urbanized locale of this study. The family's deviant order operated as a further centripetal force, encouraging the girl to remain within the domestic scene despite its drudgery. There she felt understood, accepted, and possibly appreciated, while the outside world reminded her of her abnormality and sinfulness, and of the horror and revulsion her story would evoke in others. [. . .]

Just as incest often occurs in families with exaggerated feminine subordination, so the girls' resistance to incest often assumed, perhaps had to assume, the form of resistance to the norms of feminine virtue, passivity, and subordination. One odd thing about incest is that despite the revulsion it has provoked, it opens a frightening but vital line of questioning about ordinary family relations. It identifies tensions between family solidarity and individual autonomy, between adult authority and children's rights, between women's status as victims and their responsibility as parents, tensions that one should not expect to resolve easily. It shows that many feminine virtues can support victimization, not only those one might want to reject such as obedience, quietness, or obligingness, but also those one might want to preserve—discipline, responsibility, loyalty. Incest, the most rare and deviant of family scandals, in some ways reveals the ordinary as much as the extraordinary.

"Beatrice Palmato"

Edith Wharton

The outline and fragment of the story "Beatrice Palmato" were discovered in the Wharton Papers at the Beinecke Library at Yale University. The fragment contains a bold and erotically charged account
of sexual relations between a father and daughter. The theme of incest occurs subtly in *Ethan Frome* (Ethan and Zeena are cousins) and
more forcefully in *Summer,* with its suggestion of inbreeding among
the inhabitants of the Mountain and the unwelcome overtures of
Lawyer Royall toward his surrogate daughter, Charity. [Ed.]

———

"I have been, you see," he added gently, "so perfectly patient —"

The room was warm, and softly lit by one or two pink-shaded lamps. A
little fire sparkled on the hearth, and a lustrous black bear-skin rug, on
which a few purple velvet cushions had been flung, was spread out before it.

"And now, darling," Mr. Palmato said, drawing her to the deep divan,
"let me show you what only you and I have the right to show each other."
He caught her wrists as he spoke, and looking straight into her eyes, repeated in a penetrating whisper: "Only you and I." But his touch had never
been tenderer. Already she felt every fibre vibrating under it, as of old, only
now with the more passionate eagerness bred of privation, and of the dull
misery of her marriage. She let herself sink backward among the pillows,
and already Mr. Palmato was on his knees at her side, his face close to hers.
Again her burning lips were parted by his tongue, and she felt it insinuate
itself between her teeth, and plunge into the depths of her mouth in a long
searching caress, while at the same moment his hands softly parted the thin
folds of her wrapper.

One by one they gained her bosom, and she felt her two breasts pointing up to them, the nipples as hard as coral, but sensitive as lips to his approaching touch. And now his warm palms were holding each breast as in
a cup, clasping it, modelling it, softly kneading it, as he whispered to her,
"like the bread of the angels."

An instant more, and his tongue had left her fainting mouth, and was
twisting like a soft pink snake about each breast in turn, passing from one

———

Edith Wharton: A Life, by R. W. B. Lewis. New York: Harper, 1975.

to the other till his lips closed hard on the nipples, sucking them with a tender gluttony.

Then suddenly he drew back her wrapper entirely, whispered: "I want you all, so that my eyes can see all that my lips can't cover," and in a moment she was free, lying before him in her fresh young nakedness, and feeling that indeed his eyes were covering it with fiery kisses. But Mr. Palmato was never idle, and while this sensation flashed through her one of his arms had slipped under her back and wound itself around her so that his hand again enclosed her left breast. At the same moment the other hand softly separated her legs, and began to slip up the old path it had so often travelled in darkness. But now it was light, she was uncovered, and looking downward, beyond his dark silver-sprinkled head, she could see her own parted knees and outstretched ankles and feet. Suddenly she remembered Austin's rough advances, and shuddered.

The mounting hand paused, the dark head was instantly raised. "What is it, my own?"

"I was—remembering—last week—" she faltered, below her breath.

"Yes, darling. That experience is a cruel one—but it has to come once in all women's lives. Now we shall reap its fruit."

But she hardly heard him, for the old swooning sweetness was creeping over her. As his hand stole higher she felt the secret bud of her body swelling, yearning, quivering hotly to burst into bloom. Ah, here was his subtle fore-finger pressing it, forcing its tight petals softly apart, and laying on their sensitive edges a circular touch so soft and yet so fiery that already lightnings of heat shot from that palpitating centre all over her surrendered body, to the tips of her fingers, and the ends of her loosened hair.

The sensation was so exquisite that she could have asked to have it indefinitely prolonged; but suddenly his head bent lower, and with a deeper thrill she felt his lips pressed upon that quivering invisible bud, and then the delicate firm thrust of his tongue, so full and yet so infinitely subtle, pressing apart the close petals, and forcing itself in deeper and deeper through the passage that glowed and seemed to become illuminated at its approach . . .

"Ah—" she gasped, pressing her hands against her sharp nipples, and flinging her legs apart.

Instantly one of her hands was caught, and while Mr. Palmato, rising, bent over her, his lips on hers again, she felt his firm fingers pressing into her hand that strong fiery muscle that they used, in their old joke, to call his third hand.

"My little girl," he breathed, sinking down beside her, his muscular trunk bare, and the third hand quivering and thrusting upward between them, a drop of moisture pearling at its tip.

She instantly understood the reminder that his words conveyed, letting herself downward along the divan till her head was in a line with his middle she flung herself upon the swelling member, and began to caress it insinuatingly with her tongue. It was the first time she had ever seen it actually exposed to her eyes, and her heart swelled excitedly: to have her touch confirmed by sight enriched the sensation that was communicating itself through her ardent twisting tongue. With panting breath she wound her caress deeper and deeper into the thick firm folds, till at length the member, thrusting her lips open, held her gasping, as if at its mercy; then, in a trice, it was withdrawn, her knees were pressed apart, and she saw it before her, above her, like a crimson flash, and at last, sinking backward into new abysses of bliss, felt it descend on her, press open the secret gates, and plunge into the deepest depths of her thirsting body . . .

"Was it . . . like this . . . last week?" he whispered.

"New England's Mountain-Child"

Frances Sargent Osgood

American poet Frances Sargent Osgood (1811–50) published "New England's Mountain-Child" in her volume *A Wreath of Wild Flowers from New England,* in 1838. [Ed.]

Where foams the fall—a tameless storm—
    Through Nature's wild and rich arcade,
Which forest-trees entwining form,
    There trips the Mountain-maid!

She binds not her luxuriant hair
    With dazzling gem or costly plume,
But gayly wreathes a rose-bud there,
    To match her maiden-bloom.

She clasps no golden zone of pride
    Her fair and simple robe around;
By flowing riband, lightly tied,
    Its graceful folds are bound.

A Wreath of Wild Flowers From New England. London: Edward Churton, 1838.

And thus attired,—a sportive thing,
　　Pure, loving, guileless, bright, and wild,—
Proud Fashion! match me, in your ring,
　　New England's Mountain-child!

She scorns to sell her rich, warm heart,
　　For paltry gold, or haughty rank;
But gives her love, untaught by art,
　　Confiding, free, and frank!

And once bestow'd, no fortune-change
　　That high and generous faith can alter;
Through grief and pain—too pure to range—
　　She will not fly or falter.

Her foot will bound as light and free
　　In lowly hut as palace-hall;
Her sunny smile as warm will be,—
　　For Love to her is all!

Hast seen where in our woodland-gloom
　　The rich magnolia proudly smiled?—
So brightly doth she bud and bloom,
　　New England's Mountain-child!

From *American Women in the Progressive Era, 1900–1920*

Dorothy Schneider and Carl H. Schneider

Among the points made by the Schneiders in their comprehensive study of America's Progressive era—a period that saw a significant number of political, social, and economic reform movements—is that women in the early twentieth century (particularly those who were uneducated) had few opportunities to engage in meaningful work outside the home. Those women who did work earned low wages and were often subjected to extraordinarily long workdays in

New York: Doubleday, 1992.

sweatshop conditions in mills and factories. Both Mattie Silver and Charity Royall have limited options in the work force. [Ed.]

"The Work Experience: Factory Workers"

Factory work was just one step up from domestic work. In 1900, factories employed about a quarter of women workers—almost 1,250,000. [. . .]

They worked in many industries. They stripped tobacco and rolled and packed cigars. They assembled paper boxes. They dipped and wrapped candies. They made artificial flowers and feathers. They processed and canned food. Almost 40 percent of them labored in the needle trades, some in an "inside shop" that did cutting and sewing, some in a "contracting shop" that hired workers to finish garments, and some in their tenement dwellings as home workers. No one knew how many women toiled at home in such jobs, with or without the help of their families; they were paid on a piecework basis. [. . .]

In such work most women could not earn a living wage. Indeed most male factory workers had trouble supporting their families, in 1905 averaging $400 yearly when $800 was considered the minimum needed for a family of four.

Employers usually paid women a quarter to two-thirds of what men earned. Sometimes they argued that women needed no more, since they could look to their husbands or fathers for support. Anyway, they said, women were only working temporarily, until marriage. In fact, uncontrolled by minimum-wage laws, employers paid only what they had to. Worse still, they eroded even the pittances they paid by such mean devices as forcing waitresses to pay for unsatisfactory food which customers sent back to the kitchen or requiring glove makers to buy their own machines, charging as much as $65 for a machine that cost them only $35. Fringe benefits, of course, did not exist. No sick days: sometimes women even gave birth on the mill floor between the looms.

On the $5 or $6 a week that the average *experienced* factory woman earned for her 60-hour week, she almost had to live at home with her family. Most of the "women adrift," as the society called working women living alone in boarding houses or rented rooms, barely eked out enough for room, board, and clothing even though they earned higher-than-average wages. All of them scrimped, sleeping three to a bed, skipping meals. [. . .] Truly desperate women without families had to resort to 10-cent-a-night beds in strictly regulated dormitories sponsored by charitable organizations—if they could find them.

From *Women and Reform in a New England Community, 1815–1860*

Carolyn J. Lawes

In this excerpt, Lawes discusses the importance of sewing in the lives of young New England women. Sewing is an activity that both Mattie Silver and Charity Royall engage in. [Ed.]

"The Sewing Circle"

Through most of American history sewing was central to the female life. Learning to sew was an integral part of the training for womanhood and entailed painstaking hours of practice under the guidance of a mother, a relative, or a teacher. At the age of six or seven, girls began to make "samplers" of the various stitches and techniques demanded of a competent seamstress. [. . .] Mastering the art of sewing was a rite of passage, a sign that a girl was mastering the skills of womanhood. [. . .]

Sewing was also one of the few skilled occupations open to women. Although dressmakers, milliners, mantua makers and "tailoresses" were notoriously underpaid, theirs was a profession in which only women catered to women. Moreover, dressmakers and milliners were also merchants who sold wreaths, fake curls, trimmings, artificial flowers, ribbons, laces, plumes, handkerchiefs, shell combs, and, as one Worcester advertisement declared, "a variety of other articles too numerous to mention." [. . .]

Sewing also brought women together for communal labor. Sewing circles were the oldest and most common form of New England women's voluntary associations. The colonial Puritan economy depended upon the informal networks of exchange of its "good wives," and quiltings and sewing "frolics" were common. The American Revolution prompted women to offer their associated labor in the service of the nation. "Spinning bees"

Lexington: UP of Kentucky, 2000.

spun wool into cloth to substitute for British imports while sewing circle members raised money for the cause, helped to clothe the revolutionary army, and wove patriotic themes into their needlework. After the Revolution, sewing circles continued to provide a venue for socializing and afforded farm women the all too rare opportunity to spend time with other women. However, in the antebellum years the sewing circle assumed an even greater importance as it emerged as a permanent, constitutionally based organization with explicit ties to social activism. From sewing to benefit one's family to sewing to benefit society was a charge many women eagerly embraced.

Part Four

———◆———

CRITICAL READINGS

"The Sledding Accident in *Ethan Frome*"

Jean Frantz Blackall

Ethan Frome and Mattie Silver agree to commit suicide by running their sled into the big elm tree at the bottom of School House Hill. But they argue over who is to sit in front:

> "Get up! Get up! he urged her; but she kept on repeating: "Why do you want to sit in front?"
> "Because I—because I want to feel you holding me," he stammered, and dragged her to her feet."[82][1]

Kenneth Bernard says that Ethan's wanting to sit in front of Mattie on the sled is an indication of his weakness. Ethan sincerely "wants to die being cuddled and comforted, leaving to Mattie the role of protector and shelterer."[2] Cynthia Wolff supports Bernard in this interpretation,[3] which accords with her own sentiment that Ethan demonstrates passivity, lack of normal sexual initiative, infantile and regressive behavior. This is a view Wolff otherwise argues by pointing out how Ethan's vision of living with Mattie is purely domestic; Mattie would be cook and both of them caretakers.[4]

Studies in Short Fiction (21.2) Spring: 1984.

[1] All parenthetical references are to this New Riverside Edition. [Ed.]

[2] Kenneth Bernard, "Imagery and Symbolism in *Ethan Frome,*" *College English,* 23 (December 1961), 181.

[3] Cynthia Griffin Wolff, *A Feast of Words* (Oxford: Oxford University Press, 1977), pp. 180 and 427, n. 132.

[4] Wolff, *A Feast of Words,* pp. 178–79.

As regards this domestic ideal, it is instructive to juxtapose other Wharton fictions. In *Summer,* for example, the overtly sexual character of the relationship between Lucius Harney and Charity Royall cannot be doubted. Yet their scenes together at the abandoned house in the woods emulate conventional domestic rituals. They decorate their room with flowers and leaves. They share meals and drink tea together (176–77). Lucius expresses his affection for Charity by bringing her chocolate and cold water from a spring (159). In *The Reef* George Darrow, whose sexuality is explicit, yet demonstrates a reticence similar to Ethan's, kissing Anna's scarf as Ethan kisses Mattie's sewing stuff rather than touching the woman.[5] At the end, when Anna Leath hopes that a life for herself and George Darrow may still be possible, she dreams that she is sitting on the hearth beside his chair. It would seem that in such moments Wharton is celebrating the idea of domestic community, of what she spoke of to Charles Du Bos as the desirable condition of "'a sharing of all'" between lovers, not only the sexual relationship.[6]

Ethan's wanting to sit ahead of Mattie on the sled can be understood as manifesting a similar nuance in his behavior rather than as a regressive or infantile attitude. Ethan's idea of love is nurture. He wants to sit ahead of Mattie on the sled so that he, not Mattie, will hit the elm tree first. Perhaps his solicitude is misplaced since their objective in common is to commit suicide. But throughout the scene it is Mattie who has pressed for this choice and Ethan who resists. Yielding to her insistence, he yet holds back by making a protective gesture toward her which is quite consistent with his attitude of caretaking elsewhere, as when he decides to remain with Zeena despite his love for Mattie, when he initially balks at expelling Mattie from the household as Zeena desires, and in these very moments when he worries about his horse's going without food. Such protective attitudes may not manifest an aggressive sexuality in Ethan, but they can more plausibly be interpreted as adult sentiments than as infantile ones. Ethan's sensibility affirms the values of home (hearth) and protectiveness.

Corroboration for interpreting Ethan's choice as being a protective gesture is provided by a newspaper account undoubtedly known to Wharton when she devised this final episode of *Ethan Frome.*[7] The *Berkshire Evening*

[5] Edith Wharton, *The Reef* (New York: D. Appleton and Company, 1912), p. 115.[. . .]

[6] Wolff, *A Feast of Words,* p. 293.

[7] See R. W. B. Lewis, *Edith Wharton* (New York: Harper Colophon Books, 1975), p. 308. Cf. David H. Wood, *Lenox: Massachusetts Shire Town* (Lenox: Published by the Town, 1969), esp. pp. 109 and 114, n. 2.

Eagle for March 12, 1904, reports a disastrous sledding accident on Court House Hill in Lenox, Massachusetts, in which Hazel Crosby was fatally injured when she insisted on steering the sled: "Mansuit Schmitt, the only young man in the party, had been steering the sled on its course until the accident. Miss Crosby expressed a desire to guide the sled on one trip, and the permission was reluctantly granted. She took her position in front of the party of coasters." In this position, according to the *Eagle,* "Miss Crosby received the full force of the collision and it is a wonder that she was not instantly killed."[8] From this circumstantial account Wharton would have understood Ethan's choice to sit in front on the sled as one involving greater danger. Miss Crosby, who sat forward, was killed. That Edith Wharton had intimate access to the details of this accident is a matter of local record, as reported at the time of the death of Katherine P. Spencer: "Miss Spencer was the last survivor of the five who were aboard the sled. For five years after the accident, 1904–1908, she was an assistant librarian at the Lenox Library, after which she had to resign because of impaired hearing caused by the accident. During that time, Mrs. Wharton was an associate manager at the library, and knew and consulted Miss Spencer in research for her novel."[9]

From "Frozen Hell: Edith Wharton's Tragic Offering"

Samuel Fisher Dodson

In her introduction to *Ethan Frome,* Wharton mentions twice that her short novel is a tragedy. Certainly, many people use the term tragedy very loosely and frequently imply disaster rather than actual tragedy. Robert B. Heilman distinguishes between the two terms by suggesting that disasters are everyday, external occurrences (e.g., a car crash in which teenagers are killed), whereas tragedies are profound in nature with divided characters struggling among themselves against larger values or desires.

Edith Wharton Review 16.1 (Spring 1999).

[8]Unsigned article, *The Berkshire Evening Eagle,* Pittsfield, Mass., Saturday, March 12, 1904, pp. 1, 7. [For the text of this article, see pages 218–23.]

[9]Richard V. Happel, "Notes and Footnotes," *The Berkshire Eagle,* Wednesday, Feb. 25, 1976, p. 20. [...]

Regrettably, Wharton does not record many of her views on the nature of tragedy in either her letters or essays. Yet from the gravity with which she discusses her characters, we may infer that she does not use the word lightly. In [Marilyn Jones] Lyde's words, Wharton "believed that suffering is the inevitable result of an offense against the moral order of the universe; . . . more accurately, it is an error in judgment, a failure to deduce the right course of action from the facts, to balance individual morality with social convention in order to arrive at moral truth."[1] Wharton not only called *Ethan Frome* a tragedy of isolation, but "a tragedy of human waste and suffering."[2] In her book *The Writing of Fiction,* Wharton leads us to an understanding of her sense of tragedy when she writes: "In any really good subject one has only to probe deep enough to come to tears . . . ; that is, if one really pierces to the meaning of life, he will eventually find tragedy" (qtd. in Lyde 125).

Through her portrayal of Ethan's struggle in *Ethan Frome,* Wharton does indeed pierce to the meaning of life. To Aristotle, "character is whatever reveals a person's habit of moral choice — whatever he tends to choose or reject when the choice is not obvious."[3] Similarly, when Wharton's Ethan makes specific choices, e.g., not to leave Zeena and Starkfield, he reveals his nature. On the first page of *Ethan Frome* the narrator, upon initially seeing Ethan, tells us, "Even then he was the most striking figure in Starkfield, though he was but the ruin of a man" (13).[4] Shortly thereafter, the narrator reveals that Ethan's ordeals would have been enough to kill a normal man. But then Ethan is above the normal man, and Wharton's narrator reinforces Ethan's heroic stature early on as he drives his sleigh, "his brown-seamed profile, under the helmet-like peak of the cap, relieved against the banks of snow like the bronze image of a hero" (18). As Blake Nevius notes, "no element in the characterization of Ethan is more carefully brought out than the suggestion of his useful, even heroic possibilities."[5]

A number of personal traits lift Ethan above the common lot into the heroic: for instance, "He had always been more sensitive than the people

---

[1] Marilyn Jones Lyde, *Edith Wharton: Convention and Morality in the World of the Novelist* (Norman: U of Oklahoma P, 1959). 129–30. [Ed.]

[2] Quoted in Janet Goodwyn, *Edith Wharton: Traveller in the Land of Letters* (New York: St. Martin's, 1990) 74. [Ed.]

[3] Aristotle, *Poetics,* trans. James Hutton (New York: Norton, 1982) 52. [Ed.]

[4] All parenthetical references to *Ethan Frome* are to this New Riverside Edition. [Ed.]

[5] Blake Nevius, *Edith Wharton: A Study of Her Fiction* (Los Angeles: U of California P, 1953) 119. [Ed.]

about him to the appeal of natural beauty" (26). At his most articulate when discussing the stars and their constellations, Ethan first enters his elevated, eloquent state as a result of Mattie's presence. He experiences "other sensations, less definable but more exquisite, which drew them together with a shock of silent joy: the cold red sunset behind winter hills, the flight of cloud-flocks over slopes of golden stubble, or the intensely blue shadows of hemlocks on sunlit snow" (27). This sensitivity and heightened awareness initiates Ethan's first communication with Mattie, who understands and taps into Ethan's "secret soul," a soul of high morals, compassion and dreams. Ethan tries to elevate his already good and kind nature by emulating Abraham Lincoln through his plan of self education. He sets up his study with a few books and attempts, "with these meager properties, to produce some likeness of the study of a 'minister' who had been kind to him" (65–66). Generously, he cares for his injured father, his ill mother, and then his invalid/psychosomatic wife. Even after Ethan is severely injured, when the narrator suggests to Harmon Gow that Zeena, not Ethan, is doing the caring now, Gow corrects him: "Oh, as to that: I guess it's always been Ethan done the caring" (14). Ethan's kind manner does not desert him after his recovery from the accident, as evinced by the hospitality he extends to the narrator when inviting him into his home during the storm. Lyde points out that Ethan's "moral superiority," although "not without blemish," still rises "above the common level" (136).

Ethan has the makings of a real hero: he is kind, gentle, and unfailingly considerate of others. But somehow his early promise flickers; Ethan becomes "a prisoner for life, and now his one ray of light was to be extinguished" (68). The narrator tells us, "he was too young, too strong, too full of the sap of living, to submit so easily to the destruction of his hopes" (66); but he is brutally forced into an acceptance of his destruction. A look at the way Ethan arrived at this insurmountable impasse reveals the way his tragic flaw and certain outside forces coalesce into his tragedy.

Mrs. Hale tells Ethan that she admires him for taking care of his parents, and then Zeena; she knows he's "had an awful mean time" (71). It was just chance that his father was injured, forcing Ethan to curtail his education and, as the good son, stay home to honor his filial obligations. Then his mother's illness prolongs his confinement as caretaker. Upon the arrival of his cousin Zenobia with her excellent nursing skills, Ethan's life looks as though it will resume its promising course, aided by his nurturing cousin. After his mother dies, Ethan, reduced to a lonely orphan imprisoned in the silence of the empty house, hears "Zeena's volubility" as "music in his ears" (41). His loneliness and fear of solitude, an offshoot of his inability to communicate, together with his sense of obligation, awakens his *hamartia,* or tragic flaw—asking Zeena to wed: "He had often thought since that it would not have happened if his mother had died in spring instead of winter" (42).

On the surface Ethan and Zeena do not look like such a bad match. Zeena demonstrates considerable skill as a nurse and caretaker: "her efficiency shamed and dazzled him" (41). They agree to sell the farm and move to a large town so Ethan may fulfill his dreams: to rise above his humble beginnings, become an engineer and, eventually, unravel the "huge cloudy meanings behind the daily face of things" (23). But in fact the problem lies in appearances; Zeena is not who she appears to be. She doesn't share the same dreams as Ethan, and Ethan lacks the ability to communicate enough with Zeena to recognize their incompatibility before they are married.

Zeena shows her true colors soon after the wedding. She is in reality a human being petrified of life, and this phobia manifests itself in snobbery and eventually hypochondria: "She chose to look down on Starkfield, but she could not have lived in a place which looked down on her. Even Bettsbridge or Shadd's Falls would not have been sufficiently aware of her, and in the greater cities which attracted Ethan she would have suffered a complete loss of identity" (42). Within a year Zeena becomes "sick" and, in a clinically-ill manner, controls Ethan's existence, adding one more wall to shut in Ethan from the outside world. The arrival of Mattie Silver threatens this structure, of course, and in this dynamic of love for Mattie versus obligation to Zeena, Ethan's tragedy pushes toward its dark climax.

Ethan's fate is that he was born in a region of the country where the harsh weather and poverty contribute to a meager, agricultural existence. His tragic flaw goes beyond his choosing to marry a woman who, rather than help him, hinders him both economically (little work, medical costs) and emotionally. His flaw, however, goes further than making a bad decision. It extends to and encompasses his inability to communicate his thoughts to other human beings. When Ethan becomes aware that he loves Mattie, and that Zeena will dismiss her unless he intervenes, a conflict arises that threatens his very soul: "He had made up his mind to do something, but he did not know what it would be" (70). Given Ethan's deficiencies, this dilemma is pathetic but all too real. He is a kind man. He doesn't want to hurt Zeena; even in the final letter he writes, but never delivers, he maintains a gentleness in tone, never blaming her for the unhappiness of their relationship. And ultimately, because he realizes the highly mortgaged farm will probably not sell, he does not abandon her because to do so would leave Zeena destitute.

Wharton introduces the problem of communication before the story ever begins when she reveals [in her introduction to the 1922 reprint edition] that she chose an outside narrator because the people of Starkfield have a "deep rooted reticence and inarticulateness" (viii).[6] Ethan and Zeena never communicate. He does not confront her. They have their first fight in their seventh year of marriage. A marriage without arguments is not only unhealthy, it is bizarre. In Blake Nevius' opinion, "it is in view of his potentialities that Ethan's marriage to Zeena is a catastrophe" (120). Perhaps Zeena wouldn't have been so "sick" had Ethan confronted her early on and talked to her about their individual fears and dreams.

Ethan's lack of communication skills trips him up with Mattie as well as with Zeena. When they have their one night alone, the best he can do is to kiss the material she was sewing, a pathetically inadequate demonstration of his strong feelings for her. While he does manage to sooth her feelings over the broken pickle dish—a symbol of Zeena's inability to live life, her prized possession sits in a closet, away from anyone's view and performs neither a utilitarian nor an aesthetic function—he does not communicate to Mattie just how much he has longed for the domestic scene that their after-dinner respite intimated.

Ethan, moreover, simply cannot bring into the open even his simplest thoughts. The mentioning of Zeena's name throws him into a stupor from which he cannot break free. In Cynthia Griffin Wolff's words, "it is not that he [Ethan] does not feel deeply, for he does. However, one mark of maturity is the ability to translate desire into coherent words, words into action; and Ethan Frome is incapable of such translations."[7] As a married man in a Puritanical society, when Ethan finally and feebly tries to communicate with a young, single woman, he is punished for his indiscretion. Eugene Kaelin writes that the contemporary "noble protagonist must possess some tragic flaw—otherwise his or her tragic suffering would appear unjust to the audience which would respond in moral outrage rather than in pity and fear."[8] It is difficult not to feel outrage at Ethan's outcome, but most of that anger shoots to a world where such a good man, no matter how inarticulate, could end up so abominably. Ethan's inability to express his feeling within his trapped existence caused by a despicable fate is made more intense since he has done nothing as "bad" as, say, Oedipus, who killed his father, married his mother, and fated his children to tragic lives, or Macbeth, who killed many, including women and children. Grace Kellogg writes,

---

[6] In the introduction that Wharton wrote to the 1922 reprint edition of *Ethan Frome* she addressed the novel's narrative voice and structure. [Ed.]

[7] Cynthia Griffin Wolff, *A Feast of Words: The Triumph of Edith Wharton* (New York: Oxford UP, 1977) 174. [Ed.]

[8] Eugene Kaelin, "Toward a Theory of Contemporary Tragedy," *The Existential Coordinates of the Human Condition: Poetic—Epic—Tragic,* ed. Anna-Teresa Tymieniecka (Boston: Reidel, 1984) 347. [Ed.]

"Nowhere in literature is it easy to find a more tragic story-end than *Ethan Frome* has provided."[9]

[. . .] [D]id Ethan Frome's life have to become a tragedy, and, if so, how should we view such a story? Ethan's inability to communicate led him to marry a "sick" woman who dragged him down into the isolated despair engulfing her. And once in the quagmire of Zeena's pathology, Ethan could only sink deeper with every futile move toward Mattie. At the core of Ethan's personality is a code of self-sacrifice which appears good until it progresses to the point of erasing his identity and his spiritual and emotional needs. Ethan's inability to distinguish between when self-sacrifice is noble and when it is martyrdom really constitutes the major part of his flaw—his failure to communicate his thoughts. He cannot make such subtle distinctions; Starkfield society has never asked him to do so. He honors family ties; he even argues with Zeena, protesting that she cannot evict Mattie because of the young woman's kinship to Zeena. For the most part, he remains loyal to Zeena: even though he eventually realizes that she "at every turn barred his way" until finally "a flame of hate rose in him" (61), ultimately, he is too kind to leave her in the lurch. Anna-Teresa Tymieniecka notes that "the tragic feeling expresses the moral conflict and the impossibility of solving it."[10] Ethan and Mattie's suicide attempt is not really a solution; rather, it provides a grimly ridiculous example of Ethan's inability to communicate with life. Certainly, Wharton offers no solution with her darkly ironic table-turning ending: Zeena is now the good, healthy nurse and Mattie the sullen, crippled patient, both locked in a futile struggle for the wounded Ethan to view.

This irony is the bane of Ethan's present, tortured existence and is what Mrs. Hale alludes to when she says, "it's him that suffers the most" (86). She further develops this irony in her dreary, hopeless closing words of the story: "And I say, if she'd [Mattie] ha' died, Ethan might ha' lived; and the way they are now, I don't see's there much difference between the Fromes up at the farm and the Fromes down in the graveyard, 'cept that down there they're all quiet, and the women have got to hold their tongues" (87). Nevius sees this speech as "one of despair arising from the contemplation of spiritual waste" (118). Ultimately, however, he acknowledges Ethan's own part in his tragedy: "it is Ethan's own sense of responsibility that blocks the last avenue of escape and condemns him to a life of sterile expiation" (Nevius 121). [. . .]

---

[9] Grace Kellogg, *The Two Lives of Edith Wharton* (New York: Dover, 1965) 171. [Ed.]

[10] Anna-Teresa Tymieniecka, "Tragedy and the Completion of Freedom," in *Existential Coordinates* 298. [Ed.]

Even with a belief in the sanctity of marriage, one has difficulty not viewing Ethan's inability to leave the wicked Zeena and start life over with Mattie as a tragic mistake different from, but related to, his inability to communicate. Kaelin writes that our sympathy for the character's plight is generated by the moral worth of his struggles against surrounding circumstance (350). Yet the fact remains that, even if the bars are reinforced by people and forces meaner and greater than himself, Ethan fails to break out of the caged life he creates for himself. When a kind man struggles and suffers immensely, the audience cringes for his (and subsequently, their own) relief. Edith Wharton, as a good modern, sends us home with no such consolation. Ethan Frome does not deserve the catastrophic life dealt him, and therein lies the modern tragedy so close to that of real life. If, however, our reactions to our plights determine our heroic natures, then Ethan's ability to continue to care for the women at home and show kindness to the narrator reveals an uncommon and admirable strength. Ethan's final resolve and acceptance of his lot place him among the great anguished characters of tragic literature who have still found dignity and humanity in defeat.

From "*Ethan Frome:* A Controversy about Modernizing It"

"Zeena: A Compelling Portrait of a Neurotic"

Richard B. Hovey

[. . .] [U]nmistakably in Zeena, Wharton not only renders a compelling portrait of a neurotic; she also brings that neurosis front and center in the drama and the theme.

[. . .] The starting point suggested is to look more closely at Zeena.

Rightly, her undefined sickliness is never a clear-cut disease; it is psychosomatic and hence more problematic to deal with. She is hypochondriac, for Freud one of the more recalcitrant manifestations of neurosis. Thus, the basic components of the husband-wife duel are set up. Zeena has her sickliness, to use as well as she can in her discontent. Ethan has his conscientiousness, his sense of being indebted to her at his time of greatest need. Much of the story depends on how these two forces interact. Whose weakness — or strength — will win out?

American Literary Realism 19.1 (Fall 1986).

Zeena's debility brings Mattie to the Frome farm to help. Before Ethan and Mattie are fully aware of their shy love, Zeena is alerted. In her taciturn way she begins to manipulate to get rid of the girl. She catches Ethan furtively doing some of Mattie's tasks, then makes him further uneasy by remarking that he has started to shave every morning. Hers is a "way of letting things happen without seeming to remark them, and then weeks afterward, in a casual phrase, revealing that she had all along taken her notes and made her inferences" (29).[1] Her next tactic is to break the routine of placing the key under the rug on one of those few evenings Mattie attends a church social and Ethan goes to walk her home. When she comes to let them in, Zeena's self-pitying misery and unattractiveness, contrasted with the momentary cheer Ethan and Mattie have shared, evidently make him feel shame and malaise of conscience. Next, in announcing she is going to another town to consult a new doctor, Zeena jabs again: If Ethan is too busy, the hired man, Jotham Powell, can drive her to the train station. Never suspecting her deviousness and buoyed by anticipating that she can hardly return before the following evening, Ethan is led to tell his first lie: "'I'd take you over myself, only I've got to collect the cash for the lumber'" (40).

Wharton's exquisite rendering of the tryst during Zeena's absence—the Puritan ethos intensifies its poignancy—and the cat breaking the red-glass dish are too well known for recounting. What might be marked about Ethan's attempt the next day to buy glue (in hope of mending the dish before Zeena returns) is that when, after galling delays, he does get the item at a store, its proprietress, well-meaning Mrs. Homans, calls to him as he turns for home, "'I hope Zeena ain't broken anything she sets store by'" (55). We sense how Ethan feels: as if this villager is somehow reading his secret. Returned, he learns that Zeena has already gotten back. Circumstances and timing are kinder to her than to him.

The climactic chapter VII exemplifies Wharton's dramaturgic powers at their best. We discover how carefully Zeena has planned, how decisive she has been, how swiftly and surely she has acted. Ethan is no match for her cunning. Dutifully calling her to supper, he gets "the consecrated formula": "'I don't feel as I could touch a morsel.'" Her hypochondria is in fine fettle: she is "'a great deal sicker'" than he supposes and has "'complications'" (57). Though such news produces mixed feelings in Ethan, "for the moment compassion prevailed" (57). Looking for "a consolatory short cut," he asks how reliable is this new doctor (57).

---

[1] All parenthetical references are to this New Riverside Edition. [Ed.]

Zeena opens the attack: "'I didn't need to have anybody tell me I was losing ground every day. Everybody but you could see it'" (58). Regularly now, she uses another formula as *the* authority to justify her claims: the-doctor-says. Ethan agrees she must follow the physician's orders. Whereupon he hears a "new note" in his wife's voice, "drily resolute" (58). Her medical ally has instructed her that she must not do "'a single thing around the house'"—that she must get a hired girl. In fact, she already has the girl, who will arrive the next day and be paid an extra dollar weekly. The added expense dismays and angers Ethan: "'Did Dr. Buck tell you how I was to pay her wages?'" (58).

In battle, Zeena is superb. Her every move counts. She goes for the jugular:

> "No, he didn't. For I'd 'a' been ashamed to tell *him* that you grudged me the money to get back my health, when I lost it nursing your mother!"
> "*You* lost your health nursing mother?"
> "Yes; and my folks told me at the time you couldn't do no less than marry me after—"
> "Zeena!" (58)

Ethan is horrified and shamed by this exchange. Marriage has not made him a seasoned fighter. Zeena's arsenal is full: "'The doctor says it'll be my death if I go on slaving the way I've had to. He doesn't understand how I've stood it as long as I have'" (59). Next, she is at him with self-pity. When he promises he will do all the housework, she rejoins, "'Better send me over to the alms house and done with it'" (59). By declaring it is settled because he does not have the money, Ethan has dropped his guard. Zeena catches him in a lie, and deception is a skill he is not disciplined in. In "a level voice," she can now say:

> "I thought you were to get fifty dollars from Andrew Hale for that lumber."
> "Andrew Hale never pays under three months." (59)

She sees his face redden. She nails him again: "'Why you told me yesterday you'd fixed it up with him to pay cash down. You said that was why you couldn't drive me over to the Flats'" (59). He stammers "'a misunderstanding.'" Quiet comes for a moment. Her change to seeming mildness so far misleads Ethan that he goes on about how much he can still do for both her and Mattie. Then: "Zeena, while he spoke, seemed to be following out some elaborate mental calculation. She emerged from it to say: 'There'll be Mattie's board less, anyhow'" (60). Ethan scarcely knows what has hit him. But he hears a sound he has never heard before—Zeena is laughing! "'You didn't suppose I was going to keep two girls, did you? No wonder you were scared of the expense'" (60).

Ethan is all but done for, though some further hammering awaits him as Zeena finishes him off. When he reminds her that Mattie is no hired girl but her own relative, Zeena is rock-hard. When he asks her what "'folks'll say'" if she ousts Mattie, Zeena, secure enough in the community's approval, can parry in a "smooth voice: 'I know well enough what they say of my having kep' her as long as I have'" (61). In fury, Ethan starts to strike his wife, then checks himself. He has no way to force Zeena to keep her own cousin. "Now she had mastered him and he abhorred her" (61).

Triumphing, Zeena has more weapons. Again, timing and circumstance aid her. Ethan goes downstairs, Mattie promptly knows something is wrong, and they embrace and kiss passionately—for the first time. Desperate, he exclaims: "'You can't go, Matt! I won't let you! She's always had her way, but I mean to have mine now—'" (63). Suddenly Zeena is behind him. She has overheard. But, acting her usual self, she reports feeling "'a mite better'" (63). She eats well, looking "straight at Mattie" with "a faint smile" (64). Then, in quest of her stomach powders on a high closet shelf, she finds the fragments of the pickle-dish where Ethan had hoped to conceal them. She faces the culprits with her query. Ethan, with his wretched ineptitude for duplicity, tells part of the truth, blaming the cat. How did that creature get into the closet? "'Chasin' mice, I guess'" is his explanation. Once more from Zeena comes "a small strange laugh" (65). Mattie then tells the whole truth. Zeena thus gets the indisputable evidence she requires. Weeping for the loss of her treasure, she turns on Mattie: "'You're a bad girl, Mattie Silver, and I always known it. . . . If I'd 'a' listened to folks, you'd 'a' gone before now, and this wouldn't 'a' happened'" (65). In the ethos of Starkfield, "bad girl" may be translated as seducing adulteress, if not as whore. Mattie's fate is sealed. The rest is denouement, relentless in its logic. What action can Ethan take?

> He was too young, too strong, too full of the sap of living to submit so easily to the destruction of his hopes. Must he wear out all his years at the side of a bitter querulous woman? Other possibilities had been in him, possibilities sacrificed, one by one, to Zeena's narrow-mindedness and ignorance. And what good has come of it? She was a hundred times bitterer and more discontented than when he had married her: the one pleasure left her was to inflict pain on him. All the healthy instincts of self-defence rose up in him against such waste. . . . (66)

Faced with no guilt-free exit, Ethan vacillates, fumbles among tangled alternatives. He has heard of one divorce that worked out well. So, maybe he can go out West with Mattie and turn over to Zeena the proceeds from the farm and sawmill? Money and the nitty-gritty of practicalities block this hope. The property, mortgaged to the limit, would not clear a thousand dollars; and even if Zeena's illness is a sham, she could not manage alone. "Well, she could go back to her people, then, and see what they would do for her. It was the fate she was forcing on Mattie—why not let her try it herself?" (67). Such appears fair-minded. Briefly Ethan's hopes rise when he runs across an advertisement: "'Trips to the West: Reduced Rates'" (67). But he lacks cash for the fare; lacks enough collateral even to borrow ten dollars in Starkfield (67).

After a sleepless night, he and Mattie try to show hopefulness toward each other. Again, however, Zeena has acted swiftly. She has arranged that Mattie's departure will be so prompt that, in a single trip to the railroad station, Mattie will make the train for Stamford and the new girl will be picked up and brought back to the farm. Her plans working neatly, Zeena is feeling better, has "an air of unusual alertness and activity" (69).

Ethan feels passionately rebellious, but "his manhood . . . humbled by the part he was compelled to play" (70). He must do something. One hope occurs to him. If he tells kind-hearted Andrew Hale that he needs the advance of a small sum on their lumber deal because Zeena's illness necessitates a servant, he may be able to ask "without too much loss of pride" (70). If he reaches Hale's wife beforehand, success may be more nearly possible; "and with fifty dollars in his pocket nothing could keep him from Mattie" (70). He does encounter Mrs. Hale first. Well-meaning, she probes Ethan's exposed nerve: She has heard the news of Zeena trying a new doctor. Then she adds:

> I don't know anybody round here's had more sickness than Zeena. I always tell Mr. Hale I don't know what she'd 'a' done if she hadn't 'a' had you to look after her; and I used to say the same thing 'bout your mother, You've had an awful mean time, Ethan Frome. (71)

These remarks set Ethan's ethical dilemma. Most Starkfielders were indifferent to or routinized his troubles; Mrs. Hale makes him feel less alienated in his misery. Maybe, in their compassion, the Hales will help? Then a second thought comes: "He was planning to take advantage of the Hales' sympathy to obtain money from them on false pretences" (71). His integrity gives him his answer: He cannot do it. A conscience and heart less tender would never have hesitated to mislead the Hales and abandon Zeena. Does his decision instance quixotism, weakness, morbid scrupulousness, regression? [Cynthia Griffin] Wolff summarizes: "Ethan and Zeena have been brought together by their mutual commitment to the habits of care-taking; now they have become imprisoned by them."[2] Wharton concludes the chapter: "even if he had had the heart to desert her [Zeena] he could have done so only by deceiving two kindly people who had pitied him" (71–72). Duty wins, love loses.

Only a splinter of self-assertion remains to Ethan. Against Zeena's preference, he, not Jotham, will drive Mattie to the station. The couple is fully aware of the power of their love and of its hopelessness. On their way, they stop at the sled-track. To be sure, theirs is a romanticized love: They cannot part, ever; death is preferable—the *Liebestod* motif included. Their attempted suicide by crashing into the big elm is familiar enough not to call for rehearsing. As everyone knows, these lovers win not the gift of death but the curse of death-in-life. [. . .]

Yet there is a victory, human, recognizably Freudian, and of course Zeena's. Her deepest wishes are fulfilled. She wins her power struggle with Ethan. She defeats a rival who threatened her marriage. Her sadism is gratified: She can dominate and further hurt two other persons. Her masochism is appeased: She can inwardly praise herself for her dutiful martyrdom. She has earned social approval for taking in Mattie and devoting her life to the cripples. More needed now, she feels more important. Extra demands put upon her, she can no longer be quite so attentive to her own symptoms; so her hypochondria diminishes. With the blessings of her conscience, she can spend out her days punishing the sinners in her charge. Granted, the formula oversimplifies, but we might say of *Ethan Frome*: Neurosis conquers all.

"The Two Faces of Mattie Silver"

Gary Scharnhorst

Read through a critical lens that focuses on the ambiguous character of Mattie Silver, *Ethan Frome* becomes a very different story indeed. Rather than a tale of doomed or tragic love as it is usually understood,[1] the novel

---

[This essay is previously unpublished.]

[2] Cynthia Griffin Wolff, *A Feast of Words: The Triumph of Edith Wharton* (New York: Oxford UP, 1977) 177. [Ed.]

[1] For example, in his essay "*Ethan Frome*: A Controversy about Modernizing It," in *American Literary Realism* 19 (Fall 1986) 4–20, Richard B. Hovey writes that "The couple is fully aware of the power of their love and of its hopelessness" (17). [For excerpts from Hovey's essays see pp. 257–62 in this New Riverside Edition.]

permits another interpretation entirely. Far from reciprocating Ethan's affection, Mattie seems a conniving minx who plays on his goodwill in a vain
attempt to remain in Starkfield.[2] Despite the critical consensus that Wharton's narrator is "unreliable," despite the narrator's own reference in the
frame-tale to his "vision" of events that occurred twenty-four years before,
Wharton's contention in her introduction to the novel that "only the narrator" has "the scope enough to see it all, to resolve it back into simplicity,
and to put it in its rightful place"[3] has misled readers into assuming that
Mattie is as one-dimensional as she appears to be, that she somehow loves
Ethan as much as Ethan protests he loves her.[4] On his part, the narrator insists that "the deeper meaning of the story was in the gaps" (14)[5] or holes
in the text, what Wolfgang Iser has termed "gaps of indeterminacy." Wharton's radical experiment in point of view in *Ethan Frome* has gone largely
unrecognized. The novel is no more the simple story of a hopeless love triangle than Henry James's "The Turn of the Screw" is a straightforward and
unambiguous ghost story.

Whatever else may be said of Mattie, she is (as the narrator envisions
her) a flirt and tease with whom Ethan is smitten. From her first days in
Starkfield, we learn, she has toyed with the "facetious youths" in the town.
Sitting among them at a picnic, she drops a gold locket and "set the youths"
to searching for it before Ethan finds it (76) — crucial moment in the
progress of their affair, at least as he remembers it months later. As Mattie
reminisces with characteristic inanity, "I never saw anybody with such
sharp eyes" (76). Zeena, Ethan's wife, declares in chapter I that she expects
"a poor girl like Mattie" to marry "a smart fellow like Denis Eady" (28), the
rich son of the town grocer, who has plied his wiles "to the conquest of the
Starkfield maidenhood" (25). As the chapter closes, Ethan watches Mattie
at the church dance "spinning down the floor with Denis Eady" as he waits

---

[2] See Cynthia Griffin Wolff, "Cold Ethan and 'Hot Ethan,'" in *College Literature* 14
(1987): 230 – 44. As Wolff notes, "Mattie Silver had seemed to offer warmth and love, but
in Mattie (as in Morton Fullerton), this promise could not be realized in any sustained
and socially acceptable mode" (240). Wharton fictionalizes in Mattie the same type of
false-hearted lover she knew in Morton Fullerton.

[3] Edith Wharton, introduction, *Ethan Frome* (1911; New York: Scribner's 1922) xvi.

[4] See Stuart Hutchinson, "Unpackaging Edith Wharton: *Ethan Frome* and *Summer*,"
Cambridge Quarterly 237. (1998): 219 – 32. Incredibly, Hutchinson asserts that the narrator's "account of Mattie" is "entirely realistic and authoritative. [. . .] To the contrary, so
*un*problematic is the prose [in the example he cites], so authoritative its account, that we
lose all sense of a characterized first-person narrator (and, therefore, of the possibility of
subjectivity or partiality)" (222, 223).

[5] All parenthetical references are to this New Riverside Edition.

in the darkness outside to walk her home. She lifts "her rapt face" to his and holds his hands "without appearing to feel the offence of his look and touch" (25). As Ethan observes her "whirl down the floor from hand to hand" he wonders—as must the reader by the end of the novel—"how he could ever have thought that his [Ethan's] dull talk interested her" (27). He "even noticed two or three gestures which, in his fatuity, he had thought she kept for him" (27). He must stifle a pique of jealousy stirred up by "a throng of disregarded hints and menaces" related to her past coquettish behavior (29).

In chapter II, Mattie stands outside the church "looking uncertainly around her as if wondering" where Ethan is (30), until Denis offers her a ride home. She twirls the end of her scarf provocatively, and then "Frome noticed that she no longer turned her head from side to side, as though peering through the night for another figure" (30). She "let Denis Eady lead out the horse" before eluding his embrace and escaping into the shadows—not because she is still waiting for Ethan but because she is flirting with Denis, the real object of her desire, who is rarely even mentioned in scholarship on the novel. Significantly, Denis addresses her familiarly as "Matt"—the only character in the novel to do so routinely besides Ethan. (Though Mattie is her cousin, Zeena "seldom abbreviated the girl's name" [64]). Denis follows her into the shade, "beyond Frome's earshot," before driving away a few moments later. They apparently plan to rendezvous the next day.

I believe Marlene Springer errs in asserting that "Mattie is offered a ride home but refuses it, hoping for Ethan."[6] Mattie has no romantic interest in Ethan, save what he imagines. When he finally emerges into the light, she is startled to see him. When he asks why she didn't "ride back with Denis Eady"—he "could not pronounce the name without a stiffening of the muscles of his throat" (32)—she laughs as if she has been detected in her flirtation while under parental surveillance: "Why, where *were* you? How did you know? I never saw you!" (31). Misunderstanding her reply, inbued with a mistaken "sense of having done something arch and ingenious," Ethan slips his arm through hers "as Eady had done" and "*fancied* it was faintly pressed against her side" (31; my emphasis). Within a page, however, Mattie has extricated herself and pressed ahead of Ethan "with a rapid step" (32); he is struck by her "alterations of mood" and "her indifference" to him (32).

Then Ethan lets slip the cruel truth that Zeena is no longer entirely "suited" with her housekeeping, and Mattie faces the prospect of leaving

---

[6]Marlene Springer, *Ethan Frome: A Nightmare of Need* (New York: Twayne, 1993) 72.

the farm. When a tree branch overloaded with snow crashes in the woods and a fox barks, she shrinks "closer to Ethan" (33) as if seeking his protection. "Where'd I go," she asks plaintively, were she to leave (33). To reassure her, he "pressed her against him so closely that he *seemed* to feel her warmth in his veins" (33; my emphasis). Her options are severely limited, to be sure—she "had no natural turn for house-keeping, and her training had done nothing to remedy the defect" (27). The orphaned child of penniless parents, Mattie by the age of twenty has ruined her health as a stenographer and bookkeeper "and six months on her feet behind the counter of a department store did not tend to restore it" (37). The only other immediate alternative is prostitution. "[W]hat chance had she, inexperienced and untrained, among the million bread-seekers of the cities?" Ethan later reflects. "There came back to him miserable tales he had heard at Worcester, and the faces of girls whose lives had begun as hopefully as Mattie's. . . . It was not possible to think of such things without a revolt of his whole being" (63). Even more than Ethan and Zeena, Mattie faces an uncertain future if she is "turned out." As Elizabeth Ammons explains, "She can work in a factory and lose her health; she can become a prostitute and lose her dignity; she can marry a farmer and lose her mind."[7]

Better to remain in Starkfield, if possible, and perhaps even marry Denis Eady.[8] Mattie has exactly one asset: her family tie to Zeena. As long as Mattie is confident that she is in Zeena's favor and may share her home, she is indifferent to Ethan. Only after she learns of Zeena's dissatisfaction with her and desire to send her away does she begin to look upon Ethan as her protector, her sole buffer against indigence if not indignity. It is at this early point in the novel that, for the first time, she invites him to embrace her and she yields to his embrace:

> Half-way up the slope Mattie stumbled against some unseen obstruction and clutched his sleeve to steady herself. The wave of warmth that went through him was like the prolongation of his vision. For the first time he stole his arms about her, and she did not resist. (34)

If, on her part, Mattie feigns romantic interest in Ethan, on his part Ethan fantasizes in a "rosy haze" about Mattie (35). "We'll always go on living here together," he thinks, "and some day she'll lie [in the cemetery]

---

[7]Elizabeth Ammons, *Edith Wharton's Argument with America* (Athens: U of Georgia P, 1980) 71.

[8]I believe Wolff overstates the point when she suggests that Mattie "could easily have married and joined the well-fed matrons of Starkfield village" (239). I argue in this essay that Mattie aspires to such a marriage but her abrupt dismissal from Starkfield by Zeena confounds her plans.

beside me" (34). He was "never so happy with her as when he abandoned himself" to such dreams (34). He remembers "the warmth of Mattie's shoulder against his" and regrets his failure to kiss her "when he held her" during the walk home from the church dance: "since he had seen her lips in the lamplight he felt that they were his" (36). As Cynthia Griffin Wolff fairly observes, Mattie for Ethan is "the embodiment of sexual promise," though "this promise is largely a figment of Ethan Frome's imagination."[9]

Ironically, Ethan is largely oblivious to the infatuation of Mattie and Denis. As Mattie washes the dishes the next morning, she hums "one of the dance tunes of the night before" (40) when she had danced with Denis. There are strong hints that Denis visits her this day when Zeena is away at Bettsbridge. Ethan sees him in the village sporting "a handsome new fur cap" before he heads his cutter "in the direction of the Frome farm, and Ethan's heart contracted as he listened to the dwindling bells. What [was] more likely than that Denis Eady had heard of Zeena's departure for Betts-bridge, and was profiting by the opportunity to spend an hour with Mattie?" (44–45). As he begins to walk home, Ethan spies Ned Hale and Ruth Var-num kissing in the shadows of the Varnum spruces—near the spot where Mattie had left Denis the night before—though Ethan regards it as "the spot where he and Mattie had stood with such a thirst for each other in their hearts" (45). Denis has apparently come and gone by the time Ethan reaches the farm—his colt is not stabled in the barn, to Ethan's relief—but Mattie has forgotten to unlock the kitchen door after his departure. Ethan spies a light in her room as he arrives at the house. He rattles the door handle and then rationalizes that "Mattie was alone and that it was natural she should barricade herself at nightfall" (46). Still, it takes her "a minute or two" to reach the door, time enough for her to throw on a dress, partic-ularly one with "no bow at her neck" (46). Ethan wonders if it was his sud-den arrival "that gave her such a kindled [i.e., excited] face" (47), though her excitement is more plausibly the result of Denis's discreet visit. Jealous, Ethan asks Mattie whether she had received any visitors that day, and she replies, "Yes, one." When he asks who it was, her "eyes danced with mal-ice" before she mentions the handyman's name (47). When Ethan casually observes that evening that he had seen "a friend of yours getting kissed," however, Mattie overreacts to the news. He had "imagined that his allusion might open the way to the accepted pleasantries, and these perhaps in turn

---

[9]According to David Eggenschwiler in his essay "The Ordered Disorder of *Ethan Frome*," *Studies in the Novel* 9 (Fall 1977): 237–46, Mattie "is a perfectly imagined object for Ethan's confused desires" (239). Ethan had been similarly duped by his imagination into marrying Zeena: her willingness to nurse his mother and so free him "to go about his business again" in turn "magnified his sense of what he owed her" (Wolff 52).

to a harmless caress" (51). Instead, she "blushed to the roots of her hair and pulled her needle rapidly twice or thrice through her work." Mattie suddenly "seemed infinitely farther away from him and more unapproachable" (51). But why should she blush, why the sexual image, and why the sudden withdrawal—unless she had been visited by Denis that afternoon? She remarks that Ned and Ruth plan a summer marriage, and she "pronounced the word *married* as if her voice caressed it. It seemed a rustling covert leading to enchanted glades" (51). Clearly, as the pun on "covert" would suggest, she secretly contemplates marriage—but with Denis, I believe, not with the already-married Ethan.[10]

Nowhere in the novel is the confusion of motives more apparent than in the narrator's account of the evening Mattie and Ethan spend together in Zeena's absence. Ethan fantasizes about their evening together:

> For the first time they would be alone together indoors, and they would sit there, one on each side of the stove, like a married couple, he in his stocking feet and smoking his pipe, she laughing and talking in that funny way she had. (41)

Mattie has "carefully" prepared Ethan's supper and has adorned her hair (for Denis?) with a "streak of crimson ribbon" and the table with the red pickle dish. She wishes to please Ethan, to enlist his help should Zeena try to turn her out. The ribbon associates Mattie with the character of Faith in Nathaniel Hawthorne's "Young Goodman Brown," who wears pink ribbon and who is also an ambiguously eroticized figure. Though often interpreted as a sexual symbol—e.g., "it is the broken pickle plate that becomes the symbolic disclosure of secret desires between Mattie and Ethan"—the dish does not require such a reading.[11] To paraphrase Sigmund Freud, sometimes a red pickle dish is just a red pickle dish. It need *not* signify sexual desire at all, much less the mutual desire of Ethan and Mattie.[12]

In the course of the evening, Mattie "*feigned* great interest" in Ethan's conversation (47; my emphasis). Trivial events are again charged with significance by his adolescent fantasizing: "The scene was just as he had

---

[10] The term *covert* may mean "secret" or "hidden" as well as "sheltered," as in a covered drain leading to a glade or even a wife under the protection of her husband.

[11] See, for example, Jennifer Travis, "Pain and Recompense: The Trouble with *Ethan Frome*," *Arizona Quarterly* 53 (Autumn 1997): 37–64, at p. 50.

[12] Significantly, Ethan spends part of his day looking for a bottle of glue to mend the broken pickle dish—and he looks first in Eady's store. Denis makes "an ineffectual search in the obscurer corners of the store" for the glue before admitting it "Looks as if we were all sold out" (55). If the pickle dish is a sexual symbol, it may just as easily represent the pending rupture in Denis's relations with Mattie on the eve of her departure from Starkfield and his disinterest or inability to repair them.

dreamed of it that morning" (49). They "talk easily and simply," and their informality "produced in Ethan an *illusion* of long-established intimacy [. . .] and he set his imagination adrift on the fiction that they had always spent their evenings thus and would always go on doing so" (50; my emphasis). Of course, Mattie has an ulterior motive: she asks him what he knows of Zeena's plans for her. He imagines ("it seemed to him that") a "warm current" flowed between them in the kitchen. He touches the tip of the material she is hemming and a "faint vibration of her lashes *seemed* to show that she was aware of his gesture" (52; my emphasis). "I've been in a dream," he thinks, and his "return to reality was as painful as the return to consciousness after taking an anaesthetic" (52). Still, some critics read the scene much too literally or superficially. Jennifer Travis asserts, for example, that "Ethan and Mattie are bound by a length of thread, a thin 'strip' that acts as a conduit for their feelings."[13] But when he kisses the cloth, Mattie abruptly leaves the room—a departure prompted less perhaps by her wish to resist Ethan's erotic overtures than simply to escape them for the moment. After all, as he realizes after her door has closed, "he had not even touched her hand" during the evening (53).

His fantasies about her multiply the next day. The evening "had given him a vision of what life at her side might be" (53) and, incredibly, he thinks *he* is the one who stopped before things went too far: "He had a fancy that she knew what had restrained him . . ." (53). He also imagines that "she nodded her comprehension" at his promise to "be back early" that night (54). When Zeena returns from Bettsbridge and announces to Ethan that Mattie must leave their house the very next day, he is alarmed. Zeena remains in her room, leaving the erstwhile lovers "to have one more evening together," as Mattie's "happy eyes *seemed* to say" to him (62; my emphasis). But her motives are the same as before: she needs his protection, and she will do whatever is necessary to enlist his help. When he cannot disguise his concern for her, however, she again reacts to the danger:

> "Ethan, there's something wrong! I *knew* there was!"
> She seemed [sic] to melt against him in her terror, and he caught her in his arms, held her fast there, felt her lashes beat his cheek like netted butterflies.
> "What is it—what is it?" she stammered; but he had found her lips at last and was drinking unconsciousness of everything but the joy they gave him. (62)

Mattie "slipped from him" and stepped back, "pale and troubled." How far exactly must she go to enlist him in her cause? As yet, she does not realize

---

[13] Travis 50.

he is helpless, "a prisoner for life" in his own home (68) and but a "helpless spectator" at her "banishment" (70).

The final chapter opens as Mattie sobs in her room the next morning — not because she is about to leave Ethan's side, but because she is about to be expelled from the only home she knows and, with her abrupt exile, she will lose any chance she has of marrying Denis Eady. As she leaves the farm for what she believes is the last time, she takes a final look around "with a wavering smile" (74). On this day, she makes a final desperate appeal to Ethan to help her remain there. After all, she has read the note Ethan had written to Zeena the night before in which he announced his plan to light out for the West with Mattie, so she knows she has some leverage. She does not resist when he takes her in his arms or when he "laid his lips on her hair" (73). She even draws closer to him under the bearskin during their sleigh ride. They reminisce about the church picnic the preceding summer, and Ethan says, "You were as pretty as a picture in that pink hat." Mattie replies with a laugh, "Oh, I guess it was the hat!"—whereupon the narrator reports that "They had never before avowed their inclination so openly" (76). Surely this is a peculiar lovemaking, if lovemaking at all. True to his character, Ethan suffers under "the illusion that he was a free man, wooing the girl he meant to marry," gazing "at her vaguely, only half-roused from his dream." As they leave the spot, the narrator says, "They stood looking at each other *as if* the eyes of each were straining to absorb and hold fast the other's image" (76; my emphasis). The narrator, with his qualification, scarcely insists upon Mattie's sincerity. "There's never anybody been good to me but you" (78), Mattie twice reminds Ethan; she still wants him to protect her.

In the end, she offers herself sexually to him, and when that shameless ploy fails, she resolves to commit suicide, preferring death to homelessness and disgrace. Marlene Springer notes that Mattie "kisses Ethan and pleads that they not separate,"[14] but the episode is more complex than such a statement may suggest:

> "Is this where Ned and Ruth kissed each other?" she whispered breathlessly, and flung her arms about him. Her lips, groping for his, swept over his face, and he held her fast in a rapture of surprise.
> "Good-bye—good-bye," she stammered, and kissed him again.
> "Oh, Matt, I can't let you go!" broke from him in the same old cry.
> She freed herself from his hold and he heard her sobbing. "Oh, I can't go either!" she wailed. (80)

---

[14] Springer 83.

Mattie's final line here is telling. In reply to his "I can't let you go" she does *not* say "I can't let you go either" but "I can't go either." It's not that she can't leave *him,* but that she doesn't want to leave. To be sure, on the next page she tells Ethan that she "will be [crazy] if I leave you" and she asks "where'll I go if I leave you?" (81)—but by this time her sexual negotiation has failed. Ethan asks, "What's the good of either of us going anywheres without the other one now?"—a question Mattie greets with silence, "as if she had not heard him" (80). Ethan has closed definitively the option of her remaining in Starkfield. She realizes her gambit has failed. Though he kisses her twice more, she does not kiss him again. She decides to die rather than suffer the indignities of homelessness and to use him as her executioner. Ethan, ever a dupe to his illusions, misunderstands her "avowal"; he thinks "that all that happened to him had happened to her too" (81). But it has not: Mattie's ostensible love for him is nothing more than her desire to exploit him refracted through his starved imagination.

Their double suicide attempt fails, of course, because Ethan sits in front on the sled so he can be held by Mattie and thus he absorbs the brunt of the impact with the elm tree. Still, as the sled hurdles down the slope, Ethan retains the foolish illusion that a lover's death awaits him at the elm below: "As they flew toward the tree Mattie pressed her arms tighter, and her blood *seemed* to be in his veins" (82; my emphasis). After the crash, Mattie is carried to the Varnum house, where she regains consciousness the next morning. "[S]he woke up just like herself, and looked straight at me out of her big eyes," Ruth Varnum Hale tells the narrator twenty-four years later, "and said ... Oh, I don't know why I'm telling you all this" (86). What does Mattie say when she regains consciousness? No critic, to my knowledge, has speculated on this question or tried to fill this gap in the text. My guess is that Mattie damns Ethan for his utter incompetence even to kill her and himself in the bargain.

Ironically, Mattie's desperate desire to remain in Starkfield is realized, though at an awful price. She is paralyzed (and so effectively desexualized) and nursed in her invalidism by Zeena. No one, perhaps not even the narrator who depicts her, has fully recognized her duplicity in her affair with Ethan. He is destined to live the remainder of his life with two women who scorn him. Meanwhile, Denis Eady, as we learn in the opening frame, becomes a "rich Irish grocer" and the "proprietor of Starkfield's nearest approach to a livery stable."

In all, *Ethan Frome* is a sad naturalistic tale set in a stark New England village, but it is a story of tragic love only in the most superficial sense. It is also an experiment in point of view that has misdirected readers with narrative sleight-of-hand for nearly a century. Rather than the sympathetic damsel in distress, Mattie Silver is a two-faced *femme* near-*fatale*, a scheming temptress who not only lures Ethan to a worse hell than he could have imagined but in the end is consigned to it, too.

From "The Continued Popularity of *Ethan Frome*"

R. Baird Shuman

There is probably no more pervasive single element in *Ethan Frome* than the symbolism. [Blake] Nevius and other writers have pointed out specific examples in which the landscape and the Frome dwelling are clearly related to the action of the story and to the development of characters within it. However, other symbolic elements have not been fully explored and these should be noted, because they are central to the work on a psycho-sexual level, and this level is very important to the novel because of the underlying sexual tensions which motivate its three central characters. Through the use of carefully chosen symbols, Mrs. Wharton consistently emphasizes problems which are basic to the central action, and she also gives a very strong clue regarding the basis of Zeena Frome's hypochondria.

One of the most notable symbols in *Ethan Frome* is the symbol of the elm tree into which Ethan and Mattie crash their sled during their ill-fated suicide attempt. It is evident that this tree might have been used by Mrs. Wharton, either with conscious intent or subconsciously, as a phallic symbol. Note that the reader is told of the tree long before the suicide attempt is made and is thus prepared for what is later to happen. However, such advanced preparation is not entirely necessary; enough is said of the elm just before the accident to convince the reader of the danger it presents to anyone sledding down the slope which it partially obstructs. Mattie, speaking to Ethan about the elm, says, "Ned Hale and Ruth Varnum came just as *near* running into the big elm at the bottom. We were all sure they were killed. . . . Wouldn't it have been too awful?" [31–32] [1] Read on a symbolic level, and in light of the fact that later in the narrative the reader is told that Ethan had seen Ned Hale and Ruth Varnum kissing under the Varnum spruces (50), there is a clear indication that the elm stands as a rep-

Revue des Langues Vivantes 37.3 (1971).

[1] All parenthetical references are to this New Riverside Edition. [Ed.]

resentation of sexual temptation, that it draws to it those whose resistance is weak enough that they might violate the puritanical moral codes of a small New England community. Ned and Ruth, though tempted by love, are not pressed to the point that they violate the community mores. But Ethan and Mattie, though their love has not transgressed these mores in any physical sense, cannot long resist their physical natures and will soon be sufficiently dominated by these natures to violate the established codes.

Physical reality is hard and relentless; Mrs. Wharton, in her introduction, warns the reader that it is with this "harsh and beautiful land" that she will concern herself. The harsh moral structures of this land prevent Ethan and Mattie from finding fulfilment for their love, and even the fulfilment of a death together is denied them. They collide head-on with the symbolic tree, and are doomed to a life of unbearable agony, both physical and mental. Marilyn J. Lyde notes that in *Ethan Frome* ". . . there is no element of justice in the catastrophe. This is explained by the fact that Mrs. Wharton was writing with the explicit purpose of counteracting the New England literary tradition of sweetness and light."[2] The means which Ethan and Mattie chose for their suicide would lead a sensitive reader to expect some symbolic shadings to be apparent. These shadings are quite evident both in the fact of what the tree itself represents and in the fact that Ethan and Mattie run into it on a borrowed sled, on a sled which technically they have no right to, any more than Ethan technically has a right to Mattie's love, nor she to his.

There is, throughout the novel, an emphasis upon the barrenness of the Fromes' lives and surroundings. The graveyard is constantly, mockingly in the background. Very early in the novel, the reader is told that Ethan has had to take down the "L" from his house, and Mrs. Wharton, in a lengthy paragraph, tells that the "L" in a New England house is the center of all life, the hearth-stone of the dwelling (21). Zeena, presumably, is barren, and her barrenness pervades the atmosphere of the house and is constantly in direct contrast to Mattie's vitality. The illusion of barrenness is supported by such statements as "Zeena always went to bed as soon as she had had her supper, and the shutterless windows of the house were dark." And the statement which immediately follows this one is directly applicable to Ethan: "A dead cucumber-vine dangled from the porch like the crape streamer tied to the door for a death." (34) The Freudian overtones of the shutterless windows and of the dead cucumber-vine are clearly apparent. Death surrounds Ethan; the graveyard is a constant reminder of death's in-

---

[2] Marilyn Jones Lyde, *Edith Wharton: Convention and Morality in the World of a Novelist* (Norman: U of Oklahoma P, 1959) 130, fn. 17. [Ed.]

evitability; and even as he looks ahead, there is no hope. He is the last of the Fromes. The future of his family, the hope of continuance, have been killed by his marriage to Zeena. Mattie presents a momentary hope of something wholesome and satisfying, but Ethan knows that she is what might have been, not what might ultimately be.

Although Mattie is not overly strong, she appears strong in contrast to Zeena. The reader is told that she has gained a great deal of strength during her year at Starkfield. She is often described in terms of the strong color red and its variations: "Mattie came forward, unwinding her wraps, the colour of the cherry scarf in her fresh lips and cheeks." (35) ". . . through her hair she [Mattie] had run a streak of crimson ribbon." (46) "Her [Mattie's] cheeks burned redder." (50) "She [Mattie] looked so small and pinched, in her poor dress, with the red scarf wound about her." (68) However, before Ethan's passion for Mattie had developed, she was sallow; and when she is described in terms of color, the color is more moderate: "You were as pretty as a picture in that pink hat." (76) Red is also used symbolically in relation to the sun: "The sunrise burned red in a pure sky." (36) "Now, in the bright morning air, her [Mattie's] face was still before him. It was part of the sun's red and of the pure glitter of the snow." (36) This use of "red" and "pure" in the same sentence would seem almost to provide an element of mockery, for Mattie is the pure, the virginal figure, but the red heat of passion is intruding upon her life and is leading her irresistibly into a hopeless situation.

Perhaps the most telling symbolic element in *Ethan Frome* is the cherished pickle dish which Zeena received as a wedding gift and has never used. When Zeena goes to Bettsbridge and leaves Mattie and Ethan alone overnight, Mattie takes this pickle dish from its accustomed place and uses it for its intended purpose. The cat, used symbolically throughout this part of the book to represent Zeena's inescapable presence, knocks the dish to the floor, and it is smashed. Zeena, almost immediately upon her return, discovers what has happened to the dish and blames Mattie for having used it. For the first time in the book, Zeena shows true emotion. "Her voice broke, and two small tears hung on her lashless lids and ran slowly down her cheeks." (64)

This is a major tragedy for Zeena as Mrs. Wharton presents the episode. The question, of course, arises of why this particular incident should be given such play. The smashing of the dish is not used as a pretext for sending Mattie away; Zeena has already reached the decision to do this. The incident might have been used as a turning point in the action of the novel, but it occurs after any turning point with which it might be directly associated. It is not used for characterization, because the characterization has been achieved as fully as it is to be by this point. However, on a symbolic level, it serves as explanation for Zeena's hypochondria and insecurity. The dish was a wedding gift and this, in itself, is significant. The fact that it was red and that it was a *pickle* dish adds to the sexual connotations which it might possess as a symbol. And the fact that Zeena cries because it is broken would point to the fact that Zeena is bemoaning her lost virginity and that her hypochondria is attributable to her fear of her husband's, and perhaps her own, animal nature. Zeena finds that her marriage has placed her in conflict with the codes which her New England upbringing instilled in her; her inhibitions have become so great that she is made pathological by them. Zeena is a pitiable woman. For one reason or another, she has never been able to find fulfilment. Her life is barren. Her future is dark. She reacted well to the responsibility of caring for Ethan's mother, because it was necessary to Zeena that she be needed. But with the death of Ethan's mother, there was a gap in Zeena's life. This gap might have been filled had she had children, but she was denied this satisfaction. Hence, her concern turned inward and her hypochondria, which apparently had moderated when she began caring for Ethan's mother, returned in full force.

To an extent, Zeena was rewarded for the suffering which she endured during the first seven years of her marriage when Mattie and Ethan were injured and needed Zeena to look after them. Zeena—like Ethan—is strongly masochistic throughout the novel. Her hypochondria provided her with masochistic satisfaction, just as her leaving Ethan and Mattie alone for the night did. But when she could become the martyred servant of the sharp-tongued wretch which Mattie became after the accident, her masochistic satisfaction found its greatest fulfilment. She could simultaneously feel that she was needed, that she was morally superior, and that she had been sinned against but had had the humanity to be forgiving.

One critic has written that "Mrs. Wharton conceived of the novel as an organism, the germ or controlling principle of which was character."[3] Certainly the character of Zenobia Frome represented a controlling principle in the novel at hand, for in this character Mrs. Wharton represents in a single person the generalized, warped manifestation of New England puritanism in its most unwholesome extremes.

Alfred Kazin has quoted Edith Wharton as saying that "Life is the saddest thing next to death."[4] Yet in *Ethan Frome* life has become much sadder than death. Starkfield, the name of which sounds funereal, is a

---

[3] Melvin Wayne Askew, "Edith Wharton's Literary Theory," *Dissertation Abstracts* 17 (1957): 3009. [Ed.]

[4] Alfred Kazin, *On Native Grounds: An Interpretation of Modern American Prose Literature* (New York: Harcourt 1942) 58. [Ed.]

cemetery for those who are still physically alive. There is not "much difference between the Fromes up at the farm and the Fromes down in the graveyard; 'cept that down there they're all quiet, and the women have got to
hold their tongues." (87)

   [. . .] *Ethan Frome* remains a monument in the Edith Wharton canon.
It is probably valid to say that it is the Edith Wharton novel which has been
most read in the past two or three decades. It retains a freshness in dealing
with the problem of the marriage triangle from a relatively impersonal
viewpoint. Nature and life and moral codes move steadily forth, drawing
with them such as Ethan and Mattie. Mrs. Wharton does not sentimentalize; indeed, she cannot sentimentalize if she is to achieve her end of pro-
ducing a work which will counter the sweetness and light in which other
novelists had steeped New England. [. . .]

"Charity at the Window: Narrative Technique in Edith Wharton's *Summer*"

Jean Frantz Blackall

In her Introduction to *Ethan Frome,* one of Edith Wharton's infrequent statements about her own purposes as a writer, she addresses the question of how she can represent inarticulate persons realistically.[1] She is speaking of the hill people of western Massachusetts, like Ethan Frome and his wife Zeena in that work and, again, like Charity Royall in *Summer,* Wharton's other principal fiction set in the Lenox environs. Such people, she says, are inert as stones, uncomplicated, reticent, simple. Much of the narrative space in *Ethan Frome* is devoted to recording moments of silence that overlie feelings of anger, of love, of longing aspiration. Yet we know of these feelings because Wharton utilized an educated narrator and a frame story to account for his presence in the community. In her Introduction she reports her friends' admonitions as to the artificiality of insinuating the narrative frame. Yet she doggedly insists on the appropriateness of the device to her purpose. By this means she could render Ethan's inner life in a language inaccessible to Ethan himself without violating her premise of verisimilitude, that he be a wordless man, and one lacking in perspective. [. . .]

There is no comparable author's Introduction to *Summer,* but the problem remains, for like Ethan the point-of-view character, Charity Royall, lacks education, lacks words and perspective. Like Ethan too, she develops

---

Edith Wharton: New Critical Essays. Eds. Alfred Bendixen and Annette Zilversmit. New York: Garland, 1992.

[1] In the introduction that Wharton wrote to the 1922 reprint edition of *Ethan Frome* she addressed the novel's narrative voice and structure. [Ed.]

an increasingly interesting inner life under the awakening of love, and of a sense of responsibility, but has only rudimentary modes of expressing her sentiments. Her idiom is unembellished, functional, and often monosyllabic. Charity's opening speech in the novel is "'How I hate everything!'"[2] (91) Her most profound act, the renunciation of Lucius Harney, is conveyed in these words: "'I want you should marry Annabel Balch if you promised to. I think maybe you were afraid I'd feel too bad about it. I feel I'd rather you acted right'" (181). Clearly, Wharton could not sustain an engaging narrative in such an idiom [. . .]. [I]n *Summer* Wharton solved her problem of rendering the inner life of a limited character in far subtler ways than by the rather arbitrary interjection of an educated, urban narrator into a rural community; [. . .] in doing so she in effect answered those who criticized the overt narrative frame of *Ethan Frome;* and [. . .] her answer consisted specifically in her subsuming the frame that exists apart in *Ethan Frome* into the vision of the central character in *Summer.*

Dorrit Cohn remarks in *Transparent Minds,* her fine book on techniques of narration, that "Narrative fiction attains its greatest 'air of reality' in the representation of a lone figure thinking thoughts she will never communicate to anyone. This paradox lies at the very heart of narrative realism."[3] Yet Cohn goes on to observe that "Whether thought is always verbal is . . . a matter of definition and dispute among psychologists. Most people, including most novelists, certainly conceive of consciousness as including 'other mind stuff' (as William James called it), in addition to language. This 'stuff' cannot be quoted—directly or indirectly; it can only be narrated."[4] That Edith Wharton granted the wordlessness of thought is conveyed in such a passage as this one:

> [Charity] was blind and insensible to many things, and dimly knew it; but to all that was light and air, perfume and colour, every drop of blood in her responded. She loved the roughness of the dry mountain grass under her palms, the smell of the thyme into which she crushed her face, the fingering of the wind in her hair and through her cotton blouse, and the creak of the larches as they swayed to it.
>
> She often climbed up the hill and lay there alone for the mere pleasure of feeling the wind and of rubbing her cheeks in the grass. Generally at such times she did not think of anything, but lay immersed in an inarticulate well-being. (97)

---

[2] All parenthetical references are to this New Riverside Edition. [Ed.]

[3] Dorrit Cohn, *Transparent Minds: Narrative Modes for Presenting Consciousness in Fiction* (Princeton: Princeton UP, 1978) 7.

[4] Cohn 11. [Ed.]

This passage represents Charity's experience of the abstractions of love of life and personal well-being in sensuous terms—tactile, olfactory, aural, visual. Charity crushes her face into the fragrant wild thyme, presses her palms against the rough mountain grass, sensuously responds to the wind in her hair and her blouse. She listens to the creaking of the windswept trees. A state of mind is expressed as a response of "blood" to "light and air, perfume and colour." Wharton perseveres in this technique of translating "'other mind stuff'" into sensuous experience throughout the novel.

Its counterpart is that words, which commonly open the way to understanding, are represented as being obstacles in Charity's path. Crucial words, and especially those that are abstract or allusive, such as Lucius Harney's "monologue on art and life" (114), become a barrier. Of Charity's first visit to Nettleton, a larger town, the narrator remarks that "In the course of that incredible day, Charity Royall had . . . listened to a gentleman saying unintelligible things before pictures that she would have enjoyed looking at if his explanations had not prevented her from understanding them" (92). Charity's enjoyment of the pictorial lecture is negated by "explanations," because for her "understanding" is not verbal. When Lucius Harney first visits the library where Charity functions as custodian, he comments, "'You don't seem strong on architecture'" (96). "Her bewilderment was complete: the more she wished to appear to understand him the more unintelligible his remarks became. He reminded her of the gentleman who had 'explained' the pictures at Nettleton, and the weight of her ignorance settled down on her again" (96). Despite her desire for knowledge, however, the Hatchard Memorial Library remains a "prison-house" (94), because books are opaque. They thwart rather than liberate her spirit. Apart from "architecture," other words that baffle and bewilder her are "character," "garden-party," and the "unintelligible words" that people speak in a French restaurant she visits with Lucius Harney.

In lieu of words Charity is shown to develop a pictorial vocabulary, compounded of places, people, and symbolic objects such as the kinds of hats people wear and the color of their eyes, facial expression and its aural counterpart, intonation. Her sense of her own value is a compound of visual images, discerned in the mirror: "The dresses in the shops had so impressed her that she scarcely dared look at her reflection; but when she did so, the glow of her face under her cherry-coloured hat, and the curve of her young shoulders through the transparent muslin, restored her courage; and when she had taken the blue brooch from its box and pinned it on her bosom she walked toward the restaurant with her head held high" (146). Charity assesses persons' attitudes by their tone of voice. It is good to have "character," whatever that is, because Harney's "tone was expressive of admiration" (116). North Dormer, her home, is located in Charity's mental landscape midway between Nettleton, her norm for the unvoiced concept of sophistication, and the Mountain whence she came, regarded by the town as being "a bad place, and a shame to have come from" (93). Within the domestic sphere Charity assesses her own well-being by placing the red house where she lives with Mr. Royall, her guardian, midway between Miss Hatchard's white house and the ramshackle brown hovel of the Hyatts halfway up the mountain. The stranger who has arrived in town, Miss Hatchard's cousin, is distinguished by laughter, youth, and fine hands. Annabel Balch's blue eyes become the measure for brown-eyed Charity of her own lack. The narrator employs this vocabulary of symbolized visual images to represent Charity's thought processes in such a passage as this one:

> She looked up at the Mountain, thinking of these things [that she had been brought down from this shameful place], and tried as usual to be thankful. But the sight of the young man turning in at Miss Hatchard's gate had brought back the vision of the glittering streets of Nettleton, and she felt ashamed of her old sun-hat, and sick of North Dormer, and jealously aware of Annabel Balch of Springfield, opening her blue eyes somewhere far off on glories greater than the glories of Nettleton. (93)

Here and elsewhere, the narrative voice sustains the account of Charity's attitudes, but the focal images and the mental horizon are Charity's own: the young man, blue-eyed Annabel, hats, Nettleton vs. the Mountain, North Dormer vs. them both. The terms of Charity's pictorial vocabulary are gradually augmented to include bramble flowers, butterflies, flashes of light, a blue jewel, stars, a black-and-gold sign, a pair of shoes, false teeth and a wig, and so on. The meanings of such terms constantly accrue or modify, as for example the Mountain is "'a blot'" in Mr. Royall's esteem (118), but in Harney's it is "'a little independent kingdom'" inhabited by "'a handful of people who don't give a damn for anybody.' The words thrilled [Charity]. They seemed the clue to her own revolts and defiances" (116).[5] Mr. Royall himself alternates in her vision between a figure inspiring loathing and one inspiring awe. More generally, the register of Charity's mental activities is recorded by the narrator in such words as "sight," "vision," "picture," "signs," "divined," "instinct," and "sense." Her early life on the Mountain exists in her consciousness as an unexamined heap of "blurred images" (114).

In sum, we have a heroine who sits down to the feast of life as a spectator and an auditor. Most characteristically she is passive, often silent, a recipient, assimilating particulars into a symbolic mental mosaic compounded of sense impressions. Sometimes she turns to mirrors for insight, or to the

---

[5] Note here that it is Lucius's words that define Charity's sentiments.

figurative mirrors of other characters' faces or to the reflections of her that their words evoke. Sometimes she looks at pictures on the wall, at moving pictures, into shop windows. Most important, she may pause by a window, gazing on a familiar scene. By this latter device, frequently invoked, Wharton projects Charity's state of mind as on a screen, defining the limits, the objects, and the range of her vision. [. . .] Wordlessly, Charity Royall is drawn in to the contemplation of her own life, of her circumstances, her aspirations, the hard facts. Thus her own vision is rendered, sometimes without overt authorial intervention, at times with the same subtly intrusive interpretive voice that characterizes the third-person narrative elsewhere. This device of framing is Wharton's most subtle and innovative expository technique. Under what circumstances does Charity attain such moments of vision, we may ask, and what does she see framed there?

Characteristically, she is in a state of lassitude, even apathy. "The kitchen window was open, and Charity seated herself near it, her idle hands on her knee" (117). Or else she is in an attitude of questioning and uncertainty brought on by some prior event: "[She] began to struggle against the desire to go down and ask [Mr. Royall] what had happened [i.e., why Lucius Harney no longer comes to their house for meals, for she suspects that her guardian has sent Harney away]. 'I'd rather die than do it,' she muttered to herself. With a word he could have relieved her uncertainty; but never would she gratify him by saying it. She rose and leaned out of the window" (130). But in either instance, be it apathy or curiosity that governs her, the generalized impressions that wash over Charity as she faces the window gradually focus on some central moment of figure which fixes her attention. This figure may be one of menace, one that threatens to invade her privacy. Her friend Ally Hawes becomes emblematic to Charity of the town's curiosity and malice in its scrutinizing the friendship between herself and Harney. Mr. Royall looms there. So does the Mountain. Or this figure may be an object of her own curiosity and affection, such as Harney himself. (Harney's desertion of her is ironically prefigured in such a moment of loving scrutiny: "She . . . flung open the shutters and leaned out. He waved to her and sped by, his black shadow dancing merrily ahead of him down the empty moonlit road; and she leaned there watching him till he vanished under the Hatchard spruces" [168].) Out of this concentration on a figure of menace or of love there frequently emerges a decision to act in a specific way. Hence in the window scenes Charity characteristically passes from inertia to resolution. Such moments illustrate the pertinence of Dorrit Cohn's remark that "Narrative fiction attains its greatest 'air of reality' in the representation of a lone figure thinking thoughts she will never communicate to anyone." For we are privy to the world as it is framed in Charity's private vision. We, too, are drawn into the frame, watch as she

watches. Moreover, Charity's silent watching of a scene ever so slowly unfolded before her illustrates Wharton's own sentiment that the requisite
style for representing "the mental states" of humble characters is one which
represents "the *tempo* of their minds and their lives," "that of the deadly
monotony and mediocrity of the small town":

> Leaning from her window she looked out on the dark and empty
> scene; the ashen houses with shuttered windows, the grey road climbing
> the slope to the hemlock belt above the cemetery, and the heavy mass of
> the Mountain black against a rainy sky. To the east a space of light was
> broadening above the forest; but over that also the clouds hung. Slowly
> her gaze travelled across the fields to the rugged curve of the hills. She
> had looked out so often on that lifeless circle, and wondered if anything
> could ever happen to anyone who was enclosed in it. . . . [Wharton's
> ellipses]
> Almost without conscious thought her decision had been reached; as
> her eyes had followed the circle of the hills her mind had also travelled
> the old round. She supposed it was something in her blood that made
> the Mountain the only answer to her questioning, the inevitable escape
> from all that hemmed her in and beset her. At any rate it began to loom
> in her now as it loomed against the rainy dawn; and the longer she
> looked at it the more clearly she understood that now at last she was re-
> ally going there. (187–88)

In this passage the epithets supplied by the narrator convey Charity's
hopeless mood and the specter of death that haunts her: "dark," "empty,"
"ashen," "grey," "hemlock"; and they also adumbrate the flickering resolution of her problem: "To the east a space of light . . . but over that also the
clouds hung." Meanwhile, for Charity the images captured in the frame of
her vision bring her "[a]lmost without conscious thought" to her decision.
Here Wharton's understanding of her own technique is written into the
text: "as her eyes had followed the circle of the hills her mind had also travelled the old round."

Wharton most brilliantly exploits her framing technique in two crucial
moments. The first marks the climax in Charity's will to rise above her
class and the expectations of the town by resisting a sexual liaison with
Lucius Harney. Later, having failed in that attempt, she confronts the consequences of her choice, of her two choices. For, pregnant, acquiescent to
her abandonment because she feels unworthy, and her escape to the Mountain an abortive venture, Charity has at last yielded to the marriage proposal of her ever watchful guardian, Mr. Royall. The latter scene occurs in
a Nettleton hotel bedroom on her wedding day.

The first of these crucial moments takes place before her affair with
Harney is initiated, and Charity's instigation for becoming a watcher is

Harney's sudden unexplained withdrawal. Restless beside her own window at home, she walks out into the evening with no fixed purpose, only to discern a light at Miss Hatchard's. This gleam of light draws Charity until she finds herself crouching noiselessly outside Harney's window. What follows is in effect a dumb show in which Charity reads Harney's expression and gestures as the answer to her question. She notices the restless motions, the interlocking of his hands, the "look of weariness and self-disgust on his face: it was almost as if he had been gazing at a distorted reflection of his own features" (132). She sees a half-packed portmanteau on the floor. From these marks of Harney's irresolution and tension, Charity suspects that Mr. Royall's intervention, not Harney's disapproval of herself as being kin to the Hyatts of the Mountain, is Harney's reason for withdrawal. Then Charity moves on to a discovery about herself: in Harney's physical presence—the unbuttoned low collar of his flannel shirt, "his young throat," the muscles of his neck, his throwing himself down upon the bed—she discerns his sexuality, which has its counterpart "[i]n every pulse of her rigid body" as she gazes in at the window: "She had suddenly understood what would happen if she went in. It was the thing that *did* happen to young men and girls, and that North Dormer ignored in public and snickered over on the sly. . . . It was what happened to Ally Hawes's sister Julia, and had ended in her going to Nettleton, and in people's never mentioning her name" (133). Here the sophistication of Nettleton takes on a sinister taint for Charity as she acknowledges the threat that her own sexuality poses to herself: "One motion of her hand, one tap on the pane, and she could picture the sudden change in his face" (133). But Charity desists because she makes yet another discovery, this one about her own desires: "She did not know why he was going; but since he was going she felt she must do nothing to deface the image of her that he carried away. If he wanted her he must seek her: he must not be surprised into taking her as girls like Julia Hawes were taken . . ." (133–34). Charity's mode of expressing a decision that involves her own values is, simply, that she must not deface a picture of herself. She had "looked at him with a kind of terror" when his own face gave back "a distorted reflection of his own features" (132), that is, as the narrator obtrudes, when "a look of weariness and self-disgust [was registered] on his face" (132). She does not want, herself, to project such an image. Hence Charity's convulsive engagement with abstractions, which involves both her temporary resolution of a moral question and a question of personal volition, is rendered as a matter of the faces that people present to one another. Hereafter, her own face in the mirror will be a sign of her self-betrayal.

At the end of the novel Wharton plays with framing in an intricate and ingenious way. The hotel room in which Charity finds herself on her wedding day fronts Nettleton Lake, scene of her Fourth of July outing with Lucius Harney. Gazing down upon the lake where they had rowed together, she realizes the irretrievable nature of her own act in consenting to marry her guardian, and fleetingly contemplates flight. But just as Royall intruded upon Charity's happiness on the Fourth of July, cruelly confronting her with Lucius and calling her a whore, so now he intrudes again. Entering the room, "[h]e went up to the window to draw the blind" (206), negating Charity's vision of past happiness. Later that night, forbearing but relentless, Mr. Royall sits down by the bed in which Charity lies:

> She lay there trembling with a fear. . . . "What have I done? Oh, what have I done?" she whispered, shuddering to her pillow; and pressing her face against it to shut out the pale landscape beyond the window she lay in the darkness straining her ears, and shaking at every footstep that approached. . . .
>
> . . . A faint sound had told her that someone was in the room; but she must have slept in the interval, for she had heard no one enter. The moon was setting beyond the opposite roofs, and in the darkness, outlined against the grey square of the window, she saw a figure seated in the rocking-chair. . . . She saw that it was Mr. Royall who sat there. . . .
>
> As she continued to watch him ineffable relief stole slowly over her, relaxing her strained nerves and exhausted body. He knew, then . . . he knew . . . it was because he knew that he had married her, and that he sat there in the darkness to show her she was safe with him. (207)

Mr. Royall has taken his place against the window where the scene of happiness with Lucius Harney was framed before Royall drew the blind. (This sequence reenacts an earlier one, in which Charity awaited Lucius' arrival at their cabin in the woods, only to have Royall's shadow pass across the window and Royall himself, not Lucius, enter the room.) Yet, ironically, above the bed on which Charity lies is a picture that she could scarcely contemplate earlier that afternoon: "The engraving represented a young man in a boat on a lake overhung with trees. He was leaning over to gather water-lilies for the girl in a light dress who lay among the cushions in the stern. The scene was full of a drowsy midsummer radiance, and Charity averted her eyes from it and, rising from her chair, began to wander restlessly about the room" (205). Though Royall is framed in the window, the engraving projects Charity's inner vision, the "midsummer radiance" of her joyous and undemanding love for Lucius Harney. The man framed by the window is Charity's fate, the choice she has been forced by circumstance to make. Thus Charity's own ambivalence is expressed, and, also, the peculiar sinister dualism that the novel projects. By counterpointing the window scenes and the engraving, Wharton memorializes Charity's vision of happiness with Lucius within a scene that records her qualified acceptance of a May and December marriage. Charity is grateful for succour and for Royall's uncritical acceptance of her pregnancy, but gratitude is not love. And the image of the elderly silent watcher beside the bed, his figure framed by the grey sky and a drawn blind, evokes a bleak alternative to the "midsummer radiance" of the engraving. The view from a *North Dormer* is to remain Charity's lot in life.

From "The Desolation of Charity Royall: Imagery in Edith Wharton's *Summer*"

Linda Morante

Not until the remains of Old New York life perished in the havoc of World War I, did Edith Wharton regard the society of her birth as constituting a genuine social order. Previous to the war she contended that America lost her rightful cultural inheritance when she broke with her fatherland. Bereft of this legacy she became a country without a past or heritage.[1] [. . .]

In her unpublished autobiographical fragment, "Life and I," she censures her own childhood and youth in culturally desolate America as an "intellectual desert."[2] But even more dismal than Old New York, was rural New England: "the snowbound villages of Western Massachusetts were . . . grim places, morally and physically: insanity, incest and slow mental and moral starvation were hidden away behind the paintless wooden housefronts of the long village street, or in the isolated farm-houses on the neighboring hills. . . ."[3] In the uncultured "vast field"[4] of America, it was the most barren region of all.

Wharton's association of cultural aridity and the desert or wasteland develops into the controlling imagery and symbolic center of *Ethan Frome* and *Summer,* her nouvelles of New England life. In these nouvelles she creates a barren scene to speak for characters whose perceptions and articu-

---

Colby Library Quarterly 18.4 (Dec. 1982).

[1] See Edith Wharton, *French Ways and Their Meaning* (New York: Appleton, 1919), pp. 82, 96–97.

[2] Edith Wharton, "Life and I," (1902) Za 7, MS., p. 36. This and all other manuscript material cited is in the Wharton Archives, Beinecke Library, Yale Univ., New Haven, Conn.

[3] Edith Wharton, *A Backward Glance* (New York: Appleton-Century, 1934), pp. 293–94.

[4] See Wharton, *French Ways,* p. 38.

lateness have been limited by this very environment. The composing of the poetic fabric of landscape images becomes her principal technique for revealing and developing character as well as meaning. *Ethan Frome* pictures those who, having spent "too many winters" in the culturally destitute New England village of Starkfield, are ice-bound.[5] The stunted, under-nourished plant growth, for example, the orchard of starved apple trees "writhing over a hillside among outcroppings of slate"[20] signifies the starved, barren lives of the protagonists. Similarly, in *Summer* the wasteland imagery describing the landscapes of North Dormer and the Mountain functions to symbolically express the conditions of Charity Royall's, the nouvelle's heroine's, life.

Wharton employs images of isolation to express the land's separation from any meaningful social framework. North Dormer, situated in a "lonely valley" is "left apart by railway, trolley, telegraph, and all the forces that link life to life in modern communities." "No shops, no theatres, no lectures, no 'business block'" bring together its inhabitants (92).[6] There is no social life, only solitary existence.

In Wharton's view, without a cultural tradition to sustain vital human needs, human life disintegrates, decays, disappears. "Abandoned of men," the town is an "empty place" (92, 91). Deserted, falling-to-ruin old houses blemish its countryside. "Faded" "cheerless and untended" dwellings deface its streets (98). In its musty library "cob-webby volumes" "moulder[ed] undisturbed on the damp shelves" (95, 92). Worms feed upon these rotting books, these symbols of a carrion of culture.

The asphyxiating atmosphere of this "old vault" or "mausoleum" of a library manifests North Dormer's stultifying atmosphere of cultural deprivation (110). *Summer,* as Edith Wharton once referred to it in a letter to Gaillard Lapsley, is truly a "Hot Ethan" in which the heat suffocates as thoroughly as the burying cold.[7] The town "lies high and in the open, and lacks the lavish shade of the more protected New England villages" (91). In this

---

[5] Wharton, *Ethan Frome*, p. 14 [in this New Riverside Edition]. In *Ethan Frome* the lonely and mute, barren and stunted, frozen and still land mirrors the social and cultural isolation, the starvation, and the imprisonment of the characters. As several critics (for example Bernard) have examined the relationship between the imagery and the characters and theme in *Ethan Frome,* this article will study *Summer.*

[6] Note that as in the quoted passage, which connects isolation and emptiness, the image patterns interlock. [All parenthetical references are to this New Riverside Edition.]

[7] Edith Wharton, as quoted by R. W. B. Lewis, *Edith Wharton: A Biography* (New York: Harper and Row, 1975), p. 396.

"weather-beaten sunburnt village" the sun beats down unrelenting rays and the close air stifles (92).

Only "one street" lines North Dormer (91). The town is the enclosed, restrictive place its name suggests: like the view from the narrow windows usually found in bedrooms, North Dormer affords a sleepy, limited vista of life. Its windows face north, death-wards. In this torpid, by-passed village, life is as tedious as the prison or the grave. As Charity tells Harney, a visitor, "things don't change at North Dormer: people just get used to them" (140).

The features of this cultural desert, the interlocking image patterns at the symbolic heart of *Summer,* function as metaphors of Charity's life and character. Like North Dormer, she is isolated; alienated from tradition, estranged from the people closest to her. Just as the town is a sun-scorched and stifling place where nothing flourishes, so do her dreams wither and disintegrate. And as the land is enclosed, so is she ultimately trapped.

Edith Wharton's study of cultural deprivation is interwoven with her exploration of her adolescent heroine's sexual and emotional self-discovery, creation of dreams, and initiation into disillusionment when these aspirations perish. *Summer* recounts the aborted attempt of a young girl to set forth from the "country" and journey to the "city" of cultural plenty. Dreams of self-development kindle her longing to leave North Dormer and settle in a larger town like Nettleton, Springfield, or Boston. Harney, the architect from Springfield who even has contact with New York, could become the vital link to the experience and opportunity of metropolises. Even her post as librarian, if she would read the books she neglects, could provide a bridge to other worlds. Charity never escapes the "lifeless circle" of the barrens environing her (188). *Summer* becomes a story of enclosure, of failure; of ultimate contraction rather than unfolding, and withdrawal rather than stepping out.

"The first page of a novel ought to contain the germ of the whole," Wharton asserts in *The Writing of Fiction.*[8] Accordingly *Summer's* initial words, "A girl came out of lawyer Royall's house, at the end of the one street of North Dormer, and stood on the doorstep," picture Charity about to depart from her home (91). Before she can cross the threshold, she spies a stranger attired in "city clothes" (91). Sensing his relation to urban living and culture, she emotionally recoils and physically retreats: "Her heart contracted a little, and the shrinking that sometimes came over her when she saw people with holiday faces made her draw back into the house" (91). Gazing critically into her mirror, she wishes she were Annabel Balch,

---

[8] Edith Wharton, *The Writing of Fiction* (New York: Scribner's, 1925), p. 51.

a girl whom she also associates with bigger things and places. Once she visited one of these bigger places, Nettleton, to attend a lecture on the Holy Land, a locality with roots as deep as North Dormer's are shallow. This visit, offering vistas broader than North Dormer's narrow view, awakened her sense of privation. Afterward she read fervently, seeking to discover channels to other lands. But soon, as it intensified her feelings of destitution, she ceased reading. Now, similarly, she withdraws into the house, because "the sight of the stranger . . . revived memories of Nettleton, and North Dormer shrank to its real size" (92). The end of her story, her fate, is inherent in this initial scene. As she reenters Royall's threshold here, so does she reenter it in the nouvelle's denouement, trapped by her deprivation.

For Charity regional—and national—isolation mean personal loneliness. Living with her guardian, Royall, "lonesome" Charity "had sounded the depths of isolation" (99). From her lover, Harney, a "gulf" of privation separates her: "education and opportunity . . . divided them by a width that no efforts of hers could bridge" (120–21). She struggles ineffectually to arch this gulf and establish lasting personal connection.

When she meets Harney, who smiled "as if he knew lots of things she had never dreamed of," an immediate barrier divides them (98). Her inability to comprehend him stimulates her sense of inadequacy: "the weight of her ignorance settled down on her again like a pall" (96). With him, her already "narrow world" seems more constricted (98). Even thinking of him she emotionally contracts, overwhelmed by a sense of deficiency:

> "It's no use trying to be anything in this place," she muttered to her pillow; and she shrivelled at the vision of vague metropolises, shining super-Nettletons, where girls in better clothes than Belle Balch's talked fluently of architecture to young men with hands like Lucius Harney's. (105)

Their sexual passion eventually spans the chasm of her ignorance. He temporarily transports her "away into a new world" of communication and connection (165). Here, she blossoms sexually and emotionally; there happens "the wondrous unfolding of her new self, the reaching out to the light of all her contracted tendrils" (164).

But the ever-threatening shadow of Annabel Balch, who "represented all the things that Charity felt herself most incapable of understanding or achieving," becomes substance (181). Though Charity had given Harney "all she had," she was limited in what she had to give (171). When he departs for New York leaving but promises of his return, she recognizes that "the gulf between them was too deep, and that the bridge their passion had flung across it was as insubstantial as a rainbow" (177–78). She perceives that she can never cross the cultural abyss. Despite Charity's pregnancy—the baby to be born would bond her to Harney—"there stood between them, fixed and upright . . . the indestructible figure of Annabel Balch" (185).

Charity's origins from the lawless Mountain, as well as her upbringing in traditionless North Dormer, exclude her from Harney and encompass her in loneliness and privation. In her depiction of the pastless, institutionless Mountain, Wharton creates another metaphorical barren land to express her heroine's plight. This mountain's "scarred cliff" forms a "perpetual background of gloom" to North Dormer (93). It looms in the nouvelle's background and flashes repeatedly to the foreground of Charity's consciousness.

Charity, never having revisited the place of her birth, has no apprehension of its desolation. She has only heard that it is a "bad place" compared to which North Dormer enjoys "all the blessings of the most refined civilization" (92–93). Though the shadow of her "tainted origin" casts over her life when she discovers herself deserted and pregnant and faced with the options of abortion, life as an unwed mother in North Dormer, or forcing Harney to marry her, she believes the Mountain her sole alternative (114). As she surveys the physical scene from her home in North Dormer, images of death and entrapment express her predicament:

> . . . she looked out on the dark and empty scene; the ashen houses with shuttered windows, the grey road climbing the slope to the . . . cemetery, and the heavy mass of the Mountain black against a rainy sky. . . . She had looked out so often on that lifeless circle, and wondered if anything could ever happen to anyone who was enclosed in it. . . .
> Almost without conscious thought her decision had been reached. . . . She supposed it was something in her blood that made the Mountain the only answer to her questioning. . . . At any rate . . . she understood that now at last she was really going there. (187)

As she pilgrimages to the Mountain top she travels geographically and metaphorically farther from Harney. On her ascent the first snow falls, the wind blows fiercely, and the air becomes increasingly chilled. The desolation of the scenery, the isolation and sterility, derangement and decay, signifies the cultural and spiritual destitution of its inhabitants. The land is bleak, barren, starved: she passes "fields of faded mountain grass" (191). On the Mountain's "lonely hillside" a few houses "lay in stony fields, crouching among the rocks as if to brace themselves against the wind" (191). These dwellings, ramshackle and disordered, resemble the lives they house. "Hardly more than sheds," they are "built of logs and rough boards, with tin stove pipes sticking out of their roofs" (191).

The scene enacted in the most devastated of these shanties, where Charity's mother lies dead, dramatizes Wharton's nightmarish vision of the squalor and degradation of traditionless life. [...] Inside the lightless, dirty shed listless people sprawl about. The corpse does "not look like a dead woman":

> ... she seemed to have fallen across her squalid bed in a drunken sleep, and to have been left lying where she fell, in her ragged disordered clothes. One arm was flung above her head, one leg drawn up under a torn skirt that left the other bare to the knee: a swollen glistening leg with a ragged stocking rolled down about the ankle. (192–93)

At closer scrutiny she resembles a "dead dog in a ditch" (193). The others also, seeming "nocturnal animals," appear less than human (192). Their utterings barely sound like human speech. During the funeral ceremony, a pandemoniac travesty of ritual, their drunken outbursts, curses, and arguments ironically counterpoint the preacher's prayers. Afterward, in cold pitch-darkness, Charity's mother is buried, like an animal, coffinless in the frozen earth. Without a rooted framework of social custom and mores, communal and personal relationships degenerated until people were merely "herded together in a sort of passive promiscuity in which their common misery was the closest link" (197).

Unable to establish any relation to the "miserable herd" on the Mountain, in the "icy cold" morning Charity steals away (198). On her descent the "denuded" countryside she passes mirrors her divested dreams:

> Forty-eight hours earlier, when she had last traversed it, many of the trees still held their leaves; but the high wind of the last two nights had stripped them. . . . A few days of autumn cold had wiped out all trace of the rich fields and languid groves through which she had passed on the Fourth of July; and with the fading of the landscape those fervid hours had faded, too. (203)

She feels no kinship with anyone; she feels alone, "a mere speck in the lonely circle of the sky" (199). She ponders the alienation of someone "enclosed" in the "lifeless circle" of North Dormer and the Mountain (188). Harney, her avenue to other cultures and larger worlds, has proved impassable and the Mountain, the rootless place of her birth, has proved more desolate than she had imagined. There remains nowhere for her to go but back to North Dormer, to its single street.

Overcome with loneliness, she agrees to wed her guardian, Royall. In more than one sense, they are kinsmen: he too has dreamed of and contacted larger worlds than North Dormer, he too has failed to insure the vital connection and has returned to the town, his aspirations thwarted. Still

her marriage to him means the death of her dreams of escape, of fulfill-
ment. Her wedding threshold is the threshold over which she had retreated
in the nouvelle's beginning. Her final act is again one of contraction, of defeat. Charity returns to the red house with Royall because she is imprisoned, because she has no other place to go.

Summer's penultimate words, "Late that evening, in the cold autumn
moonlight, they [Charity and Royall] drove up to the door of the red
house," ironically echo its initial sentence (210). The nouvelle and its
heroine have come full circle. For Charity it is a "lifeless circle." Imagery of
desolation continues to reveal the silent desolation of her fate. These final
words repeat the nouvelle's beginning with significant imagistic differences.
Now, she arrives at the red house "late" in the "evening" in a "cold autumn
moonlight" that forecasts winter nights. The afternoon of the first chapter
has become night; the sunlight, darkness; the spring, fall. Her human drama
has been played out according to a drama of seasons whose finale looks forward to winter.[9] She ends, not unlike her brother Ethan Frome, in the
cold—in nights without love, in days without dreams.

In *Summer,* as in *Ethan Frome,* Edith Wharton creates a tapestry of
wasteland imagery to portray the isolation, deprivation, and entrapment of
the self in a culturally destitute New England hill town. In these works this
poetic fabric becomes the essential key to character analysis as well as thematic interpretation. [. . .]

"*Summer:* The Double
Sense of Wharton's Title"

Christine Rose

[. . .] In most of Wharton's works, interiors are notable for their detail and
correspondence to the lives of the characters within them. One always has
the sense with Wharton that the spaces which her characters occupy or
move through are significant. Houses, public buildings, fences, porches
and all manner of structures often constrict the movements of her characters, functioning thereby as reminders of their moral paralysis.

ANQ: A Quarterly Journal of Short Articles, Notes, and Reviews 3.1 (1990).

[9] Blake Nevius, *Edith Wharton: A Study of Her Fiction* (Berkeley: Univ. of California
Press, 1953), p. 171.

Summer (1917) is a novel rich in architectural detail and the imagery of houses, enclosures, and walls. Lucius Harney is a student of architecture who draws New England houses—a task which takes him to the town of North Dormer (note the architectural reference) and into the life of Charity Royall. [. . .] Some [critics] have discussed the title's implications for Charity's sexual maturation, noting the grim contrast between the lazy, warm, romancing season and the "autumn" of Harney's betrayal, Charity's out-of-wedlock pregnancy, and the final desperate wintry marriage to Lawyer Royall, Charity's aging stepfather/guardian.

Yet Wharton herself suggests a way of reading this book and understanding its title when she says of Lawyer Royall, "*he's* the book." [1] [. . .] At first we resist this focus on the paradoxical Royall, since from the very opening scene of the novel, Wharton compels us to concentrate our attention on the lively and quixotic Charity. In that first scene, Charity emerges from the Royall house murmuring, "How I hate everything!"[91] [2] and from then on, she occupies center stage. By urging readers to focus on the character of Royall, however, Wharton draws attention as well to her title, *Summer.* In architectural terms, a "summer" is a large horizontal supporting beam or girder, such as a lintel. Lawyer Royall is surely that sort of force in the novel. In this use of both the architectural and the seasonal meaning of "summer," the various elements of the novel—architecture, irony, and Wharton's consummate craftsmanship—are in particularly fine conjunction.

Two things need to be said here. First, there is no reason to assume Wharton intended this double meaning for her title. Nevertheless, given her interest in architecture and interior detail, it is certainly appropriate to see Royall as the "summer," the supporting cross-beam of the novel, and it is artistically consistent with the doubleness which pervades the novel's structure and imagery to have this twofold meaning for the title. The novel is not only about a young woman's season of blossoming, but also about the man who is at the very heart of the plot's conflict. Royall, both attractive and repellant, is clearly the beam on which the story rests, if one looks beyond the conventional seduction-and-betrayal plot thread.

Doubleness, irony, and ambiguity are the artistic underpinnings of the novel. Doubleness lies in the meaning of Charity's name, in the many characters and events with two aspects, and even in Wharton's use of a limited

---

[1] The italics are Wharton's, from a letter to Bernard Berenson, quoted in Cynthia Griffin Wolff, introduction, *Summer,* by Edith Wharton (1917; New York: Harper-Perennial, 1980) xiv. [Ed.]

[2] All parenthetical references are to this New Riverside Edition. [Ed.]

authorial perspective, which forces us to look through Charity's eyes at situations which have significance she cannot judge, but we must judge. Charity labels people and happenings, yet she either passes judgement peremptorily (and wrongly), or is unclear about the meaning of something, often seeing two sides. She sees two Harneys: "An unknown Harney had revealed himself . . ." (152); "He was the new Harney again . . ." (158); "Behind the frail screen of her lover's caresses was the whole inscrutable mystery of his life . . ." (171). To Charity, Royal is both "senile" and a "lamentable ruin" (152), and majestic—"That was a *man* talking" (170). Throughout the novel, Wharton reveals to the reader that people and events are often ominously and ironically other than what Charity has so dogmatically declared them to be. This interplay of appearance and reality is carefully controlled by Wharton, as she lets the reader gradually see that perceptions other than Charity's are possible.

There are myriad examples of doubleness other than this double vision [. . .]: the two rescues of Charity; two bedroom scenes with Royall; two trips to Nettleton with men—ending in ironically opposite sexual encounters; two views of Nettleton Lake—the second a romantic print over the chaste bridal bed, hauntingly recalling the real romance of Charity's sojourn on the lake with Harney; Charity's second-hand shoes—formerly the property of Harney's fiance, Annabel Balch; the two women in Harney's love life; and the two poignant scenes of the Royall house—mirror images at either end of the book, a hopeful exit, balanced by the final hopeless entrance. Once alerted to this structural element of duality, readers can generate even more examples, as it is pervasive.

So, perhaps Wharton used this double-sided title *Summer* to show Royall as the center support of the novel's malevolent and tragic ambiguity. However much he remains away from the main thread of the lovers' story, he influences all their actions by his mere existence. Royall buttresses Charity in the end; he is her security and salvation from prostitution or death, possible results of her summer romance. Depending upon how hopefully one reads Wharton's final scenes. Royall offers what is either selfless or selfish support to Charity, who herself despises his love and the stifling, small-town life he represents. While Royall may not provide Charity with the passion of *her* summer of sexual blossoming, *his* summer-strength will, in the regrettably "quasi-incestuous" marriage,[3] support Charity and Harney's child. She is saved, but at what cost to her?

---

[3] Elizabeth Ammons, *Edith Wharton's Argument with America* (Athens: U of Georgia P, 1979) 138. [Ed.]

This picture of Royall suggested by the title—as the supporting beam of the structure of the novel—need not, and should not, impel us to see him as a positive life-giving force. Royall himself might justly claim the name "Charity" for his own double rescue of other men's children: first Charity herself, then her illegitimate baby. The second rescue, however, is not without its own doubleness. Despite the timeliness of the rescue of Charity, weak and pregnant on "the Mountain," we cannot forget the funereal imagery of the ensuing wedding to which she numbly consents. Confused and ill after her second "rescue" by Royall, Charity catatonically marries this man, her guardian and stepfather. Later, she lies alone in bed on her wedding night "trembling with a fear that ran through her veins like ice. 'What have I done? Oh what have I done?' she whispered" (207). Likewise, despite Royall's delicacy in leaving Charity to sleep alone on this night, we cannot forget the "sick" scene[4] of another night early on in the novel where the drunken Royall enters Charity's room to seduce her. Although we may sympathize with his loneliness and need, we must despise him both for the threat of rape he represents and for his view of Charity as his possession. And, in fact, Wharton so finely balances this early scene that we simultaneously witness two sexual dynamics: Royall's weakness in pleading for Charity to accept him (but she acidly rejects him), coupled with the potentially violent sexual horror he must represent for the inexperienced Charity. Here is more duality and more insistence on the hopelessness of the ending of the book, which so many have misread as hopeful: Charity is, after all, now married to this debauched man. The trappings of a happy ending may be in evidence, but the conventional rescue of the damsel in distress is turned on its ear, and the legitimacy, stability, reputation and security that Royall can provide for the next generation is paid for at too high a price for Charity: the loss of youth and hope and sexuality. Her rescue is her entrapment, and the "good" (210) for which she returns to North Dormer is not all good.

Royall's character is a complex one. He is at once the source of Charity's oppression and her kinsman in lonely superiority to their surroundings. Charity both admires him and reviles him. Wharton asks us, it seems, both to pity him and to be disgusted by him. Reading "summer" as both a season and a support adds to the novel's ironic and ambiguous texture; this reading also gives us a way of reconciling Lawyer Royall's character to Wharton's statement, "*he's* the book." The two senses of the title can be the key to the dualism throughout the novel. Royall is the chief structural

---

[4]Ammons 133. [Ed.]

element, for good or ill, in Charity Royall's meager life during and after her brief summer of desire. Yet both seemingly positive definitions of "summer" (as season and support) are finally and ironically at odds with the grim prospect Charity faces at the end of the novel. For all the sunny images that the title evokes and the scenes of wildflowers on the hillsides and the promise of young love, it is the enclosed space of a constricting and bleak New England house and a passionless marriage, with winter closing in, that is the final image which compels us to look also at the other, darker side of this novel.

From "Becoming a 'Good Girl': Law, Language, and Ritual in Edith Wharton's *Summer*"

Rhonda Skillern

[...] In her autobiographical "A Little Girl's New York," Wharton describes an incident that occurred when she was seventeen: she and her mother passed a woman sitting in a canary-yellow carriage and wearing a hat "lined with cherry color, which shed a lovely glow on her cheeks": when the captivated young Edith asked her mother, "Do you know the lady?", Lucretia Jones replied with a "stern order not to stare at strange people" and instructed Edith to turn her head toward the other window whenever their carriage passed the yellow one. They had encountered New York's "first fashionable hetaera." Years later, Wharton commented that "in the impoverished emotional atmosphere of old New York such a glimpse was like the mirage of palm trees in the desert."[1] In some measure, Wharton recovers that woman as Charity Royall, who wears a white hat with "cherry-colored lining" and red roses on the brim to, fittingly, an Independence Day celebration. Given this context, the scarlet-lined bonnet connotes Charity's budding sexuality, an aspect of the feminine that may be present but cannot be publicly recognized or inscribed in discourse without being violently distorted by the available modes of (male-referenced) significa-

---

The Cambridge Companion to Edith Wharton. Cambridge: Cambridge UP, 1995.

[1] Edith Wharton, "A Little Girl's New York," *Harper's* (August 1938), 357.

tion. Intuitively, Charity recognizes this fact: "To avoid attracting notice, she carried her new hat carefully wrapped up, and had thrown a long grey veil of Mrs. Royall's over the new white muslin dress which Ally's clever fingers had made for her" (142).[2] Once outside the gaze of Lawyer Royall and the other townsfolk, however, Charity proudly wears the hat to the Independence Day festivities.

Susan G. Davis's *Parades and Power* (1986), which discusses the socio-historical symbolism of parades and other patriotic celebrations, sheds light on the significance of the Fourth of July celebration. In early modern Europe, only the authorities of church and the state could appropriate the power of processional display. The tradition of processionals was later transferred to America, where issues of equality eventually made the public sphere a more problematic area; street performance often proved dangerous for those who were not white and not male. Still, the participants in parades and other ceremonies attempted to portray the public arenas as neutral ground and their orations as expressions of universal values. But, as Davis cautions, the public arenas were and are contested terrain. Certain groups were intentionally denied access to the street: working-class festivities were condemned as debaucheries; women made themselves "women of the streets" when they ventured too far out of the private sphere and into the public arena.[3]

But Charity Royall is "determined to assert her independence" (142), so she has lied to Lawyer Royall, telling him that she is going alone to "the Band of Hope picnic at Hepburn" rather than the Fourth of July festivities in Nettleton. Like Lily Bart, she unfortunately accepts as universal the idea of independence, not realizing until too late its particular application to a certain class and a certain gender.

That class is an issue is evidenced by Lucius Harney's disdain for the "descending mob" of rural and town folk attending the celebration. Until this point, Harney has "never put his arm about [Charity], or sought to betray her into any sudden caress. . . . His reserve did not suggest coldness, but the deference due to a girl of his own class" (143). But in Nettleton, Charity's apparent lack of aesthetic discrimination foregrounds their class differences: she thinks that not "Springfield or even Boston had anything grander to show" than "the noise and colour of this holiday vision" in Nettleton (144); she prefers sarsaparilla to the French wine he orders; she

---

[2] All parenthetical references are to this New Riverside Edition. [Ed.]

[3] See Susan G. Davis, *Parades and Power: Street Theater in Nineteenth-Century Philadelphia* (Philadelphia: Temple University Press, 1986), pp. 13–47.

admires a gaudy lily-of-the-valley brooch instead of the elegant blue one that Harney eventually buys her. And when she gasps in ecstasy over the fireworks and a "Washington Crossing the Delaware" pageant on a lake, Harney takes the opportunity to kiss her hard on the mouth. Under the symbolic auspices of the golden "Father of Our Country," Lucius Harney can assume a sort of self-government by virtue of his gender and class, liberties not generalizable to others less fortunately male.

As the abortion clinic and Lawyer Royall are soon to remind her, such sexual and social independence are for men of means only. While waiting at the wharf, on their return from the lake, Charity and Harney encounter drunken Lawyer Royall in the company of Julia Hawes, a "bad girl" from North Dormer who has resorted to prostitution in Nettleton. When Julia declares, "Here's grandpa's little daughter come to take him home," Charity notices that Royall's "face, a livid brown, with red blotches of anger and lips sunken in like a old man's, was a lamentable ruin in the searching glare" (296). Jealous of Harney and infuriated at Charity's public exhibition of sensuality and independence, Lawyer Royall twice shouts, "you whore — you damn — bare-headed whore, you!" Suddenly Charity "has a vision of herself—hatless, dishevelled, with a man's arm about her. . . . The picture filled her with shame" (153). For anyone familiar with *Ethan Frome,* the white hat with the cherry-colored lining is the vulval equivalent to the phallic red pickle dish of that earlier work: as Lawyer Royall interprets the scene, she has lost her virginity. Thus begins Charity's initiation into the symbolic order, "The Law of the Father," which both elicits female independence and sexuality and denounces its potential.[4] Heretofore, Charity has viewed her body as her own, as living with Royall but not "belonging" to him legally. From now on, her body will be the site of struggle between her own desire and pleasure and the law. [. . .]

When her affair with Harney is about six weeks old, Charity and the other young women of North Dormer are pressed into making decorations for North Dormer's Old Home Week celebration. It has been noted by several anthropologists that, although women often make most of the preparations for festivals, they are not allowed to assume any of the main performative roles during ceremonies. So it is here. Once again, the "speaking parts" go to Reverend Miles and Lawyer Royall, the church and the law. The young women who have spent weeks fashioning flags and weaving garlands are consigned to the background where, arrayed in white dresses and

---

[4]See [Teresa] de Lauretis, *Technologies of Gender* [Bloomington: Indiana University Press, 1987),] p. 14, for a discussion of the social construction of female sexuality: although located in the woman, female sexuality is seen as "belonging to" the man.

veils, they sing "Home, Sweet Home." But once again Charity subverts the meanings culturally assigned to the "virgin whiteness" of the dresses and the song: "she no longer had such visions [of marrying Harney] . . . warmer splendours had displaced them" (167). Nor, of course, is she a virgin. And when the girls intone the paean to domesticity, we discover that

> it was a joy for Charity to sing: it seemed as though, for the first time, her secret rapture might burst from her and flash its defiance at the world. All the glow in her blood, the breath of the summer earth, the rustle of the forest, the fresh call of birds at sunrise, and the brooding midday languors, seemed to pass into her untrained voice, lifted and led by the sustaining chorus. (168–69)

Her song is decidedly *undomestic.* Like the sixteenth-century Native Americans whom Michel de Certeau describes as making of "the rituals, representations, and laws imposed on them something quite different from what their [Spanish] conquerors had in mind," Charity uses the occasion for her own "ends and references foreign to the system [she has] no choice but to accept."[5] Charity's defiant rendition of the song underscores her oppositional position within the social system: she was taken from her original home (the Mountain), and the home she has known has not been particularly sweet. But the song is an ironically appropriate one for this scene because the four walls she has dreamed of escaping soon figuratively close in on her: Lawyer Royall delivers a rousing speech about "coming home for good" (a bit hypocritical, considering that he has always regretted living in North Dormer); Charity spies Harney sitting next to the affluent Annabel Balch, to whom, she realizes, he is betrothed; and as Reverend Miles extols the purity of the virginal choir, Charity succumbs to a fainting spell brought on by her pregnancy. The circumstances emerge that will keep her home for good.

Suspicious that she and Harney are enjoying a sexual liaison, Lawyer Royall soon tries to regulate their relationship by coercing Harney into marrying Charity. When he surprises them at their trysting place, a disintegrating house furnished with a mattress and a few pretty trifles, he again takes the opportunity to humiliate his foster daughter. He turns to Harney and snarls:

> you know why you ain't asked her to marry you, and why you don't mean to. It's because you hadn't need to; nor any other man either. I'm the only one that was fool enough not to know that. . . . They all know

---

[5] Michel de Certeau, *The Practice of Everyday Life,* trans. Steven F. Rendall (Berkeley and Los Angeles: University of California Press, 1984), p. xiii.

what she is, and what she came from. They all know her mother was a woman of the town from Nettleton, that followed one of those Mountain fellows up to his place and lived there with him like a heathen. . . . I went to save her from the kind of life her mother was leading—but I'd better have left her in the kennel she came from. (175–76)

We must recall that until this point, Charity has learned very little direct information about her mother, but, according to the law of the father, Charity is a "what" born of a "what," a dog from a bitch in a "kennel." Yet we (and Charity) know that Mr. Royall himself attempted to seduce her before proposing and that he seeks the services of prostitute Julia Hawes. This knowledge undercuts the unity of his words and points not only to the double standard but also to the gaps in the symbolic order represented by Royall.

To understand Royall's virulence about Charity's affair and Charity's confused anger about his reaction, it is helpful here to turn to Gayle Rubin's essay "The Traffic in Women" (1975), which combines the anthropological theories of Claude Lévi-Strauss with the psychological schema of Sigmund Freud. Lévi-Strauss suggested that the essence of kinship systems in both capitalist and noncapitalist societies was the exchange of women: men marry women, in other words, to gain more male alliances. For Rubin, the incest taboo can be understood as a way to ensure that exchanges of women take place between men, extending their kinship. Rubin claims further that, given this social relation, men have rights to their female kin, whereas women do not have the same rights to their male kin or to themselves.[6] But Charity has already been given away by her father, a jailed outlaw who, co-opted by the law, decided he wanted his daughter to be "brought down and reared like a Christian" (119). She has already been given to Royall, who apparently thinks he should be able to keep her even though, *from Charity's point of view, Royall is her father,* and thus should not be able to keep her. He has already discouraged her from pursuing one means of independence (education), and now he is incensed that she might discover another—through her desire for someone other than himself.

[. . .] Lucius Harney, an architect who is more familiar with established social structures (and who, because of class and gender, has less to lose in them), reluctantly agrees to marry Charity as soon as he "arrange[s] some things" out of town, although he does not know of her pregnancy when he departs. Convinced that marriage to Harney would be disastrous and that she cannot stay with Royall, whom she now loathes, Charity decides that

[6] Gayle Rubin, "The Traffic in Women," *Toward an Anthropology of Women,* ed. Rayna R. Reiter (New York: Monthly Review Press, 1975), pp. 177–82.

she can seek out her mother on the Mountain or become a prostitute like Julia Hawes, "only—was there no alternative but Julia's? . . . In the established order of things as she knew them she saw no place for her individual adventure" (187). Of course, she would still be part of the "established order of things" were she to become a prostitute.

Seeking a place for her individual feminine adventure, Charity decides to flee to the Mountain, to her mother's place. Charity "supposed it was something in her blood that made the Mountain the only answer to her questioning, the inevitable escape from all that hemmed her in and beset her" (188). On the most literal level, Charity is simply looking for comfort among her own kind; in addition, like so many of Wharton's most memorable characters, Charity also seeks a space beyond the confines of the exchange market, away from a system of representation that not only fails to represent her but that renders her own desires virtually unrepresentable. In the established order of things as she knows them, there is no place for her individual adventures. Perhaps there is another way of knowing and another order of things: she will try to find out.

Charity's quest for alternative signification begins with her acceptance of her desire. According to Luce Irigaray, any possible attempt at defining woman outside of the established symbolic order would have to start with *jouissance,* or feminine sexual pleasure, because the woman's experience of her own body lies beyond phallic description and representations. Irigaray even equates the clue to woman's desire with discovering an ancient maternal civilization.[7] To reach her mother, Charity has to "retrace the road over which she had so often flown to her lover" (188). The landscape of *Summer* is highly suggestive, and so it is fitting that, in her search for another way of knowing and thinking about herself, Charity must "retrace"—reconfigurate her desire. Charity has already gotten beyond conventional thinking about her state: she recalls "her start of involuntary terror when the fat evangelist" had said, "Your saviour knows everything. Come and confess your guilt"; however, "there was no sense of guilt in her now . . . only a desperate desire to defend her secret from irreverent eyes, and begin life again among people to whom the harsh code of the village was unknown" (188). What is a secret but something kept out of the circulating symbolic order, often because one fears misinterpretation if the secret is known—sometimes, in fact, because the symbolic order cannot accurately represent the secret? Charity seeks a maternal place where she can live according to a different code, one in which her baby will be received and not

[7] Luce Irigaray, *The Sex Which Is Not One,* trans. Catherine Porter (Ithaca, N.Y.: Cornell University Press, 1985), pp. 15–25.

delegitimized, where she can represent herself and her experiences without being expected to feel shame and regret.

But patriarchal law and Christian religion prove, in the end, too powerful for Charity and her quest for nonpatriarchal representation. Irigaray and other scholars suggest that the clue to a feminine language lies in an ancient civilization: it probably does, in the ancient pre-Judeo-Christian civilizations of the Neolithic period (9000 B.C.), or possibly even the Upper Paleolithic (up to 25,000 B.C.), when goddesses were worshiped in Europe and the Middle East. Many of these societies were matrilocal (the man moved to live with the woman's family) and matrilineal (the children took the mother's name). Women had rights to themselves, were artists and held the highest religious positions: they could, and did, have powers of representation. But eventually tribes worshiping the newer male deities persecuted and suppressed goddess-worshiping ones, and consequently women lost status, lost rights, lost the power of representation. A brief survey of Judeo-Christian history reveals what ensued: women were supposedly cursed with subservience to men and pain in childbirth because of Eve's transgressions (Genesis 2). Women became property—although a father could sell sexual access to his daughter and then later marry her off, a woman who "gave her self away," thereby depriving her father of a fee, was stoned to death (Deuteronomy 22:20–2). Hebraic law reveals a phobic attitude toward women's sexuality, perhaps in response to the ritual sex associated with worship of the Great Mother, Yahweh's early competition. This fear of women's contaminating power, manifested in their flesh, continued to be expressed in the Christian teachings of Paul, Saint Augustine, Thomas Aquinas, Sprenger and Kramer (authors of the infamous *Malleus Maleficarum,* 1486), and even Pope John Paul II, who suggested as late as 1980 that a man who took pleasure in looking at his wife's body committed a sin. In such a patriarchal religion, women are portrayed as necessary for procreation, but otherwise morally weak, infectious to men, and consequently in need of suppression.[8]

Historically, then, the church has buried the Great Mother and her progeny, woman (I use the lower-cased term here as a metaphor for all that patriarchal representation has left out of its conception of "Woman"), marking the grave with the dual image of the virgin and the whore, the very dichotomy that Charity Royall wishes to escape by uncovering her mother. So it is fitting that a man of the church is the one to say "Your mother is *dead,* Charity; you'd *better come with me*" (192; my emphasis): something

---

[8] Many social, historical, and feminist studies make this point. See, for instance, Elizabeth R. Allgeier and Albert R. Allgeier, *Sexual Interactions* (Lexington, Mass.: Heath, 1984), chaps. 1–3.

is better than nothing.[. . .] Charity does go with Mr. Miles, following his lead throughout the nightmarish burial scene, viewing her mother's body by the light that he casts upon it:

> they stood before a mattress on the floor in a corner of the room. A woman lay on it, but she did not look like a dead woman; she seemed to have fallen across her squalid bed in a drunken sleep, and to have been left lying where she fell, in her ragged disordered clothes. One arm was flung above her head, one leg drawn up under a torn skirt that left the other bare to the knee: a swollen glistening leg with a ragged stocking rolled down about the ankle. The woman lay on her back, her eyes staring up unblinkingly at the candle that trembled in Mr. Miles's hand. . . .
>
> He knelt down by the mattress, and pressed the lids over the dead woman's eyes. Charity, trembling and sick, knelt beside him, and tried to compose her mother's body. She drew the skirt down to the battered up-turned boots. As she did so, she looked at her mother's face, thin yet swollen, with lips parted in a frozen gasp above the broken teeth. There was no sign in it of anything human: she lay there like a dog in a ditch. (192–93)

Supine on a seamy mattress, sweaty legs apart, swollen mouth open, Mary Hyatt's body is revolting, frozen in a kind of horrific ecstasy like a backwoods Bernini *Saint Theresa*. Yet because of her overt corporeality, she does not look human by the light of Reverend Miles's candle or his religion: "human" women should not look so—well, nasty. But clearly she is a woman—too much of a woman to be human, perhaps, so that according to patriarchal thought she spills over into the animal category, just as "kennel"-begotten Charity did when Lawyer Royall caught her on a mattress with Lucius Harney.

On a literal level, Charity helps Mr. Miles bury her mother, but on a psychological level Reverend Miles (and all that he represents) helps Charity repress her own desires, including her desire for her mother (a metaphor for non-patriarchal representations). For the moment, Charity is comforted by Mr. Miles's "mighty words" that have the power of "soothing the horror, subduing the tumult, [and] mastering her":

> "Through our Lord Jesus Christ, who shall change our vile body that it may be like unto His glorious body, according to the mighty working, whereby He is able to subdue all things unto Himself. . . ." The last spadeful of earth fell on the vile body of Mary Hyatt. (196; Wharton's ellipsis)

In many ways, this ritual signals the turning point for Charity Royall, the point at which she has internalized the symbolic order that is based upon the depression of the mother. It is, in the narrator's words, Charity's "tragic initiation" (197). Charity will hereafter find it impossible to sustain her resistance because she has found no way to adequately represent it. "He is able to subdue all things unto Himself": potential polyphony is subdued by monologism; a unifying masculine voice covers over feminine difference. The mother's body, a potential power source for women, is buried beneath the word "vile."

Charity had turned to her mother for another system of thought and expression, but her mother's open mouth could utter nothing. The operating system of representation necessitates her repression. Variations of this scene recur in women's fiction, as Margaret Homans's *Bearing the Word* (1986) and Deborah Kelly Kloepfer's *The Unspeakable Mother* (1990) illustrate. Margaret Homans has argued, "Women's place in language, from the perspective of an androcentric literary tradition (and the psycholinguistic theory it generates), is with the literal, the silent object of representation, the dead mother, the absent referent."[9] Kloepfer, in her discussions of Jean Rhys and H.D., discovers that "a dead mother is a trope for textlessness, a way of speaking the unspeakable, a way of inscribing a silencing, a failure, or a repression of the female speaking subject."[10]

Still, Charity tries to "*compose* her mother's body" (193, my emphasis) — to arrange it not only for burial, but to *give it form* for remembering. She succeeds to some degree. Although Charity never discovers an external place for her individual adventure, she does find a place in her own psyche for her experience of her mother. Her quest for her maternal home at least enables her to challenge Lawyer's Royall's version of her own history:

> she remembered what Mr. Royall had said in telling her story to Lucius Harney: "Yes, there was a mother; but she was glad to have the child go. She'd have given her to anybody. . . ."
>
>   Well! after all, was her mother so much to blame? Charity, since that day, had always thought of her as destitute of all human feeling; now she seemed merely pitiful. What mother would not want to save her child from such a life? Charity thought of her own child, and tears welled into her aching eyes, and ran down over her face. If she had been less exhausted, less burdened with his weight, she would have sprung up then and there and fled away. . . . (197; Wharton's ellipses)

She recognizes what her mother must have known: that the maternal community has neither sustained economic power nor representational power. Mary Hyatt was not an evil mother; she was simply a mother caught in the

[9]Margaret Homans, *Bearing the Word: Language and Female Experience in Nineteenth-Century Women's Writing* (Chicago: University of Chicago Press, 1986), p. 32.

[10]Deborah Kelly Kloepfer, *The Unspeakable Mother: Forbidden Discourse in Jean Rhys and H.D.* (Ithaca, N.Y.: Cornell University Press, 1989), p. 15.

same dilemma as all mothers. In an essay about another Mary, entitled "Stabat Mater," [Julia] Kristeva explains that mothers in particular engage in the masochistic behavior of erasing themselves for the sake of their children's socialization, for the sake of continuity, for the sake of law.[11] Determined not to "add another life to the nest of misery on the Mountain" (198), and yet equally resolved that "she could not remain at North Dormer, and the sooner she got away from it the better" (199), Charity decides to return to the established of things a whore: masochistically, she accepts this fate as the only one that will provide financial support for her baby.

As Charity leaves the Mountain, she is physically and emotionally exhausted, a state Royall takes advantage of when he takes her into town for marriage. It is only under coercion that she submits to the ritual that will mark her final capitulation to the Law of the Father. Indeed, during the wedding ritual, she no longer even controls her own voice or body; she merely repeats what she is told to say, and the minister's wife places her hand in Royall's. While it can be argued that Royall proves extremely kind and understanding in his willingness to marry a woman impregnated by another man (although this view would only be produced in patriarchy), we must wonder at his haste: undoubtedly he senses that Charity's resistance is down.

Gayle Rubin, echoing Freud, explains that a girl's turning away from her mother to her father is marked by an "ascendancy of passivity" because she is aware of "the futility of realizing her active desire, and of the unequal terms of the struggle."[12] Before and during the ceremony in which Charity marries Royall, she is described as "confused" and "dazed"; she follows Mr. Royall "as passively as a tired child" (203). In fact, Charity neither agrees to marry him nor actively participates in the ritual that will bind her to him for life:

> The clergyman began to read, and on her dazed mind there rose the memory of Mr. Miles, standing the night before in the desolate house on the Mountain, and reading out of the same book words that had the same dread sound of finality. . . .
> She was so busy trying to understand the gestures that the clergyman was signalling to her that she no longer heard what was being said. After another interval the lady on the bench stood up, and taking her hand put it in Mr. Royall's. It lay enclosed in his strong palm and she felt a ring that

---

[11] Julia Kristeva, "Stabat Mater," in [*The Kristeva Reader,* ed. Toril Moi (Oxford: Blackwell, 1986).]

[12] Rubin, "Traffic in Women," p. 195.

was too big for her being slipped on her thin finger. She understood then that she was married. (204–05)

Thus Charity emerges with a legal identity based on the rejection of the mother. According to the traditional marriage ceremony, the "two become one," the provisional maiden name gives way to permanent masculine nomenclature, the semiotic succumbs to the symbolic, difference consolidates into unity under the power of the closed system of word and symbol. Were this truly to happen, death—absolute stasis—would result, as suggested by the fact that this ceremony reminds Charity of her mother's funeral.

But in what is basically a coda to *Summer,* we find that marriage has not, as the traditional novel of manners would have it, resolved all differences. This marriage signals both Charity's capitulation to the Law of the Father and her subversion of it: the two newlyweds have not (yet) become one in the wedding bed; moreover, the child made legitimate by this union also exposes the fictionality of that legitimacy and that unity. And though Royall tries to tempt Charity into becoming an object for display, giving her forty dollars for clothes that "will beat 'em [all the other girls] hollow," Charity resists (207). She may wear a wedding ring—a public symbol—on her finger, but she uses the forty dollars to recuperate a private sign of her mother's rebellion and her own feminine desire, a brooch with a stone as blue as a mountain lake ("mountain" suggests her mother, while "lake"— like the brooch itself—is reminiscent of her Independence Day excursion with Harney). Charity's decision to recuperate the brooch suggests that she has preserved a space within herself that neither Lawyer Royall nor the Law of the Father can invade. [. . .]

From "The Politics of Maternality in *Summer*"

Monika M. Elbert

[. . .] In [*Summer*] motherhood is depreciated, disdained, and ultimately destroyed. None of the mothers thrives: Mrs. Royall cannot have children and she becomes the absent mother to foster child Charity with her untimely death; Charity's mother is robbed of her maternity with Lawyer Royall's en-

Edith Wharton Review 7.2 (1990).

try onto the Mountain in the name of bringing "civilization" to the daughter; Miss Hatchard, the stereotypical barren spinster, is a poor excuse for a surrogate mother to Charity; Charity's friend Julia avoids the consequences of an unwanted pregnancy and poverty by having an abortion; Dr. Merkle, who could have been a surrogate mother, instead preys upon the likes of Charity for material gain [. . .]; and finally, Charity, though she decides to keep her baby, cannot be a mother freely, but ironically must rely upon her guardian's "charity" to afford the baby. Mothering does not have a chance of triumphing, let alone surviving, in Wharton's world, this as a result of man's willful distortion of motherhood. There are two negative forces at work in the novel: man's fear of the dark continent, of mothering, which is embodied in the Mountain, and man's need to control a foreign nature by giving it market value, by gaining access to the realm of the "other" in making sexuality, motherhood and its attendant housewifely duties a commodity. [. . .]

To Charity, the Mountain represents mothering—a return to her real mother and to her own ability to mother, a return to the mystery of her origins, and finally, to the mystery of her mortality.[1] In her recreation of the myth of the Mountain, she sees an antitype of Eden, a procreative wilderness, a lawless place settled by men who tried to escape from the police and where "others joined them—and children were born" (116).[2] She wants to "explore the corner of her memory where certain blurred images lingered" (113–14), and that entails a reunion with the mother/Mountain. When she feels the first stirrings of sexuality with the arrival of Harney to North Dormer, she begins to feel obsessed with ascending the Mountain. As she feels more entrapped by her feelings and by the conflicting signals from Royall's law, she threatens escape: to "go to the Mountain," "go back to my own folks" (156). Finally, in the end, when she is pregnant, she needs to encounter her mother once and for all, a mother who happens to be dying. In this respect, too, Charity, herself, takes on the mythmaking of the males: the thought of giving birth is allied to that other taboo mystery, dying. According to Otto Rank, a discipline of the matriphobic [. . .] Freud, man feels an "ideological need" to "blot out the mother-origin in order to deny his mortal nature."[3] This implies that the beginning and the end is in the Great Mother, the giver and destroyer of life, and Charity, frightened

---

[1] Traditionally, in classical mythology, the earth has been regarded as feminine, either as maternal and sensual or as barren and virgin. [. . .]

[2] All parenthetical references to *Summer* are to this New Riverside Edition. [Ed.]

[3] Otto Rank, *Beyond Psychology* (New York: Dover, 1958) 236. [Ed.]

by the manifestation of her own limitations, sees her dead mother as the horrible destroyer: her mother's face was "thin yet swollen, with lips parted in a frozen gasp above the broken teeth. There was no sign in it of anything human: she lay there like a dead dog in a ditch" (193).

If Charity cannot accept her mother's death as something natural, on feminine terms, if she sees it as something ugly, as men would have it, she will not be able to accept her pregnancy without the feeling that mothering is somehow as dirty and obscene as the Mountain. She actually loses her fight towards independence when she buys into Minister Miles' funeral oration for her mother: "We brought nothing into this world and we shall take nothing out of it . . ." (194). These are male terms which equate birth with death, because they are outside the realm of maternal creation. Indeed, in the middle of the funeral, there is a moment of black humor, as an elderly man, worn down by life in his inability to produce, states pugnaciously (as if to contradict the minister's "Nothing is brought into this world . . ."),

> "I brought the stove . . . I wen' down to Creston'n bought it . . . n' I got a right to take it outer here . . . n' I'll lick any feller says I ain't" (194).

This certainly shows man's confused belief that he can produce something material that is of significance; this buying of the stove is much different from Charity's impending birthing of a child. Yet, by returning to Royall's civilization, she gives up her mothering rights and her bond to the primeval mother within her. In fact, when she gives herself up to Royall, she attempts to block out the "white autumn moon," a reminder of the Mountain. Before she had pressed her head sensuously into the grass; now she "press[es] her face against [the pillow] to shut out the pale landscape beyond the window" (206–07). She lies in the "darkness," because she has alienated herself from the maternal landscape; but she also does not fit the "other" interior landscape of Royall's civilized world: she does not know how to "manipulate" the "electric button" to turn on the light (206).

Royall has spoiled Charity so that her maternal traits have atrophied, and she has lost touch with the meaning of mothering. In part, this is due to her many empty hours of leisure. [Charlotte] Perkins Gilman, in her then revolutionary text on mothering in *Women and Economics* (1898),[4] shows that women are trained to be consumers and not self-reliant producers, thus perpetuating the myth of the helpless woman: "Because of her maternal duties, the human female is said to be unable to get her own living . . . Is this the condition of motherhood? Does the human mother, by

---

[4] Charlotte Perkins Gilman, *Women and Economics* (Boston: Small, Maynard & Co., 1898). [Ed.]

her motherhood, thereby lose control of brain and body, lose power and skill and desire for any other work?" (18–19). Gilman suggests that in cutting themselves off from other social activities and productivity, they resign themselves to a "pathological motherhood" (181) that denies complete self-realization; they cannot fulfill themselves simply as mothers who rely upon husbands. This has produced "an enormous class of non-productive consumers,—a class which is half the world and mother of the other half" (118). This type of limiting motherhood leads to a debilitating feminine condition, with women dabbling in frivolous activity. While men are allowed to explore the world, women wait at home dutifully; thus, in North Dormer, "at three o'clock on a June afternoon its few able-bodied men are off in the fields or woods, and the women indoors, engaged in languid household drudgery" (91). To her credit, Charity refuses to do the housework after refusing to become Royall's wife at the start of the novel; he hires a domestic servant, which enables Charity to take on her job at the library, but still, because she lacks education, she spends most of her time wanting to escape to the "outside," or sewing and embroidering lacy frivolous items for herself. Charity becomes what Gilman would call, a "priestess of the temple of consumption," a victim of male market created for women, a "market for sensuous decoration and personal ornament, for all that is luxurious and enervating" (*Women and Economics* 120). Gilman warns that this relationship between men and women "sexualizes our industrial relation and commercializes our sex-relation" (121).

Charity, from the start, is never given an opportunity to go beyond the stereotypical consumer-female who ends up relinquishing her "self" by the "maternal sacrifice," as Gilman would put it (*WE* 191); indeed, when Charity writes her last letter to Harney, she thinks of the sacrifice she is making for her unborn child. From the start, we realize that Charity is burdened with her guardian's consumer-producer mentality, and she realizes that her assets revolve around her sexuality: she knows what kind of effect she has had on Harney, "She had learned what she was *worth* when Lucius Harney, looking at her for the first time, had lost the thread of his speech" (115, my emphasis), and she knows that if her indiscretions with Harney become too obvious to Royall, she will have to "pay for it" (115). She is aware of her effect on all men, as she sits in front of the mirror repeatedly and preens herself, and her purchases are meant to ornament her. Thus, for example, she gazes in the mirror and adores that hat Ally Hawes had secretly made for her: "It was of white straw, with a drooping brim and a cherry-coloured lining that made her face glow like the inside of the shell on the parlour mantelpiece" (141). Realizing that she has to compete with Annabel Balch's blue eyes to capture a man, she sits in front of the mirror for long periods of time and futilely wishes her brown eyes to turn blue, and fantasizes walking down the aisle with Lucius Harney, a bride in "low-necked satin" (106). Even in the end, when her pregnancy puts an end to her quest for self in the mirror, she is still as aware as ever of ornate surroundings. During her "honeymoon" with Royall, though she is too "ashamed" to catch a glimpse of herself in the looking glass (204), she notices in the reflection of the mirror the intricate details of the hotel room: there was "the high head-board and fluted pillow slips of the double bed, and a bedspread so spot-lessly white that she had hesitated to lay her hat and jacket on it" (205); even in her exhaustion from the trip to the Mountain, she does not miss for a second absorbing the gold-framed paintings around her bed (205) and the chandeliers and "marble-panelled hall" of the dining-hall (206). As Liff Hyatt had told her early on, as he looked at her lying in the grass with her "new shoes" and "red ribbon": "They won't any of 'em touch you up there, f'ever you was to come up . . . But I don't s'pose you will" (112). With her exorbitant taste in clothing and furnishings, Charity alienates herself fur-ther from the secrets of the primeval mother.

Though her hunger is a manifestation of the emptiness within her, her taste in food is also luxurious and frilly. In this realm too, she craves superfluities, the sweets which men have created as a steady diet for the consumer-woman. For Charity, civilization means visiting Nettleton, the closest thing to a city, and devouring bonbons that men will buy her or gawking hungrily at the sumptuous clothes in the store fronts. She remi-nisces lovingly about the "cocoanut pie" she had eaten in Nettleton during the course of a field trip to "hear an illustrated lecture on the Holy land" (92); she craves chocolate that Harney can provide for her, munches on the party sandwiches Harney brings her "from the love-feast at Hamblin" (176); and is absolutely mesmerized by the garden of delights which Net-tleton offers her when Harney takes her to the Fourth of July celebration: there were "fruit and confectionary shops stacked with strawberry-cake, cocoanut candy, boxes of caramels and chewing-gum, baskets of sodden strawberries, and dangling bunches of bananas" (144–45). Indeed, she spends most of her time with Harney and with Royall eating. Too late she realizes that they cannot satisfy her appetite: immediately after her mar-riage to Royall, she loses her appetite, "the thought of food filled her with repugnance" (206), but eats to pacify Royall. Perhaps the most revealing scene focusing on food occurs when Charity has spent the night at Liff Hy-att's house, on the evening of her mother's death. After her aunt's family has showered what little hospitality on her (the children's blanket) as they can afford, she herself raids the pantry: "faint with hunger" (198) in the middle of the night, she breaks off some bread from the half of a stale loaf. Driven by her hunger, she disregards the hunger of the others: "No doubt it was to serve as the breakfast of old Mrs. Hyatt and the children; but Charity did not care; she had her own baby to think of" (198). In the name of mother-ing, she steals from other children: this is the height of narcissistic individ-ualistic mothering as promoted by the competitive and capitalist men around her. After she devours the bread "greedily," she leaves one of her "dainty things," a "pretty chemise" (198), in exchange. She does not un-derstand the true meaning of mothering and productivity: her gesture in-dicates that she values luxuries more than necessities.

It is not just man's fear and jealousy of the primeval mother that makes him destroy her. It is his attempt to supplant feminine creativity with male productivity, with his sense of order and civilization. Thus, Charity has learned from her "avaricious" [guardian] (118), the Hometown spokes-man, who has shown her the value of woman's sexuality. For example, when he first receives Harney's payment for use of his buggy (and indi-rectly but perversely for the use of Charity), he gives Charity the money, a ten-dollar bill, to make herself look good (for him): "Here—go get your-self a Sunday bonnet that'll make all the other girls mad" (118). He teaches her the male value of competition. Later Royall begrudgingly approves of Charity's choice of Harney as lover, ". . . I don't blame you. You picked out the best when you seen it . . . well, that was always my way" (138). Finally, when he has caught her as his wife, he hands her two twenty-dollar bills and triumphantly advises her to "buy yourself whatever you need . . . You know how I always wanted you to beat all the other girls" (207).

[Charlotte] Perkins Gilman said that lack of productivity is destroying women and motherhood, and it is true in the context of this novel that capitalist male productivity, which promotes the notion of idle women or women competing for eligible bachelors, is destructive. And it is male civilization that comes out ahead of female nurturing in *Summer*. There is no true community of women here: the only bonding occurs when Miss Hatchard's circle of girls makes the garlands, decorative frills, for home-coming week. And, of course, in contrast to the Mountain, we have an im-age competing for prominence, and that is Dr. Merkle's office. Her house in Nettleton with the sign, "Private Consultations," is as foreboding to the women in the town (to Charity and her only ally, Ally), as the Mountain is to the men. Dr. Merkle robs women of their motherhood, and Julia "came as near as anything to dying" (141). Just as male civilization is glutted with ugly superfluities, and the excessive food and clothing imagery in the novel makes one nauseous, so too is Dr. Merkle's office decorated gaudily. More-over, she is a "plump" woman (the devouring mother) with "unnaturally white and even teeth" (182–83). What makes her most hideous is that she has picked up all of men's worst vices; she encompasses the competitive business mentality in its most grotesque aspects. Though her smile appears "motherly" (183), she thrives on her illicit market. And her character beneath the artificial appearance is utterly false: Charity perceives her as having "false hair," "false teeth," and a "false murderous smile" (183).

All the excessive productivity and destruction comes as a result of man's rule. Royall, whom Charity aptly describes as the "very symbol of household order" and who is adept at giving patriotic orations (with Daniel Webster as his guide), is at the heart of the "pattern" of civilization which destroys through its rigidity. When asked about the character of Lawyer Royall by the art historian and friend Bernard Berenson, Wharton said "*he's* [Royall is] the book"[5] [emphasis Wharton's]. This is certainly true if one were to judge which values triumph in *Summer*. [. . .] When Edith Wharton records her writing of *Summer* as being outside the realm of her wartime experience, she is deceiving herself: war does permeate the pages, though subtly so. She writes in *A Backward Glance* that despite being "steeped in the realities of the war," she "began to write a short novel, *Summer*, as remote as possible in setting and subject from the scenes about me; and the work made my other tasks seem lighter. The tale was written at a high pitch of creative joy."[6] Yet, the subject matter of *Summer* is closely allied with the wartime destruction, the lack of respect for life, around her: the sensuous indulgence and excessive materialism of war are rampant in *Summer*.

In *The Man-Made World* (1911), a prophetic vision of the war to come and a sociological work which predates *Summer* by six years, Charlotte Perkins Gilman warns about the evils brought about by a "man-made" civilization and she advocates a government based on mothering, "a peaceful administration in the interest of the family that comes of motherhood" (189).[7] She sees the arbitrary law of male government as a "fine machine of destruction" (184) and "free competition" as the battle cry of the "predaceous male" (192); the "iron weight" of male authority reaches its "most perfect expression in the absolutely masculine field of warfare" (183). Gilman asserts that "the tendency to care for, defend and manage a group, is in its origin maternal" (210), and she calls for more of this maternal expression in society. When Charity renounces the Mountain and drives up "to the door of the red house" [210] as Mrs. Royall, she has closed the door on maternal possibilities. Her brand of motherhood is not so far removed

---

[5] Quoted in Cynthia Griffin Wolff, Introduction, *Summer*, by Edith Wharton (1917; New York: Harper Perennial, 1979). [Ed.]

[6] Edith Wharton, *A Backward Glance* (New York: D. Appleton-Century, 1934) 356. Also see p. 215 in this New Riverside Edition. [Ed.]

[7] Charlotte Perkins Gilman, *The Man-Made World, or, Our Androcentric Culture* (New York: Charlton Co., 1911). [Ed.]

from Julia's prostitution; they have both sold into the consumer society produced by men. Not much has changed. The Mountain stands alone and abandoned. And the Dr. Merkles of the cities are still doing good business.

" 'Seduced and Abandoned': Convention and Reality in Edith Wharton's *Summer*"

Nancy A. Walker

The complexity of *Summer* is due in large measure to Wharton's use of the conventional "seduced and abandoned" theme so pervasive in both popular and serious fiction of the period. The usual heroine in such a story is either a naive young girl who succumbs to the charm of the heartless seducer or (and especially in fiction in which the central consciousness is male) the virgin-turned-bitch who hounds the man into a hasty marriage, thus ruining his chances for success. Wharton's characterizations are far more realistic, and the novel enlarges upon the conventional theme to become a story about the ambiguity of human relationships. Charity Royall is admirably shrewd and strong rather than merely an innocent victim; Lucius Harney, the young architect with whom she has her first sexual experience, is, despite his air of worldliness, more weak than opportunistic; and lawyer Royall, Charity's guardian and eventually her husband, is both would-be seducer and rescuer of the seduced.

Wharton emphasizes the complexity of human character and motivation by creating tension in *Summer* between the inevitability of fate—represented most strikingly by images of animals, prisons, seasonal cycles, and the Fall—and the suggestions of human sympathy and endurance. The name of the main character is the emblem of this tension. Charity Royall is on one hand the recipient of the charity of North Dormer's nearest approach to royalty. Her guardian is twice her savior—first when he brings her down from the Mountain when she is a child, and finally when he marries her and provides her unborn child with some degree of legitimacy. But just as important, she herself is charitable, particularly to Lucius Harney, whom she absolves of all responsibility for his actions. To be the object of charity is itself an ambiguous condition, provoking both gratitude and

Studies in American Fiction 11.1 (Spring 1983).

resentment, but Charity Royall both recognizes and practices human compassion, and that fact raises her out of the pathos of her situation. In the end she is trapped in North Dormer, and the Mountain will continue to loom over the town to remind her of her barbarous origins, but though she is without choice, she is not without love.

The novel is structured to present two different patterns of movement. The dominant pattern takes Charity first out of the narrow, isolated world of North Dormer and then back into that world. The second movement ameliorates the final grimness of the first by easing Charity closer to lawyer Royall. The first design is rendered primarily in the imagery and settings of the novel; the second is conveyed in three key conversations between Charity and her guardian, the occasions of his three proposals of marriage.

In the dominant pattern of movement in the novel, Charity inhabits, actually or imaginatively, three distinct worlds. Most primitive is the Mountain, from which, at the age of five, she was rescued by Royall. The people on the Mountain are a kind of outlaw colony, removed from and disdainful of the rest of society. Drunken and inbred, they are described by Royall as "half human"(119).[1] The sense of bestiality is reinforced by animal imagery. When Charity attends the strange funeral of her mother and sees her face for the first time in seventeen years, "there was no sign in it of anything human; she lay there like a dead dog in a ditch" (193). Later, as Charity tries to sleep among the mountain folk that night, she sees children nestled next to their grandmother "like sleeping puppies" (197). So far removed are the Mountain people from the conventions of civilized life that only death has sanctity: they request the minister for burials but not for marriages and births.

Charity's link with her origins on the Mountain is conscious as well as symbolic and serves to remove her from the "pure" origins of the heroine of romantic fiction. She sees herself as having a "tainted origin" (114), though at moments of crisis she considers the Mountain a possible refuge. She is in part guided by instinct: "Whenever she was unhappy she felt herself at bay against a pitiless world, and a kind of animal secretiveness possessed her" (131). After Royall's drunken accusations on the Fourth of July, she reacts with "the secretive instinct of the animal in pain" (154). When she discovers that she is pregnant, her first impulse is to return to the Mountain:

> Almost without conscious thought her decision had been reached; as her eyes had followed the circle of the hills her mind had also travelled the

---

[1] All parenthetical references are to this New Riverside Edition. [Ed.]

old round. She supposed it was something in her blood that made the Mountain the only answer to her questioning, the inevitable escape from all that hemmed her in and beset her (188).

If Charity is linked by heritage with the people of the Mountain, she nonetheless inhabits and perfectly understands the town of North Dormer over which it looms. North Dormer is a mean and petty town, in which convention exerts as strong an inhibiting influence as the absence of convention does upon the people of the Mountain.[. . .] The library in which Charity works—a job for which she is ill-suited by education or temperament—represents Charity's trapped feelings at the beginning of the novel. It is described as a "prison-house" (94), a "vault-like room" (94), a "mausoleum" with a "melancholy penumbra" (110).

But Charity Royall is too shrewd to be completely at the mercy of the town. She has a certain status as the ward of lawyer Royall, "the biggest man in North Dormer," and from this vantage point she has "taken the measure of most things about her" (98, 99). She understands the desperate gentility of Ally Hawes, the seamstress whose sister Julia has become a "loose woman"; the innocence and "long immaturity" (102) of the spinster Miss Hatchard; and most particularly she understands Royall, who, beneath his aura of power and respectability, is a defeated man. Though successful by the standards of North Dormer, Royall has failed to make a name for himself in the world outside it and has come back "for good," as he says in his Old Home Week speech. He lives on the remnants of a law practice, and his office is "dusty" and "clerkless" (104). But, as Charity is aware, "it was the fact of having lived in Nettleton that made lawyer Royall, in spite of his infirmities, the strongest man in North Dormer" (110). Charity understands that power is related to position; that reputation is seldom based on innate worth.

Lucius Harney represents Charity's third world: the wide range of possibilities beyond North Dormer and its surrounding towns. From the first, she is aware of the differences between herself and Harney; she feels her ignorance and lack of sophistication in sharp contrast to his urbanity. The fact that life very far from North Dormer is not a real possibility for Charity is underscored by her inability to imagine correspondence over long distances. When she considers writing to Harney in New York, "she had the feeling that her letter would never reach its destination." She reads his letter to her "with a strange sense of its coming from immeasurable distances and having lost most of its meaning on the way" (178). Lucius Harney himself is mysterious and unattainable:

> She had always dimly guessed him to be in touch with important people, involved in complicated relations—but she felt it all to be so far beyond

her understanding that the whole subject hung like a luminous mist on the farthest verge of her thoughts (171).

When she sees him with his fiancée, Annabel Balch, she feels not jealousy but "a terror of the unknown" (171).

This world outside North Dormer is most concretely represented by the Fourth of July outing in Nettleton, which occupies the center of the novel both thematically and structurally. Everything that has happened to this point has led Charity out of the world of the town; everything that happens afterward leads her back to it. Appropriately, the celebration is described in terms both exciting and decadent, both stimulating and sinister. To Charity, the crowds and decorations make Nettleton "resplendent"; she feels "as if she had always strolled through tessellated halls beside young men in flannels" (146). Here Harney buys her the blue brooch, and they attend the theatre, where she is dazzled by the images on the screen. Finally, they go to the fireworks display and Charity feels "as if all the latent beauty of things had been unveiled to her" (151). But mingled with these images of splendor are the images of decay and mystery. The fruit displayed along the street is "sodden," "spotted," and "dusty," and the air "reeked" with aromas (145). Significantly, Charity and Harney have lunch at a French restaurant, where they eat "queerly flavoured things" and Charity imagines herself "alone with him in foreign countries" (146). Later, just before they see Julia Hawes, and before Royall drunkenly calls Charity a whore, Wharton describes the trolleys from Nettleton to the lake as "great luminous serpents." The implication of the Fall, of the sin of Adam and Eve, is made complete when, at the end of the chapter, Charity first sees the office of Dr. Merkle, the abortionist to whom she will later go for confirmation of her pregnancy but whose other services she will refuse.

Each of these three worlds—the Mountain, the town, and the wider world—is embodied in a particular woman who represents a possible future for Charity. Two of these women, Charity's mother and Ally Hawes, are trapped in their respective environments; the third, Annabel Balch, is the image of a world for which Charity realizes she is not suited. Although Charity is initially devastated by the knowledge that her mother is a "half human" woman who has rejected her, once she learns she is pregnant she feels a need to go to her for help. But after her mother's funeral she loses any sense of kinship with the Mountain people:

> Charity's bewildered brain laboured with the attempt to picture her mother's past, and to relate it in any way to the designs of a just and merciful God; but it was impossible to imagine any link between them. She herself felt as remote from the poor creature she had seen lowered into her hastily dug grave as if the height of the heavens divided them (197).

Ally Hawes represents another possible fate. Considered unmarriageable because of a limp, Ally earns a slender living as a seamstress to North Dormer. To Charity, Ally's "pale face" looks like "the ghost of wasted opportunities" (141). In the second half of the novel, after the Fourth of July sequence, Ally's access to local gossip makes her seem to represent the town itself, "with all its mean curiosities, its furtive malice, its sham unconsciousness of evil" (155), in short, everything that Charity wants to escape.

The distance between Charity and Annabel Balch emerges first in the fact that Charity usually thinks of her as "Miss Balch," a habit of mind that reveals more than a difference of social class. Although Charity at one point quite literally wears Annabel's shoes, Wharton makes it clear that Charity will never enter Annabel's world of garden parties and concerts. Even before she realizes that Annabel and Lucius Harney are engaged, Charity senses that they belong to the same world and feels "the uselessness of struggling against the unseen influences in Harney's life" (129). Later, Annabel comes to represent "all the things that Charity felt herself most incapable of understanding or achieving." As Charity writes the letter releasing Harney from any obligation to her—before she knows she is pregnant—Wharton writes:

> Annabel Balch was, if not the girl Harney ought to marry, at least the kind of girl it would be natural for him to marry. Charity had never been able to picture herself as his wife; had never been able to arrest the vision and follow it out in its daily consequences; but she could perfectly imagine Annabel Balch in that relation to him (181).

Charity's letter to Lucius Harney is simple and short, but its language is a telling instance of Charity's moral ascendancy. After telling Harney that he should marry Annabel if he has so promised, she ends by saying, "I'd rather you acted right." Although the reader recognizes the irony of this statement, Charity's message is straightforward and unironic: in her morality, a promise is a promise. Further, she has a perfect understanding of their equal responsibilities for her condition:

> She could not see anything more reprehensible in his conduct than in her own. From the first she had needed him more than he had wanted her, and the power that had swept them together had been as far beyond resistance as a great gale loosening the leaves of the forest (185).

The fact that Charity never tells Harney about her pregnancy has nothing to do with shame: a forced marriage to Harney would be as abhorrent to her as an abortion. So Charity is left in the world of North Dormer.

The countermovement of the novel, which leads Charity to marry her guardian, further reveals the complexity of these two characters and lifts the story even further out of its origins in stereotype. Royall's three proposals of marriage indicate the shifting balance of their relationship. The first proposal takes place several years before the summer of the novel's main action and is prompted by Royall's sense of guilt at having tried to seduce Charity, then a girl of seventeen. His attempted seduction is a mild, non-violent one, but Charity's calm, contemptuous refusal, coupled with his bad conscience, gives her the upper hand in their relationship. When he abruptly proposes to her a few days later, she sees him as "a hideous parody of the fatherly old man she had always known" and laughs scornfully at him, accusing him of wanting a hired girl without having to hire one. He quails before her indignant response: "His face was ash-coloured and his black eyebrows quivered as though the blaze of her scorn had blinded him" (104).

By the time of the second proposal, Royall and Charity are on a more equal footing. She is four years older, but she is also more vulnerable, having discovered first hand how cruel the gossip of the townspeople can be. Although she is at this point innocent of any wrongdoing, having merely sat outside Harney's window for several hours, the townspeople assume that she and Harney have spent those hours together. Royall's proposal is this time another of his acts of "charity": he will make an "honest woman" of her; they will move somewhere else, "some big town, where there's men, and business, and things doing." But Charity "saw the old life closing in on her, and hardly heeded his fanciful picture of renewal." After she again refuses him, they look at each other "with the terrible equality of courage that sometimes made her feel as if she had his blood in her veins" (138). At this moment, just before the pivotal Fourth of July scene, Royall and Charity are equal: his desire to escape from North Dormer is almost as strong as hers, but the "old life" is closing in on both of them.

When Royall proposes for the third time, in the penultimate chapter of the novel, Charity makes only a feeble protest, and one which very subtly reveals her own perception of his moral quality: "She was not sure if she was rejecting what he offered, or already struggling against the temptation of taking what she no longer had a right to" (202). Royall is described as "kindly" in this scene; he is once again her protector, and she has moved from the scorn of the first incident, to the courage of the second, and finally to acquiescence. As they start for the train that will take them to Nettleton and the minister who will marry them, "she had only a confused sensation of slipping down a smooth irresistible current" (203). At the end of the same day, "in the cold autumn moonlight, they drove up to the door of the red house" (210). Thus ends the novel that began with Charity coming out of the same house in June.

Wharton has prepared for the conclusion of the novel in several ways. Because she uses a limited omniscient point of view, most of the story is related through Charity's consciousness. Thus when Royall is presented in a more and more positive way toward the end of the novel, the reader is seeing him as Charity does. The scene in which she first perceives him as a man of substance and sense is the occasion of his Old Home Week address, at the conclusion of which she symbolically (if somewhat too obviously so) falls at his feet in a faint. Imagery drawn from the natural world also contributes an inevitability to Charity's final acceptance of Royall. In a negative sense, the seasonal cycle reinforces the theme of Charity's entrapment by circumstances. The novel begins with the promise of summer and ends with the closing in of autumn. But Wharton also moves Charity toward the natural and away from the artificial. She describes Charity's joy in nature, her love of flowers and earthy fragrances; in a significant scene early in the novel Charity tries to stop Liff Hyatt from trampling some bramble flowers. The abortionist, Dr. Merkle, represents interference with natural process and is fittingly described as a woman with "the false hair, the false teeth, the false murderous smile" (183). If abortion is an artificial and therefore unacceptable option for Charity, marriage to Royall, to whom she already feels somehow related, is the only natural one.

The major force in *Summer* lies in the realistic, unsentimental portrait of Charity Royall, who has a strength and dignity seldom found in the depictions of women in similar situations drawn by other writers of the period. Wharton persuades the reader to feel sympathy, not pity, for Charity, who is not merely a victim of either biology or conventional morality. The classic "seduced and abandoned" story presents the woman as the passive and often pious figure ruined by her own sexuality, and there is little doubt that society usually viewed such women in that light. But Wharton explores the reality behind the cliché. Limiting though Charity's circumstances may be, she is not the pale, clinging wraith of melodrama but rather the strongest moral force in the novel—not as an embodiment of conventional morality, but as a woman of integrity and insight. *Summer* is thus an important work not only in Edith Wharton's impressive canon but also in the continuing reassessment of women's role and image in American life.

WORKS CITED

Ammons, Elizabeth. *Edith Wharton's Argument with America.* Athens: U of Georgia P, 1980.

Bell, Millicent, ed. *The Cambridge Companion to Edith Wharton,* Cambridge: Cambridge UP, 1995.

Bendixen, Alfred and Annette Zilversmit, eds. *Edith Wharton: New Critical Essays.* New York: Garland, 1992.

Blackall, Jean Frantz. "The Sledding Accident in *Ethan Frome.*" *Studies in Short Fiction,* 21.2 (Spring 1984): 145–46.

Dodson, Samuel Fisher. "Frozen Hell: Edith Wharton's Tragic Offering." *Edith Wharton Review* 16.1 (Spring 1999): 10–15.

Elbert, Monika M. "The Politics of Maternality in *Summer.*" *Edith Wharton Review* 7.2 (Winter 1990): 4–9.

"Fatal Coasting Accident." *Berkshire Evening Eagle,* Pittsfield, Massachusetts. 12 March 1904, pp. 1, 3.

Gordon, Linda. "Incest and Resistance: Patterns of Father-Daughter Incest, 1880–1930." *Social Problems* 13:4 (1986): 253–67.

Hovey, Richard B. "*Ethan Frome*: A Controversy About Modernizing It." *American Literary Realism, 1870–1910,* 19:1 (Fall 1986), 4–19.

Lawes, Carolyn J. *Women and Reform in a New England Community, 1815–1860.* Lexington: UP of Kentucky, 2000.

Lewis, R.W.B. *Edith Wharton: A Life.* New York: Harper, 1975.

Morante, Linda. "The Desolation of Charity Royall: Imagery in Edith Wharton's *Summer.*" *Colby Library Quarterly,* 18:4 (Dec. 1982): 241–48.

Osgood, Frances. *A Wreath of Wild Flowers From New England.* London: Edward Churton, 1838.

Peattie, Roderick, ed. *The Berkshires: The Purple Hills.* New York: Vanguard P, 1948.

Reid, John. *Essays on Hypochondriacal and Other Nervous Affections.* Philadelphia: M. Carey & Son, 1817.

Robinson, Rowland Evans. "Glimpses of New England Farm Life." *Scribner's Monthly* Aug. 1878: 510, 511, 514–15, 516–17, 519.

Rose, Christine M. "*Summer*: The Double Sense of Wharton's Title." *ANQ* 3.1 (1990): 16–19.

Schneider, Carl H. and Dorothy Schneider. *American Women in the Progressive Era, 1900–1920.* New York: Anchor Books, 1993.

Shuman, R. Baird. "The Continued Popularity of *Ethan Frome.*" *Revue Des Langues Vivantes,* 37:3 (1971): 257–63.

Walker, Nancy A. " 'Seduced and Abandoned': Convention and Reality in Edith Wharton's *Summer.*" *Studies in American Fiction* 11.1 (Spring 1983): 107–114.

Wharton, Edith. *A Backward Glance.* 1934. New York: Scribner's, 1985.

———. *The Letters of Edith Wharton.* Ed. R. W. B. Lewis and Nancy Lewis. New York: Collier, 1988.

———. "The Writing of *Ethan Frome.*" *The Colophon: The Book Collectors Quarterly* Pt. II, no. 4 (Sept. 1932).

White, Barbara A., ed. *Wharton's New England: Seven Stories and Ethan Frome.* Hanover: UP of New England, 1995.

FOR FURTHER READING

Ammons, Elizabeth. *Edith Wharton's Argument with America*. Athens: U of Georgia P, 1980.

Benstock, Shari. *No Gifts from Chance: A Biography of Edith Wharton*. New York: Scribner's, 1994.

Bernard, Kenneth. "Imagery and Symbolism in *Ethan Frome*." *College English* 22 (1961): 178–84.

Bloom, Harold. *Edith Wharton*. New York: Chelsea, 1986.

Campbell, Donna M. "Rewriting the 'Rose and Lavender Pages': *Ethan Frome* and Women's Local Color Fiction." *Speaking the Other Self: American Women Writers*. Ed. Jeanne Campbell Reesman. Athens: U of Georgia P, 1997. 263–77.

Crowley, John W. "The Unmastered Streak: Feminist Themes in Wharton's *Summer*." *American Literary Realism, 1870–1910* 15 (1982): 86–96.

Farland, Maria Magdalena. "*Ethan Frome* and the 'Springs' of Masculinity." *MFS: Modern Fiction Studies* 42.4 (1996): 707–29.

Goodman, Susan. *Edith Wharton's Women: Friends and Rivals*. Hanover: UP of New England, 1990.

Grafton, Kathy. "Degradation and Forbidden Love in Edith Wharton's *Summer*." *Twentieth Century Literature* 41.4 (1995), 350–66.

Hattenhauer, Darryl. "Wharton's *Ethan Frome*." *Explicator* 51.4 (1993): 226–27.

Hays, Peter L. "Signs in *Summer:* Words and Metaphors." *Papers on Language and Literature* 25.1 (Winter 1989): 114–20.

Hill, William Thomas. "'Man-Like, He Sought to Postpone Certainty': Shadows of Truth and Identity in Edith Wharton's *Ethan Frome*." *Studies in the Humanities* 56 (1995): 63–82.

Hoeller, Hildegard. *Edith Wharton's Dialogue with Realism and Sentimental Fiction.* Gainesville: UP of Florida, 2000.

Hummel, William E. "My 'Dull-Witted Enemy': Symbolic Violence and Abject Maleness in Edith Wharton's *Summer.*" *Studies in American Fiction* 24.2 (1996), 215–36.

Hutchinson, Stuart. "Unpackaging Edith Wharton: *Ethan Frome* and *Summer.*" *Cambridge Quarterly* 27.3 (1998): 219–32.

Khan, D. Noor. "The Arrival at Selfhood of the Wharton Woman: A Fresh Glance at *Ethan Frome* and *Summer.*" *Panjab University Research Bulletin* 20.1 (1989): 81–88.

Lewis, R. W. B. *Edith Wharton: A Biography.* New York: Harper, 1975.

Marshall, Scott. "Edith Wharton, Kate Spencer, and *Ethan Frome.*" *Edith Wharton Review* 10.1 (1993): 20–21.

McDowell, Margaret B. *Edith Wharton.* Rev. ed. Twayne Ser. Boston: Hall, 1991.

Murad, Orlene. "Edith Wharton and *Ethan Frome.*" *Modern Language Studies* 13 (Summer 1983): 90–103.

Nettels, Elsa. "Thwarted Escapes: *Ethan Frome* and Jean Stafford's 'A Country Love Story.'" *Edith Wharton Review* 11.2 (1994): 6–8, 15.

Nevius, Blake. *Edith Wharton.* Berkeley: U of California P, 1953.

Nilsen, Helge Normann. "Naturalism in Edith Wharton's 'Ethan Frome.'" *Performances in American Literature and Culture: Essays in Honor of Professor Orm Overland on His 60th Birthday.* Ed. Vidar Pedersen and Zeljka Svrljuga. Bergen: University of Bergen, 1995. 179–88.

Rose, Alan Henry. "Such Depths of Sad Initiation: Edith Wharton and New England." *New England Quarterly* 50 (1977): 423–39.

Singley, Carol J. "Calvinist Tortures in Edith Wharton's *Ethan Frome.*" *The Calvinist Roots of the Modern Era.* Ed. Aliki Barnstone, Michael Tomasek Manson, and Carol J. Singley. Hanover: UP of New England, 1997. 162–80.

Smith, Christopher, ed. *Readings on Ethan Frome.* San Diego: Greenhaven P, 2000.

Springer, Marlene. *Ethan Frome: A Nightmare of Need.* New York: Twayne, 1993.

Travis, Jennifer. "Pain and Recompense: The Trouble with *Ethan Frome.*" *Arizona Quarterly* 53.3 (1997): 37–64.

Werlock, Abby H. P. "Whitman, Wharton, and the Sexuality in *Summer*. *Speaking the Other Self: American Women Writers.* Ed. Jeanne Campbell Reesman. Athens: U of Georgia P, 1997. 246–62.

Wharton, Edith. *A Backward Glance.* 1934. New York: Scribner's, 1985.

——. *The Letters of Edith Wharton.* Ed. R. W. B. Lewis and Nancy Lewis. New York: Collier, 1988.

——. *Novellas and Other Writings:* Madame de Treymes, Ethan Frome. Summer, Old New York, The Mother's Recompense, A Backward Glance. Ed. Cynthia Griffin Wolff. New York: Library of America, 1990.

——. "The Writing of *Ethan Frome.*" *The Colophon: The Book Collectors Quarterly* Pt II, no. 4 (Sept. 1932).

White, Barbara A. "Edith Wharton's *Summer* and Women's Fiction." *Essays in Literature* 11 (1984): 223–35.

——, ed. *Wharton's New England.* Hanover: U Press of New England, 1995.

Wolff, Cynthia Griffin. "Cold Ethan and 'Hot Ethan.'" *College Literature* 14.3 (1987): 230–44.

CREDITS

Reprinted by permission of Jean Frantz Blackall, Professor of English, Emerita, Cornell University and Alfred Bendixen, Professor of English, California State University.

Linda Morante from "The Desolation of Charity Royall: Imagery in Edith Wharton's *Summer*," *Colby Library Quarterly*, 18:4 (Dec. 1982) 241–48. Reprinted by permission.

Christine M. Rose, from "*Summer*: The Double Sense of Wharton's Title" in *ANQ* 3.1. 1990. 16–19. Lexington: The University Press of Kentucky, © 1999. Reprinted by permission.

Rhonda Skillern from "Becoming a 'Good Girl': Law, Language, and Ritual in Edith Wharton's *Summer*" in *The Cambridge Companion to Edith Wharton*, edited by Millicent Bell, Cambridge: Cambridge UP, 1995, pp. 117–136. Excerpts from pp. 117–136, "Becoming a 'Good Girl': Law, Language and Ritual in Edith Wharton's *Summer*", by Rhonda Skillem, edited by Millicent Bell. Copyright © 1995 by Cambridge University Press. Reprinted with the permission of Cambridge University Press.

Monika M. Elbert, from "The Politics of Maternality in *Summer*" in *Edith Wharton Review* 7.2 (Winter 1990), 4–9. 24. Reprinted with permission.

Nancy A. Walker, from "'Seduced and Abandoned': Convention and Reality in Edith Wharton's *Summer*" in *Studies in American Fiction* 11.1, Spring 1983, pp. 107–114.

Gary Scharnhorst, "The Two Faces of Mattie Silver," is reprinted by permission of the author.